Machine Learning and Blockchain – Challenges, Future Trends and Sustainable Technologies

Edited by

Keshav Kaushik
Center for Cyber Security and Cryptology
Sharda School of Computer Science & Engineering
Sharda University, Greater Noida
India

Rewa Sharma
J.C Bose University of Science and Technology
YMCA, Faridabad, India

&

Ayodeji Olalekan Salau
Department of Electrical and Electronics
and Computer Engineering, Afe Babalola University
Ado Ekiti, Nigeria

Machine Learning and Blockchain – Challenges, Future Trends and Sustainable Technologies

Editors: Keshav Kaushik, Rewa Sharma and Ayodeji Olalekan Salau

ISBN (Online): 978-981-5324-21-1

ISBN (Print): 978-981-5324-22-8

ISBN (Paperback): 978-981-5324-23-5

© 2026, Bentham Books imprint.

Published by Bentham Science Publishers Pte. Ltd. Singapore. All Rights Reserved.

First published in 2026.

BENTHAM SCIENCE PUBLISHERS LTD.
End User License Agreement (for non-institutional, personal use)

This is an agreement between you and Bentham Science Publishers Ltd. Please read this License Agreement carefully before using the ebook/echapter/ejournal (**"Work"**). Your use of the Work constitutes your agreement to the terms and conditions set forth in this License Agreement. If you do not agree to these terms and conditions then you should not use the Work.

Bentham Science Publishers agrees to grant you a non-exclusive, non-transferable limited license to use the Work subject to and in accordance with the following terms and conditions. This License Agreement is for non-library, personal use only. For a library / institutional / multi user license in respect of the Work, please contact: permission@benthamscience.org.

Usage Rules:

1. All rights reserved: The Work is the subject of copyright and Bentham Science Publishers either owns the Work (and the copyright in it) or is licensed to distribute the Work. You shall not copy, reproduce, modify, remove, delete, augment, add to, publish, transmit, sell, resell, create derivative works from, or in any way exploit the Work or make the Work available for others to do any of the same, in any form or by any means, in whole or in part, in each case without the prior written permission of Bentham Science Publishers, unless stated otherwise in this License Agreement.
2. You may download a copy of the Work on one occasion to one personal computer (including tablet, laptop, desktop, or other such devices). You may make one back-up copy of the Work to avoid losing it.
3. The unauthorised use or distribution of copyrighted or other proprietary content is illegal and could subject you to liability for substantial money damages. You will be liable for any damage resulting from your misuse of the Work or any violation of this License Agreement, including any infringement by you of copyrights or proprietary rights.

Disclaimer:

Bentham Science Publishers does not guarantee that the information in the Work is error-free, or warrant that it will meet your requirements or that access to the Work will be uninterrupted or error-free. The Work is provided "as is" without warranty of any kind, either express or implied or statutory, including, without limitation, implied warranties of merchantability and fitness for a particular purpose. The entire risk as to the results and performance of the Work is assumed by you. No responsibility is assumed by Bentham Science Publishers, its staff, editors and/or authors for any injury and/or damage to persons or property as a matter of products liability, negligence or otherwise, or from any use or operation of any methods, products instruction, advertisements or ideas contained in the Work.

Limitation of Liability:

In no event will Bentham Science Publishers, its staff, editors and/or authors, be liable for any damages, including, without limitation, special, incidental and/or consequential damages and/or damages for lost data and/or profits arising out of (whether directly or indirectly) the use or inability to use the Work. The entire liability of Bentham Science Publishers shall be limited to the amount actually paid by you for the Work.

General:

1. Any dispute or claim arising out of or in connection with this License Agreement or the Work (including non-contractual disputes or claims) will be governed by and construed in accordance with the laws of Singapore. Each party agrees that the courts of the state of Singapore shall have exclusive jurisdiction to settle any dispute or claim arising out of or in connection with this License Agreement or the Work (including non-contractual disputes or claims).
2. Your rights under this License Agreement will automatically terminate without notice and without the

need for a court order if at any point you breach any terms of this License Agreement. In no event will any delay or failure by Bentham Science Publishers in enforcing your compliance with this License Agreement constitute a waiver of any of its rights.
3. You acknowledge that you have read this License Agreement, and agree to be bound by its terms and conditions. To the extent that any other terms and conditions presented on any website of Bentham Science Publishers conflict with, or are inconsistent with, the terms and conditions set out in this License Agreement, you acknowledge that the terms and conditions set out in this License Agreement shall prevail.

Bentham Science Publishers Pte. Ltd.
No. 9 Raffles Place
Office No. 26-01
Singapore 048619
Singapore
Email: subscriptions@benthamscience.net

CONTENTS

PREFACE	i
LIST OF CONTRIBUTORS	ii
CHAPTER 1 BLOCKCHAIN: A SUSTAINABLE TECHNOLOGY	1
Renu Singh, Ashlesha Gupta and *Poonam Mittal*	
INTRODUCTION TO BLOCKCHAIN	1
History of Blockchain	2
Centralized	4
Decentralized	4
Distributed	4
What is Blockchain?	4
Fundamentals of Blockchain Technology	5
Transaction	5
Block	6
Categories of Blockchain Structure	6
Public Blockchain	6
Private Blockchain	6
Consortium/Federated Blockchain	6
Characteristics of Blockchain	7
Decentralization	8
Immutability	8
Persistency	8
Security	8
Capacity	8
Anonymity	8
Auditability	8
Architecture of Blockchain	9
Block	9
Digital Signature	10
Workflow of the Blockchain Process	10
Components of Blockchain	12
Transactions	12
Node	12
Wallet	12
Nonce	13
Cryptography	13
Hash	13
Consensus Algorithm	13
Versions of Blockchain	13
Blockchain Version 1.0 (Cryptocurrency)	14
Blockchain Version 2.0 (Smart Contracts)	14
Blockchain Version 3.0 (DApps)	15
Blockchain Protocols	15
Proof-of-work (PoW)	15
Proof-of-stake (PoS)	15
Applications of Blockchain	16
Blockchain in the Financial Domain	16
Blockchain in Healthcare	17
Blockchain for Unmanned Aerial Vehicles (UAVs)	18

CONCLUSION AND FUTURE SCOPE	19
REFERENCES	20

CHAPTER 2 MAPPING OF BLOCKCHAIN TECHNOLOGY WITH THE INDIAN FINTECH SECTOR FOR SECURING FINANCIAL OPERATIONS 23

Khushwant Singh, Mohit Yadav, Yudhvir Singh and Dheerdhwaj Barak

INTRODUCTION	24
Existing Fintech Sector in India	26
Potential Solution Using Proposed System	27
Proposed Methodology	31
USE CASES FOR BLOCKCHAIN IN FINTECH	35
Payment Processing and Peer-to-Peer Lending	36
Identity Verification and Supply Chain Finance	36
BENEFITS OF THE SYSTEM	38
Payments and Trade Finance	39
Crypto Lending and Digital Identity	39
CHALLENGES ASSOCIATED WITH BLOCKCHAIN	40
CONCLUSION	42
REFERENCES	43

CHAPTER 3 BLOCKCHAIN TECHNOLOGY AND SMART CONTRACTS FOR FINANCIAL TRANSACTIONS IN VIRTUAL ENVIRONMENTS 50

Pooja Sharma, Sangeet Vashishtha, Neeraj Saxena and Shruti Saxena

INTRODUCTION	50
Predictive Analytics	51
Fraud Detection	52
Automated Audits and Reporting	52
Natural Language Processing (NLP) for Contract Interpretation	53
Traditional Contracts vs. Smart Contracts	53
Real Estate Purchase Agreement	54
Example of Smart Contract	54
Hybrid Approach Example	54
Impact of Blockchain-Based Smart Contracts	55
Increased Efficiency:	55
Enhanced Security	55
Transparency and Trust	55
Global Accessibility	56
Innovation and Disruption	56
Decentralization and Democratization	56
Compliance and Governance	56
BLOCKCHAIN TECHNOLOGY: FOUNDATIONS AND KEY CONCEPTS	56
Decentralization and Distributed Ledger	57
Immutable Record through Cryptography	58
Consensus Mechanisms	59
Smart Contracts	60
Transparency and Pseudonymity	60
Tokenization	60
SMART CONTRACTS: SIGNIFICANT BREACHES AND VULNERABILITIES	61
Example 1: The DAO Hack (2016)	61
Example 2: Parity Wallet MultiSig Bug (2017)	62
Example 3: KuCoin Exchange Hack (2020)	62
Example 4: bZx Flash Loan Attack (2020)	62

Example 5: Cream Finance Exploit (2021)	63
Example 6: Ronin Network Hack (2022)	63
PERFORMANCE METRICS AND BENCHMARKS FOR SMART CONTRACT EXECUTION	64
Efficiency Metrics	64
Cost Metrics	64
Security Metrics	64
Interoperability in Blockchain Technology and Smart Contracts for Financial Transactions in Virtual Environments	65
Key Interoperability Challenges in Financial Transactions	65
Solutions for Achieving Interoperability in Financial Transactions	65
Importance in Virtual Financial Environments	66
APPLICATIONS OF BLOCKCHAIN TECHNOLOGY IN VIRTUAL FINANCE	66
REIMAGINING BUSINESS PROCESSES THROUGH BLOCKCHAIN AND SMART CONTRACTS	66
INDUSTRIES BENEFITING FROM SMART CONTRACTS: PRACTICAL IMPLEMENTATION AND ADVANTAGES	73
INSURANCE	73
ADVANTAGES	73
REAL ESTATE	73
ADVANTAGES	73
SUPPLY CHAIN AND LOGISTICS	74
ADVANTAGES	74
HEALTHCARE	74
ADVANTAGES	74
SMART CONTRACTS: ENABLING AUTOMATED VIRTUAL FINANCIAL TRANSACTIONS	74
Understanding Smart Contracts	75
Decentralized Execution	75
Transparency and Immutability	76
Trustless Transactions	76
Cost Efficiency and Speed	76
Programmable Financial Logic	76
BENEFITS AND CHALLENGES OF BLOCKCHAIN AND SMART CONTRACTS IN VIRTUAL FINANCE	76
Benefits	77
Challenges	77
FUTURE PROSPECTS AND CONCLUSION	78
Future Prospects	78
CONCLUSION	79
REFERENCES	79
CHAPTER 4 BLOCKCHAIN: USE OF SMART CONTRACTS IN FINANCE	82
Ambika R. Thakur, Chetna Tiwari, Kartikey Vats and Garima Sharma	
INTRODUCTION	82
BLOCKCHAIN	85
Architecture of Blockchain	85
Blocks	85
Consensus Mechanism	86
Cryptographic Hashing	86
Decentralized Ledger	87

Nodes	88
Working of Blockchain	89
Applications of Blockchain in the Financial Sector	90
Cryptocurrencies and Digital Assets	91
Cross-Border Payments	91
Trade Finance	91
Identity Verification	92
Stock Trading and Settlement	92
Regulatory Compliance	92
Tokenization of Assets	92
Central Bank Digital Currencies (CBDC)	92
Peer-to-Peer Lending	92
SMART CONTRACT	92
Architecture of Smart Contracts	92
Trading and Transaction Rules	93
Key Aspects of Transaction Rules	93
Power and Responsibility Analysis	94
Key Elements of Rights and Responsibilities Analysis	94
Reward and Punishment Mechanism	94
Key Elements of the Reward and Punishment Mechanism	94
Data Traceability	95
Working on Smart Contracts	95
Applications of Smart Contract	97
Loan Agreements	97
Derivatives Trading	97
Insurance Claims Processing	97
Token Offerings (ICOs/STOs)	98
Mortgage Agreements	98
Tokenization of Assets	98
Royalty Agreements	98
Cross-Border Payments	98
P2P Lending and Crowdfunding	98
SYMBIOTIC RELATIONSHIP BETWEEN BLOCKCHAIN TECHNOLOGY AND SMART CONTRACTS	98
BENEFITS	101
CHALLENGES	103
COMPARISON BETWEEN TRADITIONAL FINANCE SYSTEM AND BLOCKCHAIN-BASED FINANCE SYSTEM	104
CONCLUDING REMARKS	108
REFERENCES	109
CHAPTER 5 BLOCKCHAIN IN AGRICULTURAL INFORMATION SYSTEMS AND NETWORKS: FOUNDATION AND FUTURE POTENTIALITIES - A SCIENTIFIC REVIEW	111
P. K. Paul, M. Kayyali, Nilanjan Das and *Ritam Chatterjee*	
INTRODUCTION	112
WORK OBJECTIVE AND AIM	113
METHODS	113
Related Existing Works	114
BASICS OF BLOCKCHAIN AND ML: THE STORY BEHIND BLOCKCHAIN IN THE AGRO FIELD	116
Technologies in Supply Chain Management and Agriculture	116

  Blockchain Technology in Agriculture 117
  Machine Learning in Agriculture 118
  Agriculture as a Career and the Role of Technology 118
AGRO INFORMATICS AND AGRICULTURE 4.0 FOR SOPHISTICATED AGRO DEVELOPMENT 118
FUNDAMENTALS AND EMERGING BLOCKCHAIN APPLICATIONS IN THE AGRICULTURAL SECTOR 121
  Blockchain Technologies in Agro and Food Sectors 122
  Blockchain with Machine Learning Technologies in Improving Supply Chain Management in Agriculture 124
  Blockchain Applications and Agro Enhancement 125
  Enhanced Transparency and Traceability 125
  Improved Efficiency and Cost Reduction 126
  Increased Security and Fraud Prevention 126
  Empowerment of Small-Scale Farmers 126
  Machine Learning Applications in the Agricultural Sector 126
ISSUES, CHALLENGES, AND PROBABLE SOLUTIONS IN AGRO MANAGEMENT USING BLOCKCHAIN SYSTEMS AND MACHINE LEARNING 128
  Core Challenges of ML in Agriculture 132
  Future Potentials of Blockchain & Machine Learning-Supported Agricultural Systems 133
CONCLUDING REMARKS 134
REFERENCES 135

CHAPTER 6 DEEP LEARNING-BASED INTRUSION DETECTION SYSTEM FOR IOT-BASED BLOCKCHAIN SYSTEM 140
J. Jayaganesh, Sreenivas Mekala, M. Kalyan Chakravarthi, R. Sundarrajan, Belsam Jeba Ananth M., Mohit Tiwari and *Manika Manwal*
 INTRODUCTION 141
  Research Objective 141
  Scope and Limitations of Study 141
 LITERATURE REVIEW 142
  Internet of Things Definition 142
  IoT Security Issues and Existing Intrusion Detection Methods 142
  IoT Security Vulnerabilities 143
  Attack by Remote Control 143
  Bricking Attack 143
  Weaponization of Devices 143
  Attack using Wormhole Tunnel 143
  Enhanced Rank Attack on RPL 144
  Attacks Using Sinkholes 144
  Attack by Ballot Stuffing 144
  Attacks using Opportunistic Services 144
  Attacks that Distribute Denial of Service 144
  Botnet Participation 144
  Ransomware 144
 METHODOLOGY 145
  Network Architecture 145
  Architecture of the System 146
  Deep Learning-based Detection 148
  Anomaly Detection based on Deep Learning 148
  Algorithm 1: Deep learning-based intrusion detection model. 150

RESULTS	151
Blackhole Attack	151
Opportunistic Service Attack	151
DDoS Attack	153
Sinkhole Attack	155
Wormhole Attack	156
DISCUSSION	158
Analysis	158
CONCLUSION	160
REFERENCES	160

CHAPTER 7 E-ANALYSIS AND NOTARIZATION OF SOCIAL MEDIA BASED ON BLOCKCHAIN TECHNOLOGY — 162

K. Santhanalakshmi, G. Madhumita, Martin Selvakumar Mohanan, Sathish Kumar R., Belsam Jeba Ananth M., Subhrajit Chanda and Gunjan Chhabra

INTRODUCTION	163
Objective of Study	164
LITERATURE REVIEW	164
Notarization	164
History of Blockchain	165
Attack using False Data	166
Social Media Security based on Blockchain	167
METHODOLOGY	168
Notarization Approach	168
Approach for Proof of Credibility (POC)	169
RESULTS	171
Proof-of-concept	171
PoC Results	173
CONCLUSION	178
REFERENCES	178

CHAPTER 8 DEVELOPMENT OF SMART CITY USING BLOCKCHAIN AND ARTIFICIAL INTELLIGENCE — 181

Caetan Shelke, Preeti Gupta, Binod Kumar, Abhijeet Kaiwade, Belsam Jeba Ananth M., Sumeet Gupta and Satvik Vats

INTRODUCTION	182
Study Objective	184
LITERATURE REVIEW	184
A Sneak Peek at the Two Business Plans	184
AI Business Model	184
Blockchain Business Model	186
The Business Models' Effect	188
An Overview of Smart Cities and Emerging Markets	189
METHODOLOGY	190
Qualitative Methodology	190
The Quantitative Method	191
Population Target	191
Research Instrumentation	191
Analyzing Data	191
Ethical Consideration	191
RESULTS	192
Blockchain and AI's Contributions to Business Development	192

    Modern Businesses' Readiness to Adopt Blockchain and AI Technologies 194
    Obstacles in the Adoption of Blockchain and AI Technology 194
    Contributions, both Theoretical and Practical 195
  CONCLUSION 195
  REFERENCES 196

CHAPTER 9 BLOCKCHAIN, BIG DATA, AND DEEP LEARNING-BASED FRAUD DETECTION SYSTEM FOR CREDIT CARD FRAUD 199
Nur Mohammad Ali Chisty, Shweta Gakhreja, Yogita Satish Garwal, Belsam Jeba Ananth M., Tripti Tiwari, Dharamvir and *Kamreed Udham Singh*
  INTRODUCTION 200
  LITERATURE REVIEW 201
  METHODOLOGY 202
    Pre-applying Phase 202
    Implementing Phase 203
    LSTM Variables and Performance Measurements 205
    The Post-applying Phase 205
    Database of Credit Card Fraud Detection 206
    Research Setup 206
  RESULTS 207
    Research Outcomes 208
    Result Assessment 210
    Comparison with Other DL Algorithms 212
    Comparing with Current ML-based Methods 212
  CONCLUSION 214
  REFERENCES 214

CHAPTER 10 IOT-DRIVEN BLOCKCHAIN SYSTEM FOR PREDICTION OF HEART DISEASE USING SMART HEALTHCARE MONITORING DEEP LEARNING MODEL 216
Mrunal K. Pathak, Shaik Balkhis Banu, Anupama Chadha, Gaurav Kumar, Shashi Kant Mishra, Tarun Jaiswal and *Vikrant Sharma*
  INTRODUCTION 217
  LITERATURE REVIEW 218
  METHODOLOGY 219
    Data Collection Layer 219
    Data Preprocessing Layer 220
    FIS 221
    Prediction Data Layer 222
  RNN 222
  LSTM 223
    Research Setup 225
    Performance Assessment 225
  RESULTS 226
  CONCLUSION 234
  REFERENCES 234

CHAPTER 11 ADOPTION OF MACHINE LEARNING TECHNIQUES IN SMART APPLICATIONS BASED ON BLOCKCHAIN TECHNOLOGY 238
K.M. Rashmi, Balraj Kumar, K.T. Thilagham, Harish Kumar, S. Aswath, Mohit Tiwari and *Rahul Chauhan*
  INTRODUCTION 239
  LITERATURE REVIEW 240

METHODOLOGY	241
Adoption of Blockchain and DRL in Smart House	241
DRL	242
Blockchain-Based Gateway System for Smart Houses	242
RESULTS	246
Study Setup	246
Data	247
Performance of the Blockchain Architecture in Smart Houses	248
Performance of DRL in Smart Houses	249
CONCLUSION	255
REFERENCES	255
SUBJECT INDEX	257

PREFACE

Machine Learning and Blockchain-Challenges, Future Trends and Sustainable Technologies (MLB) by Bentham Science is a brainchild of Keshav Kaushik, Rewa Sharma, and Ayodeji Olalekan Salau. The goal of this book is to make it easier for academics and prospective readers to grasp blockchain technology and machine learning. They will be able to practice and gain expertise with ML techniques thanks to this book. The book will provide readers with a thorough grasp of the cutting-edge technologies around blockchain, artificial intelligence, and machine learning. These technologies have the ability to collect and process enormous amounts of data from the real world. The edited book will be set up with distinct chapters to provide readers with maximum readability, flexibility, and adaptability. We are very grateful to all of our co-authors for sharing their expertise and experience; they are all authorities in their fields. This book is an attempt to gather their thoughts and share them with the world in the format of chapters. This book offers insights into AI, FinTech, Deep Learning, Blockchain, Machine Learning, and Blockchain applications. Academicians, industry professionals, researchers, undergrads, and grads will all find the book useful. We acknowledge Bentham Science Publishers and all of the authors of this book for their cooperative efforts.

Keshav Kaushik
Center for Cyber Security and Cryptology
Sharda School of Computer Science & Engineering
Sharda University, Greater Noida
India

Rewa Sharma
J.C Bose University of Science and Technology
YMCA, Faridabad, India

&

Ayodeji Olalekan Salau
Department of Electrical and Electronics
and Computer Engineering, Afe Babalola University
Ado Ekiti, Nigeria

List of Contributors

Ambika R. Thakur	Department of Computer Science and Engineering, The NorthCap University, Gurugram, India
Abhijeet Kaiwade	Institute of Management and Research., Abhinav Education Society's Institute of Management and Research, Pune, India
Anupama Chadha	Department of Computer Applications, Manav Rachna International Institute of Research and Studies, Faridabad, India
Belsam Jeba Ananth M.	Department of Mechatronics Engineering, SRM Institute of Science and Technology, Kattankulathur, India
Binod Kumar	Department of Computer Applications, JSPM's Rajarshi Shahu College of Engineering, Pune, India
Balraj Kumar	School of Computer Application, Lovely Professional University, Phagwara, Punjab, India
Chetna Tiwari	Department of Computer Science and Engineering, The NorthCap University, Gurugram, India
Chetan Shelke	Alliance College of Engineering and Design, Alliance University, Bangalore, India
Dharamvir	Department of Computer Application, The Oxford College of Engineering, Bengaluru, India
Dheerdhwaj Barak	Department of Computer Science & Engineering, Vaish College of Engineering, Rohtak, India
G. Madhumita	Department of Management Studies, Vels Institute of Science Technology and Advanced Studies (VISTAS), Chennai, India
Garima Sharma	Department of Computer Science and Engineering, The NorthCap University, Gurugram, India
Gunjan Chhabra	Department of Computer Science and Engineering, Graphic Era Hill University, Dehradun, India
Gaurav Kumar	School of Computer Application, Lovely Professional University, Phagwara, Punjab, India
Harish Kumar	Department of Computer Science, King Khalid University, Abha, Saudi Arabia
J. Jayaganesh	Department of Computer Science, Government Arts and Science College Perumbakkam, Chennai, India
K. Santhanalakshmi	Faculty of Management, SRM Institute of Science and Technology, Kattankulathur, India
Kamreed Udham Singh	School of Computing, Graphic Era Hill University, Dehradun, India

K.M. Rashmi	Department of Electronics and Communication Engineering, Manipal Institute of Technology, Manipal Academy of Higher Education, Bengaluru, Manipal, Karnataka, India
K.T. Thilagham	Department of Metallurgical Engineering, Government College of Engineering Salem, Salem, India
Khushwant Singh	Department of Computer Science & Engineering, University Institute of Engineering and Technology, Maharshi Dayanand University, Rohtak, India
Kartikey Vats	Department of Computer Science and Engineering, The NorthCap University, Gurugram, India
Mohit Yadav	Department of Mathematics, University Institute of Sciences, Chandigarh University, Mohali, India
M. Kayyali	Department of Quality Assurance and Accreditation Directorate, Al Maaref University of Applied Sciences, Sarmada, Syria
M. Kalyan Chakravarthi	School of Electronic Engineering, Vellore Institute of Technology, Amaravathi, Andhra Pradesh, India
Manika Manwal	Department of Computer Science and Engineering, Graphic Era Hill University, Dehradun, India
Martin Selvakumar Mohanan	Department of Organization & Human Resource Management, Great Lakes Institute of Management, Chennai, India
Mohit Tiwari	Department of Computer Science and Engineering, Bharati Vidyapeeth's College of Engineering, Delhi, India
Neeraj Saxena	Sandip University, Nashik, India
Nilanjan Das	Siliguri Institute of Technology, Siliguri, India
Nur Mohammad Ali Chisty	Cyber Crime Wing, Anti-Terrorism Unit, Bangladesh Police, Dhaka, Bangladesh
Pooja Sharma	IIMT University, Meerut, India
P. K. Paul	Department of Computer & Information Science, Raiganj University, Raiganj, India
Preeti Gupta	Department of Computer Science and Engineering, Jain University (Deemed-to-be-University), Bangalore, India
Poonam Mittal	Faculty of Informatics and Computing, J.C. Bose University of Science and Technology, YMCA, Faridabad, India
Renu Singh	Faculty of Informatics and Computing, J.C. Bose University of Science and Technology, YMCA, Faridabad, India
Ritam Chatterjee	Department of Computer & Information Science, Raiganj University, Raiganj, India
R. Sundarrajan	Department of Information Techology, Kalasalingam Academy of Research and Education (Deemed to be University), Virudhunagar, India
Rahul Chauhan	Department of Computer Science, Graphic Era Hill University, Graphic Era Deemed to be University, Dehradun, Uttarakhand-248007, India

Sangeet Vashishtha	IIMT University, Meerut, India
Sreenivas Mekala	Department of Information Technology, Sreenidhi Institute of Science & Technology, Hyderabad, India
Sathish Kumar R.	Department of Artificial Intelligence and Machine Learning, Faculty of Engineering and Technology, Jain University (Deemed-to-be-University), Bengaluru, India
Subhrajit Chanda	Jindal Global Law School, OP Jindal Global University, Sonipat, India
Sumeet Gupta	Global Economics and Finance Cluster, School of Business, University of Petroleum and Energy Studies, Dehradun, India
Satvik Vats	Department of Computer Science and Engineering, Graphic Era Hill University, Dehradun, India
Shweta Gakhreja	Manipal University Jaipur, Jaipur, India
S. Aswath	Department of Electronics & Communication Engineering, Vel Tech Rangarajan Dr Sagunthala R&D Institute of Science and Technology, Chennai, India
Shaik Balkhis Banu	Department of Physiotherapy, Fatima College of Health Sciences, Al Ain, UAE
Shashi Kant Mishra	Guru Nanak Institute of Technology, Hyderabad, India
Tripti Tiwari	Department of Management Studies, Bharati Vidyapeeth (Deemed to be University) Institute of Management and Research, Delhi, India
Tarun Jaiswal	National Institute of Technology, Raipur, India
Vikrant Sharma	Department of Computer Science and Engineering, Graphic Era Hill University; Adjunct Professor, Graphic Era Deemed to be University, Dehradun, India
Yudhvir Singh	Department of Computer Science & Engineering, University Institute of Engineering and Technology, Maharshi Dayanand University, Rohtak, India
Yogita Satish Garwal	Manipal University Jaipur, Jaipur, India

CHAPTER 1

Blockchain: A Sustainable Technology

Renu Singh[1,*], **Ashlesha Gupta**[1] **and Poonam Mittal**[1]

[1] *Faculty of Informatics and Computing, J.C. Bose University of Science and Technology, YMCA, Faridabad, India*

Abstract: In recent years, blockchain has become one of the most booming technologies. It has completely revolutionized industries and academia by creating a transparent system of trading money. The blockchain industry has started to get significant investments from corporations and tech mega-corporations. In the upcoming years, its net worth is expected to increase more than three times. Blockchain Technology has grown in popularity because of its trust, transparency, and data security. As a result, everyone, either from academics or industry, wants to learn the Blockchain. This chapter provides a detailed overview of Blockchain Technology, which will help researchers and scholars quickly understand Blockchain. Firstly, we introduce blockchain along with its history and a thorough understanding of different types of networks. Then, the definition of Blockchain, fundamentals, categories of Blockchain structure, characteristics, architecture, workflow, components, version, Blockchain protocols, and finally, applications of Blockchain are discussed.

Keywords: Blockchain technology, Consensus, Cryptography, Distributed, Decentralized applications.

INTRODUCTION TO BLOCKCHAIN

Blockchain Technology (BT) can transform ongoing business methods. Blockchain Technology has now become very popular in both academics and industries. All the technologists, researchers, and research scholars are just picking up the books on blockchain and beginning to study them to master the concepts of Blockchain. Also, people from different backgrounds are very much interested in becoming professionals in blockchain application development. Until one picks up a good source, it becomes extremely difficult to clear the basic concepts of Blockchain Technology. So, to aid one in comprehensively gaining the concepts of Blockchain, we have written this chapter on Blockchain, a Sustainable Technology. This chapter is intended for all levels of software

---

[*] **Corresponding author Renu Singh:** Faculty of Informatics and Computing, J.C. Bose University of Science and Technology, YMCA, Faridabad, India; E-mail: renus2344@gmail.com

Keshav Kaushik, Rewa Sharma & Ayodeji Olalekan Salau (Eds.)
All rights reserved-© 2026 Bentham Science Publishers

engineers, developers, researchers, scholars, and anyone from academia and industry who wants to learn Blockchain Technology in detail.

This chapter includes a very detailed discussion of Blockchain, including the history of Blockchain, Blockchain and its fundamentals, categories, characteristics, architecture, workflow of Blockchain process, components, version, blockchain protocols, and applications. Lastly, we end our chapter with the conclusion.

History of Blockchain

The Distributed ledger concept was introduced in 1976 [1]. After the evolution of cryptography, "Scott Stornetta" and "Stuart Haber" presented a paper titled [2], which provides the concept for time stamping the data in place of the medium. Another idea that plays a major role in Blockchain is "Electronic cash" or "Digital Currency," which was presented by David Chaum. He has also made a major contribution to e-cash schemes and double-spending detection.

Adam Back, in 1997, presented a concept known as "hashcash", which provides a means to control spam emails. Then Wei Dai created money known as "b-money", a peer-to-peer network.

Blockchain originated from Satoshi Nakamoto [3] and was created using Bitcoin paper [3]. This paper focuses mainly on electronic payment systems using cryptography. In this paper, Nakamoto presented a technique that prevents double-spending. The idea of a public ledger was introduced in this paper to track and confirm the transaction history of digital coins.

After some months, an open-source program for implementing Bitcoin was released. Beginning in 2009, Satoshi Nakamoto introduced the first bitcoin. The inventors of Bitcoin are unanimous, but Bitcoin still has a very large community that supports and addresses the different issues of the code.

While there are various cryptocurrencies like Dogecoin, Litecoin, *etc*, Bitcoin holds a maximum market share. The main feature of Bitcoin that attracts users is its capacity to maintain the anonymity of users and transparency. Afterward, the use of Bitcoin grew, and in 2013, investors started to invest heavily in contract-starting. Ethereum has become popular as it provides safety, speed, and a more efficient environment [4]. To understand the major contributions of Blockchain, a summary of its history is shown in Fig. (**1**).

Blockchain is a distributed form of the network. The other two ways in which nodes in the network can be arranged are centralized and distributed, as shown in

Fig. (**2**). To understand the difference between these three network types and distinguish why the distributed form of network is preferred for blockchain, here, we provide a detailed discussion of them.

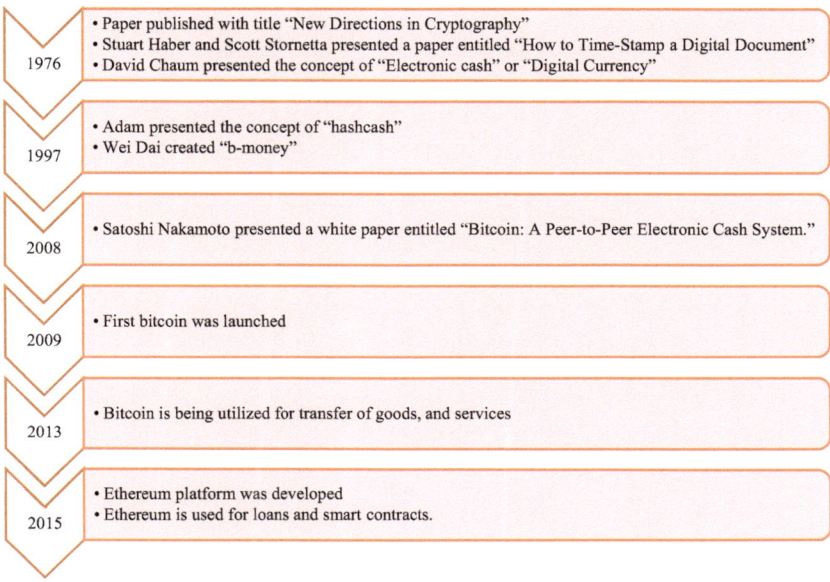

Fig. (1). History of blockchain.

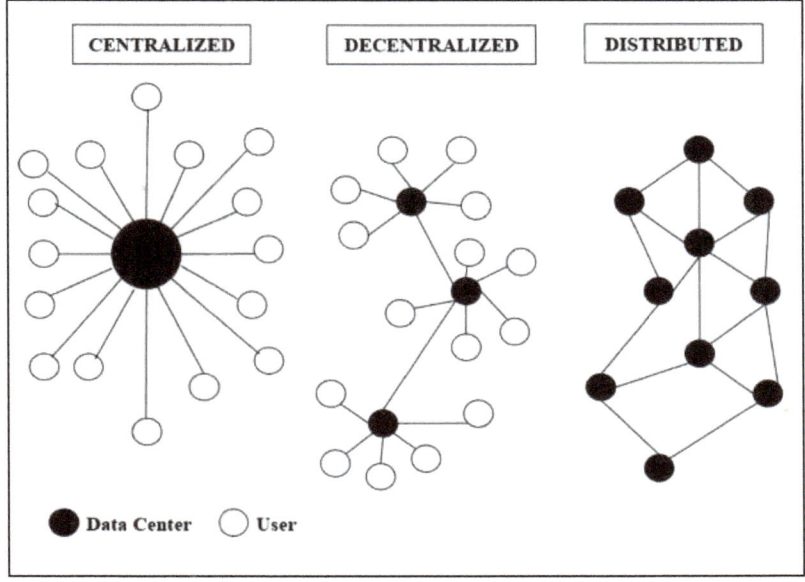

Fig. (2). Types of network.

Centralized

A centralized network is one in which all the users or stations are interconnected with a single network owner or server. This central server stores users' data, which different server users can access.

The problem with a centralized network is that if the central server crashes, the network cannot work properly, and all the data is lost. Moreover, it is possible that the owner of the central server is unavailable, and hence, other users cannot access the data. Also, this type of network is more prone to attacks.

Decentralized

A decentralized network is one in which there is no central owner. Instead, multiple servers store copies of all the data and other users' information.

The decentralized network is also prone to attacks. However, it is more fault-tolerant to attacks than a centralized network.

Distributed

Distributed network is one step further from a decentralized network. In this network, all the users have same access to data. However, user privileges can be enabled if needed [5].

Blockchain follows the distributed network. The benefit of having a distributed network is that all the users have a copy of the data and are more fault-tolerant than other types of networks.

What is Blockchain?

In 1991, the word "blockchain" was introduced. When a team of researchers developed a method for timestamping digital documents in such a way that it is impossible to modify or backdate them. In 2008, Satoshi Nakamoto modified and innovated this technique and developed the first cryptocurrency, Bitcoin.

Blockchain can be defined as a method of recording unviable information for hacking, changing, or cheating data. Another way of defining blockchain is as a network of peer-to-peer blocks that are connected and store some information securely.

In simple words, one can understand Blockchain as a group of computers connected, making the entire network decentralized [6].

The term Blockchain has become very popular in today's world. Hence, various researchers from different backgrounds define blockchain according to their perspective. Some of the popular definitions given by researchers are mentioned below.

According to a study [7], "Blockchain is an open, distributed ledger that can record transactions between two parties efficiently and in a verifiable and permanent way".

According to a study [8], Blockchain can be defined as: "A blockchain is a distributed database of records or public ledger of all transactions or digital events executed and shared among participating parties".

According to a study [9], "A blockchain is a distributed ledger structured into a linked list of blocks. Each block contains an ordered set of transactions. Typical solutions use cryptographic hashes to secure the link from a block to its predecessor".

To understand the Blockchain with the help of an example, consider the time before Google Docs, where, for any update, the administrator must send the document to all participants for updates. Then, each participant will perform the updates on their system and send the updated document to the administrator. The administrator will then combine the participants' updates to prepare the updated document. This process, therefore, consumes a lot of time. But now, with Google Docs, the document can be distributed among all participants, and every participant can make the necessary changes simultaneously.

Blockchain Technology permits digital information to be distributed instead of different copies.

Fundamentals of Blockchain Technology

This section focuses on the fundamentals of BT. A blockchain in the network includes two components – Transaction and Block.

Transaction

In blockchain, a transaction is a transfer of both tangible and non-tangible assets from one person to another person. It is a participant-initiated action.

Block

A block is a data structure inside the Blockchain. It records the transactions and other information like correct sequence, timestamp creation, *etc*. Block, once created, cannot be altered or removed.

Categories of Blockchain Structure

Depending upon the scope of use, blockchain can be public, private, consortium or federated blockchain. Each type of blockchain is discussed below:

Public Blockchain

A public blockchain is one in which everyone inside the network can read and add transactions until they are valid for the applied protocol. Every node inside the public blockchain can do the consensus process. The consensus protocols that are used are Proof-of-Work and Proof-of-Stake.

The disputable thing about public blockchain is that it is very sleepy when including a transaction in the network.

Private Blockchain

Unlike Public Blockchain, there is an access control in Private Blockchain. It can limit the access of data to nodes present in the network and can decide whether a particular node can transact and view within the network [10].

From the perspective of governance and participation, a private blockchain is not decentralized. Moreover, as a single trusted individual or entity manages the whole network, it may be possible that there is no reward for mining. Mining for participants is a form of agreement that transactions cannot be changed.

Consortium/ Federated Blockchain

The private blockchain of different organizations is combined with the consortium blockchain. Each of these blockchains of an organization acts as a node in the network and a stakeholder in alliance, and it is possible only for them to join or quit the network after obtaining permission from the stakeholders. A consortium blockchain is preferred by organizations that work on the same objective [11].

A detailed comparison of these blockchain structures is depicted in Table **1**.

Table 1. Comparison of Blockchain structures.

Feature	Public	Private	Consortium/ Federated
Centralization	No	Yes	Partial
Consensus method	Permissionless	Requires permission	Requires permission
Consensus determination	All miners	Miners of organization	Selected nodes
Read permission	Public	Public/ Restricted	Public/ Restricted
Immutability	Impossible to tamper	Modifiable	Modifiable
Efficiency	Low	High	High
Example	Bitcoin, Bitcoin, Ethereum	R3, Corda, Hyperledger Fabric	IBM Food Trust, Energy Web Foundation

Characteristics of Blockchain

The utilization of blockchain in different applications has become famous due to the characteristics of the blockchain, as shown in Fig. (3). Below are the well-known characteristics of the blockchain.

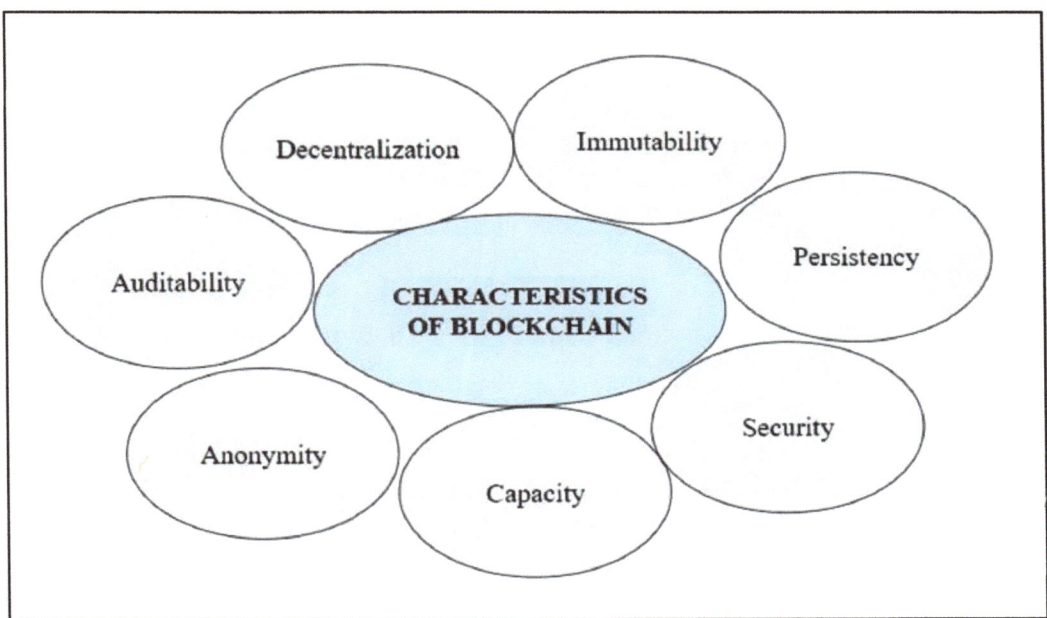

Fig. (3). Characteristics of blockchain.

Decentralization

Blockchain Technology is decentralized; no single entity or individual controls the whole network. In blockchain, there is a group of multiple organizations or nodes that help in the functioning of a network and make it decentralized.

Immutability

Immutability is the feature in blockchain that prevents transactions of the blockchain ledger from being changed or altered. It can convert the auditing process into a fast, adequate, and minimized cost method, providing more trust and integrity to businesses' data.

Persistency

While validating the transactions, the genuine miners will quickly validate the valid transactions, and invalid transactions won't be approved. Also, the transactions included in the blockchain cannot be deleted or rolled back afterward. In this way, blocks that contain invalid transactions can be determined effortlessly.

Security

Blockchain ensures more security as the network is not in the hands of a particular individual or organization. For each node to enter the network, it must be approved by the genuine miners. A proper consensus mechanism is to be followed before entering any node or transaction in the network.

Capacity

In blockchain, multiple computers work together, having more capacity than the centralized network.

Anonymity

Every user of the blockchain interacts with an address, which means the actual identity of the user remains anonymous. However, due to intrinsic limitations, blockchain does not ensure 100% privacy preservation.

Auditability

The user bitcoin balances are stored in the Unspent Transaction Output (UTXO) model [13], which says that any transaction to be added to the blockchain must refer to the previous unspent transaction. When the ongoing transaction is considered, the status of the unspent transaction is changed from unspent to spent.

In this manner, transactions in the blockchain can be effortlessly approved and tracked.

Architecture of Blockchain

Fig. (4) illustrates the sequence of blocks of blockchain. The block stores the complete record of transactions like the traditional public ledger [12]. Every block contains one parent block—the block header stores the previous block's hash value [13]. In the Ethereum blockchain, the hash of the successor blocks is also stored [14]. The block having no parent block is termed a Genesis Block.

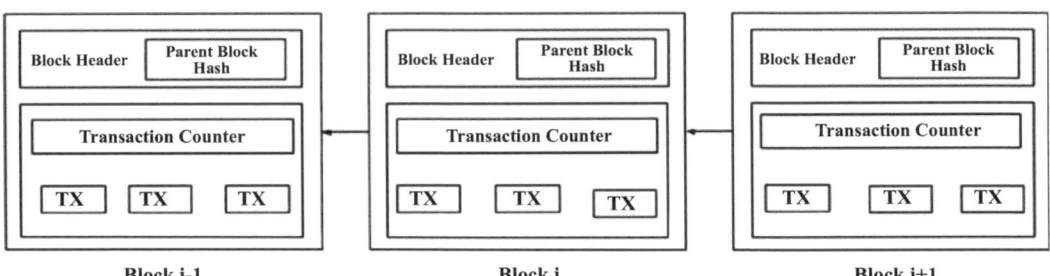

Fig. (4). Sequence of blocks.

The internal parts of the block in the Blockchain are discussed below:

Block

As shown in Fig. (5), a block includes a block header and a body. Block header particularly includes,

Block Version: It includes the group of validation rules to be implemented for a block.

Merkle Tree Root Hash: The collection of all hashes of the transactions in a block.

Timestamp: It is the time in seconds according to universal time, January 1, 1970.

nBits: It is the required limit for the hash of the valid block.

Nonce: Nonce is a 4-byte value that begins from 0 and grows with each hash value computation.

Parent Block: This is a 256-bit hash value directed to the preceding block.

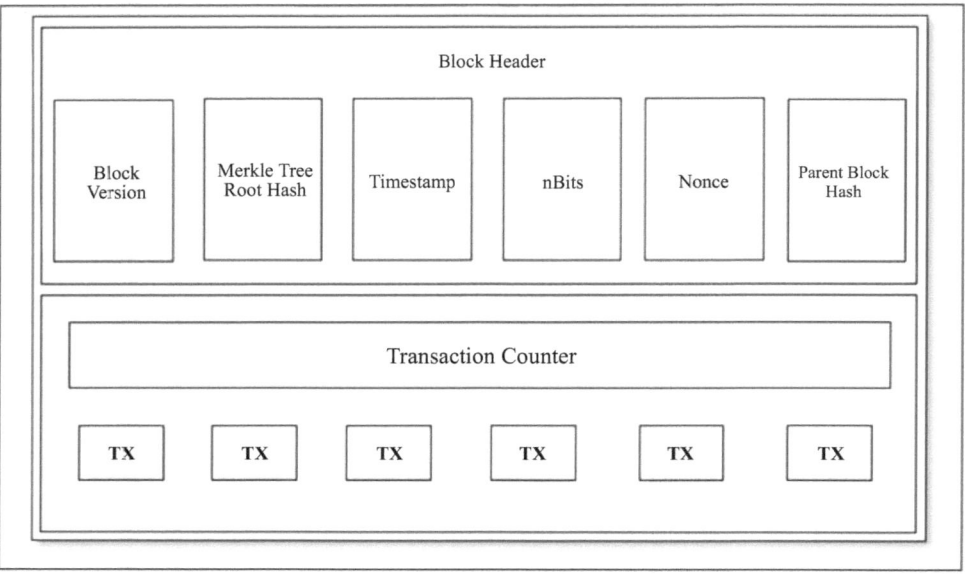

Fig. (5). Structure of a block.

The block body is comprised of transactions and a transaction counter. The number of transactions included in a block is based on two parameters. One is the size of each transaction, and the other is the block size. Blockchain validates the authenticity of transactions using the asymmetric cryptographic algorithm [15]. Next, we discussed the digital signature.

Digital Signature

Every blockchain user has a public and private key. The private key is the secret key used to sign the transactions. Digitally signed transactions are disseminated across the whole network. Digital signature comprises two phases: the signing phase and the verification phase. Blockchain's most popular digital signature method is the elliptic curve digital signature algorithm (ECDSA) [16].

Workflow of the Blockchain Process

To add a new transaction to the blockchain, it must be validated by every participant of the related blockchain ecosystem. Participants apply a specific algorithm to validate and verify a new transaction. The related blockchain ecosystem determines what is valid, which differs for different ecosystems. All the transactions validated and verified by this process are grouped in a block.

All other nodes are subsequently informed about the newly prepared block and added to the existing blockchain, as shown in Fig. (**6**). Every succeeding block comprises a hash and a unique digital fingerprint of the previous block [17].

Fig. (**7**) provides a step-by-step breakdown of how blockchain transactions are carried out. Bob wants to send some money to Alice. Once Bob initiates and triggers the financial transaction, it will be represented as a "transaction." Then, it is broadcast to all the parties included in the network. Now, this transaction is being approved by the network participants. When the transaction is approved as "valid," it is fed into the new block along with the hash value, and all the participating nodes are informed to append the previous chain of blocks in the Blockchain distributed ledger. In this way, the money is transferred from Bob to Alice.

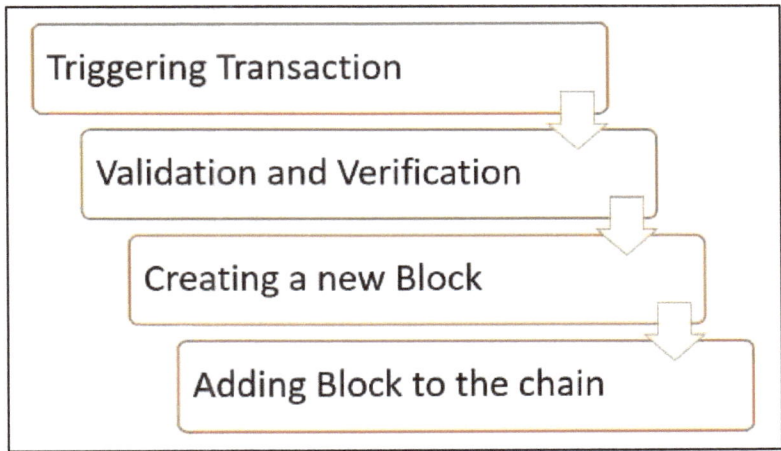

Fig. (6). A general workflow of Blockchain.

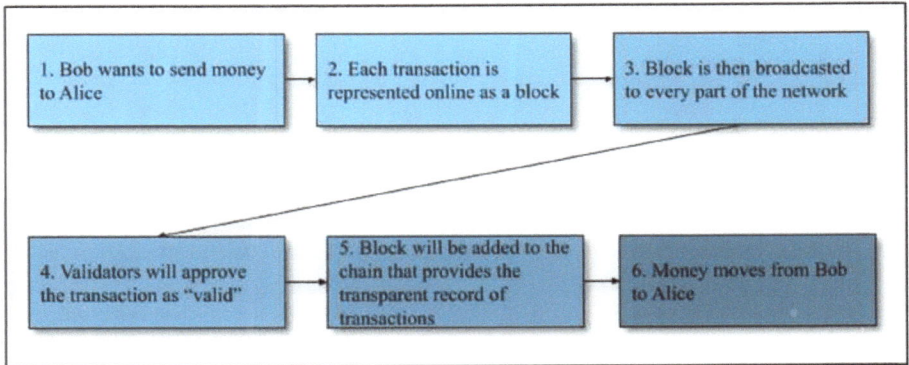

Fig. (7). Working of Blockchain for transfer of money.

Components of Blockchain

As the name itself, blockchain tells that the information will be stored in blocks. Various components are to be utilized to store the information in the blocks in the form of chains in a secure way. The following are the components of blockchain technology:

Transactions

The Blockchain digital ledger contains a list of transactions that occurred on the network.

Node

It can be in two forms - Full node and Partial node. Full nodes keep a complete copy of every transaction. Full nodes are used to approve, validate, and reject the transactions. Partial nodes are also known as lightweight nodes, as they do not keep a complete copy of the blockchain ledger. Partial nodes only store the hash value for a particular transaction. All the transactions of partial nodes are accessed with hash values. Also, they have low computational power and low storage.

Wallet

The wallet can be linked to a bank account. It can be stored on different platforms and devices, enabling users to send and receive cryptocurrency. Below, we explained the criteria for wallet selection and the various types of wallets.

Criteria for Wallet Selection

- Security
- Use of cryptography algorithms
- Personal spending *vs.* investments
- Ease of Use

Types of Wallets

- **Desktop:** Wallet can be installed on a computer or a laptop. They can only be accessed from the computer where they were downloaded. It provides excellent security. However, if a computer crashes, one is likely to lose money.
- **Cloud:** They are available from any device or location because they are cloud-based and online. Other parties may access your wallet since private keys are stored online (Hack).
- **Mobile Device:** It can be easily downloaded on your mobile device *via* the App Store or Play Store. Many are safe, having multiple signature access and backup

options if the phone is lost.
- **Hardware:** The storage of crypto money on a USB or hard drive is called a H/W wallet. Even though H/W wallets execute transactions online, they are held offline, which increases security.
- **Paper:** They are printed out on a piece of paper. It can be carried easily and stored in a safety deposit box. They provide a high level of security because they are printed. Here, the paper is on par with the money.

Nonce

Nonce is the abbreviation for "number only used once". Nonce is added to the hash or the encrypted block of the blockchain. This is a random 32-bit integer that helps in the generation of new blocks or for validating the transaction. Nonce is utilized to increase the security of a transaction.

To find a number that can be nonce is quite difficult. A substantial amount of trial and error is needed [9].

Cryptography

To protect the information across the network based on code.

Hash

Hashing is very important in Cryptography. It maps the information inside the blockchain to a fixed size. In blockchain, the hash value of a particular transaction is the input value for the other transaction. The hash function of the blockchain must have Puzzle friendliness, Hidden, and Collision resistance as a property.

Consensus Algorithm

Consensus is a mechanism that allows all blockchain network nodes to agree on the present state of the ledger and generate trust with non-identified network partners. A network with multiple nodes or users is designed to provide reliability through a consensus mechanism. As a result of consensus procedures, blockchain can achieve dependability and trust with other nodes while assuring the network. It is beneficial when it is utilized to keep records.

Versions of Blockchain

The benefits of Blockchain Technology show that it is a disruptive technology that can completely restructure society and how it functions. To understand Blockchain Technology better and from an organization and convenience point of view, the current and potential activities in the blockchain revolution are divided into three categories, as shown in Fig. (8).

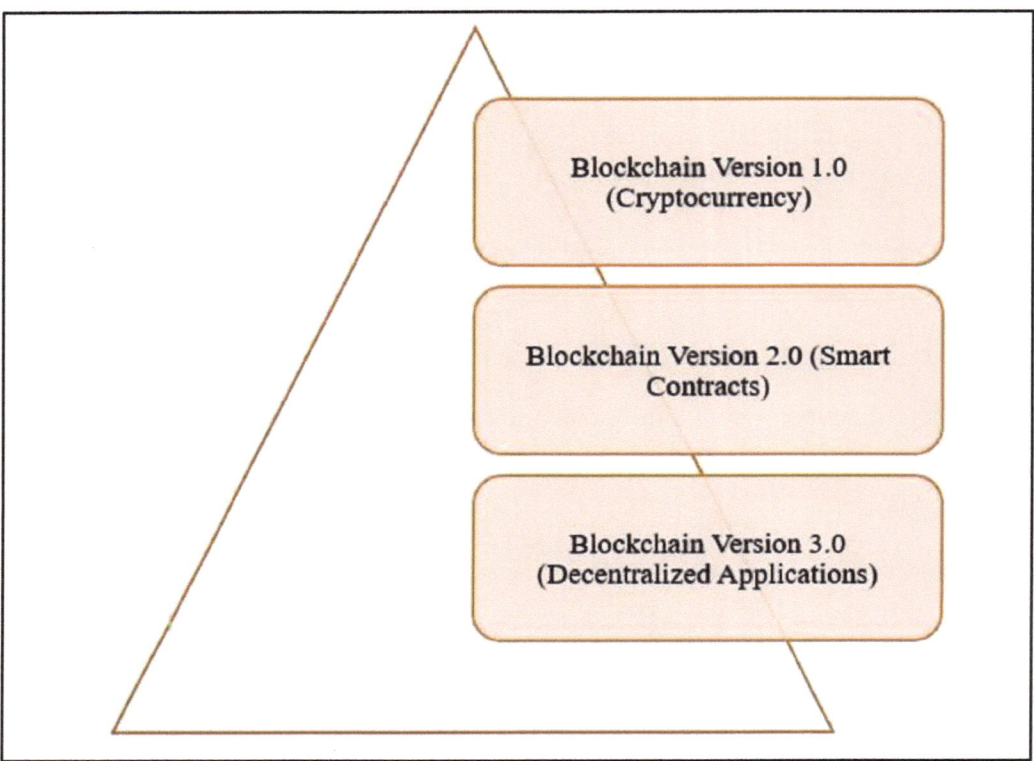

Fig. (8). Different versions of blockchain.

These versions of the Blockchain revolution were first described in the book by Melanie Swan [18].

Blockchain Version 1.0 (Cryptocurrency)

Hall Finley, 2005, developed blockchain 1.0. He implemented Distributed Ledger Technology (DLT), the first application of Cryptocurrency. Cryptocurrency helps in financial transactions and is implemented with the help of Bitcoin. This version of Blockchain includes all the alternative coins [4] and the fundamental applications like currency transfer and digital payment systems.

Blockchain Version 2.0 (Smart Contracts)

In Version 1.0 of blockchain, the mining was wasteful, and the network couldn't be scaled. This limitation was resolved by version 2.0. Version 2.0 of Blockchain is not restricted to cryptocurrency but is extended to smart contracts. The small computers that reside in the chain of blocks are smart contracts. These small computers are free programs that run automatically, according to the defined conditions. In blockchain version 2.0, Bitcoin was changed with Ethereum.

Blockchain Version 3.0 (DApps)

This version of blockchain includes DApps called decentralized applications. DApp is the same as a regular app with a frontend written in any language called backend code, and then backend code is performed with a decentralized P2P network [19].

Some examples of DApps include BitMessage, Tor, Popcorn, and BitTorrent.

Blockchain Protocols

Consensus methods are used to validate the transactions of a public blockchain so that there will be no involvement of third parties like banks.

The two such methods are: "Proof-of-work (PoW)" and "Proof-of-stake (PoS)". Their major goal of consensus is to know that the transaction is valid and the same, but how they do it is slightly different [20].

Proof-of-work (PoW)

Proof-of-work was the first consensus mechanism. It has been used for writing Ethereum and Bitcoin till now. However, starting in 2022, Ethereum will move to Proof-of-Stake. The foundation of PoW is cryptography, which relies on mathematical formulations that computers can use to solve problems.

PoW has two major limitations. Firstly, it consumes a lot of power. Secondly, it can only examine a certain number of transactions simultaneously. Bitcoin can handle only seven transactions at a time. The average completion time of a transaction is at least ten minutes, which increases with the busy network conditions. Due to these limitations of PoW, another consensus method, PoS, is being used.

Proof-of-stake (PoS)

This consensus method also uses cryptographic algorithms to validate the transactions, but the difference is that a designated validator determines whether a transaction is valid. The designated validator is chosen based on the number of coins it has or its stake.

In PoS, technically, no one is mining, and there is no block reward. The blocks are forged instead. A certain amount of coins are locked on the network by participating in this.

The higher a person's stake, the higher the mining strength and the likelihood of choosing them as the validator for upcoming blocks.

Techniques like randomized block selection and coin age selection ensure that those with the maximum coins are not always chosen for validating the new block. While incorporating randomized block selection, the forgers with a maximum stake and minimum hash are chosen.

The outcomes of PoS are faster transaction time and lower costs. Transactions in cryptocurrencies like NEO and DASH can be sent and received in seconds.

Applications of Blockchain

Blockchain technology is the leading technology in today's world and has the potential to dominate every field, from financial to supply chain and health care. Blockchain technology eliminates the need for mediators and promotes digital trust. In blockchain technology, digital trust is achieved by storing the information so no one can remove it. Blockchain has applications in the supply chain, health care, the Internet of Things, International payments, peer-to-peer transactions, copyright and ownership protection, building a full-proof voting system (EVoting), and many more. Here, we discuss some of the applications of Blockchain in detail.

Blockchain in the Financial Domain

Blockchain in the financial domain can provide private securities and insurance.

Private Securities: An organization spends a lot of money to go public. A syndicate bank is required to underwrite the deals and recruit the investors. The secondary market for the organization's shares is mentioned on stock exchanges, allowing it to operate safely and swiftly settle and clear trades. Businesses can now be shared immediately *via* blockchain technology [8].

Insurance: Blockchain can be used to register assets with unique identification by one or more identifiers and is challenging to copy or destroy. These identifiers can be used to trace the transactions' history and confirm who owns an asset. Property like automobiles, real estate, laptops, physical assets, and other valuable items may be registered on the blockchain, and everyone's transaction history may be verified, particularly insurance companies.

Blockchain in Healthcare

Initially, Blockchain Technology was implemented for financial applications, but now it is being utilized in different areas like the biomedical field [21]. The capability of BT to stabilize and secure the dataset with which network users can engage with distinct categories of transactions in neuroscience, EHR Medical, Clinical Research, Medical fraud detection, Neuroscience, and Pharmaceuticals in Industry & Research [22], is shown in Fig. (**9**).

EHR (Electronic Health Records): Interacting with a patient's current and historical health data becomes challenging for doctors. That is why many researchers have introduced blockchain technology to maintain patients' health records.

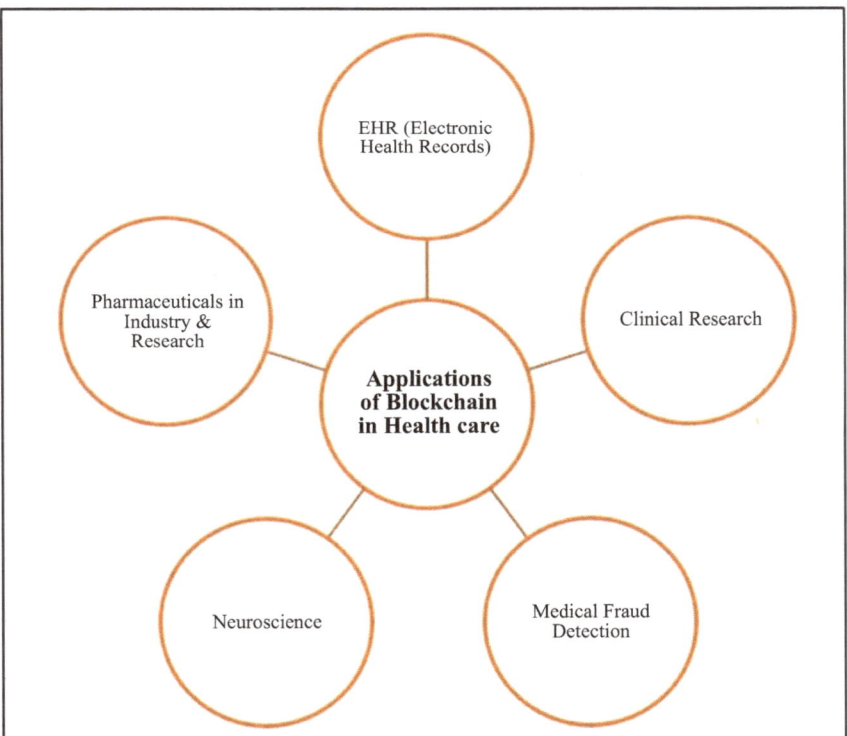

Fig. (9). Applications of blockchain in healthcare.

"MedRec" [23], a prototype, is a decentralized record management method that gives patients a comprehensive and immutable history of their health records. It helps different providers and therapy institutions access healthcare information easily.

Clinical Research: Clinical studies may encounter various problems such as data integrity, data privacy, data sharing, keeping records, and enrollment [24] of patients. Blockchain technology, the next generation [25], can offer workable solutions to these problems.

A framework [26] is proposed that takes the patient's informed consent and uses it for storing and tracking the clinical records to be publicly verifiable, secure, and not falsifiable.

Medical fraud detection: The management of healthcare supply chains is a major application of Blockchain. Any compromise to the supply chain in healthcare will impact the patient's health [27]. Supply chains are vulnerable to fraudulent attacks and have gaps that can be exploited. By offering data transparency and product traceability, blockchain provides a safe and secure technology to solve this issue. Manipulating the blockchain is difficult as it is implemented with smart contracts [28].

Neuroscience: BT has various applications in neuroscience, like the reenactment of the brain, brain augmentation, and brain thinking. A medium is to be used to store the entire digitization of the human brain, and blockchain innovation comes into play here.

Pharmaceutical Industry & Research: One of the fastest-growing sectors in healthcare is the pharmaceutical industry. This industry assists and guarantees safe and valid health products and drugs to the market. Additionally, this sector helps in the examination [31] and processing of safe medications, promoting faster patient recovery.

Blockchain for Unmanned Aerial Vehicles (UAVs)

UAVs are a subset of robotic aircraft that may carry payloads and carry out autonomous or remotely controlled aerial missions [29]. Due to their high mobility, UAVs can be operated even in distant locations without physical and technological infrastructure. UAVs were first only employed in military settings. However, due to their rising popularity, technological development, and increased awareness among professionals in business and academia, their uses are no longer restricted to the military [30].

As shown in Fig. **(10)**, the major applications that are in use of UAVs are [31]: saving lives [32], rescue operations [33], agriculture and farming [34], inspecting pipelines [35], constructing structures [36], delivering commodities and medical supplies [37], recording and editing video [38].

With more UAVs in the air, new difficulties must be overcome, including increased air traffic, choosing the best routes, creating flight plans, handling collisions, cyber-physical attacks, and UAV swarms. As per research, these difficulties can be overcome with tools like blockchain. Blockchain is considered a method of empowering UAVs and enhancing their safety, accuracy, and controllability [39].

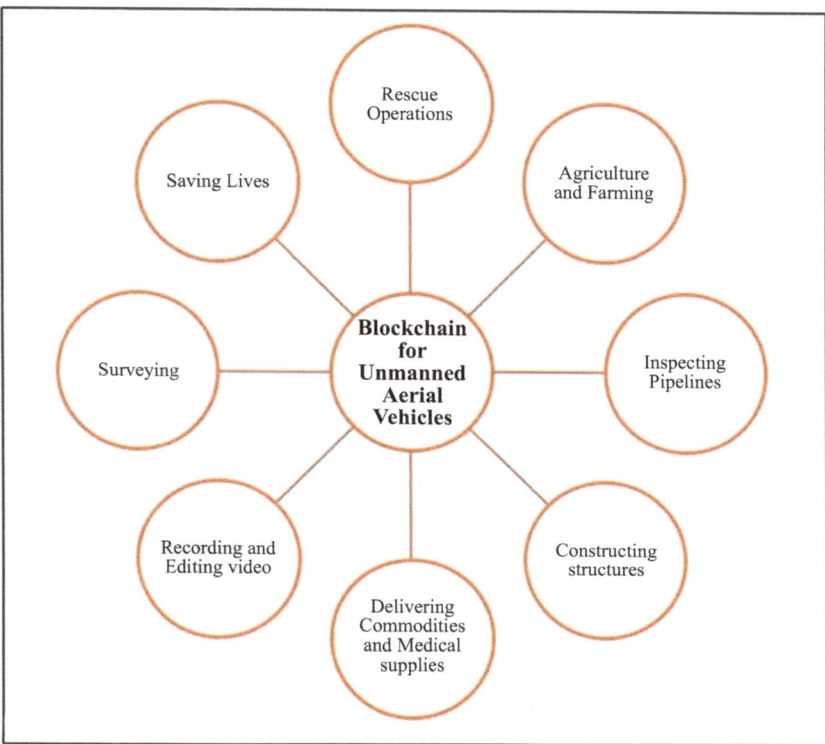

Fig. (10). Applications of blockchain for unmanned aerial vehicles.

CONCLUSION AND FUTURE SCOPE

The four main qualities of blockchain—decentralization, persistency, anonymity, and audibility—have demonstrated their potential to revolutionize traditional industries and academia. Hence, we wrote this book chapter to help everyone get a quick start to Blockchain Technology. Firstly, we introduce blockchain, its history, and types of networks. Then, we provided some popular definitions of Blockchain, its fundamentals, categories, characteristics, architecture, workflow, components, versions, and protocols. Lastly, we offered the applications of Blockchain in different domains.

REFERENCES

[1] W. Diffie, and M.E. Hellman, "New directions in cryptography", In: *Democratizing Cryptography: The Work of Whitfield Diffie and Martin Hellman*, vol. 42, New York, NY, USA: Association for Computing Machinery, 2022, pp. 365-390.
[http://dx.doi.org/10.1145/3549993.3550007]

[2] S. Haber, and W. Scott Stornetta, "How to time-stamp a digital document", In: *Advances in Cryptology-CRYPTO '90*, A. J. Menezes and S. A. Vanstone, Eds., Lecture Notes in Computer Science, vol. 537, Berlin, Heidelberg: Springer, 1991, pp. 437–455.
[http://dx.doi.org/10.1007/3-540-38424-3_32]

[3] S. Nakamoto, "Bitcoin: A Peer-to-Peer Electronic Cash System," 2008. [Online]. Available: https://bitcoin.org/bitcoin.pdf

[4] S. S. Sarmah, "Understanding Blockchain Technology," *Computer Science and Engineering*, vol. 8, no. 2, pp. 23–29, 2018.
[http://dx.doi.org/10.5923/j.computer.20180802.02]

[5] G.R. Nair, S. Sebastian, G. R. Nair, and S. Sebastian, Blockchain technology centralised ledger to distributed ledger. *Int. Res. J. Eng. Technol.*, vol. 4, pp. 2395–0072, 2017. Available from:https://www.academia.edu/download/53539998/IRJET-V4I3711.pdf

[6] A. Lastovetska, "Blockchain Architecture Basics: Components, Structure, Benefits & Creation," MLSDev, 2021. Available: https://mlsdev.com/blog/156-how-to-build-your-own-blockchain-architecture. [Accessed: Feb. 21, 2023].

[7] M. Iansiti, and K. R. Lakhani, "The truth about blockchain", *Harv. Bus. Rev.*, vol. 2017, 2017. Available from:https://e-tarjome.com/storage/btn_uploaded/2019-09-25/1569393941_10128-etarome-English.pdf

[8] M. Crosby, and P. Nachiappan, Pattanayak, S. Verma, and V. Kalyanaraman, "Blockchain Technology - BEYOND BITCOIN". *Berkley Eng.*, p. 35, 2016. Available from:https://scet.berkeley.edu/wp-content/uploads/AIR-2016-Blockchain.pdf

[9] X. Xu, I. Weber, and M. Staples, *Architecture for Blockchain Applications*, Lecture Notes in Computer Science, vol. 11474, Springer, 2019. Available from:https://link.springer.com/content/pdf/10.1007/978-3-030-03035-3.pdf
[http://dx.doi.org/10.1007/978-3-030-03035-3]

[10] R. Bhandari, and U. Suman, "Broker based secure web service composition using star topology", *CSI 6th Int. Conf. Softw. Eng. (CONSEG)*, 2012, pp. 1-7..
[http://dx.doi.org/10.1109/CONSEG.2012.6349493]

[11] O. Dib, K. Brousmiche, and A. Durand, "Consortium blockchains: Overview, applications and challenges", Available: https://www.researchgate.net/publication/328887130_Consortium_Blockchains_Overview_Applications_and_Challenges

[12] D.L.K. Chuen, *Handbook of Digital Currency: Bitcoin, Innovation, Financial Instruments, and Big Data*, Amsterdam, Netherlands: Academic Press (Elsevier), 2015.
[http://dx.doi.org/10.1016/C2014-0-01905-3]

[13] Z. Zheng, S. Xie, H. Dai, X. Chen, and H. Wang, An overview of blockchain technology: Architecture, consensus, and future trends. *Proc. - 2017 IEEE 6th Int. Congr. Big Data*, 2017, pp. 557-564.
[http://dx.doi.org/10.1109/BigDataCongress.2017.85]

[14] V. Buterin, "A next-generation smart contract and decentralized application platform," Ethereum White Paper, 2014. [Online]. Available:https://finpedia.vn/wp-content/uploads/2022/02/Ethereum_white_papera_next_generation_smart_contract_and_decentralized_application_platform-vitalik-buterin.pdf

[15] Information Economy Division and Commerce and Information Policy Bureau, "Survey on Blockchain Technologies and Related Services FY2015 Report: The Aim of the Survey Background," Ministry of Economy, Trade and Industry (METI), Japan, 2016. [Online]. Available: https://smallake.kr/wp-content/uploads/2016/06/0531_01e.pdf

[16] A. Triwinarko, *Elliptic Curve Digital Signature Algorithm.* ECDSA, 2005, pp. 1-6. [Online] Available from:contecsi.tecsi.org

[17] M.H. Miraz, and M. Ali, "Applications of blockchain technology beyond cryptocurrency", *Annals of Emerging Technologies in Computing,* vol. 2, no. 1, pp. 1-6, 2018. [http://dx.doi.org/10.33166/AETiC.2018.01.001]

[18] M. Swan, *Blockchain: Blueprint for a New Economy,* uploaded by K. Rarhi, Academia.edu, 2020.

[19] "Different Version of Blockchain - GeeksforGeeks," GeeksforGeeks, Jul. 23, 2025 Available from:https://www.geeksforgeeks.org/different-version-of-blockchain/ (accessed Feb. 21, 2023).

[20] A. Rosic, "What is Blockchain Technology? A Step-by-Step Guide For Beginners", Blockgeeks. [Online]. Available: https://blockgeeks.com/guides/what-is-blockchain-technology/. [Accessed: Feb. 21, 2023].

[21] T.T. Kuo, H.E. Kim, and L. Ohno-Machado, "Blockchain distributed ledger technologies for biomedical and health care applications", *J. Am. Med. Inform. Assoc.,* vol. 24, no. 6, pp. 1211-1220, 2017.
[http://dx.doi.org/10.1093/jamia/ocx068] [PMID: 29016974]

[22] A.A. Siyal, A.Z. Junejo, M. Zawish, K. Ahmed, A. Khalil, and G. Soursou, "Applications of blockchain technology in medicine and healthcare: Challenges and future perspectives", *Cryptography,* vol. 3, no. 1, p. 3, 2019.
[http://dx.doi.org/10.3390/cryptography3010003]

[23] A. Ekblaw, A. Azaria, J. D. Halamka, and A. Lippman, "A Case Study for Blockchain in Healthcare: MedRec Prototype for Electronic Health Records and Medical Research Data," MIT Media Lab and Beth Israel Deaconess Medical Center, White Paper, Aug. 2016. [Online]. Available: https://www.media.mit.edu/publications/medrec-whitepaper/

[24] "How blockchain will revolutionise clinical trials | pharmaphorum." Available from:https://pharmaphorum.com/views-and-analysis/how-blockchain-will-revolutionize-clinical-trials-clinical-trials/ (accessed Feb. 21, 2023).

[25] M. Alsumidaie, "Blockchain Concepts Emerge in Clinical Trials", 2018. Available from: https://www.appliedclinicaltrialsonline.com/view/blockchain-concepts-emerge-clinical-trials

[26] M. Benchoufi, R. Porcher, and P. Ravaud, Blockchain protocols in clinical trials: Transparency and traceability of consent. In: *F1000Res.* vol. 6, p. 66, 2018.
[http://dx.doi.org/10.12688/f1000research.10531.5]

[27] K.A. Clauson, E.A. Breeden, C. Davidson, and T.K. Mackey, "Leveraging Blockchain Technology to Enhance Supply Chain Management in Healthcare: An exploration of challenges and opportunities in the health supply chain", *Blockchain in Healthcare Today,* vol. 1, no. 0, 2018.
[http://dx.doi.org/10.30953/bhty.v1.20]

[28] "Blockchain for fraud prevention: Industry use cases IBM Supply Chain and Blockchain Blog." Jul. 2017. Available:https://www.ibm.com/blogs/blockchain/2017/07/blockchain-for-fraud-prevent-on-industry-use-cases/

[29] I.J. Jensen, D.F. Selvaraj, and P. Ranganathan, "Blockchain technology for networked swarms of unmanned aerial vehicles UAVs", *20th IEEE International Symposium on A World of Wireless, Mobile and Multimedia Networks, WoWMoM 2019,* Washington, DC, USA, 2019, pp. 1-7..
[http://dx.doi.org/10.1109/WoWMoM.2019.8793027]

[30] M. Alwateer, S.W. Loke, and A.M. Zuchowicz, "Drone services: issues in drones for location-based

[31] M. Alwateer, and S. Loke, Enabling drone services: drone crowdsourcing and drone scripting. *IEEE Access,* vol. 7, pp. 1-1, 2019.
[http://dx.doi.org/10.1109/ACCESS.2019.2933234]

services from human-drone interaction to information processing", *J. Locat. Based Serv.,* vol. 13, no. 2, pp. 94-127, 2019.
[http://dx.doi.org/10.1080/17489725.2018.1564845]

[32] A. Claesson, L. Svensson, P. Nordberg, M. Ringh, M. Rosenqvist, T. Djarv, J. Samuelsson, O. Hernborg, P. Dahlbom, A. Jansson, and J. Hollenberg, "Drones may be used to save lives in out-o--hospital cardiac arrest due to drowning," *Resuscitation,* vol. 114, pp. 152–156, 2017.
[http://dx.doi.org/10.1016/j.resuscitation.2017.01.003]

[33] S. W. Loke, M. Alwateer, and V. S. A. Abeysinghe Achchige Don, Virtual space boxes and drone-a--reference-station localisation for drone services: An approach based on signal strengths. In *Proc. DroNet '16: 2nd Workshop on Micro Aerial Vehicle Networks, Systems, and Applications for Civilian Use,* Singapore, 2016, pp. 45–48.
[http://dx.doi.org/10.1145/2935620.2935627]

[34] M. Bacco, A. Berton, E. Ferro, C. Gennaro, A. Gotta, S. Matteoli, F. Paonessa, M. Ruggeri, G. Virone, and A. Zanella. "Smart farming: Opportunities, challenges and technology enablers", In: *in Proc. 2018 IoT Vertical and Topical Summit on Agriculture - Tuscany (IOT Tuscany),* Tuscany, Italy, 2018, pp. 1–6.
[http://dx.doi.org/10.1109/IOT-TUSCANY.2018.8373043]

[35] A. Shukla, H. Xiaoqian, and H. Karki, , pp. 194-200, 2016. Autonomous tracking and navigation controller for an unmanned aerial vehicle based on visual data for inspection of oil and gas pipelines.*International Conference on Control, Automation and Systems (ICCAS),* Gyeongju, Korea (South),. 2016, pp. 194-200.
[http://dx.doi.org/10.1109/ICCAS.2016.7832320]

[36] S. Daftry, C. Hoppe and H. Bischof, "Building with drones: Accurate 3D facade reconstruction using MAVs," *2015 IEEE International Conference on Robotics and Automation (ICRA),* Seattle, WA, USA, 2015, pp. 3487-3494.

[37] C.A. Thiels, J.M. Aho, S.P. Zietlow, and D.H. Jenkins, "Use of unmanned aerial vehicles for medical product transport", *Air Med. J.,* vol. 34, no. 2, pp. 104-108, 2015.
[http://dx.doi.org/10.1016/j.amj.2014.10.011] [PMID: 25733117]

[38] E. Natalizio, R. Surace, V. Loscrì, F. Guerriero, and T. Melodia. Filming sport events with mobile camera drones: Mathematical modeling and algorithms. Research Report, 2012. Available from:https://hal.inria.fr/hal-00801126/

[39] T. Alladi, V. Chamola, N. Sahu, and M. Guizani, "Applications of blockchain in unmanned aerial vehicles: A review", *Vehicular Communications,* vol. 23, p. 100249, 2020.
[http://dx.doi.org/10.1016/j.vehcom.2020.100249]

CHAPTER 2

Mapping of Blockchain Technology with the Indian Fintech Sector for Securing Financial Operations

Khushwant Singh[1,*], Mohit Yadav[2], Yudhvir Singh[1] and Dheerdhwaj Barak[3]

[1] *Department of Computer Science & Engineering, University Institute of Engineering and Technology, Maharshi Dayanand University, Rohtak, India*

[2] *Department of Mathematics, University Institute of Sciences, Chandigarh University, Mohali, India*

[3] *Department of Computer Science & Engineering, Vaish College of Engineering, Rohtak, India*

Abstract: The term "Fintech" (Financial Technology) refers to software and other spearheading technologies adopted by different organizations to automate and enhance financial services. It refers to the technology that improves the backend system at traditional financial institutions. In FY22, $8.53 billion was invested in India's Fintech industry. It has been anticipated that the FinTech industry will generate around $200 billion in revenue by the year 2030 and overall throughput will be $1 trillion. Fintech is expanding quickly, yet there are several problems in the current fintech market including interacting with legacy systems like banks, data and payment security, compliance, lack of end-user awareness, retaining users, and user experience. Due to the development of fintech, more data is now accessible in digital formats, which facilitates analysis and the generation of insights but also increases the risk of security breaches. Blockchain is disruptive technology using which one can securely move money from one account to another without using a bank or any financial organization The term "distributed ledger technology" is often used interchangeably with "blockchain technology" in the financial services corporation. Each transaction has a trustworthy record, thus there is no chance of changing to earlier ones. In essence, blockchain technology can completely ensure the accuracy of every transaction. In this study, the problems facing India's fintech industry are described in detail, and possible solutions employing blockchain distributed ledger technology are suggested. Additionally, it finds blockchain technology has the ability to enhance the security and competence of financial operations in the Indian fintech sector, there are challenges such as regulatory uncertainty and scalability that require to be addressed. The paper concludes with recommendations for the upcoming development and adoption of blockchain technology in the Indian fintech sector.

---

* **Corresponding author Khushwant Singh:** Department of Computer Science & Engineering, University Institute of Engineering and Technology, Maharshi Dayanand University, Rohtak, India; E-mail: erkhushwantsingh@gmail.com

Keshav Kaushik, Rewa Sharma & Ayodeji Olalekan Salau (Eds.)
All rights reserved-© 2026 Bentham Science Publishers

Keywords: Blockchain, Cryptocurrency, DeFi, FinTech India, FinTech, Security.

INTRODUCTION

Fintech is a word used to explain companies that incorporate technology to boost or automate financial services and processes [1]. The combination of "financial" and "technology" forms the term and refers to a rapidly growing sector that caters to the needs of both businesses and consumers [2, 3]. Fintech includes a broad variety of uses, like mobile banking, cryptocurrency, insurance, and investment apps [4, 5]. It encompasses a variety of financial transactions that are often done without human intervention, such as money transfers, smartphone check deposits, credit applications, raising capital for startups, and investment management [6 - 8]. According to a report titled "The winds of change: Trends shaping India's Fintech Sector," released in September 2022, the global financial services sector has been greatly impacted by fintech in the past decade [9 - 11]. However, in the first half of 2022, fintech investment growth slowed down due to increased regulation, shifting customer preferences, uncertain global events, and ongoing geopolitical unrest [10 - 12]. In spite of the obstacles, the global fintech industry experienced significant growth in 2021, although the pandemic caused some disruptions [13 - 15]. Supernova cryptocurrencies such as Bitcoin and Ethereum have clinched prominence and brought blockchain technology into the spotlight [16 - 18]. The extensive implementation of blockchain has caught the attention of the finance and corresponding industry, resulting in the development of new cryptocurrencies such as ZCash, NameCoin, PrimeCoin, and LightCoin) [19 - 21]. This has consequences for the appearance of a novel way of financing innovative ventures and products, known as Initial Coin Offerings (ICO) [22 - 25]. In current times, there has been rising attention to the utilization of blockchain beyond cryptocurrencies, driven by the distinctive characteristics of distributed ledger technologies (DLT) such as cryptographic security, immutability, decentralization, and transparency [26 - 29]. These features present exciting possibilities for a variety of industries. The fintech industry, including major financial organizations, insurance companies, and exchange corporations, has recently turned its focus toward blockchain technology [30 - 32]. The term "distributed ledger technology" is often used instead of simply "blockchain" as it highlights the security, immutability, reliability, and auditability that the technology provides [33 - 35]. Additionally, the utilization of efficient contracts in financial operations is a significant advantage of DLT. As a consequence of circulated ledger technology, blockchain uses a one-way cryptographic hash function to maintain a secure, replicated, and distributed ledger of transactions that cannot be altered or disputed [36 - 39]. This consensus-verified, unchanging record of transactions among peers results in a single, agreed-upon version of the truth within the system [40 - 42]. Due to the temper-proof nature of DLT, it is difficult for anyone to alter records, which boosts trust between parties [43 - 46]. By using a DLT platform, fintech companies can improve their bank-to-bank (B2B) transactions and reach agreements faster compared to traditional centralized systems, which may take one to several days to process [47, 48]. DLT's ability to securely record digital representations of fiat currency, securities, and physical goods opens numerous opportunities for fintech to build smart contracts and provide secure and innovative financial services. This allows for seamless trading and settlement of securities without manual intervention [49, 50].

Various blockchain platforms and technologies can be utilized in the Indian FinTech sector. Ethereum is a decentralized stage that permits the formation of smart contracts and decentralized applications (DApps) using blockchain technology. It is widely used in the FinTech space due to its open-source nature, strong set of tools, and frameworks for developing blockchain-based FinTech solutions. Hyperledger Fabric, on the other hand, is a key blockchain proposal that is planned for enterprise employment cases. Its modular architecture enables customizations and integrations with existing enterprise systems, making it ideal for FinTech utilization that needs safe and proficient processing of financial transactions and data. Ripple is a payment procedure and cryptocurrency that enables faster, cheaper, and more reliable cross-border payments. It uses a consensus algorithm called the Ripple Protocol Consensus Algorithm (RPCA) to authenticate transactions on its distributed ledger. Other blockchain technologies and protocols, such as Corda, Quorum, and Stellar, are also being developed and adopted in the Indian FinTech space. The choice of platform and technology relies on the particular needs and use case of the FinTech solution, as well as factors such as security, scalability, and regulatory compliance.

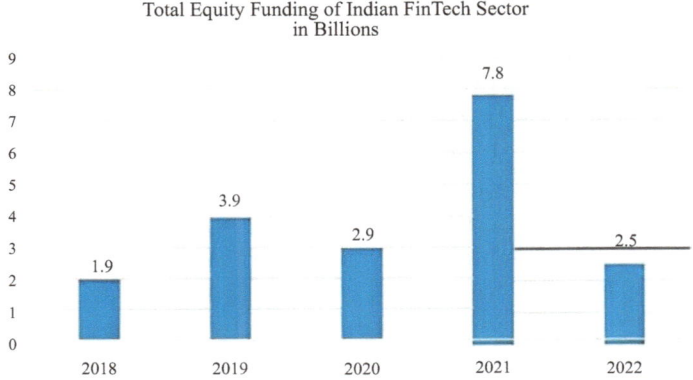

Fig. (1). FinTech adoption in India.

Existing Fintech Sector in India

Fintech demonstrates the utilization of digital technology to increase and automate financial services and operations. According to the Financial Stability Board, fintech is defined as "financial innovation allowed by technology that may guide to novel business models, applications, processes, or products that have a significant impact on financial markets and institutions and the provision of financial services". India is among the world's fastest-growing fintech markets, with over 2,000 recognized fintech businesses by DPIIT and counting. It has the highest global fintech adoption rate at 87%. Factors such as India's demographic advantage, rising national disposable income, large unbanked population, growing internet and smartphone usage, and booming e-commerce market are driving the enlargement of fintech in India. Twenty three fintech companies in India have achieved "unicorn" status, with one-fifth of these being in the fintech sector. In 2021, India had the most real-time transactions globally, reaching 48 billion, or 6.5 times more than the combined volume of the five largest economies. This resulted in savings of $12.6 billion for the Indian consumers and enterprises in 2021. The digital investment market is projected to grow in value from $6.4 billion to $14.3 billion by 2025. India has a very high rate of fintech adoption as compared to Global fintech adoption in all the aspects of fintech such as financial planning, savings and investment, money transfer, borrowing as well as insurance. As shown in Fig. (**1**), the market saw a substantial fall in equity FinTech funding in areas such as geopolitical and macroeconomic issues such as the conflict in Ukraine, rising inflation, and underwhelming financial and stock market achievement of prominent fintech organizations, which eroded investors' trust in the potential for future exits. Various famous Fintech businesses face several problems, like extended funding cycles, overlooking objectives, and escalating losses [51, 52]. However, the fintech sector is continually confronted with several additional serious issues like dependency on centralized systems, regulatory laws, liking of cash transactions, numerous people without bank accounts, threats of cyber security, lack of government support, and industry-specific issues. Fintech may appear to be user-friendly, yet the real control remains in the hands of other organizations. Even though transactions are carried out with approval from the higher-ups, consumers are still awaiting an endorsement that works in their favor. Regulations inevitably impede the escalation of Fintech startups in India's banking sector. These restrictions, which are not only difficult to comply with but also hinder the entry of Fintech companies into the Indian market, were created as a stringent regulatory framework to prevent fraud. However, they also present significant barriers to entry for new Fintech businesses, as they must meet a lengthy list of standards before they can even begin operations. Most Indians have a conservative stance and choose to conduct daily transactions in cash. Their long-standing reliance on money as a sales tool makes it difficult for them to break old habits and implement fresh approaches. Because financial services are commonly linked to internet fraud, providing them to an unbanked market is difficult. Many Indians lack the financial literacy necessary to fully appreciate the worth that FinTechs offer through their cutting-edge supplies and services. The development of FinTechs was delayed because of the inadequate framework, as well as little internet access and low literacy rates in India. The benefits would not be felt right now, even though the Indian government is tackling these issues with liberal policies. Another obstacle to the growth of fintech in India is the low level of financial knowledge in Indian society. Private customer information is handled by financial technology companies. Numerous cybersecurity issues result in huge financial losses for online transactions. These are unnecessary for the customers. The same technology that simplifies daily tasks also makes it simpler for con artists to steal money from online accounts. This is a constant driver of FinTech expansion. Threats issued by hackers must be avoided by FinTechs. Massive amounts of digitally available financial data about individuals and companies. The likelihood of cybersecurity breaches increases as a result. Government encouragement and support for fintechs to protect their attention in the Indian financial markets are severely missing. This can be quite discouraging for up-an--coming Fintech players. Fintechs are essential for promoting economic growth, so it is critical to provide them with all the tools necessary for success. Fintechs are designed to operate using a sophisticated operating model. As a result, they find it difficult to maintain positive relationships with other financial organizations like banks. In contrast, banks are reluctant to work with fintechs because they are worried about their reputation.

Potential Solution Using Proposed System

Blockchains are networks of distributed digital ledgers that record all transactions. With distributed ledger technology, any transactions—in text, picture, spreadsheet, or PDF format can be stored across the whole network. Every member or node in the blockchain network has an entire copy of the blockchain, which facilitates a peer-to-peer distributed network. Decentralization, immutability, and transparency are the three pillars on which the blockchain's whole operation is built. As blockchain operates on a dispersed network, decentralization means that there is no single governing organization. Transparency means that a copy of every transaction in the form of a ledger is available, and immutability means that if an operation has been evidenced on the blockchain, it is permanently set and cannot be changed or modified. Numerous research articles and projects on Blockchain primarily concentrate on Bitcoin. However, Blockchain has vast potential and can be utilized in many different fields. By combining Blockchain with other technologies, the impact can be significant. Unlike the centralized banking system, Blockchain is decentralized.

Therefore, if the technology underlying Blockchain can be implemented in centralized systems, it could also be applied in the banking sector. One example of blending Blockchain with other technologies is by combining it with big data, as the transactions on Blockchain can be utilized for big data analysis. Additionally, users can forecast the latent growth of trading actions. The enhancement of Blockchain technology can lead to numerous novel opportunities, with the exception being that it may create some unforeseen challenges as well [53 - 58].

Blockchain technology is considered a latent game-changer for financial services due to its capability to offer efficient, cost-effective, and secure solutions. The financial sector can benefit from blockchain in various areas, including cross-border payments, remittances, digital identity verification, and trade finance. Traditional cross-border payments and remittance services are often time-consuming, expensive, and lacking transparency. Blockchain can address these issues by reducing intermediaries, fees, and increasing transparency. For trade finance processes, blockchain can streamline documentation, reduce fraud, and enhance trust [60 - 65]. Lastly, blockchain can offer a more protected and reliable path to verify digital identities, which is crucial in the digital age where traditional identity verification techniques can be costly, prone to data breaches, and lack interoperability. Blockchain is a decentralized distributed ledger technology that operates on a dispersed network of computers called nodes. Each node in the network runs the blockchain software and has a copy of the blockchain ledger. When a transaction is made, it is broadcast to the entire network and each node validates it using a consensus system. After validation, the transaction is integrated with the blockchain ledger, which is a continuous chain of blocks, with every block integrated with the proceeding one [66 - 68]. This confirms that the information in the blockchain is immutable and tamper-proof. The consensus system confirms that every node agrees on the condition of the blockchain, preventing malicious actors from tampering with it. Incentives such as earning cryptocurrency are often used to encourage nodes to maintain the network. This decentralized approach offers a high degree of safety and transparency, making the blockchain resistant to tampering. In blockchain, data encryption can be achieved using hashing, asymmetric encryption, as well as homographic encryption [69 - 71]. Commercial banks are increasingly leveraging Blockchain technology to boost the present centralized banking system [72 - 76]. By utilizing the security, immutability, and transparency of Blockchain, financial organizations can bypass intermediaries [77 - 80]. However, Blockchain can carry both opportunities and challenges to the banking sector. Banks' approach towards Blockchain is often conflicted as they have traditionally acted as intermediaries and received compensation for their trust-building role [81 - 86]. Blockchain, on the other hand, is a technology that seeks to eliminate the need for intermediaries.

To overcome different issues related to the FinTech sector of India, Blockchain technology can be used, which can provide the following security solutions as shown in Table 1.

Table 1. FinTech potential solutions using blockchain.

FinTech Issues	Potential Solution Using Blockchain
Centralized Dependency	Blockchain is a decentralized and peer-to-peer system, where data and transactions can be accessed by every individual connected to the system, so no dependency on centralized financial institution's confidentiality and data Integrity blockchain uses different cryptographic algorithms like asymmetric cryptography, digital signature, and hashing to provide security for financial transactions. Also, to maintain the confidentiality of data, third-party removal, and consensus mechanisms will be used. It uses the concept of smart contracts to maintain the conditions and terms for financial transactions.
Authentication	Membership Service Provider (MSP) is used to identify every user and only authenticated users can join the network and participate in transactions.
Access Control	Only those members, who have corresponding rights can access or execute the transactions, which can be achieved using MSP.
Non-Repudiation	Blockchain uses digital signatures for transactions in a block and once the transaction is recorded, it cannot be reverted. Also, even if fraudulence activity is done, it can be easily detected and punished.
Verification and Validation	No third party is involved, all the members and minors can be used to verify and validate every transaction, whether it is valid or not.
Transparency	Blockchain protects transparency by storing information in a manner that it cannot be altered without leaving a record of the modifications made, as well as by implementing the required encryption and control systems.
Tracking	Tracking and traceability can be achieved using smart contracts and distributed ledgers always ensure that all the information is available to all users at the same time.
Temper-proof Transactions	For temper-proof transactions, blockchain uses a consensus mechanism, and a digital signature is used for digitization operations.

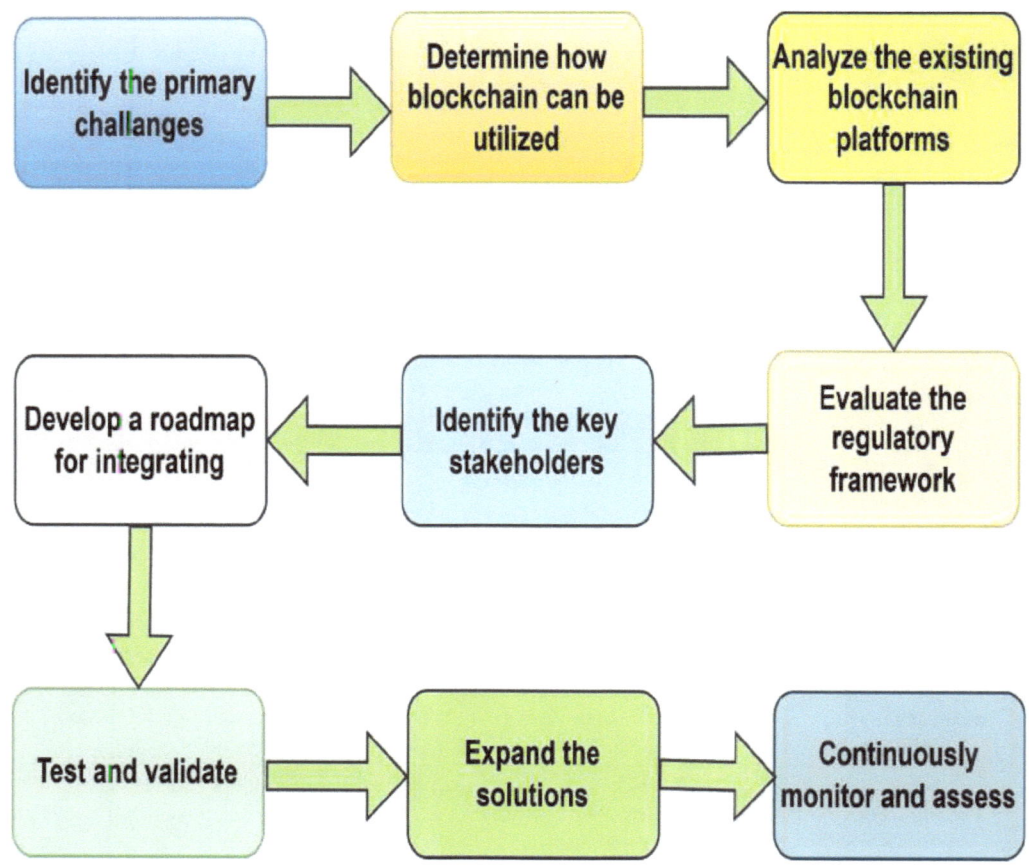

Fig. (2). Steps for integrating blockchain technology with the Indian FinTech sector.

Fig. (2) depicts the various steps for integrating blockchain technology with the Indian FinTech Sector in a flowchart. We can identify the primary challenges that the Indian FinTech industry is facing when it comes to securing financial operations. Examples of such challenges include fraud, data breaches, and a lack of transparency. How blockchain technology can be utilized to tackle these challenges needs to be determined, for instance, blockchain can offer decentralized identity management, secure data sharing, and transparent record-keeping. The existing blockchain platforms and technologies that are suitable for FinTech use cases in India are analyzed. Ethereum, Hyperledger Fabric, and Ripple are some of the platforms that can be leveraged. We also evaluate the regulatory framework for blockchain and FinTech in India, including government policies, regulations, and guidelines, and identify the key stakeholders in the Indian FinTech ecosystem, such as banks, financial institutions, startups, and regulators. We develop a roadmap for integrating blockchain technology into the Indian FinTech ecosystem, considering the technical and regulatory challenges, as well as the interests and incentives of different stakeholders. We test and validate the blockchain-based FinTech solutions through pilots and prototypes, and measure their efficacy in terms of safety, efficiency, and cost-effectiveness. We expand the successful blockchain-based FinTech solutions and promote their adoption across the Indian financial industry. Continuously monitor and assess the effect of blockchain technology on the Indian FinTech sector, and adjust the strategy as needed to address emerging challenges and opportunities.

The popularity of blockchain can be attributed to its favorable features, including transparency, security, immutability, and lower transaction costs. Distributed operations can be conducted either on a key ledger or a public ledger. The effective handling of key storage is ensured through several stages, including public key cryptography, encryption service, and double signing and verification.

As shown in Fig. (**3**), every customer who wishes to participate in a blockchain-enabled FinTech ecosystem needs to have his/her corresponding public and private key wallet. The transaction can be signed by the initiator's private key and broadcast to the blockchain network for miners' approval. A miner or blockchain validator will verify the transaction using ledger data and validate it through customers' public keys. If the result happens to be successful, then the validator will approve the transaction or if some error occurs during the validation or verification phase then the validator can reject the transaction.

Proposed Methodology

Various modules can be used in FinTech financial operations when integrating with blockchain such as issuer, receiver, and validation. It is used to transfer funds from the source entity through an online blockchain system by entering details such as information of sender, and recipient as well as information about transaction details. Upon successful completion and acceptance of the blockchain validation process by the financial organization or other approving authority, this module is used to receive the transferred funds from the issuer entity at the end of the settlement. Validation elements with their operations have been depicted in Table **2**. Validation contains the following different elements:

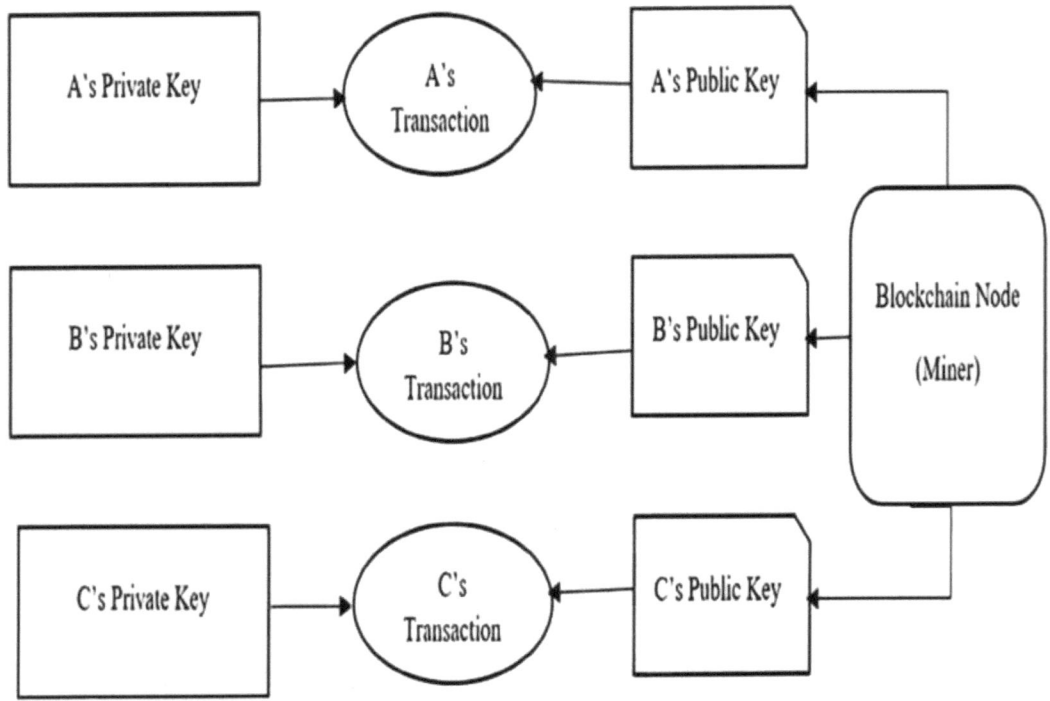

Fig. (3). Security handling in transactions.

Table 2. Validation elements and operations.

Validation Elements	Operations
Key Generator	This component generates header information, which includes information in encrypted form about the transaction and data validation. The header information is transmitted as part of a blockchain transaction.
Key Validator	This component utilizes a,n interpreter to gather transaction data and validation information depending on the financial organization's regulatory requirements, which are specified by the approving body. It retrieves the transaction block node that is received from the sender.
Key Interpreter	As directed by the approving entity, this component transforms the encrypted data received by the sender into the validation comments that are used by the validation component during the validation.

The process of recording transactions on a blockchain involves broadcasting each transaction to the network, where it is validated by multiple nodes using a consensus mechanism. This ensures that the transaction is verified and accurate before it is added to a block with other validated transactions. To initiate a money transfer, the user visits the appropriate financial institution or organization. They obtain the necessary information for both the sender's and recipient's accounts before beginning the process through a web-based platform. The information is then consolidated into a single block of data, with separate sections for the sender's information and the details of the transaction, and transmitted *via* the blockchain channel for processing. The gathered data is encrypted and kept in the node's header for the transaction's initial block of data. Until it reaches the receiving bank, the transaction information is used in its current form throughout the blockchain communication. Every block transfer in the channel updates customer information according to the specifications of the receiving bank. For instance, while a few banks prefer to require the customer's address or contact number as part of the transfer, others may not be interested in these details. FinTech architecture with blockchain integration has been depicted in Fig. (**4**).

The overall procedure consists of the following steps:

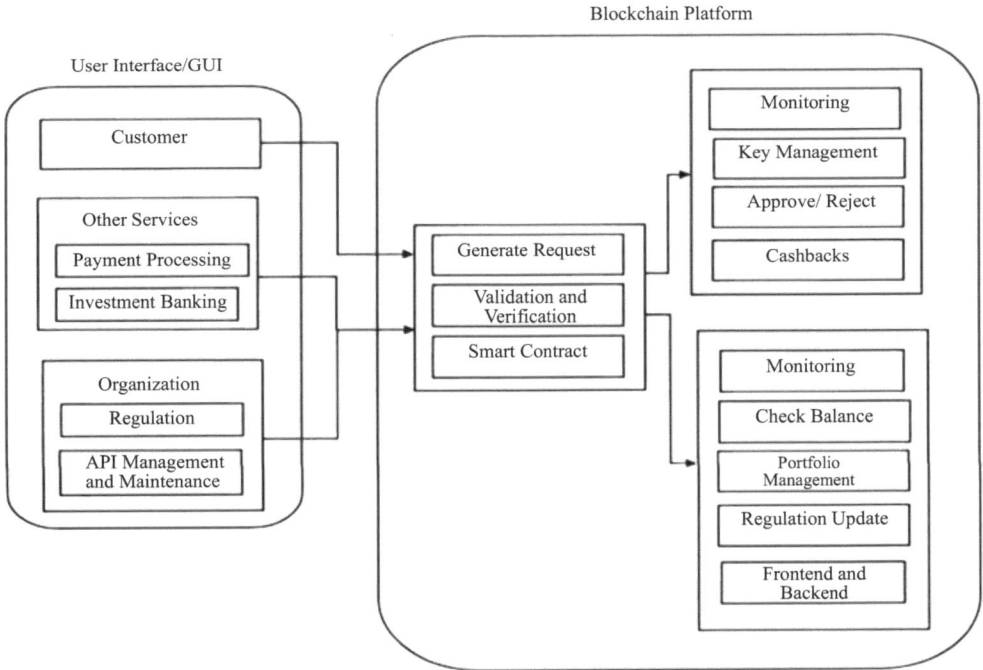

Fig. (4). FinTech architecture with blockchain integration.

Every block ID is unique to the group that issues it or sends it, so if the same user tries to create duplicate transactions, they will be rejected when a block is created because they will have the same ID as another transaction. To establish a connection between nodes in blockchain communication, the receiving bank determines the location for a new node to be created and linked to the received node through a smart contract. This chain of nodes continues to grow until the validation process is initiated by a validating bank. The consortium responsible for creating the underlying blockchain platform prioritizes security by using encryption to protect the data as it is transferred among the network's nodes throughout the transaction. The blockchain transmission process involves grouping nodes generated during a transaction into a cluster of transactions, resulting in a single, unified network of nodes. The sender bank initiates a transaction block that holds client and transaction information, as well as a unique identification generated in the block's header. This header information is transmitted through all blocks under the blockchain transmission protocol and is replicated to each new block as it is formed. The customer data is then transmitted under validation requirements. The process of broadcasting the block ID and header continues with every new block that is created until the last block is formed at the receiver or when the transaction is validated and completed by the validator. A practical clustered data store approach is introduced to improve the validation process for various blockchain transactions. The network of nodes is organized into a cluster, and the information exchanged between the transaction's nodes is stored in this tree structure and included in the node when the customer's information block is created and sent for validation. The validation node then uses the clustering data in the node to connect to the approval process used by the receiving bank to either accept or reject the transaction. Additional communication components within the transaction chain can also be added to the clustered information to enhance it. Once the validation process is completed, the information is recorded in the ledger transaction of the receiving bank. In the banking process for transactions, the validation unit takes the block for validation and separates the significant customer information from the node. This extracted data is then prepped for approval by an authorized individual and once the green light is given, the transaction is finalized. The data is decrypted and transmitted to the approver through a non-volatile memory transfer and then deleted after the validation process is completed to ensure that the transaction is only handled between the sender and recipient banks. Once the validation is completed, the approval status information is added to the last block of the transaction and has been sent to the receiving bank. The sender initiates the transaction by instructing the receiver bank to either actualize or credit the transaction to the receiver's account, and the receiver bank follows these instructions. A node that includes information about the customer, account, and currency is created in the validation process based on the specifications of the approver. The node is then utilized in the subsequent stage to transfer data to the approver for further processing. This is the outcome of a typical blockchain hierarchy process after validation. Based on the validation outcome, the next step is either to complete the payment or reject the transaction. This verification step sets a boundary for the information necessary to assemble a clustered block in a ledger-based blockchain transaction that adheres to specific conditions. The information transfer encompasses crucial details from customers, accounts, and currency blocks. Blockchain technology and machine learning (ML) can be integrated to considerably improve the efficiency and security of the fintech sector. A robust framework for securely storing financial transactions is provided by the decentralized and immutable ledger of blockchains. Additionally, ML algorithms can be employed to analyze the immense amount of data in realtime, detecting patterns, anomalies, and potential fraud with greater accuracy. The predictive capabilities of machine learning (ML) can be utilized by fintech platforms to develop more dynamic fraud detection and risk management systems that are perpetually enhanced by learning from new data. Furthermore, ML has the potential to enhance the operational efficacy and adaptability of smart contracts on the blockchain, thereby reducing execution times. A more secure, transparent, and efficient financial ecosystem can result from the synergy between ML and blockchain. The integration of machine learning (ML) with blockchain in financial technology (fintech) presents significant potential to improve security and operational efficiency. Blockchain offers a secure, decentralized ledger for financial transactions, whereas machine learning can analyze blockchain data to identify fraud, forecast risks, and enhance operations. For instance, employing machine learning to analyze transaction patterns on a blockchain enables fintech organizations to detect anomalous or fraudulent actions more swiftly than conventional approaches. This is seen in practical applications, such as the utilization of machine learning in cryptocurrency trading platforms to improve fraud detection, exemplified by projects like Chainalysis, which employs machine learning to monitor criminal activities throughout blockchain networks. Theoretical frameworks such as "Decentralized Autonomous Organizations" (DAOs) propose the implementation of machine learning-driven smart contracts that adapt and self-execute according to real-time data inputs, thereby enhancing efficiency and minimizing human error. The integration of these technologies provides a fintech ecosystem that is more safe, transparent, and adaptive to changing threats and market dynamics.

USE CASES FOR BLOCKCHAIN IN FINTECH

Incorporating case studies of successful blockchain implementations in Indian fintech would yield useful, region-specific insights into the transformation of the financial landscape by this technology. Yes Bank established a blockchain-based vendor financing system in collaboration with fintech company Cateina Technologies, which optimized the loan approval process and markedly decreased the time required for payouts. A notable instance is the National Payments Corporation of India's (NPCI) implementation of blockchain *via* its Vajra platform, which improves transaction security and transparency in real-time payments, hence improving many banking services. Furthermore, firms such as Instamojo and WazirX have included blockchain technology for international payments and cryptocurrency trading, providing secure and efficient alternatives to conventional methods. These case studies demonstrate how blockchain may effectively tackle the distinct issues of scalability, transparency, and efficiency within the Indian financial sector, facilitating wider adoption and regulatory conformity. Practical examples are crucial for elucidating theoretical notions, since they offer concrete evidence of the application of ideas, rendering the knowledge more accessible and comprehensible; for example, while examining blockchain's possibilities in financial technology, referencing instances such as Ripple's blockchain-driven cross-border payment solutions or Yes Bank of India utilizing blockchain for vendor financing might illustrate how decentralized ledgers enhance transaction speed and security. In the domain of machine learning, organizations such as PayPal utilize AI to identify fraudulent transactions, exemplifying the application of algorithms to address tangible business concerns. These examples contextualize the content for readers, illustrating the shift from theory to real-world impact, thus enhancing their comprehension of the concepts and fostering trust in the technology's practical advantages.

Payment Processing and Peer-to-Peer Lending

One of the well-promising utilization of blockchain technology in the FinTech industry is for secure and transparent payment processing that minimizes the danger of fraud and other economic crimes. This can improve the efficiency and speed of payment processing, such as Ripple, a global payment solutions platform that uses blockchain technology for fast, secure, and low-cost cross-border payments. Blockchain technology can also be utilized to construct a decentralized platform for peer-to-peer (P2P) lending that allows borrowers and lenders to connect directly without the need for intermediaries like banks. Bitbond is a blockchain-based P2P lending stage that provides loans to small business owners. Bitbond uses blockchain technology to create a safe and transparent stage that connects borrowers and lenders directly.

Identity Verification and Supply Chain Finance

By creating a decentralized identity system on the blockchain, users can verify their identity without relying on third-party identity verification providers. Civic is a blockchain-based identity verification platform and another possible case study. Civic employs blockchain technology to construct a decentralized identity system that enables users to verify their identity securely and anonymously.

Blockchain technology can improve supply chain finance by creating a safe and apparent platform that shortens the danger of fraud and other financial crimes. For example, IBM's Food Trust platform is a blockchain-based supply chain management system for the food industry. Food Trust leverages blockchain technology to create an apparent and safe platform that mitigates the risk of food fraud and enhances food safety.

Insurance and Stock Trading

A decentralized platform for insurance on the blockchain can decrease the threat of fraud and advance the pace and efficiency of insurance payouts. For example, Etherisc a blockchain-based insurance stage that provides parametric insurance solutions, is another potential case study. Etherisc utilizes blockchain technology to create a transparent and decentralized stage that minimizes the risk of fraud and facilitates fast, automated insurance payouts. Blockchain technology can improve stock trading by creating a safe and apparent platform that reduces the risk of fraud and improves the speed and efficiency of trades, such as Nasdaq's Linq platform, a blockchain-based platform for private market trading, is another example that can be explored. Linq harnesses blockchain technology to construct a secure and transparent stage that decreases the risk of fraud and streamlines the trading process.

Asset Management

Creating a decentralized platform for asset management on the blockchain can assist in decreasing the possibility of fraud and advance the pace and efficiency of asset transfers; for example, Harbor is a blockchain-based platform for alternative investments. Harbor employs blockchain technology to create a safe and transparent platform that simplifies the process of buying and selling alternative investments. The potential future developments in blockchain technology are numerous and could greatly impact the Indian FinTech sector. Decentralized Finance (DeFi) and Central Bank Digital Currencies (CBDCs) have emerged as potential game-changers that could revolutionize the financial sector. Additionally, researchers are actively addressing the challenge of scalability and interoperability, and the development of more efficient and interoperable blockchain platforms could further enhance the effect of blockchain on the Indian FinTech sector. Other areas of development include blockchain-based identity management, smart contracts, and supply chain management. Given the dynamic nature of blockchain technology, there are likely to be numerous other developments that could impact the Indian FinTech sector in the future. The future of fintech will likely be influenced by the convergence of artificial intelligence, machine learning, and blockchain, with breakthroughs in these technologies set to transform the industry. As AI and ML advance, its amalgamation with blockchain may facilitate more sophisticated, automated financial systems. AI-driven smart contracts can autonomously execute depending on real-time data inputs, facilitating more dynamic and adaptive financial arrangements. Machine learning algorithms can evaluate blockchain data to enhance fraud detection, forecast market trends, and optimize transaction procedures. Nonetheless, these developments present hurdles, including the necessity of safeguarding data privacy and maintaining compliance within decentralized networks, managing the computing requirements of integrating AI with blockchain, and maneuvering through legislative frameworks that may not keep pace with technological progress. It is plausible that decentralized AI marketplaces or blockchain-based AI auditing tools may arise, promoting openness and equity in machine-generated judgments. The advancing integration of AI, ML, and blockchain will create new opportunities, necessitating a careful study of scalability, security, and ethical dilemmas in fintech.

BENEFITS OF THE SYSTEM

A comparison of blockchain technology with other technologies used for securing financial operations in the Indian FinTech sector involves an evaluation of the strengths and weaknesses of each technology to determine their effectiveness in securing financial transactions. This comparison typically involves analyzing the features, benefits, and limitations of blockchain technology against those of other technologies such as traditional databases, encryption, and biometrics. For instance, traditional databases are known for their high speed and ease of use in storing financial data, but they are also vulnerable to hacking and data breaches. Encryption, which is used to protect data from unauthorized access, can also be vulnerable to attacks and can be difficult to manage on a large scale. Biometrics, such as fingerprints and facial recognition, are increasingly used in financial transactions to enhance security, but they are also subject to privacy concerns. In contrast, blockchain technology, with its distributed and decentralized nature, offers unique benefits such as immutability, transparency, and security. It has the potential to prevent fraud and enhance transparency in financial transactions. However, blockchain technology is still in the early phase of development and faces challenges like scalability, interoperability, and regulatory uncertainty. By comparing these technologies, it is possible to identify the most suitable technology for securing financial operations in the Indian FinTech sector based on the specific needs of each application. This analysis can help better recognize the strengths and weaknesses of each technology and to determine the most effective approach to securing financial transactions in the Indian FinTech sector.

One example of Blockchain and FinTech integration is, Yes Bank, which collaborated with Cateina Technologies to develop a blockchain-based solution for supply chain financing in India, called "Yes Transact". The solution leverages the safety and precision of blockchain technology to process invoices and payments between parties involved in the supply chain, reducing turnaround time and improving cash flow management. This adoption has resulted in several benefits for Yes Bank, including an increased customer base, reduced operational costs, and improved risk management practices. Furthermore, the success of this solution has inspired other banks and financial institutions in India to explore the utilization of blockchain technology for various FinTech use cases, driving innovation and growth in the Indian FinTech sector.

Payments and Trade Finance

Peer-to-peer (P2P) demonstrates a decentralized network architecture where a node interacts directly without the requirement for intermediaries. In the context of cryptocurrencies, P2P transactions permit users to directly exchange cryptocurrencies with one another without the involvement of a central authority, such as a bank or exchange. P2P transactions are facilitated using blockchain technology, which enables safe, apparent, and tamper-proof transfers of digital assets. The utilization of encryption ensures the anonymity of the parties involved in the transaction, further increasing the safety and privacy of the exchange. The implementation of blockchain-based smart contracts in financial trading will do away with the need for manual data element validation and verification. Blockchain technology can offer authorized access with real-time visibility for all parties including regulators. Blockchain offers a secure shared ledger that can produce a clear shared understanding of the terms and conditions of a contract as well as provide the status of commodities for importers, exporters, banks, shipping companies, port authorities, and customs. Additionally, blockchain offers automation that enhances accuracy and transparency and incorporates flexibility to model a range of restrictions.

Crypto Lending and Digital Identity

Crypto lending provides an alternative to traditional lending methods in the banking sector. The utilization of cryptocurrencies and blockchain technology offers advantages such as efficiency, transparency, and flexibility in the lending process. Borrowers can use their crypto assets as collateral and receive loans in either fiat currencies or stablecoins, while lenders can earn interest on their assets. This new lending mechanism can revolutionize the traditional banking system and bring novel opportunities to both borrowers and lenders. Blockchain technology offers a solution for digital identity management. Once individuals have undergone verification, they can utilize their digital identity to carry out global transactions. Moreover, the use of blockchain can improve the experience of financial consumers by giving them control over their identity data, allowing for electronic signatures of documents like claims and transactions, and minimizing security risks during data sharing with others.

Crowdfunding and Auditing

Crowdfunding aims to gather funds by soliciting a few roles from a huge number of individuals, often through online stages. As opposed to conventional financing methods, blockchain-based fundraising is more efficient and transparent, facilitated by the use of Initial Coin Offerings (ICOs) and similar approaches. The integration of a transaction into a reliable blockchain can provide adequate evidence for auditing specific financial statement claims, like the existence of the transaction [57, 58]. To boost the safety of financial operations in the Indian FinTech sector, it can leverage blockchain technology by adopting several solutions. Firstly, it develops interoperability standards to enable seamless transactions across different blockchain networks. Secondly, it explores the use of smart contracts for automating payment processing, settlement times, and financial reporting. Thirdly, it implements blockchain-based Know Your Customer (KYC) and Anti-Money Laundering (AML) solutions to streamline compliance processes and enhance security. Fourthly, it develops decentralized identity solutions that offer greater privacy and control over personal data. Additionally, exploring blockchain technology for cross-border payments can reduce transaction costs and improve efficiency. Finally, developing blockchain-based solutions for supply chain finance can increase transparency, traceability, and efficiency in supply chain finance operations. These solutions can provide greater efficiency, transparency, and security while reducing costs for the Indian FinTech sector.

CHALLENGES ASSOCIATED WITH BLOCKCHAIN

The decentralized or peer-to-peer structure of blockchain technology enables all participants in the network to view transaction records and add new information to the database [59 - 61]. The open and decentralized characteristics of the system, which also pose challenges and limit its use, are the foundation of blockchain technology [62 - 64]. Most of the challenges associated with the blockchain are scalability, potential vulnerability, privacy, high energy, cybercrime, and regulatory laws.

Blockchain grows as there are more transactions, and it has been noted that these transactions take longer to complete because they are complicated, encrypted, and distributed. A 51% attack is a potential vulnerability in public blockchain systems, caused by the architecture of blockchain technology. When a group of attackers acquires more than half of a blockchain's computational power, those nodes can launch a 51% attack and gain control over the network, effectively dominating it. Blockchain technology enables users to create multiple addresses, rather than using their real-world identities, which is considered a secure way to prevent information leakage. However, due to the transparent nature of blockchain, which makes all transactions and balances information publicly accessible, it is not possible to prevent transactional information from being disclosed. The Bitcoin network requires a significant amount of energy, with a single Bitcoin transaction consuming several terawatt-hours of electricity. Public blockchains foster innovation, efficiency, and competition, but because they do not enforce participant authentication, they can pose challenges for laws related to money laundering, terrorism financing, and tax evasion. In 2017, the Reserve Bank of India (RBI) issued a circular that prohibited banks and other regulated entities from providing services to individuals or entities involved in cryptocurrency trading. As a consequence of this buying or selling of cryptocurrencies by Indian citizens is effectively illegal. The RBI's directive effectively banned the provision of banking services to anyone dealing with cryptocurrencies. The regulatory framework for blockchain technology in India refers to the set of laws, policies, and regulations that govern its use in the country's financial sector. The Reserve Bank of India is responsible for overseeing blockchain technology and has issued several guidelines and regulations related to its use. While blockchain technology is generally recognized as legally valid in India, there are still uncertainties about how blockchain transactions and contracts are treated under Indian law. Other regulatory issues include Know-Your-Customer (KYC) and Anti-Money Laundering (AML) regulations, data protection and privacy laws, and intellectual property issues. The dynamic regulatory landscape presents both challenges and opportunities for businesses and investors seeking to leverage blockchain technology in the Indian market. Although blockchain technology offers various benefits for the fintech industry, there are also potential drawbacks to consider. Regulatory challenges can make it difficult to comply with regulations and laws that are still developing. Scalability issues can slow down the overall speed of the blockchain network as the dimension of the blockchain grows. Energy consumption can be a concern, as the process of verifying transactions can be energy-intensive and increase a business's carbon footprint. Adoption barriers may exist for businesses that lack the necessary resources to invest in new technology. Lastly, while blockchain technology is generally considered secure, security breaches and hacks have occurred in the past. Thus, businesses that use blockchain technology must ensure the security of their networks and data. It is crucial to evaluate both the benefits and risks of integrating blockchain technology into fintech before deciding. The fintech industry encounters substantial regulatory obstacles, especially over adherence to anti-money laundering (AML), know-your-customer (KYC), and data privacy requirements. As financial transactions become increasingly computerized, fintech companies must comply with more intricate regulatory frameworks. Blockchain technology can significantly address compliance challenges by providing transparent, immutable transaction records, thereby facilitating more clear and efficient audits and regulatory reporting. Blockchain-based KYC solutions facilitate the secure sharing of verified client identities among institutions, minimizing redundancy and assuring real-time compliance. Nonetheless, the regulatory environment is diverse across several locations, and the incorporation of blockchain necessitates greater clarity and consistency from regulatory bodies. Moreover, scalability issues remain as blockchain networks, especially public ones, face challenges in efficiently processing high transaction volumes. Layer-2 protocols and sharding are being investigated to enhance blockchain scalability, guaranteeing that as fintech companies expand, blockchain systems can accommodate the need for rapid, compliant transactions. Confronting these regulatory and scalability concerns will be essential for the wider use of blockchain in fintech. An exhaustive examination of scalability options for blockchain in finance should encompass off-chain scaling techniques and layer-2 solutions, both of which are crucial for enhancing the network's ability to manage substantial transaction volumes. Off-chain techniques, like state channels and side-chains, provide transaction processing beyond the primary blockchain, alleviating congestion and enhancing transaction speeds while ensuring security through intermittent engagement with the main chain. Layer-2 solutions, such as the Lightning Network for Bitcoin and Optimistic Rollups for Ethereum, enhance transaction speed for micro-transactions on secondary layers, with intermittent settlement on the primary blockchain. Companies such as Binance and Kraken have effectively implemented these solutions by adopting layer-2 technology to enhance transaction throughput and minimize expenses. Ethereum's Optimism rollup has been employed to scale decentralized financial (DeFi) applications, markedly improving transaction performance while preserving blockchain integrity. These case studies illustrate that scalable blockchain infrastructures are not merely theoretical but are actively functioning, proving essential to the growth and broad adoption of fintech.

CONCLUSION

The gap in financial services in developing countries is filled by mobile money offerings from financial technology companies. Mobile banking and agent banking serve to bridge the infrastructure gap for these populations. Blockchain technology, with its decentralized and unalterable database, is becoming increasingly popular among fintech companies to increase profits, improve customer experiences, streamline operations, enhance efficiency, and reduce business risks. By using blockchain, financial transactions can be securely made directly between individuals, bypassing the need for banks or other financial intermediaries. The financial sector often refers to blockchain as "distributed ledger technology" and it is considered a more reliable alternative to traditional databases. Although the potential benefits of Blockchain and financial technology have spread quickly, their associated concerns have not yet been adequately addressed. Currently, there are many issues in the current fintech sector of India, but to overcome security-related issues like transparency, trust, privacy, and programmability, blockchain is proven to be a good solution. Using blockchain we can implement the entire fintech ecosystem which will be beneficial in all security aspects for the issuer, receiver as well as validator.

REFERENCES

[1] V. Murinde, E. Rizopoulos, and M. Zachariadis, "The impact of the FinTech revolution on the future of banking: Opportunities and risks", *Int. Rev. Financ. Anal.,* vol. 81, p. 102103, 2022.
[http://dx.doi.org/10.1016/j.irfa.2022.102103]

[2] W. Lu, Blockchain technology and its applications in FinTech, in *Intelligent, Secure, and Dependable Systems in Distributed and Cloud Environments,* I. Traore, I. Woungang, S. Ahmed, and Y. Malik, Eds., vol. 11317, *Lecture Notes in Computer Science,* Springer, Cham, 2018.
[http://dx.doi.org/10.1007/978-3-030-03712-3_10]

[3] C. Vijai, "Fintech in India-opportunities and challenges", *SAARJ Journal on Banking & Insurance Research,* vol. 8, no. 1, pp. 42-54, 2019. [SJBIR].
[http://dx.doi.org/10.5958/2319-1422.2019.00002.X]

[4] A. Mehrotra, and S. Menon, Second round of FinTech-Trends and challenges, *Proc. 2021 Int. Conf. on Contemporary Advances in Knowledge Management (ICCAKM),* 2021.
[http://dx.doi.org/10.1109/ICCAKM50778.2021.9357759]

[5] N. Jain, and R.R. Sedamkar, A blockchain technology approach for the security and trust in trade finance, *2020 14th International Conference on Innovations in Information Technology (IIT),* Al Ain, United Arab Emirates, 2020, pp. 192-197.
[http://dx.doi.org/10.1109/IIT50501.2020.9299060]

[6] S. Mengi, and A. Gupta, "P2P Payment using Blockchain Technology", *International Journal of Advanced Research in Science, Communication and Technology (IJARSCT),* vol. 11, no. 1, 2021.
[http://dx.doi.org/10.48175/IJARSCT-2071]

[7] S. Sonawane, and D. Motwani, Issues of commodity market and trade finance in India and its solutions using blockchain technology in *Emerging Technologies in Data Mining and Information Security,* P. Dutta *et al.,* Eds., *Lecture Notes in Networks and Systems,* vol. 491, Springer, Singapore, 2023.
[http://dx.doi.org/10.1007/978-981-19-4193-1_44]

[8] M.C. Dyball, and R. Seethamraju, "Client use of blockchain technology: exploring its (potential) impact on financial statement audits of Australian accounting firms", *Account. Audit. Account. J.,* vol. 35, no. 7, pp. 1656-1684, 2022.
[http://dx.doi.org/10.1108/AAAJ-07-2020-4681]

[9] V. Chang, P. Baudier, H. Zhang, Q. Xu, J. Zhang, and M. Arami, "How Blockchain can impact financial services – The overview, challenges and recommendations from expert interviewees", *Technol. Forecast. Soc. Change,* vol. 158, p. 120166, 2020.
[http://dx.doi.org/10.1016/j.techfore.2020.120166] [PMID: 32834134]

[10] S. Sonawane, and D. Motwani, Investigating the pervasiveness of existing fintech sector of India. *In AIP Conference Proceedings,* vol. 2930, p. 020007, 2023.
[http://dx.doi.org/10.1063/5.0175287]

[11] H. Han, R.K. Shiwakoti, R. Jarvis, C. Mordi, and D. Botchie, "Accounting and auditing with blockchain technology and artificial Intelligence: A literature review", *Int. J. Account. Inf. Syst.,* vol. 48, p. 100598, 2023.
[http://dx.doi.org/10.1016/j.accinf.2022.100598]

[12] L. Di, Z. Yang, and G.X. Yuan, The consensus games for consensus economics under the framework of blockchain in Fintech, *Game Theory,* D. F. Li, Ed., *Communications in Computer and Information Science,* vol. 1082, Springer, Singapore, 2019, pp. 1-26.
[http://dx.doi.org/10.1007/978-981-15-0657-4_1]

[13] P.K. Priya, and K. Anusha, "Fintech issues and challenges in India", *International Journal of Recent Technology and Engineering,* vol. 8, no. 3, pp. 904-908, 2019.

[14] A. Polyviou, P. Velanas, and J. Soldatos, Blockchain technology: Financial sector applications beyond cryptocurrencies, *Proceedings,* vol. 28, no. 1, p. 7, 2019.
[http://dx.doi.org/10.3390/proceedings2019028007]

[15] W. Jerbi, O. Cheikhrouhou, H. Hamam, H. Trabelsi, and A. Guermazi, "A blockchain-based storage intelligent", In: *In 2022 International Wireless Communications and Mobile Computing (IWCMC)* Dubrovnik, Croatia,, 2022, pp. 635-640.
[http://dx.doi.org/10.1109/IWCMC55113.2022.9824790]

[16] R. Verma and G. Indra, "AI-driven dynamic trust management and blockchain-based security in industrial IoT," *Computers and Electrical Engineering,* vol. 123, pt. C, p. 110213, 2025.
[http://dx.doi.org/10.1016/j.compeleceng.2025.110213]

[17] M. Grossman, "Blockchain in the Middle East and North Africa (MENA): opportunities for regional integration and economic growth", *Journal of International Business and Management,* vol. 5, no. 5, pp. 01-19, 2022.

[18] K. Singh, Y. Singh, D. Barak, M. Yadav, and E. Özen, "Parametric evaluation techniques for reliability of Internet of Things (IoT)", *International Journal of Computational Methods and Experimental Measurements,* vol. 11, no. 2, pp. 123-134, 2023.
[http://dx.doi.org/10.18280/ijcmem.110207]

[19] A.B. Chavan, and K. Rajeswari, "The design and developement of decentralized digilocker using blockchain", *Int. J. Comput. Sci. Eng. Inf. Technol. Res. (IJCSEITR),,* vol. 9, pp. 29-36, 2019.
[http://dx.doi.org/10.24247/ijcseitrdec20195]

[20] M. T. Hasan, M. M. Alam, S. Sarkar, M. H. Miraz, and M. H. Masum. Factors affecting consumers intention to use Blockchain-based services (BBS) in the hotel industry. *Int. J. Mech. Prod. Eng. Res. Dev.* vol. 10, no. 3, pp. 8891-8902, 2020.
[http://dx.doi.org/10.24247/ijmperdjun2020846]

[21] M.H. Miraz, M.T. Hasan, F.R. Sumi, S. Sarkar, and M.I. Majumder, "Understanding, supervision, strategy and acceptance effect into the blockchain employment in Malaysia", *Int. J. Mech. Prod. Eng. Res. Dev. (IJMPERD),,* vol. 10, pp. 8339-8360, 2020.
[http://dx.doi.org/10.24247/ijmperdjun2020793]

[22] K. Kaushik, S. Tayal, S. Dahiya, and A.O. Salau, Eds., *Sustainable and Advanced Applications of Blockchain in Smart Computational Technologies,* 1st ed., Chapman & Hall/CRC, 2023.
[http://dx.doi.org/10.1201/9781003193425]

[23] E. Elgeldawi, A.A. Radwan, F. Omara, T.M. Mahmoud, and H.V. Madhyastha, "Detection and characterization of fake accounts on the pinterest social networks", *Int. J. Comput. Netw. Wirel. Mob. Commun,* vol. 4, pp. 21-28, 2014.

[24] K.H. Alturki, Corporate Governance and the Role of Forensic Accountants in Saudi Arabia. *Int. J.*

Account. Financ. Manag. Res. [IJAFMR]. vol. 7, no. 2, pp. 17-24, 2017.

[25] S. Bhatia, A.K. Goel, B.B. Naib, K. Singh, M. Yadav, and A. Saini, "Diabetes Prediction using Machine Learning", *Proc. 2023 World Conf. on Communication & Computing (WCONF),* 2023, pp. 1–6.

[26] K. Singh, Y. Singh, D. Barak, and M. Yadav, "Comparative Performance Analysis and Evaluation of Novel Techniques in Reliability for Internet of Things with RSM", *Int. J. Intell. Syst. Appl. Eng.,* vol. 11, no. 9s, pp. 330-341, 2023.

[27] K. Singh, Y. Singh, D. Barak, and M. Yadav, "Detection of Lung Cancers From CT Images Using a Deep CNN Architecture in Layers Through ML", In: *AI and IoT-Based Technologies for Precision Medicine.* IGI Global, 2023, pp. 97-107.
[http://dx.doi.org/10.4018/979-8-3693-0876-9.ch006]

[28] A. Kaushik, S. Gahletia, R.K. Garg, P. Sharma, D. Chhabra, and M. Yadav, "Advanced 3D body scanning techniques and its clinical applications", *2022 International Conference on Computational Modelling, Simulation and Optimization (ICCMSO),* Pathum Thani, Thailand, 2022, pp. 352-358.
[http://dx.doi.org/10.1109/ICCMSO58359.2022.00074]

[29] M. Yadav, A. Kaushik, R.K. Garg, M. Yadav, D. Chhabra, S. Rohilla, and H. Sharma, "Enhancing dimensional accuracy of small parts through modelling and parametric optimization of the FDM 3D printing process using GA-ANN", *2022 International Conference on Computational Modelling, Simulation and Optimization (ICCMSO),* Pathum Thani, Thailand, 2022, pp. 89-94.
[http://dx.doi.org/10.1109/ICCMSO58359.2022.00030]

[30] M. Yadav, S. Kumar, A. Kaushik, and D. Chhabra, "Piezo-beam structure in a pipe with turbulent flow as energy harvester: Mathematical modeling and simulation", *J. Inst. Eng. India Ser. D,,* vol. 104, no. 2, pp. 739-752, 2023.
[http://dx.doi.org/10.1007/s40033-022-00440-z]

[31] M. Yadav, D. Yadav, R.K. Garg, R.K. Gupta, S. Kumar, and D. Chhabra, Modeling and optimization of piezoelectric energy harvesting system under dynamic loading, in *Advances in Fluid and Thermal Engineering,* B. S. Sikarwar, B. Sundén, and Q. Wang, Eds., *Lecture Notes in Mechanical Engineering,* Springer, Singapore, 2021, pp. 339-353.
[http://dx.doi.org/10.1007/978-981-16-0159-0_30]

[32] S. Bhatia, N. Goel, V. Ahlawat, B.B. Naib, and K. Singh, "A Comprehensive Review of IoT Reliability and Its Measures: Perspective Analysis", In: *Handbook of Research on Machine Learning-Enabled IoT for Smart Applications Across Industries.* N. Goel and R. Yadav, Eds., IGI Global Scientific Publishing, 2023, pp. 365–384.
[http://dx.doi.org/10.4018/978-1-6684-8785-3.ch019]

[33] K. Singh, D. Barak, and Y. Singh, "Reviewing the IOT systems reliability and accuracy", *Pharma Innovation Journal,* vol. 12, no. 3, pp. 2775-2780, 2023.

[34] A.K. Bharti, A study of emerging areas in adoption of blockchain technology and it's prospective challenges in India, in *Proc. WITCON ECE,* Maharishi University of Information Technology, Lucknow, India, 2019, pp. 146–153.

[35] M. Yadav, D. Yadav, D.S. Kumar, D.R.K. Garg, and D.D. Chhabra, "Experimental & mathematical modeling and analysis of piezoelectric energy harvesting with dynamic periodic loading", *International Journal of Recent Technology and Engineering (IJRTE),* vol. 8, no. 3, pp. 6346-6350, 2019.
[http://dx.doi.org/10.35940/ijrte.C6107.098319]

[36] A. Ahmi, A. Tapa, and A.H. Hamzah, Mapping of financial technology (FinTech) Research: A bibliometric analysis, *Int. J. Adv. Sci. Technol.,* vol. 29, no. 8, pp. 379-392, 2020.

[37] K. Singh, Y. Singh, D. Barak, and M. Yadav, "Evaluation of Designing Techniques for Reliability of Internet of Things (IoT)", *International Journal of Engineering Trends and Technology,* vol. 71, no. 8, pp. 102-118, 2023.

[http://dx.doi.org/10.14445/22315381/IJETT-V71I8P209]

[38] S. Sonawane, and D. Motwani, "Identifying business models for blockchain-based FinTech solutions in India", *International Journal of Blockchains and Cryptocurrencies,* vol. 4, no. 3, pp. 202-227, 2023.
[http://dx.doi.org/10.1504/IJBC.2023.135002]

[39] K. Singh, M. Yadav, Y. Singh, and D. Barak, Reliability techniques in IoT environments for the healthcare industry in *AI and IoT-Based Technologies for Precision Medicine,* A. Khang, Ed., IGI Global Scientific Publishing, 2023, pp. 394–412.
[http://dx.doi.org/10.4018/979-8-3693-0876-9.ch023]

[40] K. Singh, M. Yadav, Y. Singh, D. Barak, A. Saini, and F. Moreira, "Reliability on the Internet of Things with designing approach for exploratory analysis", *Front. Comput. Sci.,* vol. 6, p. 1382347, 2024.
[http://dx.doi.org/10.3389/fcomp.2024.1382347]

[41] M. Yadav, D. Yadav, S. Kumar, and D. Chhabra, "State of art of different kinds of fluid flow interactions with piezo for energy harvesting considering experimental, simulations and mathematical modeling", *J. Math. Comput. Sci.,* vol. 11, no. 6, pp. 8258-8287, 2021.

[42] K. Singh, M. Yadav, Y. Singh, and D. Barak, "Finding security Gaps and vulnerabilities in IoT devices", In: *Revolutionizing Automated Waste Treatment Systems: IoT and Bioelectronics,* IGI Global, 2024, pp. 379-395.
[http://dx.doi.org/10.4018/979-8-3693-6016-3.ch023]

[43] V.A. Hajimahmud, Y. Singh, and M. Yadav, "Using a Smart Trash Can Sensor for Trash Disposal", In: *Revolutionizing Automated Waste Treatment Systems: IoT and Bioelectronics,* IGI Global, 2024, pp. 311-319.
[http://dx.doi.org/10.4018/979-8-3693-6016-3.ch020]

[44] M. Yadav, V.A. Hajimahmud, K. Singh, and Y. Singh, "Convert waste into energy using a low capacity igniter", In: *Revolutionizing Automated Waste Treatment Systems: IoT and Bioelectronics,* IGI Global, 2024, pp. 301-310.
[http://dx.doi.org/10.4018/979-8-3693-6016-3.ch019]

[45] K. Yadav, S. Rohilla, A. Ali, M. Yadav, and D. Chhabra, "Effect of speed, acceleration, and jerk on surface roughness of FDM-fabricated parts", *J. Mater. Eng. Perform.,* vol. 33, no. 14, pp. 6998-7007, 2024.
[http://dx.doi.org/10.1007/s11665-023-08476-2]

[46] S. Kumar, A. Kumar, N. Parashar, J. Moolchandani, A. Saini, and R. Kumar, "An Optimal Filter Selection on Grey Scale Image for De-Noising by using Fuzzy Technique", *International Journal of Intelligent Systems and Applications in Engineering,* vol. 12, pp. 322-330, 2024.

[47] K. Singh, M. Yadav, and V.H. Abdullayev, "Prediction of Flight Areas using Machine Learning Algorithm", *LatIA,* vol. 2, pp. 93-93, 2024.
[http://dx.doi.org/10.62486/latia202493]

[48] K. Singh, M. Yadav, and R.K. Yadav, "IoT-based automated dust bins and improved waste optimization techniques for smart city", In: *Revolutionizing Automated Waste Treatment Systems: IoT and Bioelectronics.* A. Khang, H. V. Abdullayev, E. Litvinova, G. E. Musrat, and Z. Avramovic, Eds., IGI Global Scientific Publishing, 2024, pp. 167–194.
[http://dx.doi.org/10.4018/979-8-3693-6016-3.ch012]

[49] A. Khang, K. Singh, M. Yadav, and R.K. Yadav, "Minimizing the Waste Management Effort by Using Machine Learning Applications", In: *Revolutionizing Automated Waste Treatment Systems: IoT and Bioelectronics.* A. Khang, H. V. Abdullayev, E. Litvinova, G. E. Musrat, and Z. Avramovic, Eds., IGI Global Scientific Publishing, 2024, pp. 42–59.
[http://dx.doi.org/10.4018/979-8-3693-6016-3.ch004]

[50] R.K. Sudhamathi, "Fintech as a road map to enhance business operations and delivery of financial services", *Asian Journal of Research in Business Economics and Management,* vol. 12, no. 3, pp. 1-9,

2022.
[http://dx.doi.org/10.5958/2249-7307.2022.00017.2]

[51] S. Trivedi, K. Mehta, and R. Sharma, "Systematic literature review on application of blockchain technology in E-finance and financial services", *J. Technol. Manag. Innov.,* vol. 16, no. 3, pp. 89-102, 2021.
[http://dx.doi.org/10.4067/S0718-27242021000300089]

[52] M. Yadav, S. Kumar, R. Yadav, D. Yadav, R.K. Garg, A. Kaushik, A. Ahlawat, and D. Chhabra, "Analysis of Renewable Energy Harvesting Sources with Interaction of Piezoelectric Materials", *2023 2nd International Conference on Computational Modelling, Simulation and Optimization (ICCMSO),* Bali, Indonesia, 2023, pp. 73-78.
[http://dx.doi.org/10.1109/ICCMSO59960.2023.00025]

[53] H. I. Reddy, M. Yadav, and H. Kumar, "Stochastic Analysis of The Utensil Industry Subject to Repair Facility", *Reliability: Theory & Applications,* vol. vol .19, no. 2 (78), pp. 170-177, 2024.

[54] M. Yadav, S. Gupta, and S. Singh, "Applications of Simulation and Queuing Theory in Scooter Industry", *Reliability: Theory & Applications,* vol. 19, no. 2 (78), pp. 655-660, 2024.

[55] M. Yadav, and H. Kumar, "Profit Analysis of Repairable Juice Plant", *Reliability: Theory & Applications,* vol. 19, no. 1 (77), pp. 688-695, 2024.

[56] S. Khwaldeh, M. Yadav, and K. Singh, "Defensive Auto-Updatable and Adaptable Bot Recommender System (DAABRS): A New Architecture Approach in Cloud Computing Systems", *International Congress on Human-Computer Interaction, Optimization and Robotic Applications (HORA), Istanbul, Turk,* 2024pp. 1-6
[http://dx.doi.org/10.1109/HORA61326.2024.10550519]

[57] T. Askerov, V. Abdullayev, V. Abuzarova, Y. Niu, and K. Singh, "Data processing in internet of things networks", In: *LatIA* vol. 2. p. 91, 2024.

[58] K. Singh, and D. Barak, "Healthcare Performance in Predicting Type 2 Diabetes Using Machine Learning Algorithms", In: *Driving Smart Medical Diagnosis Through AI-Powered Technologies and Applications*.* A. Khang, Ed., IGI Global Scientific Publishing, 2024, pp. 130–141.
[http://dx.doi.org/10.4018/979-8-3693-3679-3.ch008]

[59] B. Asgarova, E. Jafarov, N. Babayev, V. Abdullayev, and K. Singh, "Artificial neural networks with better analysis reliability in data mining", *LatIA,* vol. 2, p. 111, 2024.
[http://dx.doi.org/10.62486/latia2024111]

[60] B. Asgarova, E. Jafarov, N. Babayev, V. Abdullayev, and K. Singh, "Improving Cleaning of Solar Systems through Machine Learning Algorithms", *LatIA,* vol. 2, p. 100, 2024.
[http://dx.doi.org/10.62486/latia2024100]

[61] E. Ducas, and A. Wilner, "The security and financial implications of blockchain technologies: Regulating emerging technologies in Canada", *Int. J.,* vol. 72, no. 4, pp. 538-562, 2017.
[http://dx.doi.org/10.1177/0020702017741909]

[62] E. Davradakis, and R. Santos, *Blockchain, FinTechs and their relevance for international financial institutions.* EIB Working Papers, no. 2019/01, European Investment Bank, Luxembourg, 2019.

[63] M. Javaid, A. Haleem, R.P. Singh, R. Suman, and S. Khan, A review of blockchain technology applications for financial services. *BenchCouncil Trans. Benchmarks, Standards and Evaluations,* vol. 2, no. 3, p. 100073, 2022.

[64] A. Nasir, and K. Shaukat, "K., A. Iqbal Khan, I. Hameed, T.M. Alam, and S. Luo, "Trends and directions of financial technology (Fintech) in society and environment: A bibliometric study", *Appl. Sci.,* vol. 11, no. 21, p. 10353, 2021.
[http://dx.doi.org/10.3390/app112110353]

[65] M.P. Rodríguez Bolívar, and H.J. Scholl, "Mapping potential impact areas of Blockchain use in the public sector", *Inf. Polity,* vol. 24, no. 4, pp. 359-378, 2019.

[http://dx.doi.org/10.3233/IP-190184]

[66] M. Khalil, K.F. Khawaja, and M. Sarfraz, "The adoption of blockchain technology in the financial sector during the era of fourth industrial revolution: a moderated mediated model", *Qual. Quant.*, vol. 56, no. 4, pp. 2435-2452, 2022.
[http://dx.doi.org/10.1007/s11135-021-01229-0]

[67] N.R. Mosteanu, and A. Faccia, "Fintech frontiers in quantum computing, fractals, and blockchain distributed ledger: Paradigm shifts and open innovation", *J. Open Innov.*, vol. 7, no. 1, p. 19, 2021.
[http://dx.doi.org/10.3390/joitmc7010019]

[68] D.K. Pandey, M.K. Hassan, V. Kumari, Y.B. Zaied, and V.K. Rai, "Mapping the landscape of FinTech in banking and finance: a bibliometric review", *Res. Int. Bus. Finance*, vol. 67, no. 4, p. 102116, 2023.

[69] P. Khanna, and A. Haldar, "Will adoption of blockchain technology be challenging: evidence from Indian banking industry", *Qualitative Research in Financial Markets*, vol. 15, no. 2, pp. 361-384, 2023.
[http://dx.doi.org/10.1108/QRFM-01-2022-0003]

[70] R. Mishra, R K. Singh, S. Kumar, S.K. Mangla, and V. Kumar, "Critical success factors of Blockchain technology adoption for sustainable and resilient operations in the banking industry during an uncertain business environment", *Electron. Commerce Res.*, vol. 25, pp. 595-629, 2023.

[71] R.R. Suryono, I. Budi, and B. Purwandari, "Challenges and trends of financial technology (Fintech): a systematic literature review", *Information (Basel)*, vol. 11, no. 12, p. 590, 2020.
[http://dx.doi.org/10.3390/info11120590]

[72] S. Dashottar, and V. Srivastava, "Corporate banking—risk management, regulatory and reporting framework in India: a Blockchain application-based approach", *Journal of Banking Regulation*, vol. 22, no. 1, pp. 39-51, 2021.
[http://dx.doi.org/10.1057/s41261-020-00127-z]

[73] R. Kumar Singh, R. Mishra, S. Gupta, and A.A. Mukherjee, "Blockchain applications for secured and resilient supply chains: A systematic literature review and future research agenda", *Comput. Ind. Eng.*, vol. 175, p. 103854, 2023.
[http://dx.doi.org/10.1016/j.cie.2022.108854]

[74] R. Jaiswal, S Gupta, and A.K. Tiwari, "Delineation of blockchain technology in finance: A scientometric view", *Annals of Financial Economics*, vol. 17, no. 4, p. 2250025, 2022.
[http://dx.doi.org/10.1142/S2010495222500257]

[75] V. Paliwal, S. Chandra, and S. Sharma, "Blockchain technology for sustainable supply chain management: A systematic literature review and a classification framework", *Sustainability (Basel)*, vol. 12, no. 18, p. 7638, 2020.
[http://dx.doi.org/10.3390/su12187638]

[76] R.K. Jena, "Examining the factors affecting the adoption of blockchain technology in the banking sector: An extended UTAUT model", *International Journal of Financial Studies*, vol. 10, no. 4, p. 90, 2022.
[http://dx.doi.org/10.3390/ijfs10040090]

[77] R. Patel, M. Migliavacca, and M.E. Oriani, "Blockchain in banking and finance: A bibliometric review", *Res. Int. Bus. Finance*, vol. 62, p. 101718, 2022.
[http://dx.doi.org/10.1016/j.ribaf.2022.101718]

[78] S. Singh, and A. Chakraborty, "Demystifying blockchain adoption in financial sector—A critical analysis", In: *Distributed Computing to Blockchain*. Academic Press, 2023, pp. 367-375.
[http://dx.doi.org/10.1016/B978-0-323-96146-2.00008-5]

[79] A. Sharma, D. Sharma, and R. Bansal, "Emerging Role of Blockchain in Banking Operations: An Overview", In: *Contemporary Studies of Risks in Emerging Technology*. Part A, 2023, pp. 1-12.
[http://dx.doi.org/10.1108/978-1-80455-562-020231001]

[80] T.A. Almeshal, and A.A. Alhogail, "Blockchain for businesses: a scoping review of suitability evaluations frameworks", *IEEE Access,* vol. 9, pp. 155425-155442, 2021.
[http://dx.doi.org/10.1109/ACCESS.2021.3128608]

[81] P. Varma, S. Nijjer, K. Sood, S. Grima, and R. Rupeika-Apoga, "Thematic Analysis of Financial Technology (Fintech) Influence on the Banking Industry", *Risks,* vol. 10, no. 10, p. 186, 2022.
[http://dx.doi.org/10.3390/risks10100186]

[82] K. Nelaturu, H. Du, and D.P. Le, "A review of blockchain in fintech: taxonomy, challenges, and future directions", *Cryptography,* vol. 6, no. 2, p. 18, 2022.
[http://dx.doi.org/10.3390/cryptography6020018]

[83] S. Sheela, A.A. Alsmady, K. Tanaraj, and I. Izani, "Navigating the Future: Blockchain's Impact on Accounting and Auditing Practices", *Sustainability,* vol. 15, no. 24, p. 16887, 2023.
[http://dx.doi.org/10.3390/su152416887]

[84] D. Appelbaum, and R.A. Nehmer, "Auditing cloud-based blockchain accounting systems", *J. Inf. Syst.,* vol. 34, no. 2, pp. 5-21, 2020.
[http://dx.doi.org/10.2308/isys-52660]

[85] R. Silva, H. Inácio, and R.P. Marques, "Effective and Potential Implications of Blockchain Technology for Auditing", In: *Trends and Applications in Information Systems and Technologies..* Á. Rocha, H. Adeli, G. Dzemyda, F. Moreira, and A. M. Ramalho Correia, Eds., *Advances in Intelligent Systems and Computing,* vol. 1368, Springer, Cham, 2021, pp. 489–498.
[http://dx.doi.org/10.1007/978-3-030-72654-6_42]

[86] A.I. Baba, S. Neupane, F. Wu, and F.F. Yaroh, "Blockchain in accounting: challenges and future prospects", *International Journal of Blockchains and Cryptocurrencies,* vol. 2, no. 1, pp. 44-67, 2021.
[http://dx.doi.org/10.1504/IJBC.2021.117810]

CHAPTER 3

Blockchain Technology and Smart Contracts for Financial Transactions in Virtual Environments

Pooja Sharma[1], Sangeet Vashishtha[1,*], Neeraj Saxena[2] and Shruti Saxena[2]

[1] *IIMT University, Meerut, India*
[2] *Sandip University, Nashik, India*

Abstract: Blockchain technology and smart contracts have revolutionized the way financial transactions are conducted in virtual environments. This review paper provides a comprehensive overview of the role of blockchain technology and smart contracts in shaping the future of virtual financial transactions. We explore the fundamentals of blockchain technology, its applications in the financial industry, and the pivotal role that smart contracts play in automating and securing virtual financial transactions. Furthermore, we discuss the benefits, challenges, and prospects of these innovations within the virtual financial landscape.

Keywords: Artificial intelligence, Blockchain technology, Cross-border payments, Cryptocurrency, Digital identity, Financial transactions, Kyc, Machine learning, Smart contracts, Virtual finance.

INTRODUCTION

In recent years, the convergence of financial transactions and virtual environments has given rise to transformative technologies that promise to redefine the way we conduct and secure digital transactions. At the forefront of this paradigm shift is blockchain technology, a decentralized and tamper-resistant ledger system originally designed to underpin cryptocurrencies like Bitcoin. However [1], its applications extend far beyond digital currencies, finding innovative use cases across various industries. One of the most noteworthy applications within the financial realm is the integration of blockchain technology with smart contracts [15].

Blockchain technology is a relatively recent innovation, which emerged within the last decade. Despite its short history, blockchains have garnered significant interest across diverse domains, including computer science, cryptography,

---

[*] **Corresponding author Sangeet Vashishtha:** IIMT University, Meerut, India; E-mail: sangeet83@gmail.com

Keshav Kaushik, Rewa Sharma & Ayodeji Olalekan Salau (Eds.)
All rights reserved-© 2026 Bentham Science Publishers

finance, economics, civil law, healthcare, rights management, real estate, auctions, gambling, and various industries where challenges such as reliability, accountability, trust, and transparency are crucial [2 - 16]. Many assert that blockchains have the potential to revolutionize asset management to a degree comparable to the transformative impact the Internet had on communication.

Specifically, within the realm of Intelligent Environments and the burgeoning domain of the Internet of Things (IoT), blockchains have the potential to be a transformative force [3 - 8].

By leveraging smart contracts, blockchains introduce a groundbreaking element—provable trust—in the interactions among sensors, actuators, and processors owned by diverse entities spanning different jurisdictions and administrative domains. This breakthrough implies that blockchains have the capacity to bring a heightened level of reliability, transparency, and trust to both existing and future designs of intelligent environments [21].

AI can significantly enhance the functionality of smart contracts, especially through predictive analytics and fraud detection. Here's how these technologies could add value:

Predictive Analytics

Smart contracts are self-executing agreements that automatically enforce the terms written into their code. By integrating AI-driven predictive analytics, smart contracts can make more informed, proactive decisions, adding layers of intelligence beyond simple automation. Here's how:

Risk Assessment and Decision Making: Predictive models can assess the likelihood of certain outcomes (*e.g.*, default risk in insurance or credit). For instance, in insurance claims, smart contracts can use predictive analytics to determine whether a claim is likely to be fraudulent or predict the future behavior of a policyholder based on historical data.

Market Predictions for Dynamic Pricing: In use cases like decentralized finance (DeFi) or supply chain contracts, smart contracts can adjust terms dynamically based on AI's market trend predictions. For instance, in supply chains, AI could predict price fluctuations for goods or services, automatically adjusting contract terms to match market conditions.

Predicting Contract Triggers: AI could foresee when certain events (*e.g.*, financial triggers or performance milestones) are likely to happen, ensuring the contract's clauses are executed at the optimal time or recommending renegotiations before breaches occur.

Personalization of Smart Contracts: Predictive analytics can also help tailor smart contract terms to individual participants by analyzing data such as past behavior, transaction history, or market conditions. For example, in the insurance industry, contracts can adjust premiums dynamically based on real-time data on a user's behavior [22 - 23].

Fraud Detection

Fraud detection is another area where AI can make smart contracts significantly more secure and reliable. By integrating machine learning models and pattern recognition algorithms, smart contracts can detect anomalies and mitigate fraud risks in several ways:

Real-Time Anomaly Detection: Machine learning models can analyze real-time transaction data to spot irregularities or suspicious patterns. If a fraudulent action or transaction attempt is detected, the smart contract could trigger specific clauses (*e.g.*, freeze funds, alert parties) to mitigate risks.

Behavioral Analysis: AI can track and analyze user behavior over time to establish a baseline of normal activity. When behavior deviates significantly from this baseline, AI could flag these transactions for further investigation before the contract is executed.

Anti-Money Laundering (AML) and KYC Compliance: AI can enhance smart contracts by screening transaction data and identifying suspicious behavior that could indicate money laundering. Smart contracts could be embedded with algorithms that enforce regulatory compliance by identifying high-risk users based on KYC (Know Your Customer) and AML policies.

Dynamic Contract Adjustments: If a smart contract detects potential fraud risks, it could dynamically adapt its terms. For instance, in peer-to-peer lending, if a borrower's creditworthiness deteriorates (detected by AI), the smart contract could adjust loan repayment schedules or interest rates to compensate for increased risk.

Automated Audits and Reporting

AI can continuously audit the execution of smart contracts, verifying compliance with contract terms and flagging any discrepancies. Predictive models can forecast potential contract breaches or regulatory non-compliance, allowing for preemptive action. This would be particularly valuable in industries such as finance and healthcare, where accurate auditing is critical for regulatory compliance.

Natural Language Processing (NLP) for Contract Interpretation

In many cases, smart contracts rely on precise conditions, but AI-powered NLP can help interpret ambiguous clauses or make more complex judgments based on the language in traditional contracts. NLP could bridge the gap between legal contracts and code-based smart contracts, enabling automation even when the inputs are less structured.

Traditional Contracts *vs.* Smart Contracts

Traditional contracts are foundational legal instruments that have long been used to formalize agreements between parties. These contracts are typically drafted in natural language, making them accessible to all involved parties. However, they often require the involvement of intermediaries such as lawyers or notaries to ensure legal validity and enforceability. The enforcement of traditional contracts relies on established legal systems within specific jurisdictions, and disputes may need to be resolved through litigation or arbitration, adding time and cost to the process. While traditional contracts offer a high degree of flexibility and can be tailored to various situations, their interpretation can sometimes be subject to ambiguity, potentially leading to disputes and delays in execution. The process of drafting, negotiating, and executing traditional contracts can also be time-consuming and costly, involving expenses related to legal fees and administrative overhead.

These contracts are self-executing and encoded directly into software code, eliminating the need for intermediaries. Smart contracts operate within decentralized networks, such as blockchain, enabling trustless execution of transactions without reliance on centralized authorities. By automating execution and eliminating manual intervention, smart contracts offer significant cost savings and operational efficiencies for parties involved in financial transactions. They can execute transactions near-instantaneously, enhancing the speed and efficiency of transactions in virtual environments.

While smart contracts offer numerous advantages, traditional contracts still have their place, especially in scenarios requiring legal nuances, human interpretation, and flexibility. Complex legal agreements and regulatory compliance may necessitate the expertise of legal professionals and the flexibility provided by traditional contract frameworks. Additionally, smart contracts may have limitations in terms of flexibility compared to traditional contracts, as they are bound by the logic written into their code. Therefore, the choice between traditional contracts and smart contracts depends on various factors, including the nature of the transaction, the level of trust required, regulatory considerations, and the desired balance between automation and human intervention. In many cases, a hybrid approach that combines elements of both traditional and smart contracts may be adopted to optimize efficiency, compliance, and risk management in virtual financial transactions. Here we can elaborate on these functions with the help of a few examples.

Real Estate Purchase Agreement

Consider a scenario where two parties are engaging in a real estate transaction. They negotiate the terms of the sale, including the purchase price, financing arrangements, and conditions of the property. Once they reach an agreement, they draft a traditional contract known as a Real Estate Purchase Agreement. This contract outlines all the terms and conditions of the sale, such as the identification of the property, the purchase price, the timeline for the transaction, and any contingencies or conditions that must be met. The contract is typically reviewed and finalized by legal professionals to ensure compliance with relevant laws and regulations. Upon execution by both parties, the contract becomes legally binding, and the transaction proceeds according to the agreed-upon terms.

Example of Smart Contract

Decentralized Exchange (DEX) Trade: In the realm of decentralized finance (DeFi), smart contracts play a pivotal role in facilitating various financial transactions. Let us consider an example of a trade on a decentralized exchange (DEX), where a user wishes to swap one cryptocurrency for another. The user interacts with a smart contract deployed on the DEX platform, specifying the details of the trade such as the amount and type of cryptocurrency to be exchanged. The smart contract automatically executes the trade based on the prevailing market rates and predefined rules encoded into its code. Once the transaction is initiated, it is processed directly on the blockchain network without the need for intermediaries. The execution of the trade is transparent, irreversible, and verifiable on the blockchain, providing security and trust without relying on a centralized authority.

Hybrid Approach Example

Tokenized Asset Offering (TAO): In a tokenized asset offering (TAO), a company seeks to raise funds by issuing digital tokens representing ownership or rights to a specific asset, such as real estate, artwork, or intellectual property. In this scenario, a hybrid approach combining traditional contracts and smart contracts may be employed. Initially, the company drafts a traditional legal agreement outlining the terms and conditions of the offering, including the rights and responsibilities of token holders, regulatory compliance requirements, and dispute resolution mechanisms. Once the legal agreement is finalized and signed by all parties, the company deploys a smart contract on a blockchain platform to tokenize the asset and manage the issuance, transfer, and redemption of digital tokens. The smart contract automates key aspects of the TAO process, such as token distribution, dividend payments, and voting rights, while the traditional contract provides the legal framework and regulatory compliance necessary to ensure the validity and enforceability of the offering.

These examples demonstrate how both traditional contracts and smart contracts are utilized in financial transactions within virtual environments, each offering distinct advantages and considerations depending on the nature of the transaction and the desired outcomes of the parties involved.

Impact of Blockchain-Based Smart Contracts

Blockchain-based smart contracts have had a profound impact on various industries and sectors, offering several benefits and opportunities:

Increased Efficiency:

Smart contracts automate the execution of agreements, eliminating the need for intermediaries and manual processing. This results in faster transaction times, reduced administrative overhead, and lower costs associated with traditional contract execution.

Enhanced Security

Blockchain technology provides a tamper-proof and immutable ledger, ensuring the integrity and security of smart contract execution. Once deployed, smart contracts cannot be altered or tampered with, reducing the risk of fraud, manipulation, or unauthorized modifications.

Transparency and Trust

Smart contracts operate within decentralized networks, enabling transparent and auditable transactions visible to all participants. This transparency fosters trust among parties, as the terms and conditions of agreements are enforced automatically and verifiably without the need for intermediaries.

Global Accessibility

Blockchain-based smart contracts operate on decentralized networks accessible from anywhere in the world with an internet connection. This global accessibility expands market reach and facilitates cross-border transactions without the need for intermediaries or complex legal frameworks.

Innovation and Disruption

Smart contracts enable novel business models and use cases, unlocking opportunities for innovation and disruption across various industries. Decentralized finance (DeFi), supply chain management, digital identity, and tokenization of assets are just a few examples of areas where smart contracts are driving innovation and reshaping traditional business models.

Decentralization and Democratization

By operating on decentralized blockchain networks, smart contracts reduce reliance on centralized authorities and intermediaries, democratizing access to financial services and empowering individuals and organizations to transact directly with one another.

Compliance and Governance

Smart contracts can incorporate predefined rules and conditions to ensure compliance with regulatory requirements and industry standards. Additionally, blockchain networks can implement governance mechanisms to enable stakeholders to participate in decision-making processes and ensure the continued integrity and evolution of smart contract protocols.

Overall, blockchain-based smart contracts offer transformative potential, revolutionizing the way agreements are executed, and transactions are conducted across various sectors. Their impact extends beyond financial transactions to encompass broader implications for transparency, security, accessibility, and innovation in the global economy. As the adoption of blockchain technology continues to grow, the influence of smart contracts is expected to expand, driving further innovation and disruption across industries.

BLOCKCHAIN TECHNOLOGY: FOUNDATIONS AND KEY CONCEPTS

Blockchain technology, a cornerstone of innovation in the digital era, has rapidly evolved since its inception [4 - 5]. This section delves into the foundational principles and key concepts that underpin this transformative technology. Blockchain technology has been recognized as a promising solution for establishing decentralized E-commerce marketplaces [6]. Functioning as a network model, a blockchain system interconnects participants, allowing transactions without the necessity of pre-established trust, a requisite in traditional marketplaces. Instead, it introduces the concept of "meta trust", wherein participants can rely on consensus mechanisms, immutable ledgers, smart contract algorithms, and the foundational infrastructure of protocols to validate trades, even with unknown or anonymous counterparts. The overall architecture of a blockchain system is illustrated in Fig. (**1**), depicting a network comprising several parties, each maintaining an identical copy of the ledger. Business transactions within this network are executed through smart contracts.

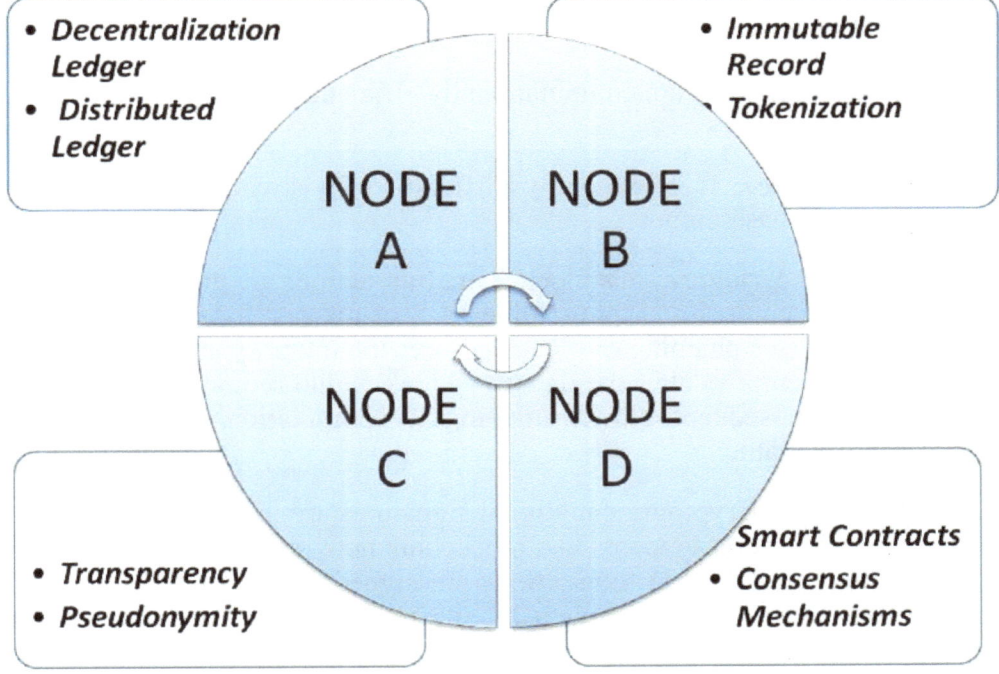

Fig. (1). Blockchain technology architecture.

Decentralization and Distributed Ledger

The fundamental concept underpinning blockchain technology is decentralization. In contrast to conventional centralized systems, wherein a solitary entity exercises control, a blockchain functions across a distributed network of nodes, with each node retaining a duplicate of the complete ledger. This distributed ledger ensures transparency, security, and resilience against single points of failure.

Immutable Record through Cryptography

An immutable record through cryptography refers to the use of cryptographic techniques to create and maintain an unchangeable and tamper-proof ledger of data. This concept is particularly prevalent in blockchain technology, where cryptography plays a central role in securing and validating transactions.

Here's how an immutable record is achieved through cryptography:

Hash Functions: Cryptographic hash functions are mathematical algorithms that take an input (data) and produce a fixed-size string of characters, known as a hash value or hash digest. These hash functions have several key properties:

Deterministic: The same input always produces the same hash output.

Fast Computation: They are computationally efficient, enabling rapid generation of hash values.

Collision Resistance: It is extremely difficult to find two different inputs that produce the same hash output.

Blockchain Data Structure: In a blockchain, transactions are grouped into blocks, and each block contains a cryptographic hash of the previous block, forming a chain of blocks. This chaining of blocks ensures the integrity and immutability of the data. Any attempt to alter the data in a block would require recalculating the hashes of all subsequent blocks, making it computationally infeasible and economically unviable.

Digital Signatures: Cryptographic digital signatures are used to authenticate and verify the identity of participants in a blockchain network. Each participant has a public-private key pair, and transactions are signed using the private key. The signature can be verified by anyone using the corresponding public key, ensuring the integrity and authenticity of the transaction data.

Encryption: Cryptographic encryption techniques can be used to secure the transmission and storage of sensitive data on a blockchain. Data is encrypted before being stored on the blockchain, and only authorized parties with the appropriate decryption keys can access the data.

By leveraging cryptographic principles and techniques, blockchain technology creates a tamper-proof and immutable record of transactions, ensuring data integrity, authenticity, and security. This immutable record is crucial in various applications, including financial transactions, supply chain management, digital identity, and decentralized governance, where trust, transparency, and reliability are paramount.

Consensus Mechanisms

Consensus mechanisms serve as the cornerstone of blockchain technology, ensuring that all nodes within the network agree on the current state of the ledger. These mechanisms are essential for maintaining the integrity and immutability of the distributed ledger by establishing a shared understanding of transaction validity and chronological order. One of the most widely recognized consensus mechanisms is Proof of Work (PoW), which involves participants, known as miners, competing to solve complex mathematical puzzles to validate and add new blocks of transactions to the blockchain.

In the Proof of Work process, the first miner to solve a cryptographic problem can add a new block to the blockchain. This involves miners using computer resources, a process known as mining, which consumes significant energy and processing capacity. However, it provides a robust and decentralized method of achieving consensus, as the probability of successfully mining a block depends on the processing power contributed by each participant.

Another prominent consensus mechanism is Proof of Stake (PoS), which operates on a different principle than PoW. In PoS, validators are selected to create new blocks based on the amount of cryptocurrency they hold and are willing to "stake" as collateral. Validators are chosen in a deterministic manner, with higher stakes increasing the probability of selection. Unlike PoW, PoS does not require extensive computational resources, making it more energy-efficient and environmentally friendly.

Both PoW and PoS mechanisms aim to incentivize honest behavior and deter malicious actors from attempting to manipulate the blockchain. In PoW, attackers would need to control a majority of the network's computational power to execute a successful attack, which becomes increasingly difficult and economically unfeasible as the network grows. Similarly, in PoS, attackers would need to control a majority of the cryptocurrency supply, which is costly and impractical.

Consensus mechanisms play a crucial role in ensuring the security, decentralization, and reliability of blockchain networks. While PoW and PoS are among the most well-known mechanisms, various other consensus algorithms, such as Delegated Proof of Stake (DPoS) and Practical Byzantine Fault Tolerance (PBFT), offer alternative approaches to achieving consensus based on different principles and objectives. Ultimately, the choice of consensus mechanism depends on factors such as network scalability, decentralization, energy efficiency, and security requirements.

Smart Contracts

Self-executing contracts containing programmed terms and conditions are known as smart contracts. When particular criteria are satisfied, these contracts automate the performance of predetermined activities. They allow for the transparent and trustless implementation of agreements without the need for middlemen because they are built on blockchain platforms like Ethereum.

Transparency and Pseudonymity

Transparency and pseudonymity are essential principles guiding the operation of smart contracts within virtual environments, particularly in blockchain networks. Transparency ensures that the code and execution logic of smart contracts are visible and accessible to all participants within the network. This openness allows for independent verification and auditing of the contract's functionality, promoting trust and confidence among stakeholders. Once deployed, smart contracts execute autonomously and immutably, with every transaction recorded on the blockchain in a transparent and verifiable manner, enabling real-time visibility into contract execution. Pseudonymity, on the other hand, protects the privacy and confidentiality of participants by concealing their real identities behind cryptographic addresses.

While transactions are recorded on the blockchain, participants interact using pseudonyms, safeguarding their personal information from exposure. Pseudonymity enhances privacy and security within virtual environments, reducing the risk of identity theft or fraud. Together, transparency and pseudonymity uphold the integrity, trustworthiness, and security of smart contracts, fostering accountability, privacy, and confidence in blockchain-based transactions and interactions.

Tokenization

Tokenization within smart contracts involves the process of representing various assets, whether physical or digital, as programmable tokens on blockchain networks. Through the use of smart contracts, these tokens are created, managed, and exchanged, adhering to predefined rules and conditions encoded within the contract's code. Such assets may include real estate properties, securities, commodities, digital collectibles, or currencies. Token standards like ERC-20 or BEP-20 ensure interoperability and compatibility with existing infrastructure and wallets. Smart contracts handle the issuance and distribution of tokens, including parameters such as total supply, distribution mechanisms, and regulatory compliance requirements. Ownership and transfer of tokens are securely managed on the blockchain ledger, enabling peer-to-peer transactions without intermediaries while enforcing rules such as ownership verification and transaction fees. Tokenization allows for fractional ownership of assets, democratizing investment opportunities by enabling smaller investors to participate in high-value asset markets. Tokens can be traded on decentralized exchanges, fostering liquidity and price discovery, while governance and utility functions within tokens incentivize user engagement and ecosystem growth. Compliance features integrated into smart contracts ensure regulatory adherence, incorporating procedures such as identity verification and anti-money laundering checks. Overall, tokenization within smart contracts unlocks new possibilities for asset management, investment, and decentralized finance, revolutionizing traditional financial systems and asset markets with transparency, efficiency, and programmability.

SMART CONTRACTS: SIGNIFICANT BREACHES AND VULNERABILITIES

Several significant breaches and vulnerabilities in the world of blockchain and smart contracts have occurred in the past, resulting in substantial losses. By examining these past incidents, we can understand how implementing AI for monitoring and detection could have prevented similar issues. Here are some notable examples:

Example 1: The DAO Hack (2016)

One of the most infamous smart contract hacks occurred when "The DAO," a decentralized autonomous organization on the Ethereum network, was exploited. Hackers found a vulnerability in the contract's recursive call function, which allowed them to drain about **$60 million worth of Ether**. The exploitation was not a flaw in the Ethereum blockchain itself but rather in the smart contract's code.

AI for Vulnerability Detection: AI-driven code analysis tools could have detected the recursive call vulnerability before the contract was deployed. Machine learning models trained on past smart contract exploits can identify patterns of faulty logic or inefficient code execution and alert developers to potential risks.

Real-time Monitoring and Anomaly Detection: AI could monitor smart contracts continuously, identifying abnormal transaction patterns. If a contract is invoked recursively in an unexpected or unauthorized manner, AI could flag it as suspicious and automatically trigger safety measures such as halting contract execution.

Example 2: Parity Wallet MultiSig Bug (2017)

The Parity Wallet, a popular Ethereum wallet, had a critical flaw in its multi-signature wallet smart contract. A user accidentally deleted the contract's library code, freezing **$300 million worth of Ether** across all affected wallets. The vulnerability was due to improper access control.

AI for Predictive Auditing: AI models can be trained to recognize risky patterns in code, such as improper or missing access control measures. Predictive analytics could have identified that the "kill" function was accessible without proper safeguards, flagging it for revision before deployment.

Real-Time Monitoring for Critical Functions: AI systems could monitor for interactions with critical functions (*e.g.*, "kill" functions or self-destruct methods). If AI detects an unauthorized or anomalous interaction, it could immediately halt the execution, preventing accidental or malicious damage.

Example 3: KuCoin Exchange Hack (2020)

In September 2020, KuCoin, a cryptocurrency exchange, was hacked, and over $275 million in cryptocurrency was stolen. The hack exploited private key leakage and targeted user wallets.

How AI Could Help: Behavioral Analysis and Fraud Detection: AI can monitor user and system behavior to detect anomalies; for example, AI could have flagged unusual withdrawal patterns or unauthorized access to private keys. Machine learning models trained to detect deviations from normal wallet activity could have detected the hack in its early stages.

AI-Driven Access Control: Implementing AI-based access control mechanisms, such as dynamic authorization, could have limited the hack's scope by preventing unauthorized access to critical wallets or systems.

Example 4: bZx Flash Loan Attack (2020)

bZx, a decentralized finance (DeFi) protocol, was targeted by a series of flash loan attacks, where the attacker took advantage of how the protocol handled leveraged trades. The attacker manipulated Oracle price feeds, resulting in a total loss of nearly $1 million.

AI-Powered Market Prediction and Oracle Security: AI can strengthen Oracle mechanisms by monitoring market conditions and spotting inconsistencies in real-time. Machine learning models can cross-validate data from multiple oracles, flagging outliers that deviate from expected market behavior.

Flash Loan Detection: AI models can detect unusual transaction patterns characteristic of flash loan attacks, such as rapid borrowing and repayment within a single transaction. Predictive models can identify and flag suspicious behavior before the attacker can fully exploit the vulnerability.

Example 5: Cream Finance Exploit (2021)

Cream Finance, a DeFi platform, suffered from a series of flash loan attacks in 2021, with one attack resulting in a loss of **$130 million**. This exploitation stemmed from vulnerabilities in the platform's price oracle and loan collateral logic.

Anomaly Detection for Oracle Manipulation: AI could have detected abnormal price fluctuations and liquidity patterns in the protocol, recognizing that they were inconsistent with regular market behavior. By learning from historical data, AI could automatically pause the contract or alert developers before significant losses occur.

AI-Based Collateral Risk Management: AI can optimize collateralization mechanisms by predicting the risk of under-collateralization based on real-time market data. If a collateralization imbalance is detected, AI could trigger additional margin calls or block new loans until the system stabilizes.

Example 6: Ronin Network Hack (2022)

The Ronin Network, associated with the popular game Axie Infinity, experienced one of the largest hacks in DeFi history, where attackers stole $625 million by exploiting the network's validators. The attackers gained access to private keys and made unauthorized transactions.

AI for Validator Behavior Monitoring: AI models could continuously analyze validator behavior to detect any signs of compromised nodes or irregular voting patterns. AI could identify when an abnormal number of validators approve a transaction outside typical operating hours or with unusual approval speeds, flagging it for immediate review.

AI-Based Key Management: AI can enhance security in multi-signature and key management systems by analyzing access behavior and adding layers of dynamic authorization. AI could detect unusual key access attempts and trigger multi-factor authentication protocols for additional security.

PERFORMANCE METRICS AND BENCHMARKS FOR SMART CONTRACT EXECUTION

In the world of blockchain, evaluating the performance of smart contracts is essential to ensure their efficiency, cost-effectiveness, and security. By establishing clear performance metrics and benchmarks, developers, and users can better understand how well a smart contract operates within its virtual environment. This approach also helps in optimizing smart contracts and making informed decisions about their deployment. Here's an elaboration of key metrics and benchmarks: To enhance the effectiveness of smart contracts, clear performance metrics and benchmarks are essential for evaluating **efficiency**, **cost**, and **security** in virtual environments:

Efficiency Metrics

Gas Usage: Measures computational resource efficiency; lower gas consumption indicates optimization.

Execution Time & Throughput: Faster execution and higher transaction throughput show better contract performance, especially in high-volume applications.

Cost Metrics

Gas Fees: Tracks transaction costs, benchmarks help optimize for lower fees without compromising functionality.

Total Cost of Ownership (TCO): Measures long-term costs, including deployment, maintenance, and audits, across blockchain platforms.

Security Metrics

Vulnerability Detection: AI tools monitor for real-time threats and anomalies, identifying security risks early.

Attack Resistance: Measures contract resilience against known exploits like reentrancy and flash loan attacks.

By defining and regularly measuring these metrics, smart contracts can be optimized for **scalability**, **affordability**, and **robust security**, ensuring their long-term viability in various blockchain ecosystems.

Interoperability in Blockchain Technology and Smart Contracts for Financial Transactions in Virtual Environments

In the context of **blockchain technology and smart contracts for financial transactions in virtual environments**, **interoperability** plays a critical role in ensuring the seamless operation of decentralized finance (DeFi) and cross-platform transactions. As blockchain platforms proliferate, each with unique protocols, achieving interoperability is essential for efficient, scalable, and borderless financial ecosystems.

Key Interoperability Challenges in Financial Transactions

Fragmented Networks: Different blockchains, such as Ethereum, Binance Smart Chain, and Solana, each have their infrastructure, making it difficult to transfer assets or data between them without intermediaries.

Cross-Chain Asset Movement: Financial transactions often require the movement of assets across multiple blockchains, but without interoperability, these transfers are complex and costly.

Data and Contract Standardization: Smart contracts on different platforms use distinct coding languages and frameworks, making it difficult to automate multi-chain financial transactions.

Solutions for Achieving Interoperability in Financial Transactions

Cross-Chain Protocols: Protocols like **Polkadot's parachains** and **Cosmos' IBC** allow multiple blockchains to interoperate by creating a unified system for transferring assets and data across platforms.

Blockchain Bridges: **Bridges** enable the transfer of assets (*e.g.*, Wrapped Bitcoin) between blockchains without central authorities, ensuring liquidity across different networks for financial transactions.

Interoperable Smart Contracts: Standardizing smart contract frameworks across blockchains (*e.g.*, ERC-20 tokens) and leveraging **cross-chain oracles** like **Chainlink** can enable automated, trustless financial contracts across different platforms.

Layer 2 Solutions: Platforms like **Polygon** provide scalability and interoperability by enabling faster and cheaper transactions across blockchain ecosystems.

Importance in Virtual Financial Environments

In virtual environments, such as DeFi platforms or metaverse economies, **interoperability** ensures that users can easily move assets, execute contracts, and perform financial transactions without being constrained by the limitations of any single blockchain. It enhances **liquidity**, **reduces costs**, and enables **global financial inclusivity**. Interoperability in blockchain technology and smart contracts is key to unlocking the full potential of decentralized financial transactions. By adopting cross-chain solutions, bridges, and interoperable smart contracts, financial operations in virtual environments can achieve the scale, security, and efficiency needed for widespread adoption.

APPLICATIONS OF BLOCKCHAIN TECHNOLOGY IN VIRTUAL FINANCE

As blockchain technology continues to mature, its applications within the realm of virtual finance have become increasingly evident [7 - 8]. Blockchain technology has found diverse applications in the realm of virtual finance, reshaping traditional financial practices and introducing novel solutions shown in Table **1**. One prominent application lies in the creation and management of crypto currencies [17], such as Bitcoin and Ethereum, providing decentralized alternatives to conventional fiat currencies. The advent of decentralized finance (DeFi) platforms is another noteworthy development, leveraging blockchain's smart contract capabilities to offer automated and trustless financial services like lending, borrowing, and trading. Beyond currency and DeFi, blockchain facilitates the tokenization of assets, allowing for the representation of real-world assets, such as real estate or art, as digital tokens on a blockchain [18]. This tokenization not only enhances liquidity but also democratizes access to traditionally illiquid assets. Moreover, blockchain technology is revolutionizing cross-border payments, making transactions more efficient and cost-effective by eliminating intermediaries [9 - 20]. The transparent and immutable nature of blockchain ledgers enhances security and traceability, making it a valuable tool in supply chain finance. As blockchain continues to mature, its applications in virtual finance are expected to expand, offering innovative solutions to longstanding challenges and fostering a more inclusive and efficient financial ecosystem.

REIMAGINING BUSINESS PROCESSES THROUGH BLOCKCHAIN AND SMART CONTRACTS

The integration of blockchain technology and smart contracts is revolutionizing the landscape of business operations, offering unprecedented opportunities for efficiency, transparency, and innovation. Here's how these transformative technologies are reshaping traditional business processes:

Table 1. Applications of blockchain technology.

Applications	Description
Cryptocurrencies and Digital Assets	The primary means by which blockchain technology transforms virtual finance are cryptocurrencies such as Ethereum and Bitcoin. Thanks to blockchain networks, these digital currencies offer safe, decentralized substitutes for conventional fiat money. Blockchain also makes it easier to create and administer a variety of digital assets, which broadens the use of virtual finance.
Decentralized Finance (DeFi)	Decentralized Finance, or DeFi, represents a revolutionary use case for blockchain in virtual finance. DeFi platforms leverage smart contracts to recreate traditional financial services such as lending, borrowing, and trading without the need for intermediaries. This decentralized approach enhances accessibility, reduces costs, and increases the efficiency of financial transactions in virtual spaces.
Tokenization of Assets	Blockchain's ability to tokenize assets has profound implications for virtual finance. Physical assets like real estate, art, and commodities can be represented as digital tokens on a blockchain. This process not only enables fractional ownership but also enhances liquidity, allowing users to trade these tokenized assets seamlessly within virtual environments.
Cross-Border Payments	Blockchain technology is transforming cross-border payments by providing a faster and more cost-effective alternative to traditional banking systems. Cryptocurrencies and blockchain-based payment systems eliminate the need for intermediaries and significantly reduce transaction times, making international transactions more efficient in virtual finance.
Supply Chain Finance	In virtual environments, blockchain is enhancing transparency and traceability in supply chain finance. By recording every step of a product's journey on an immutable ledger, blockchain ensures authenticity and reduces the risk of fraud. This transparency is particularly valuable in virtual environments where trust and verification are critical.
Supply Chain Finance	In virtual environments, blockchain is enhancing transparency and traceability in supply chain finance. By recording every step of a product's journey on an immutable ledger, blockchain ensures authenticity and reduces the risk of fraud. This transparency is particularly valuable in virtual environments where trust and verification are critical.
Smart Contracts in Financial Agreements	The integration of smart contracts in virtual finance automates and secures financial agreements. These self-executing contracts enforce predefined rules without the need for intermediaries, reducing the risk of fraud and increasing the efficiency of contract execution in virtual transactions.
Enhanced Security and Fraud Prevention	Blockchain's inherent security features, such as cryptographic hashing and decentralized consensus mechanisms, contribute to a more secure virtual finance ecosystem. The immutability of transaction records and the elimination of a single point of failure make blockchain a robust solution for preventing fraud in virtual financial transactions.
Regulatory Compliance and Auditing	Blockchain's transparent and traceable nature facilitates regulatory compliance in virtual finance. Transactions recorded on the blockchain can be audited in real time, ensuring adherence to regulatory standards. This transparency also enhances accountability, a crucial aspect of virtual financial environments.

Supply Chain Optimization: Supply chain optimization represents one of the most promising applications of blockchain technology and smart contracts, offering a transformative solution to long-standing challenges in logistics and inventory management. By leveraging blockchain's immutable ledger capabilities, businesses can achieve unprecedented levels of transparency and traceability across their supply chains. For instance, consider a global food retailer seeking to ensure the freshness and safety of its products. Through blockchain, the retailer can track the entire journey of perishable goods, from farm to shelf, recording critical information such as origin, temperature conditions, and handling procedures at each stage of the supply chain. This transparent record enhances consumer trust and enables rapid response to food safety incidents or recalls.

Smart contracts play a pivotal role in streamlining supply chain operations by automating a myriad of tasks, including order processing, inventory management, and logistics coordination. For instance, when a customer places an order for a product, a smart contract can automatically trigger a series of actions, such as initiating procurement from suppliers, updating inventory records, and scheduling transportation routes. This automated workflow minimizes manual intervention, reduces human error, and accelerates the flow of goods from production to delivery. Moreover, smart contracts can enforce predefined rules and conditions, such as quality standards or payment terms, ensuring compliance and accountability throughout the supply chain. An illustrative example of supply chain optimization through blockchain and smart contracts is seen in the automotive industry. Car manufacturers often rely on complex networks of suppliers to source components and parts for vehicle assembly. By implementing blockchain-based supply chain solutions, manufacturers can gain real-time visibility into the availability and status of critical components, enabling proactive inventory management and production planning. Smart contracts can automate the reordering process based on demand forecasts, production schedules, and inventory levels, optimizing supply chain efficiency and minimizing the risk of stockouts or production delays. Furthermore, blockchain technology facilitates collaboration and information sharing among supply chain partners while preserving data privacy and security. For instance, a consortium of pharmaceutical companies may collaborate on a blockchain platform to track the distribution of life-saving drugs. Each participant maintains a copy of the blockchain ledger, ensuring mutual trust and transparency in the exchange of sensitive information, such as batch numbers, expiration dates, and shipping details. Smart contracts can facilitate seamless coordination among stakeholders, triggering alerts or notifications when deviations from predefined standards occur, such as temperature excursions during transit. In conclusion, the integration of blockchain technology and smart contracts offers a compelling solution for supply chain optimization, revolutionizing the way businesses manage logistics, inventory, and distribution processes. By enhancing transparency, minimizing errors, and automating workflows, blockchain-based supply chain solutions drive operational efficiency, reduce costs, and improve overall supply chain resilience. As industries continue to embrace these innovative technologies, the potential for supply chain optimization and value creation remains vast, promising a future of greater transparency, agility, and sustainability in global supply chains.

Financial Services Disruption: Blockchain-powered decentralized finance (DeFi) platforms represent a groundbreaking innovation that is fundamentally reshaping the landscape of traditional financial services. These platforms leverage blockchain technology and smart contracts to create accessible and inclusive alternatives to conventional banking systems. By eliminating the need for intermediaries and embracing principles of decentralization, DeFi platforms offer a wide range of financial services to users worldwide, regardless of their geographical location or socioeconomic status.

At the heart of DeFi platforms are smart contracts, which automate complex financial processes such as lending, borrowing, and investment, without the need for traditional financial institutions. For example, consider a decentralized lending protocol that allows users to borrow funds or earn interest on their crypto assets by interacting directly with smart contracts deployed on a blockchain network. These smart contracts facilitate peer-to-peer lending and borrowing transactions, determining interest rates, collateral requirements, and repayment terms based on predefined rules encoded within their code. By automating these processes, DeFi platforms minimize reliance on centralized intermediaries, thereby reducing transaction costs, improving efficiency, and increasing accessibility to financial services for underserved populations.

One of the most significant advantages of DeFi is its democratization of finance, which opens up new avenues for individuals and businesses to access capital and investment opportunities. Unlike traditional banking systems, which often impose stringent eligibility criteria and geographic restrictions, DeFi platforms offer a level playing field where anyone with an internet connection and a digital wallet can participate in financial activities. For instance, a small business owner in a developing country can access liquidity through decentralized lending protocols to fund business expansion, without the need for a traditional bank loan. Similarly, retail investors can diversify their investment portfolios by participating in decentralized asset exchanges, tokenized securities offerings, or yield farming strategies, all facilitated by smart contracts on DeFi platforms. DeFi platforms promote financial inclusion by catering to the unbanked and underbanked populations who lack access to traditional banking services. For example, individuals in regions with limited banking infrastructure can use DeFi platforms to store value, transfer funds, or access credit without relying on brick-and-mortar banks. Moreover, DeFi's permission less nature allows users to retain full control over their funds and financial activities, mitigating the risk of censorship, account freezes, or asset seizures by central authorities. Blockchain-powered decentralized finance (DeFi) platforms are revolutionizing traditional financial services by offering accessible, inclusive, and efficient alternatives. Through the automation of financial processes *via* smart contracts, DeFi platforms democratize finance, enabling individuals and businesses worldwide to access capital, invest in diverse asset classes, and participate in a global financial ecosystem. As the DeFi space continues to evolve and mature, it holds the potential to drive financial innovation, promote economic empowerment, and foster greater financial inclusion on a global scale.

Digital Identity Management: Digital identity management represents a critical aspect of online interactions, encompassing the verification and authentication of individuals' identities in digital environments. Blockchain-based identity solutions revolutionize this process by offering a secure and self-sovereign approach to managing digital identities. Unlike traditional identity management systems, which rely on centralized authorities to verify and authenticate users, blockchain-based solutions leverage decentralized networks to empower individuals with greater control over their identity data. At the core of blockchain-based identity management are smart contracts, which facilitate identity verification and access control in a transparent and tamper-proof manner. For instance, consider a blockchain-based identity platform where users can create a digital identity profile containing personal information such as name, address, and biometric data. This profile is encrypted and stored on a blockchain, ensuring data integrity and protection from unauthorized access. Smart contracts govern the verification process, requiring users to provide cryptographic proof of their identity, such as a digital signature or biometric authentication, before granting access to their identity data. By decentralizing identity management, blockchain-based solutions reduce the risk of identity theft and data breaches associated with centralized databases. Each user retains control over their identity data, which is cryptographically secured and can only be accessed with their explicit consent. Moreover, blockchain's immutable ledger ensures that any changes or updates to identity records are transparent and traceable, enhancing trust and accountability in the digital identity ecosystem.

One of the key benefits of blockchain-based identity solutions is their self-sovereign nature, which empowers individuals to control and share their identity data on their own terms. For example, users can selectively disclose specific attributes of their identity to different service providers, depending on the context of the interaction. This granular control enhances privacy and reduces the risk of overexposure of sensitive information. Businesses stand to benefit significantly from blockchain-based identity management solutions. By integrating with decentralized identity platforms, businesses can streamline user authentication processes, reduce friction in onboarding procedures, and enhance trust in digital interactions. For instance, an e-commerce platform can leverage blockchain-based identity verification to streamline the account creation process, ensuring that new users are genuine and trustworthy. Similarly, financial institutions can use blockchain-based identity solutions to comply with Know Your Customer (KYC) regulations more efficiently, while minimizing the storage and exposure of sensitive customer data.

Blockchain-based identity management solutions offer a secure, transparent, and self-sovereign approach to managing digital identities. Through the use of smart contracts and decentralized networks, these solutions empower individuals to control and share their identity data securely, while reducing the risk of identity theft and data breaches. By streamlining user authentication processes and enhancing trust in digital interactions, blockchain-based identity management holds the potential to revolutionize online identity verification and authentication in diverse industries and applications.

Intellectual Property Rights Protection: The protection of intellectual property rights is paramount in fostering innovation and creativity, yet traditional methods often fall short in providing robust solutions. Leveraging blockchain's inherent tamper-proof nature, creators now have a powerful tool to securely register and safeguard their intellectual property rights. Through blockchain, creators can establish an immutable ledger of ownership, ensuring the integrity and authenticity of their creations. Smart contracts play a pivotal role in this process by automating various aspects of intellectual property management, including licensing agreements, royalty distributions, and copyright enforcement. For instance, consider a musician who wants to protect their original compositions. By deploying a smart contract on a blockchain network, the musician can encode the terms of their licensing agreements, specifying usage rights, royalties, and payment conditions. This automated system ensures that all parties involved adhere to the agreed-upon terms, reducing the risk of disputes and ensuring fair compensation for the creator's work. Furthermore, blockchain's transparent and immutable nature fosters trust and accountability in the management of intellectual property rights. Every transaction and modification to the intellectual property registry is recorded on the blockchain, creating an auditable trail of ownership and usage rights. This transparency not only enhances the credibility of the intellectual property system but also serves as a deterrent to potential infringements or unauthorized usage. By providing creators with greater control over their intellectual property rights, blockchain-based solutions promote innovation and creativity. Creators can confidently share their work with the knowledge that their rights are protected and enforced through smart contracts. This empowerment encourages a thriving ecosystem of content creation, collaboration, and dissemination, fueling continued innovation across diverse industries.

Streamlined Real Estate Transactions: Blockchain simplifies real estate transactions by digitizing property records and automating contract execution through smart contracts. These contracts manage tasks such as title transfers, escrow, and regulatory compliance, reducing paperwork and transaction costs. By enhancing transparency and efficiency, blockchain accelerates the buying, selling, and leasing of properties.

Healthcare Data Integrity: Blockchain secures patient records, ensuring the integrity and interoperability of healthcare data across providers. Smart contracts automate consent management, insurance claims processing, and healthcare payments, streamlining administrative tasks and improving patient care outcomes. This secure and transparent data management system enhances patient trust and enables better decision-making in healthcare delivery.

Supply Chain Finance Optimization: Blockchain-powered supply chain finance solutions leverage smart contracts to provide liquidity to suppliers based on verifiable supply chain data. These contracts automate invoice financing, trade finance, and supply chain financing processes, enabling suppliers to access working capital more efficiently. By reducing financing costs and risks, businesses can strengthen supplier relationships and drive supply chain resilience.

Efficient Cross-Border Payments: Blockchain-based payment networks facilitate fast, secure, and cost-effective cross-border transactions. Smart contracts automate currency conversion, compliance checks, and transaction settlement, enabling businesses to conduct international trade with greater efficiency and transparency. This streamlined payment infrastructure reduces currency exchange risks and enhances liquidity management for global businesses.

The integration of blockchain technology and smart contracts offers transformative potential across diverse business sectors. By reimagining traditional processes, businesses can achieve enhanced efficiency, transparency, and trust, paving the way for a more resilient and innovative future.

INDUSTRIES BENEFITING FROM SMART CONTRACTS: PRACTICAL IMPLEMENTATION AND ADVANTAGES

Smart contracts offer numerous benefits across industries by automating processes, enhancing security, and reducing costs. Key sectors like **insurance** and **real estate** have seen significant advantages from implementing smart contracts.

INSURANCE

Practical Implementation: Smart contracts automate the insurance claims process. For example, parametric insurance uses smart contracts to automatically trigger payouts when predefined conditions are met (*e.g.*, flight delays or natural disasters).

ADVANTAGES

Speed: Claims are processed instantly without human intervention.

Transparency: Policies and claim rules are embedded in the contract, reducing disputes.

Fraud Prevention: Automating claim verification reduces fraudulent claims by ensuring only legitimate conditions trigger payments.

REAL ESTATE

Practical Implementation: Smart contracts simplify real estate transactions by automating property sales, lease agreements, and escrow services. Blockchain-based smart contracts can handle deed transfers, rental payments, and contract enforcement.

ADVANTAGES

Efficiency: Eliminates the need for intermediaries (*e.g.*, brokers, banks), speeding up transactions.

Security: Transactions are encrypted and stored on the blockchain, preventing fraud.

Cost Reduction: By cutting out middlemen, smart contracts lower transaction fees and administrative costs.

SUPPLY CHAIN AND LOGISTICS

Practical Implementation: Smart contracts streamline supply chain management by automating processes like inventory tracking, payment releases, and shipment verification.

ADVANTAGES

Real-Time Tracking: Enables transparency across the supply chain, providing real-time data on product location and status.

Accountability: Automatically triggers payments upon delivery, reducing delays and ensuring all parties fulfill their obligations.

HEALTHCARE

Practical Implementation: Smart contracts in healthcare can manage patient records, insurance billing, and the sharing of medical data securely between healthcare providers.

ADVANTAGES

Data Security: Ensures patient data is stored and shared securely.

Automation: Streamlines billing and insurance claims, reducing administrative burdens and errors.

Smart contracts provide automation, security, and cost reduction across various industries like **insurance**, **real estate**, **supply chain**, and **healthcare**. These practical applications demonstrate their potential to transform traditional processes by enhancing transparency, speeding up operations, and eliminating intermediaries.

SMART CONTRACTS: ENABLING AUTOMATED VIRTUAL FINANCIAL TRANSACTIONS

Smart contracts, a pivotal innovation within the realm of blockchain technology, are revolutionizing how financial transactions unfold in virtual environments. Smart contracts, a cornerstone of blockchain technology, are catalysts for the evolution of automated virtual financial transactions [11]. These self-executing contracts, encoded with predefined rules and conditions, operate on blockchain platforms, introducing a level of automation and trust previously unparalleled in financial transactions within virtual environments [12].

The key strength of smart contracts lies in their ability to automate the execution of contractual agreements. Once deployed on a blockchain, these contracts autonomously enforce predetermined rules when specific conditions are met. This eliminates the need for intermediaries and streamlines the execution of transactions, offering a swift, efficient, and transparent alternative to traditional contract handling methods. In the context of virtual finance, smart contracts act as digital agents, facilitating a diverse range of financial operations. From executing payments and settlements to enforcing complex financial agreements, smart contracts bring a new dimension to the efficiency and precision of virtual financial transactions. The automated nature of smart contracts not only reduces the risk of errors but also significantly cuts down the time required for transaction processing.

Moreover, smart contracts operate within a decentralized network, leveraging the security features of blockchain technology. The immutability of the distributed ledger ensures that once a smart contract is executed, its outcome is permanently recorded, providing a tamper-resistant and auditable trail of transactions. This level of transparency and security is particularly critical in virtual financial transactions where trust and accuracy are paramount.

The applications of smart contracts in virtual finance are vast, ranging from decentralized finance (DeFi) platforms offering lending and borrowing services to tokenization of assets, creating digital representations of real-world valuables. As technology continues to mature, smart contracts are poised to play a central role in shaping the future of virtual finance, offering a secure, efficient, and automated foundation for a wide array of financial transactions in the digital realm.

Understanding Smart Contracts

Smart contracts are self-executing contracts with predefined rules and conditions written in code. These contracts operate on blockchain platforms and automatically execute actions when specific criteria are met. In the context of virtual finance, smart contracts enable trustless and automated transactions, reducing the need for intermediaries and streamlining processes.

Decentralized Execution

One of the key features of smart contracts is their execution on decentralized networks. This means that the code governing the contract is distributed across multiple nodes in the blockchain, ensuring transparency and eliminating the risk of a single point of failure. Decentralization enhances the reliability of virtual financial transactions.

Transparency and Immutability

Smart contracts leverage the transparency and immutability inherent in blockchain technology. Once deployed on the blockchain, a smart contract's code, and execution history are visible to all participants, fostering trust and accountability. The immutability of the blockchain ensures that once a smart contract is executed, its outcome cannot be altered.

Trustless Transactions

By automating the execution of agreements, smart contracts mitigate the need for trust between parties. The code enforces the terms of the contract, and the decentralized nature of blockchain ensures that no single entity has the power to manipulate the transaction. This trustless nature is particularly advantageous in virtual financial transactions where parties may be geographically dispersed and lack prior relationships.

Cost Efficiency and Speed

Traditional financial transactions often involve intermediaries, leading to increased costs and delays. Smart contracts, operating directly on the blockchain, eliminate the need for intermediaries, resulting in cost-efficient and swift transactions. This efficiency is crucial in virtual finance, where speed and reduced transaction costs are highly valued.

Programmable Financial Logic

Smart contracts introduce programmable financial logic into transactions. This flexibility allows for the creation of sophisticated financial instruments and agreements tailored to specific needs. From complex derivatives to automated payment schedules, smart contracts bring a new level of customization to virtual financial transactions.

BENEFITS AND CHALLENGES OF BLOCKCHAIN AND SMART CONTRACTS IN VIRTUAL FINANCE

The integration of blockchain and smart contracts into virtual finance brings forth a range of benefits and challenges, shaping the landscape of digital transactions. Blockchain technology has become a focal point for startups, offering a myriad of opportunities to disrupt traditional industries and innovate across various sectors. The decentralized and transparent nature of blockchain presents unique advantages for startups seeking to address key challenges [9 - 10].

Benefits

Enhanced Security: Blockchain's cryptographic mechanisms and decentralized nature contribute to robust security, safeguarding virtual financial transactions against hacking and fraud. The immutability of the ledger ensures that once a transaction is recorded, it cannot be altered, providing a secure foundation for virtual finance.

Transparency and Trust: Blockchain's transparent and decentralized ledger fosters trust in virtual finance. Participants can independently verify transactions, ensuring a high level of transparency. This transparency reduces the need for trust between parties and promotes accountability, a crucial element in virtual financial environments.

Efficiency and Speed: Blockchain and smart contracts streamline processes, eliminating intermediaries and reducing transaction times. The automation of tasks through smart contracts leads to quicker and more efficient virtual financial transactions. This increased speed is particularly valuable in scenarios where real-time transactions are essential.

Cost Reduction: The removal of intermediaries, coupled with automated processes, results in cost-efficient transactions. Virtual finance systems leveraging blockchain and smart contracts can significantly reduce fees associated with traditional financial services, making transactions more economical for participants.

Financial Inclusion: Blockchain's decentralized nature allows for greater financial inclusion, enabling individuals without access to traditional banking systems to participate in virtual finance. This inclusivity is empowered by the ability to create digital identities and access financial services directly through blockchain platforms.

Challenges

Scalability: As the number of transactions on blockchain networks increases, scalability becomes a critical challenge. Ensuring that the technology can handle a growing volume of transactions without compromising speed and efficiency is an ongoing concern in the adoption of blockchain in virtual finance.

Regulatory Uncertainty: The evolving regulatory landscape poses challenges for the widespread adoption of blockchain and smart contracts in virtual finance. The lack of standardized regulations can lead to uncertainty, hindering the development of clear frameworks that address legal and compliance considerations.

Smart Contract Security: While smart contracts offer automation and efficiency, vulnerabilities in their code can lead to security breaches. Flaws in smart contract programming may be exploited, resulting in financial losses. Ensuring the security and resilience of smart contracts is a continuous area of focus.

Interoperability: The interoperability of different blockchain platforms and smart contracts is a challenge that needs addressing. Seamless interaction between diverse systems is crucial for the widespread adoption of these technologies in virtual finance, but achieving this interoperability is a complex task.

Legal and Ethical Considerations: The legal recognition of smart contracts and the ethical implications of decentralized finance are subjects of ongoing debate. Determining the legal status of transactions conducted through blockchain and addressing ethical concerns, such as the potential for illicit activities, is essential for the responsible development of virtual finance.

FUTURE PROSPECTS AND CONCLUSION

The future of virtual finance holds exciting prospects as blockchain technology and smart contracts continue to evolve and shape the digital landscape. In this final section, we explore the potential trajectories and offer concluding insights into the transformative journey ahead.

Future Prospects

Integration with Emerging Technologies: The convergence of blockchain and emerging technologies like artificial intelligence, machine learning, and the Internet of Things holds the promise of creating more sophisticated and interconnected virtual financial ecosystems. Smart contracts, empowered by AI, could autonomously adapt to dynamic market conditions, enhancing the efficiency and responsiveness of virtual financial transactions.

Tokenization of Assets: The tokenization of various assets is expected to expand, allowing for the representation of real-world assets as digital tokens on blockchains This evolution has the potential to unlock liquidity in traditionally illiquid markets and democratize access to investment opportunities, further broadening the scope of virtual finance.

Regulatory Frameworks: The establishment of clear and globally accepted regulatory frameworks is crucial for the widespread adoption of blockchain and smart contracts in virtual finance. As governments and regulatory bodies continue to engage with these technologies, a harmonized and supportive regulatory environment may emerge, fostering responsible innovation and protecting participants.

Continued Innovation in DeFi: Decentralized Finance (DeFi) is likely to witness ongoing innovation, with new protocols, financial instruments, and governance models being developed. As DeFi matures, it may increasingly challenge traditional financial systems, offering more inclusive and accessible alternatives for users worldwide.

CONCLUSION

In conclusion, the integration of blockchain technology and smart contracts into virtual finance represents a paradigm shift with far-reaching implications. The benefits of enhanced security, transparency, efficiency, and financial inclusion are poised to reshape the way financial transactions occur in virtual environments.

As the technology matures, addressing challenges such as scalability, regulatory uncertainty, and security concerns will be paramount. Collaboration among industry stakeholders, governments, and regulatory bodies will play a crucial role in defining the future trajectory of virtual finance.

The transformative journey ahead involves not only technological advancements but also societal adaptation to these innovative financial paradigms. Virtual finance, powered by blockchain and smart contracts, has the potential to redefine economic landscapes, empower individuals globally, and pave the way for a more inclusive and efficient financial future. The ongoing exploration of these possibilities underscores the dynamic nature of the digital revolution and the continued evolution of virtual finance on the global stage.

REFERENCES

[1] L.W. Cong, and Z. He, "Blockchain disruption and smart contracts", *Rev. Financ. Stud.,* vol. 32, no. 5, pp. 1754-1797, 2019.
[http://dx.doi.org/10.1093/rfs/hhz007]

[2] R. Ramadoss, "Blockchain technology: An overview", *IEEE Potentials,* vol. 41, no. 6, pp. 6-12, 2022.
[http://dx.doi.org/10.1109/MPOT.2022.3208395]

[3] S.N. Khan, F. Loukil, C. Ghedira-Guegan, E. Benkhelifa, and A. Bani-Hani, "Blockchain smart contracts: Applications, challenges, and future trends", *Peer-to-Peer Netw. Appl.,* vol. 14, no. 5, pp. 2901-2925, 2021.
[http://dx.doi.org/10.1007/s12083-021-01127-0] [PMID: 33897937]

[4] M. Hamilton, "Blockchain distributed ledger technology: An introduction and focus on smart contracts", *J. Corp. Account. Finance,* vol. 31, no. 2, pp. 7-12, 2020.
[http://dx.doi.org/10.1002/jcaf.22421]

[5] S. Vashishtha, and P. Sharma, "Big Data-New Trend of Change in Complex Corporate World", *Globus An International Journal of Management & IT,* vol. 10, no. 1, pp. 4-6, 2018.
https://www.researchgate.net/publication/376046003_BIG_DATA-NEW_TREND_OF_CHANGE_

IN_COMPLEX_CORPORATE_WORLD

[6] T.T. Davarakis, G. Palaiokrassas, A. Litke, and T. Varvarigou, "Reinforcement learning with smart contracts on blockchains", *Future Gener. Comput. Syst.,* vol. 148, pp. 550-563, 2023.
[http://dx.doi.org/10.1016/j.future.2023.06.018]

[7] A. Jabbar, and S. Dani, "Investigating the link between transaction and computational costs in a blockchain environment", *Int. J. Prod. Res.,* vol. 58, no. 11, pp. 3423-3436, 2020.
[http://dx.doi.org/10.1080/00207543.2020.1754487]

[8] J.A. Fairfield, "Smart contracts, Bitcoin bots, and consumer protection", *Wash. & Lee L. Rev. Online,* vol. 71, p. 35, 2014.

[9] S. Vashishtha, P. Sharma, M.P. Gupta, M.B. Kumar, A. Singh, and M.F. Ansari, "Sustainability Of Start-Ups During Pandemic: An Analytical Study In Reference Of Indian Perspective", *J. Pharm. Negat. Results,* vol. 13, no. 8, pp. 4001-4008, 2023.
[http://dx.doi.org/10.47750/pnr.2022.13.S08.503]

[10] Y. Xu, H.Y. Chong, and M. Chi, "A review of smart contracts applications in various industries: a procurement perspective", *Adv. Civ. Eng.,* vol. 2021, no. 1, p. 5530755, 2021.
[http://dx.doi.org/10.1155/2021/5530755]

[11] E. Mik, "Smart contracts: terminology, technical limitations and real world complexity", *Law Innov. Technol.,* vol. 9, no. 2, pp. 269-300, 2017.
[http://dx.doi.org/10.1080/17579961.2017.1378468]

[12] N.W. Greenwald, "BIM, blockchain, and smart contracts", *Constr. Law.,* vol. 40, p. 9, 2020.

[13] A. Khatoon, "A blockchain-based smart contract system for healthcare management", *Electronics (Basel),* vol. 9, no. 1, p. 94, 2020.
[http://dx.doi.org/10.3390/electronics9010094]

[14] D.Y. Liao and X. Wang, "Applications of blockchain technology to logistics management in integrated casinos and entertainment", *Informatics,* vol. 5, no. 4, p. 44, 2018.
[http://dx.doi.org/10.3390/informatics5040044]

[15] A.K. Yadav, and R.K. Bajpa, "KYC optimization using blockchain smart contract technology", *International Journal of Innovative Research in Applied Sciences and Engineering,* vol. 4, no. 3, pp. 669-674, 2020.
[http://dx.doi.org/10.29027/IJIRASE.v4.i3.2020.669-674]

[16] O. Firica, "Blockchain technology: Promises and realities of the year 2017", *Calitatea,* vol. 18, no. S3, p. 51, 2017.

[17] D. Macrinici, C. Cartofeanu, and S. Gao, "Smart contract applications within blockchain technology: A systematic mapping study", *Telemat. Inform.,* vol. 35, no. 8, pp. 2337-2354, 2018.
[http://dx.doi.org/10.1016/j.tele.2018.10.004]

[18] R. Herian "Legal recognition of blockchain registries and smart contracts", *EU Blockchain Observatory and Forum,* 2018

[19] A. A. Hassanein, N. El-Tazi, and N. N. Mohy, "Blockchain, smart contracts, and decentralized applications: an introduction", *Implementing and Leveraging Blockchain Programming.* B. S. Rawal, G. Manogaran, and M. Poongodi, Eds., *Blockchain Technologies, Springer,* Singapore, 2022, pp. 103–122.
[http://dx.doi.org/10.1007/978-981-16-3412-3_6]

[20] P. Yeoh, "Regulatory issues in blockchain technology", *Journal of Financial Regulation and Compliance,* vol. 25, no. 2, pp. 196-208, 2017.
[http://dx.doi.org/10.1108/JFRC-08-2016-0068]

[21] S. Vashishtha, and P. Sharma, "Artificial intelligence and more effective advertising: unlocking the power of data and automation", In: *Advances in Digital Marketing in the Era of Artificial Intelligence,*

CRC Press, 2025, pp. 162-171.

[22]   S. Vashishtha, and P. Sharma, "Deep Learning: A state-of-the-art approach to artificial intelligence "AI"", In: *Deep Learning Concepts in Operations Research*, 2024, pp. 105-123. 1st ed., Auerbach Publications, 2024, p. 19.
[http://dx.doi.org/10.1201/9781003433309-11]

[23]   S. Vashishtha, and P. Sharma, Artificial intelligence and more effective advertising, in *Advances in Digital Marketing in the Era of Artificial Intelligence: Case Studies and Data Analysis for Business Problem Solving,* M. Ltifi, Ed., CRC Press, 2024, p. 162.

CHAPTER 4

Blockchain: Use of Smart Contracts in Finance

Ambika R. Thakur[1], **Chetna Tiwari**[1], **Kartikey Vats**[1] and **Garima Sharma**[1,*]

[1] *Department of Computer Science and Engineering, The NorthCap University, Gurugram, India*

Abstract: Through its decentralized architecture, blockchain technology has become a transforming paradigm in the banking sector, revolutionizing established procedures. This study analyzes the dynamic convergence of blockchain and finance, with an emphasis on smart contracts' essential role in altering financial transactions. It adds to the expanding knowledge of the practical uses and possibilities of this technology in the banking industry by investigating the uses, problems, and prospects of smart contracts within the financial environment. This research study digs into the many uses, effects, problems, and prospects of smart contracts in the banking industry. This chapter attempts to give a full knowledge of how smart contracts are revolutionizing financial processes and determining the future of the financial sector through theoretical studies.

Keywords: Applications, Blockchain, Decentralization, Efficiency, Finance sector, Improvements, Security, Smart contracts, Transparency.

INTRODUCTION

Blockchain technology was originally made public in 2008 when Satoshi Nakamoto released the Bitcoin software [1]. Blockchain is a system that enables many parties to have a secure, transparent, and immutable record of transactions. It was originally intended to be the core technology for the cryptocurrency Bitcoin, but its uses go well beyond that [1]. The blockchain networks can be broadly categorized into four categories, namely: (1) Public, (2) Private, (3) Hybrid, (4) Consortium. Table 1 provides a summary of the characteristics of all four blockchain networks.

This chapter delves into smart contracts, which are automated programs encoded with the terms of an agreement. These contracts, which operate on blockchain systems, automatically enforce terms when predefined criteria are satisfied, removing the need for an intermediary. By leveraging blockchain's decentralized

---

[*] **Corresponding author Garima Sharma:** Department of Computer Science and Engineering, The NorthCap University, Gurugram, India; E-mail: garimasharma@ncuindia.edu

Keshav Kaushik, Rewa Sharma & Ayodeji Olalekan Salau (Eds.)
All rights reserved-© 2026 Bentham Science Publishers

nature, platforms like Ethereum ensure transparency and resistance to tampering during contract execution [2, 3]. Originally conceptualized by computer scientist Nick Szabo in the 1990s, smart contracts found practical applications with the emergence of blockchain technology, particularly on platforms such as Ethereum [3]. Fig. (**1**) illustrates the usage statistics of smart contracts in financial organizations like banks, insurance companies, and investment businesses.

Table 1. Various blockchain and their features.

Various Blockchain	Features
Public Blockchain	- Decentralized - Open to anyone - Transparent and verifiable - High security through consensus mechanisms
Private Blockchain	- Restricted access - Controlled by a single organization or consortium - Faster transaction processing - Enhanced privacy and confidentiality
Consortium Blockchain	- Shared among a group of organizations Blockchain - Permissioned access - Collaborative decision-making - Balances decentralization and control
Hybrid Blockchain	- Combination of public and private/consortium aspects - Offers flexibility based on use case requirements - Suitable for various industries and applications

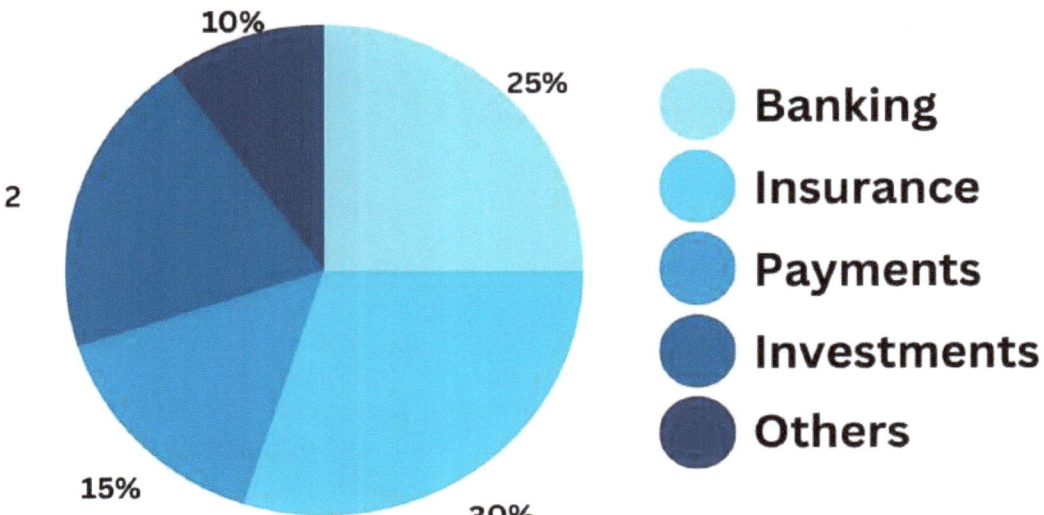

Fig. (1). Use of smart contracts in various financial sectors.

After discussing smart contracts, this chapter talks about the relationship between smart contracts and cryptocurrencies [5]. Smart contracts and cryptocurrencies are inextricably linked because smart contracts frequently run on blockchain systems that enable cryptocurrencies. To run on the blockchain, smart contracts demand computing resources. Native platform cryptocurrencies, such as Ether (ETH) in the case of Ethereum, are used to pay for the computational effort and storage required for smart contract execution [6]. This is frequently referred to as "gas" on the Ethereum network [6]. The term "gas" refers to the computing labor necessary to conduct operations or run programs (smart contracts) on the Ethereum blockchain [6]. According to 2023 data, the top 5 cryptocurrencies are (1) Bitcoin, (2) Ethereum, (3) Binance, (4) XRP, and (5) Solana as shown in Fig. (**2**) [7].

Fig. (2). Cryptocurrencies according to 2023 data.

Through its decentralized ledger, blockchain offers a platform for safe and transparent transactions [4]. On this blockchain, cryptocurrency's function, and smart contracts, which are programmable scripts, perform activities based on predetermined circumstances inside this decentralized and secure ecosystem [4]. The convergence of blockchain, cryptocurrencies, and smart contracts has resulted in novel applications and use cases that are transforming different sectors, notably banking [5].

The crux of this chapter discusses the application of smart contracts in the finance sector. The primary motivation of this study is rooted in the profound transformation and innovation that blockchain has brought to the financial sector. The aim of this chapter is to delve deep into the practical applications, advantages, and disadvantages of integrating smart contracts into financial systems.

The chapter is organized as follows:

- Section 2 discusses the basics of Blockchain and its working.
- Section 3 discusses the basics of Smart Contract and its working.
- Section 4 discusses the Symbiotic relationship between blockchain technology and smart contracts.
- Section 5 is about the benefits of symbiotic relations shown in the above section.
- Section 6 is about the challenges of symbiotic relations shown in section 4.
- Section 7 is about the comparison between traditional and blockchain-based financial systems.
- Section 8 shows future works and conclusions.

BLOCKCHAIN

This section discusses blockchain technology in-depth and provides an understanding of the basic terminologies associated with the blockchain.

Architecture of Blockchain

Blocks

This part discusses the blocks in the blockchain. Blocks are containers on the blockchain that retain a record of transactions [8]. Transactions added to the block can never be reversed. In addition, once a block is added to the chain, it cannot be changed [9]. If the blockchain survives, all information saved in blocks will be preserved in perpetuity [8]. They construct a chain one by one, containing the whole history of network transactions [8]. The actual structure of blocks might change amongst blockchains [9]. The simple block layout is depicted in Fig. (**3**).

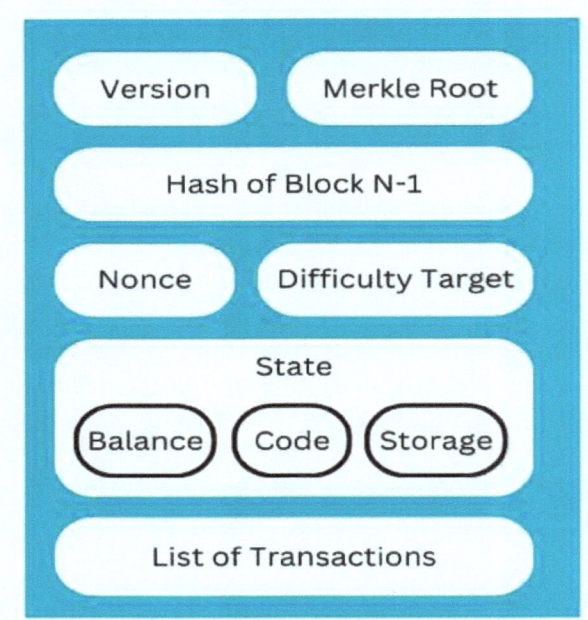

Fig. (3). Structure of a block.

Consensus Mechanism

[10] A consensus mechanism refers to a software component employed within blockchain systems to achieve unanimous agreement on the ledger's state. Typically deployed in networks involving multiple processes and users, this mechanism supplants the considerably slower processes involving human verifiers and auditors. Consequently, cryptocurrencies, blockchains, and distributed ledgers stand to gain significant advantages by incorporating consensus mechanisms into their operations. Different types of consensus mechanisms are shown in Fig. (**4**).

Cryptographic Hashing

Cryptographic hashing is the cornerstone of security and immutability in the realm of blockchain [11]. This process entails taking an input, which could be data or a transaction, and transforming it into a fixed-length string of characters, resembling a seemingly random sequence [12]. This resultant hash is distinctive to the input, and even a very small modification in the input data leads to a huge difference in the output hash [11]. The basic working of a cryptographic hash is given in Fig. (**5**). The significance of hashing lies in its role in safeguarding the integrity of data within the blockchain [11]. Once a transaction becomes part of a block and undergoes hashing, any attempt to alter that transaction would necessitate modifying the entire chain, starting from that point onward [12]. This formidable obstacle renders it exceedingly arduous for attackers to manipulate the data residing on the blockchain, thus fortifying the bedrock of trust and reliability upon which the technology relies [11].

Fig. (4). Types of consensus mechanisms.

Fig. (5). Cryptographic hashing.

Decentralized Ledger

This part talks about the decentralized ledger [13]. The core of blockchain technology revolves around a decentralized ledger, ushering in a transformative shift in the recording and maintenance of data and transactions. Diverging from conventional centralized systems, where a solitary authority or institution oversees the ledger, a decentralized ledger is distributed across a network of systems, referred to as nodes. A visual representation of a decentralized ledger is given in Fig. (6).

Fig. (6). Decentralized ledger structure.

Nodes

This part discusses the nodes in the blockchain. Nodes play a vital role in the working of a blockchain network [14]. A node essentially represents a computer or device that engages with the blockchain by preserving a copy of the ledger, verifying transactions, and contributing to the consensus mechanism that upholds network security within the context of blockchain technology [15].

Within a blockchain network, two categories of nodes exist: full nodes and lightweight nodes [14]. Full nodes retain a comprehensive copy of the blockchain ledger and actively partake in the validation and confirmation of transactions, thereby upholding the network's overall integrity [15]. On the contrary, lightweight nodes rely on full nodes for transaction validation and do not maintain the entire blockchain, enhancing their efficiency but diminishing their involvement in the consensus process [14].

Working of Blockchain

This section discusses the workings of blockchain. The complete process [16] of completing a transaction on the blockchain is as follows:

Step 1 - Initiating a Transaction: When a new transaction is initiated in the blockchain network, it undergoes a two-fold encryption process using both public and private keys to secure all necessary data.

Step 2 - Transaction Verification: Subsequently, the transaction information is distributed to a globally spread network of peer-to-peer systems, known as nodes. Within this network, all nodes undertake the verification of the transaction's legitimacy, which includes confirming the availability of sufficient funds to execute the transaction.

Step 3 - Block Formation: In a normal blockchain network with many nodes, numerous transactions are parallelly validated. Once a transaction has been confirmed as authentic, it joins a mempool, which consists of all validated transactions at a specific node. Multiple mempools are then aggregated to create a new block.

Step 4 - Consensus Mechanism: The nodes within a block commit to securely append the newly created block to the network permanently. However, permitting each node to add blocks independently would disrupt the network's operation. To address this, nodes employ a consensus process, ensuring that every new block integrated into the blockchain aligns with the collective truth accepted by all network nodes. This process also ensures that only valid blocks are securely linked to the blockchain. The miner chosen to add a block, which is also the "node," receives a reward. Additionally, the consensus mechanism generates a unique hash code for the block, which is imperative for the block's addition to the network. The blockchain hashing is shown in Fig. (**7**).

Step 5 - Adding Block: Once the new block has been assigned a hash value and authenticated, it is ready to be included in the blockchain. Every block includes a hash value from the preceding block, establishing a cryptographic link that cumulatively forms the blockchain.

Step 6 - Transaction Finalization: When the new block is successfully added to the blockchain, the transaction is considered complete, and its details are permanently preserved within the blockchain. The formation process of the blockchain structure is represented in Fig. (**8**) below.

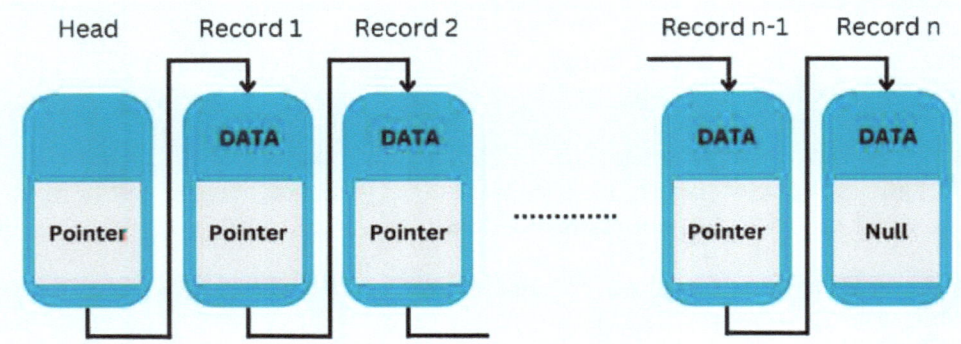

Fig. (7). Blockchain hashing.

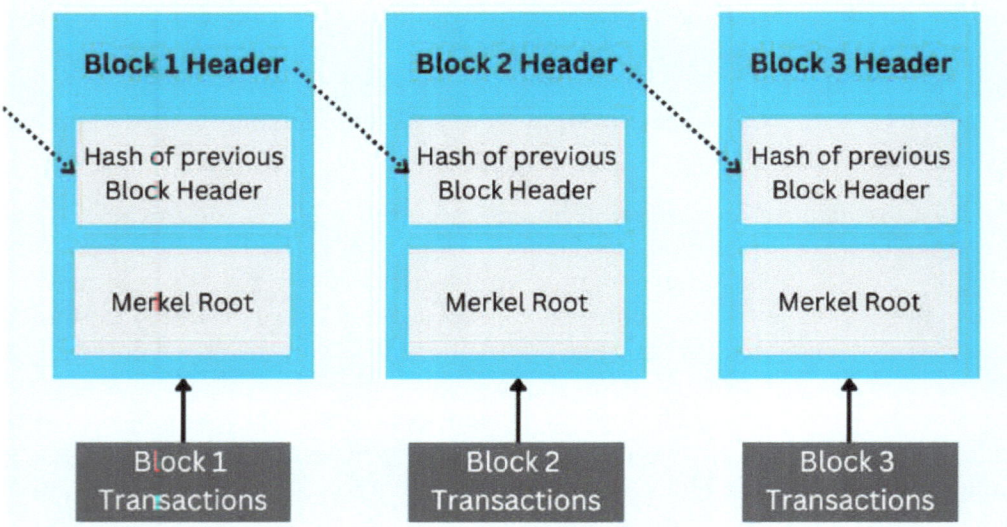

Fig. (8). Formation of blockchain structure.

Applications of Blockchain in the Financial Sector

Blockchain has several applications in the field of finance, altering existing procedures and opening new opportunities. These applications highlight the disruptive potential that is present in this technology, such as providing better efficiency, transparency, security, and accessibility to financial services [17]. Additional use cases and innovations are likely to emerge as technology matures, substantially changing the financial sector. Here are some important blockchain applications [17, 18] in finance shown in Fig. (**9**):

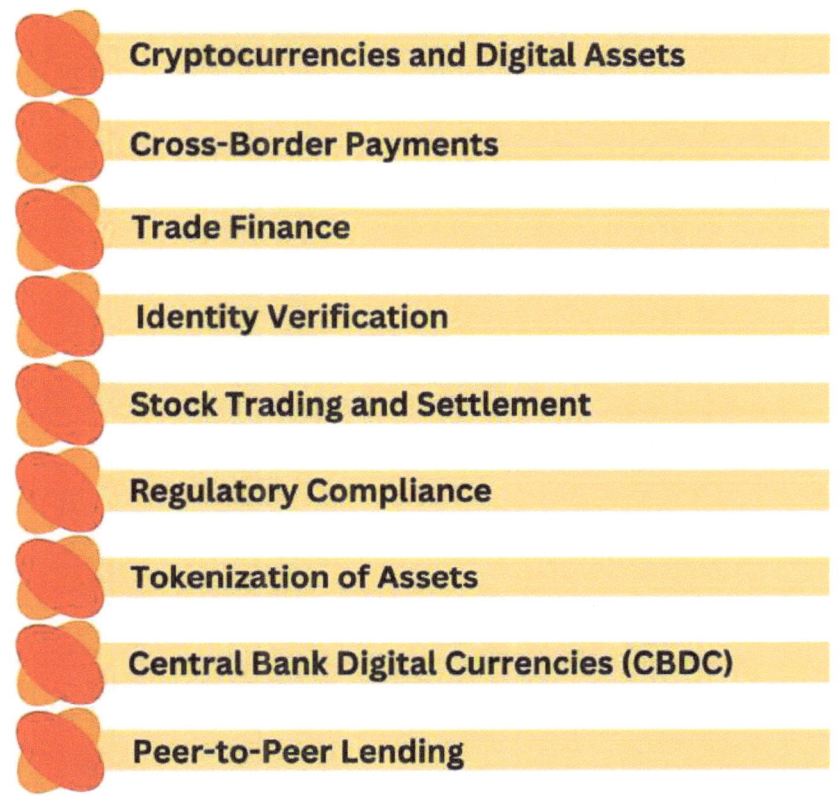

Fig. (9). Applications of blockchain in the financial sector.

Cryptocurrencies and Digital Assets

- Using digital currencies such as Bitcoin and Ethereum to provide safe and transparent transactions [12].
- Allowing for the creation and administration of digital assets and tokens.

Cross-Border Payments

- Reducing international transactions, and settling timeframes and costs.
- Improving transparency and lowering the risk of fraud in international payments.

Trade Finance

- Improving trade process efficiency through digitization and automation of documents.
- Increasing openness and reducing fraud in supply chain financing.

Identity Verification

- KYC (Know Your Customer) and AML (Anti-Money Laundering) protocols are being improved.
- Providing a safe and decentralized method of managing and verifying IDs [12].

Stock Trading and Settlement

- Facilitating the settlement of securities transactions in real time.
- Improving transparency and reducing counterparty risk in stock trading.

Regulatory Compliance

- Streamlining compliance processes by providing an auditable and transparent record of transactions.
- Real-time data availability facilitates regulatory reporting.

Tokenization of Assets

- Assets, such as art or real estate, are represented as digital tokens on the blockchain.
- Increasing liquidity and facilitating fractional ownership in historically illiquid markets.

Central Bank Digital Currencies (CBDC)

- Investigating its use in the conception of digital representations of national currencies.
- Improving the effectiveness of monetary policy and payment systems.

Peer-to-Peer Lending

- Providing transparent and automated smart contract execution to decentralized lending networks.
- Making loans more accessible to people and small companies.

SMART CONTRACT

This section [19, 20] discusses the concept of smart contracts in depth and associated terminologies in detail.

Architecture of Smart Contracts

The smart contract's structure comprises four components, which are discussed in this section. The architecture of smart contracts is further illustrated in the figure below with detailed insights (Fig. **10**).

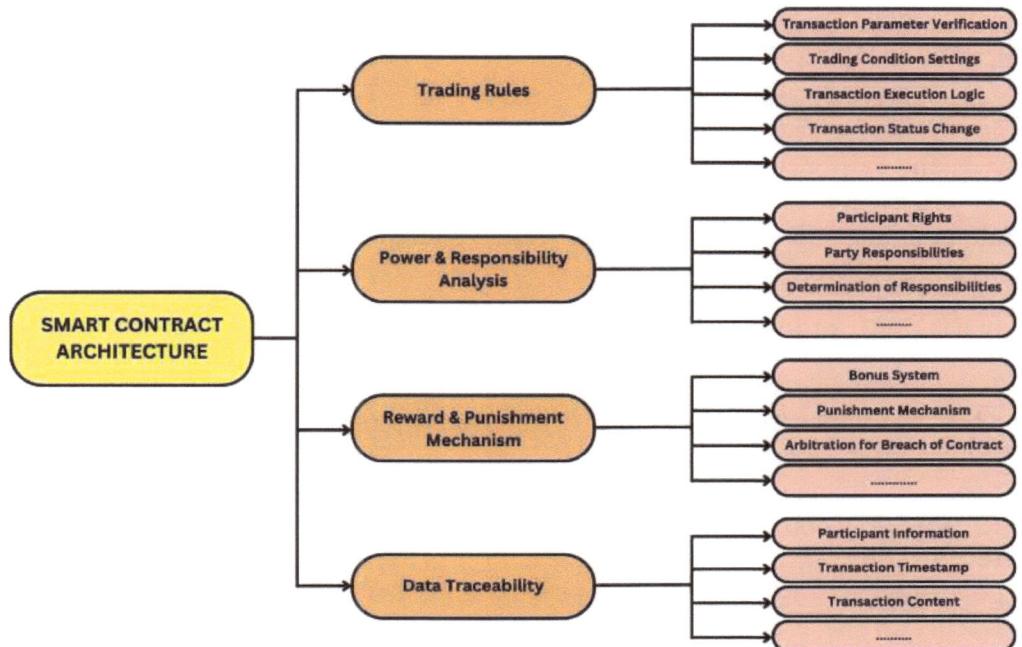

Fig. (10). Architecture of smart contract.

Trading and Transaction Rules

Smart contract transaction rules are essential conditions that govern and restrict transaction execution. By precisely defining these rules, smart contracts ensure that only transactions meeting specified criteria are executed, mitigating the risk of unauthorized or erroneous transactions.

Key Aspects of Transaction Rules

1. *Parameter Validation*: This involves establishing criteria for the validity of transaction parameters, ensuring they adhere to the correct value range, format, and type.
2. *Conditional Triggers*: Precisely defined triggers or conditional logic automatically execute specific actions when predefined criteria are met, such as value comparisons or event occurrences.
3. *Transactional Logic:* At the core of a smart contract, the transactional logic defines the precise method and processing logic for executing a transaction. Predefined rules govern the execution logic, dictating how the contract handles the transaction and evolves its state.
4. *State Transitions and Flow*: Managing the dynamic flow of states during contract execution is important. As the contract progresses through various

stages, specific states may trigger additional conditions or change the contract's overall behavior, often represented by state transition diagrams.

Power and Responsibility Analysis

Rights and responsibilities analysis in smart contracts forms an important aspect of smart contracts. A well-structured analysis contributes to achieving smart contract goals, enhancing participant satisfaction, and fostering confidence in the contract.

Key Elements of Rights and Responsibilities Analysis

1. ***Participant Rights***: Clearly defining the rights of each participant is crucial. This encompasses the ability to initiate transactions, access transaction information, check contract status, and more. Ensuring participants have the necessary rights is essential for meeting transaction demands.
2. ***Clarity of Commitments***: Every party within a transaction carries specific responsibilities. Understanding these obligations, encompassing adherence to conditions and limits, as well as compliance with contract terms, is essential. Clarity in these commitments fosters smooth execution and avoids potential roadblocks.
3. ***Shared Accountability***: Reiterating the significance of clearly defined responsibilities is crucial. By ensuring full comprehension of their duties, including respect for limitations and adherence to transactional conditions, all parties contribute to the contract's successful execution and a seamless transaction journey.

Reward and Punishment Mechanism

The reward and punishment mechanism ensures that the participating entities hold true to the conditions of the contract by using an incentivizing process. A well-designed system enhances participant motivation, leading to improved smart contract execution efficiency, network stability, and overall development impact.

Key Elements of the Reward and Punishment Mechanism

1. ***Bonus System***: Contract participants' rights and benefits may vary based on reputation points. Depending on the participant's rating, people would receive different rewards. This promotes the participants to maintain a better reputation in the network.
2. ***Punishment Mechanism***: Smart contracts can incorporate a penalty system for participants who breach terms or neglect responsibilities. The penalty's cost adjusts based on the severity of contract violation and damage degree, compensating the aggrieved party for their loss.

3. ***Arbitration for Breach of Contract***: In cases of disagreements or contract violations, arbitration serves as a dispute resolution procedure. A neutral arbitrator settles the dispute amongt the parties with the disagreement, while taking into consideration various factors such as contract conditions, performance, evidence, *etc.* before deciding on the reward. The smart contract enforces the conclusion of this arbitration procedure to resolve disputes efficiently.

Data Traceability

A thorough record of the transaction encompasses details about the identities and actions of the parties involved, along with pertinent timestamps. By retracing the history of the transaction, this information can be accessed, aiding in dispute resolution, disagreement adjudication, and supporting the arbitration process. Concurrently, it offers a comprehensive view, ensuring transparency into the transaction's past. Users have the capability to trace and authenticate the origin, participants, timing, and related details of an individual transaction.

Working on Smart Contracts

When required conditions are satisfied, a smart contract can autonomously enforce or execute the terms of the predetermined agreement. The core idea is to replace traditional, centralized middlemen with decentralized, automated code, hence increasing transaction trust and efficiency. A smart contract's operation includes many critical components [14] as shown in Fig. (**11**):

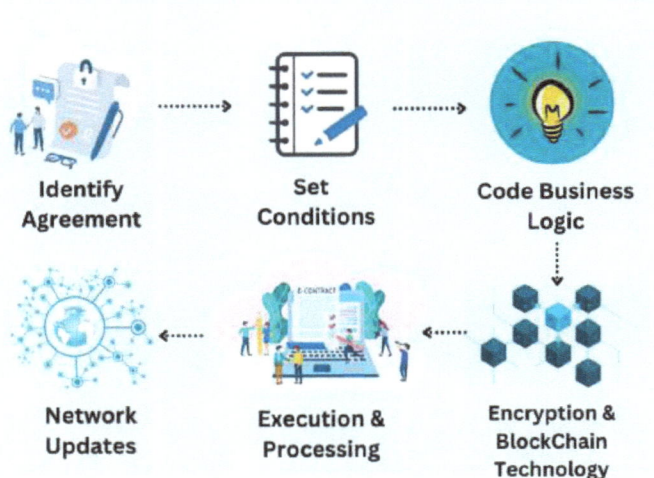

Fig. (11). How smart contract works.

Step 1 - Identify Agreement: The cooperation opportunities and intended objectives are identified by several partners.

Step 2 - Set Conditions: Smart contracts can be initiated by an organization or by preset conditions such as the performance of a crypto, the conversion rate of a currency, and much more.

Step 3 - Code Execution Logic: When the parameters are satisfied, a computer algorithm is built which executes automatically.

Step 4 - Encryption Technology: Encryption ensures the authentication, authorization, and transfer of data between smart contract parties.

Step 5 - Execution and Processing: When parties gain consensus on authentication and verification during blockchain iteration, the code is executed, and the results are recorded for authentication and authorization.

Step 6 - Network Updates: Following the deployment of the smart contract, all nodes update their ledger to show the changes.

When building a smart contract, it is critical to evaluate the transaction's characteristics as well as the design and execution of each component to match the demands and goals of the transaction. At the same time, it is vital to adhere to the blockchain platform's features and limits to ensure the efficient execution and steady functioning of smart contracts. Fig. (**12**) depicts the smart contract flow chart.

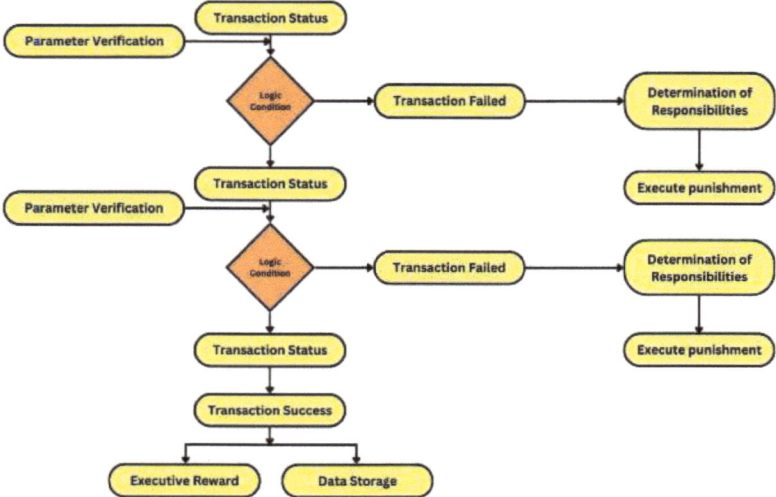

Fig. (12). Smart contracts in transaction.

Applications of Smart Contract

Smart contracts have a wide range of financial uses. Here is a list of specific applications [21] as shown in Fig. (**13**):

Fig. (13). Applications of smart contracts in the financial sector.

Loan Agreements

- The lending process, including loan origination, approval, and repayment, is becoming automated.
- In the case of a default, automatic collateral release or liquidation is triggered.

Derivatives Trading

- Complex derivatives contracts are executed automatically depending on predetermined circumstances.
- Counterparty risk is reduced by guaranteeing quick and transparent settlement.

Insurance Claims Processing

- Automating the claims process by automatically initiating payouts when certain conditions are satisfied.
- Improving openness and shortening the time it takes to settle disputes.

Token Offerings (ICOs/STOs)

- Token sales are managed by automatically distributing tokens to investors according to established conditions.
- Using programmable elements in the smart contract to enforce regulatory compliance.

Mortgage Agreements

- Mortgage operations, such as payment schedules, interest computations, and foreclosure situations, are becoming automated.
- Improving openness and lowering the likelihood of mortgage contract disputes.

Tokenization of Assets

- Smart contracts are used to represent ownership of real estate, art, or other assets as digital tokens.
- Allowing for fractional ownership and automatic return distribution.

Royalty Agreements

- Automating the payment of royalties to content creators depending on usage or sales.
- Ensure that royalties are distributed transparently and accurately among stakeholders.

Cross-Border Payments

- Cross-border payments and currency exchanges are becoming automated.
- Providing immediate settlement and minimizing the need for intermediaries.

P2P Lending and Crowdfunding

- Providing automated loan issuance and repayment on decentralized lending networks.
- Facilitating crowdfunding campaigns with transparent and programmable fund disbursement.

SYMBIOTIC RELATIONSHIP BETWEEN BLOCKCHAIN TECHNOLOGY AND SMART CONTRACTS

Smart contracts and blockchain work together to develop decentralized, tamper-resistant, and automated systems. Smart contracts enable programmable and self-executing agreements without the need for middlemen, while blockchain offers the infrastructure for safe and transparent transactions. This partnership has broad industry implications, changing established procedures and driving innovation. Here's a step-by-step breakdown of how they work together as shown in Fig. **(14)**:

1. **Blockchain as the Foundational Technology:** Blockchain is the technology that smart contracts are built on. It is a distributed ledger that keeps a secure record of all transactions that occur across a network of computers (nodes) [13].
2. **Smart Contract Development:**> Self-executing programmes or scripts that are written and deployed on a blockchain are known as smart contracts [10]. They are often built in specialized programming languages, with solidity being a popular language for Ethereum blockchain smart contracts [11].
3. **Blockchain Implementation:** When a smart contract is established, its code is distributed to a specified blockchain address [11]. This deployment is documented in a new block, and the contract is added to the blockchain's history [13].
4. **Validation of Decentralized Networks:** The blockchain network, which is made up of nodes (computers) all over the world, validates and verifies transactions as well as the deployment of smart contracts. Proof-of-work or proof-of-stake consensus procedures assure agreement on the state of the blockchain [17].
5. **Transparent and immutable record:** When a smart contract is implemented, its code and the transactions it processes become part of the blockchain's immutable and visible ledger [10]. Every network participant has access to the same historical record, increasing openness and avoiding unauthorized alterations [4].
6. **Triggering Factors:** Smart contracts have predetermined conditions, sometimes known as "if-then" expressions [19]. These criteria define the conditions under which the smart contract should carry out its planned functionality [17].
7. *Automatic Execution:* When the triggering circumstances are satisfied, the smart contract conducts the stated actions automatically. This might include sending money, altering data, or connecting with other smart contracts [11]. Automation removes the need for intermediaries and lowers the likelihood of mistakes or fraud [4].
8. **Computational Resources and Gas Fees:** Smart contracts on a blockchain necessitate the use of computing resources [10]. When users initiate transactions or engage with smart contracts, they must pay "gas" costs to compensate network nodes for processing power and storage. Petrol fees are often paid in the blockchain's native cryptocurrency [10].
9. **Decentralized Applications (DApps) Integration:** Smart contracts are frequently used as the foundation for decentralized apps (DApps) [19]. These

apps use smart contract capabilities to deliver a variety of services like decentralized finance (DeFi), supply chain management, gaming, and more [17].

10. **Trust and security:** The combination of blockchain and smart contracts improves security and trust. The decentralized and tamper-proof nature of blockchain protects the integrity of smart contract code and execution, lowering the risk of fraud and unauthorized alterations [4].

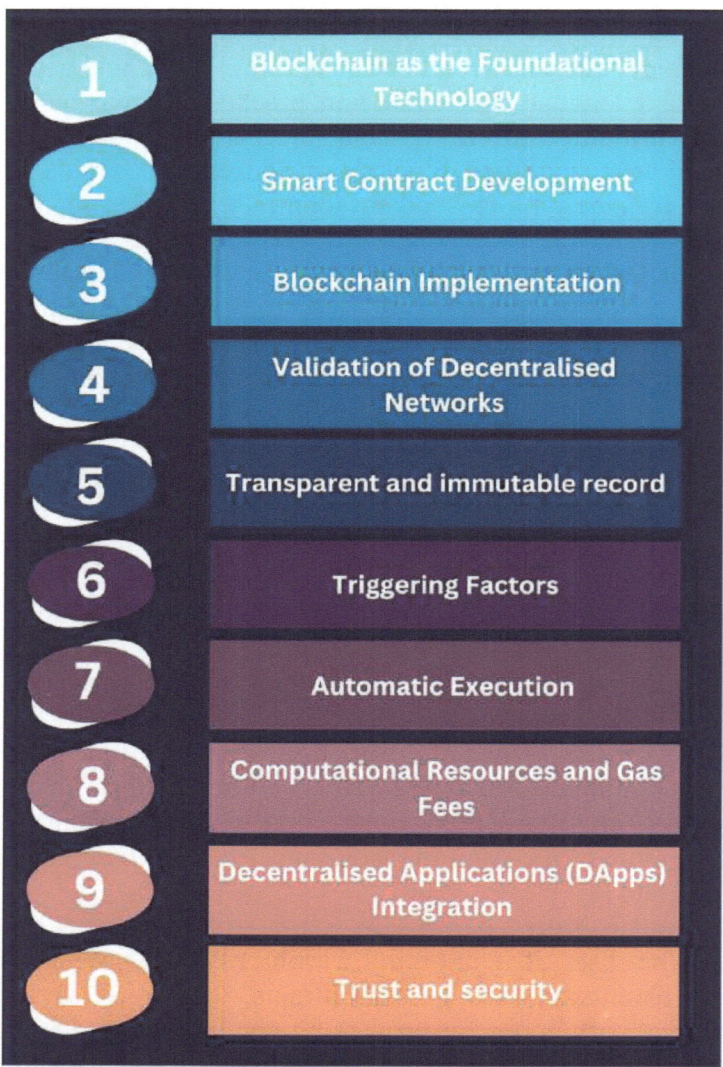

Fig. (14). Breakdown of How blockchain and smart contracts work together.

BENEFITS

The usage of blockchain and smart contracts in the financial sector has several advantages, including the ability to revolutionize existing procedures while improving efficiency, security, and transparency. Here is a list of perks in Fig. (15):

Fig. (15). Benefits of blockchain & smart contract together in finance sector.

1. **Security**
   - *Immutable Ledger:* Because blockchain offers a tamper-resistant and transparent ledger, hostile actors find it incredibly difficult to modify transaction history [4].
   - *Cryptography Security:* Smart contracts utilize cryptography techniques to improve transaction and data security [10].
2. **Transparency**
   - *Public Ledger:* The decentralized and transparent ledger of blockchain allows all parties to monitor and verify transactions, strengthening confidence among stakeholders [12].
   - *Smart Contracts with Auditable Code:* The code of smart contracts is viewable on the blockchain, allowing for easy auditing and verification [12].
3. **Efficiency**
   - *Automation Smart Contracts:* They automate the execution of set conditions, eliminating the need for human involvement in financial operations [7].
   - *Real-Time Settlement:* Blockchain provides faster and more efficient transaction settlement, particularly in cross-border payments [15].

4. Reduced Intermediaries
- *Decentralization:* By supporting node-to-node transactions, blockchain eliminates the intermediary, lowering costs and enhancing efficiency [11].
- *Trustless Transaction:* Smart contracts automate confidence in transactions, minimizing dependency on middlemen such as banks and clearinghouses [11].

5. Cost Savings
- *Lower Transaction Expenses:* Blockchain and smart contracts eliminate the expenses of middlemen, paperwork, and manual processes [10].
- *Operational Efficiency:* Automation reduces operating expenses and allows for speedier transaction processing [12].

6. Fraud Prevention
- *Immutable Record:* The immutability of blockchain avoids fraud by assuring that no recorded data can ever be changed [11].
- *Secure Execution:* Smart contracts execute automatically and securely, reducing the risk of fraud or manipulation [11].

7. Enhanced Traceability
- *Supply Chain Visibility:* Blockchain offers complete transparency in supply chain financing [12].
- *Transaction History:* The blockchain's transparent and chronological structure enables easy tracking of financial transactions [4].

8. Real-Time Access to Data
- *Data Availability:* Blockchain allows authorized parties real-time access to transaction data, which improves decision-making processes [10].
- *Immutable Data Storage:* Data cannot be changed once it is stored on the blockchain, preserving data integrity [10].

9. Global Accessibility
- *Global Knowledge Bank:* Blockchain platforms can securely store academic records, issue tamper-proof diplomas, and facilitate micro-learning opportunities, democratizing access to education and enhancing employability worldwide.
- *24/7 Availability:* Blockchain is available at all times globally, with no geographical constraints [14].

10. Smart Regulation and Compliance
- *Automated Compliance:* Smart contracts may be built to ensure regulatory compliance, lowering the chance of infractions [13].
- *Transparent Auditing:* The transparency of blockchain makes regulatory audits easier and more efficient [13].

11. Decentralized Identity Verification

○ *KYC/AML Compliance:* The use of blockchain for smooth and secure verification of credentials and identities can improve KYC/AML processes in the banking sector [11].

12. **Resilience and Disaster Recovery**
    ○ *Decentralized Architecture:* Because blockchain is decentralized, data redundancy is ensured, making it more immune to failures or assaults [11].
    ○ *Continuous Operation:* Even in the event of a network outage, blockchain systems may continue to function, assisting in disaster recovery efforts [4].

CHALLENGES

While the combination of blockchain and smart contracts provides significant benefits, there are several hurdles and impediments that must be overcome before widespread use in the financial sector. Here is a list of challenges [22, 23] as shown in Fig. (**16**):

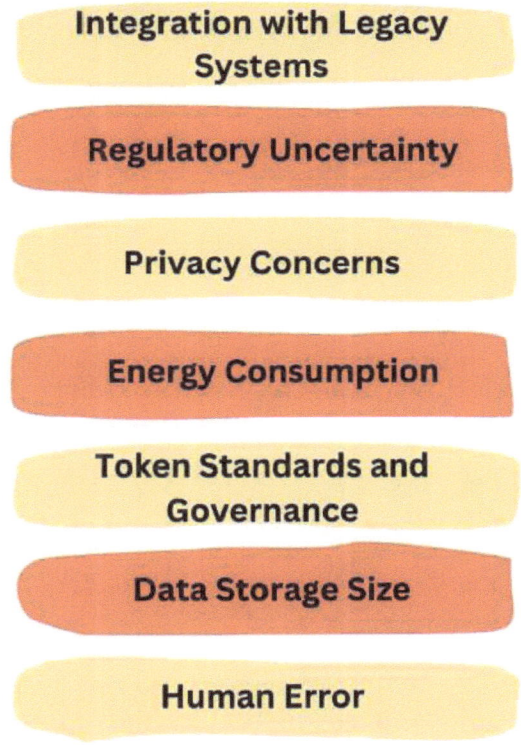

Fig. (16). Challenges for blockchain & smart contract together in the finance sector.

1. Integration with Legacy Systems

Legacy banking systems are not meant to function in tandem with blockchain technology, making integration difficult and expensive.

2. Regulatory Uncertainty

Globally changing and different regulatory regimes provide hurdles for blockchain and smart contract adoption, particularly in terms of compliance and legal recognition.

3. Privacy Concerns

While blockchain provides openness, it also raises privacy problems, particularly in financial transactions where secrecy is critical.

4. Token Standards and Governance

The absence of defined tokenization mechanisms and governance frameworks can cause confusion and impede interoperability between blockchain initiatives.

5. Data Storage Size

The size of the blockchain ledger might grow cumbersome over time, causing storage and bandwidth difficulties, particularly for nodes participating in the network.

6. Human Error

When users engage with smart contracts, they may make mistakes or misinterpret the programming, resulting in unforeseen effects and financial losses.

COMPARISON BETWEEN TRADITIONAL FINANCE SYSTEM AND BLOCKCHAIN-BASED FINANCE SYSTEM

While traditional banking systems have a lengthy history and a well-established legal framework, blockchain-based finance systems provide improved decentralization, transparency, and efficiency. Both have advantages and disadvantages, and the growth of financial systems may include a combination of traditional and blockchain-based techniques. Regulatory changes and continuous technological breakthroughs will have a significant impact on the future of finance. The comparison between traditional and blockchain-based financial systems based on different criteria is shown in Table **2**.

Table 2. Comparison of traditional and blockchain-based finance system.

Criteria	Traditional Finance System	Blockchain-Based Finance System
Centralization *vs.* Decentralization	- Institutions such as banks, governments, and financial intermediaries manage centralized financial systems.	- Decentralized finance (DeFi) operates without a central authority on blockchain networks.
Transparency and Trust	- Financial firms' reputations and regulatory control help to build trust. - Some financial operations remain opaque to clients, limiting transparency.	- The openness and immutability of blockchain ledgers foster trust. - All participants have access to a verifiable and transparent transaction record.
Transactional Speed and Accessibility	- Transactions might take longer to complete, particularly in cross-border situations. - Access may be limited, especially for people who do not have access to traditional banking.	- Transactions in decentralized finance (DeFi) systems can be near-instantaneous. - Anyone with an internet connection can gain access, promoting financial inclusivity.
Fees and Intermediaries	- Intermediaries frequently charge for their services. - A transaction may include several intermediaries, such as banks, clearinghouses, and payment processors.	- Fees tend to be cheaper, and some decentralized systems strive for charge transparency. - Transactions can take place directly between participants, requiring fewer middlemen.
Immutability and security	- Records can be modified or changed. - Because security is based on centralized databases, they are vulnerable to hacking and fraud.	- Because blockchain transactions are unchangeable, the possibility of fraud is reduced. - Cryptographic algorithms and consensus processes improve security.
Financial Inclusion	- Individuals in underserved or unbanked areas may have restricted access to financial services.	- Decentralized finance (DeFi) has the ability to make financial services available to a worldwide audience, including those who have hitherto been excluded.
Programmability and Smart Contracts	- Contracts are frequently paper-based and manually performed, resulting in delays and possible inaccuracies.	- Smart contracts allow for programmable and self-executing agreements, which automate a variety of financial procedures.
Regulatory Environment	- Traditional financial systems are governed by well-established regulatory structures.	- Regulatory clarity and frameworks are continually changing, which is causing some uncertainty.
Resilience and Redundancy	- Systemic breakdowns and single points of failure are common in centralized systems.	- Decentralized systems are more robust since data is copied across several nodes.

Now let us see the example of how traditional banking and blockchain-based banking work in the case of loan handling [24]. Numerous banks or financial institutions work together to give a loan or funding to a single borrower or project under a financial sector cooperation arrangement. This sort of banking is frequently utilized for big, complex, or high-value transactions that surpass a single financial institution's lending capacity or risk tolerance.

In October 1996, the Reserve Bank of India initiated a series of regulatory amendments aimed at enhancing the flexibility of credit delivery systems by relaxing certain requirements related to consortium, multiple banking, and syndicate arrangements. However, due to an increase in fraud activities associated with these arrangements, it wasn't safe and fast enough. Therefore, blockchain can be introduced in this scenario where the shortcomings are looked after and solved.

Fig. (**17**) shows the traditional banking system, and Fig. (**18**) shows the blockchain-based banking system which will be based on security and easy accessibility terms.

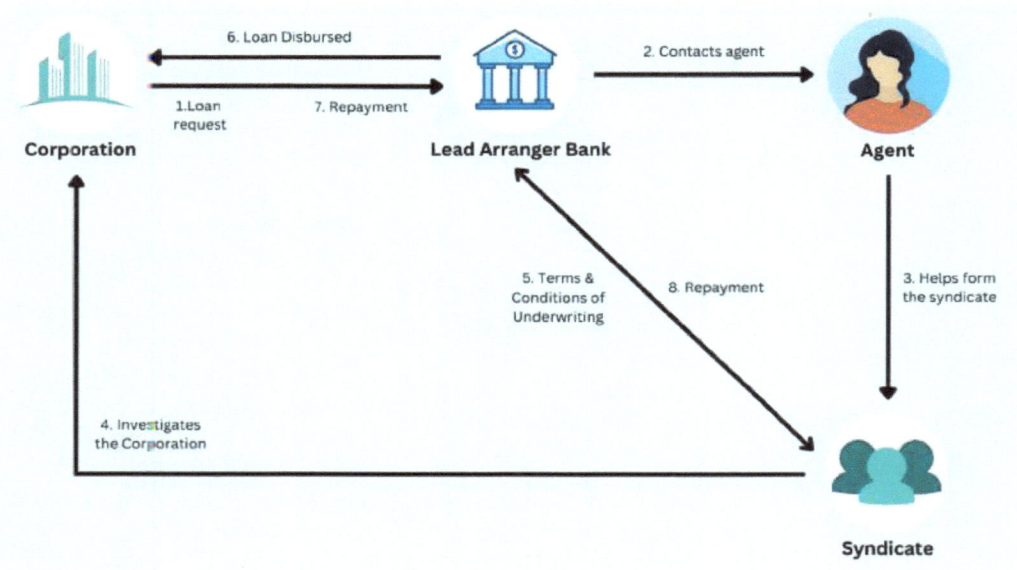

Fig. (17). Traditional banking system.

Use of Smart Contracts in Finance *Machine Learning and Blockchain* 107

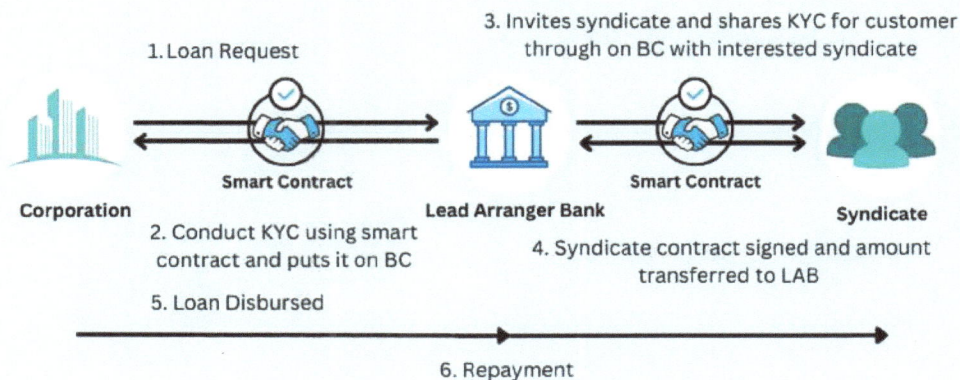

Fig. (18). Blockchain-based banking system.

Another case scenario is KYC procedures [24], where KYC processes are often marked by repetition, inconsistency, and redundancy, leading to substantial administrative burdens and costs. At present, KYC documents are managed in two ways: i) They are collected and stored internally, typically utilizing a document management system or an internal database; and ii) they are externally stored and individually shared with various external agencies for validation. Once successfully validated, these documents are updated in the internal repository of banks and then submitted to central agencies. But when blockchain gets introduced to this system, this process will be more fraud-proof, cost-effective, time-effective, and centralized.

Fig. (**19**) shows the traditional KYC system, and Fig. (**20**) shows the blockchain-based KYC system which will be based on security and easy accessibility terms.

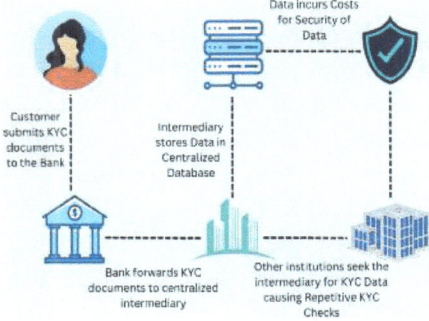

Fig. (19). Traditional KYC system.

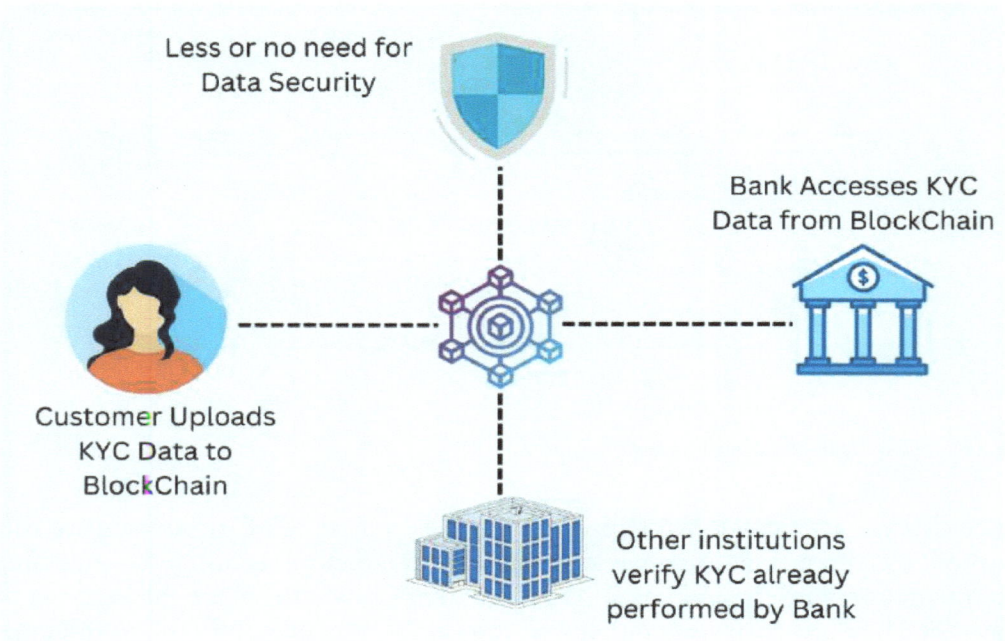

Fig. (20). Blockchain based KYC system.

CONCLUDING REMARKS

Blockchain technology is maturing to underpin a range of financial applications, fostering automation, streamlining processes, and enhancing transparency in payments, trade finance, lending, and asset tokenization. Improved interoperability and standards are set to promote collaboration among diverse blockchain networks and financial institutions, creating a more interconnected and efficient ecosystem. The synergy between blockchain and smart contracts holds promise for transforming the financial sector by addressing challenges through enhanced security, transparency, and efficiency. Ongoing research and development efforts aim to overcome challenges such as scalability, regulatory uncertainties, and interoperability. With increasing adoption, a financial landscape marked by reduced reliance on intermediaries, simplified processes, and enhanced global access to financial services is anticipated. The future suggests a paradigm shift where blockchain and smart contracts not only refine traditional financial processes but also unlock new possibilities, contributing to a resilient, inclusive, and technologically advanced financial sector.

REFERENCES

[1] Q. Wang, X. Zhu, Y. Ni, L. Gu, and H. Zhu, "Blockchain for the IoT and industrial IoT: A review", *Internet of Things,* vol. 10, p. 100081, 2020..
[http://dx.doi.org/10.1016/j.iot.2019.100081]

[2] W. Zou, D. Lo, P.S. Kochhar, X-B.D. Le, X. Xia, Y. Feng, Z. Chen, and B. Xu, "Smart Contract Development: Challenges and Opportunities", *IEEE Trans. Softw. Eng.,* vol. 47, no. 10, pp. 2084-2106, 2021.
[http://dx.doi.org/10.1109/TSE.2019.2942301]

[3] J.R. Varma, "Blockchain in Finance", *Vikalpa,* vol. 44, no. 1, pp. 1-11, 2019.
[http://dx.doi.org/10.1177/0256090919839897]

[4] V. Chang, P. Baudier, H. Zhang, Q. Xu, J. Zhang, and M. Arami, "How Blockchain can impact financial services – The overview, challenges and recommendations from expert interviewees", *Technol. Forecast. Soc. Change,* vol. 158, p. 120166, 2020.
[http://dx.doi.org/10.1016/j.techfore.2020.120166] [PMID: 32834134]

[5] M. Hashemi Joo, Y. Nishikawa, and K. Dandapani, "Cryptocurrency, a successful application of blockchain technology", *Managerial Finance,* vol. 46, Emerald Group Holdings Ltd., no. 6, pp. 715-733, 2020.
[http://dx.doi.org/10.1108/MF-09-2018-0451]

[6] L. Marchesi, M. Marchesi, G. Destefanis, G. Barabino, and D. Tigano, "Design Patterns for Gas Optimization in Ethereum", *2020 IEEE International Workshop on Blockchain Oriented Software Engineering (IWBOSE),* London, ON, Canada, 2020, pp. 9-15.
[http://dx.doi.org/10.1109/IWBOSE50093.2020.9050163]

[7] A. Afzal and A. Asif, "Cryptocurrencies, blockchain and regulation: A review," *The Lahore Journal of Economics,* vol. 24, no. 1, pp. 103–130, 2019.
[http://dx.doi.org/10.35536/lje.2019.v24.i1.a5]

[8] R. Toorajipour, P. Oghazi, V. Sohrabpour, P.C. Patel, and R. Mostaghel, "Block by block: A blockchain-based peer-to-peer business transaction for international trade", *Technol. Forecast. Soc. Change,* vol. 180, p. 121714, 2022.
[http://dx.doi.org/10.1016/j.techfore.2022.121714]

[9] K. Kaushik, S. Tayal, S. Dahiya, and A.O. Salau, *Sustainable and Advanced Applications of Blockchain in Smart Computational Technologies,* 1st ed., Chapman and Hall/CRC, 2022.
[http://dx.doi.org/10.1201/9781003193425]

[10] W. Wang, D.T. Hoang, P. Hu, Z. Xiong, D. Niyato, P. Wang, Y. Wen, and D.I. Kim, "A Survey on Consensus Mechanisms and Mining Strategy Management in Blockchain Networks", *IEEE Access,* vol. 7, pp. 22328-22370, 2019.
[http://dx.doi.org/10.1109/ACCESS.2019.2896108]

[11] P. Velmurugadass, S. Dhanasekaran, S. Shasi Anand, and V. Vasudevan, "Enhancing Blockchain security in cloud computing with IoT environment using ECIES and cryptography hash algorithm", In: *Materials Today.* Proceedings, 2020.
[http://dx.doi.org/10.1016/j.matpr.2020.08.519]

[12] A. Kuznetsov, I. Oleshko, V. Tymchenko, K. Lisitsky, M. Rodinko, and A. Kolhatin, "Performance analysis of cryptographic hash functions suitable for use in blockchain", *International Journal of Computer Network and Information Security,* vol. 13, no. 2, pp. 1-15, 2021.
[http://dx.doi.org/10.5815/ijcnis.2021.02.01]

[13] P. Lafourcade, and M. Lombard-Platet, "About blockchain interoperability", *Inf. Process. Lett.,* vol. 161, p. 105976, 2020.
[http://dx.doi.org/10.1016/j.ipl.2020.105976]

[14] H. R. Andrian, and N. B. Kurniawan, "Blockchain technology and implementation: AA systematic

[14] literature review", *in 2018 International Conference on Information Technology Systems and Innovation, (ICITSI),* Bandung, Indonesia, 2018, pp. 370-374.
[http://dx.doi.org/10.1109/ICITSI.2018.8695939]

[15] K. Wüst, and A. Gervais, "Do you need a Blockchain?", *IACR Cryptology ePrint Archive,* 2017.

[16] N. Kawaguchi, "Application of Blockchain to Supply Chain: Flexible Blockchain Technology", *Procedia Computer Science,* vol. 164, pp. 143–148, 2019.
[http://dx.doi.org/10.1016/j.procs.2019.12.166]

[17] S. Trived, K. Mehta, and R. Sharma, "Systematic Literature Review on Application of Blockchain Technology in E-Finance and Financial Services", *J. Technol. Manag. Innov.,* vol. 16, no. 3, pp. 89-102, 2021.
[http://dx.doi.org/10.4067/S0718-27242021000300089]

[18] D. Knezevic, "Impact of blockchain technology platform in changing the financial sector and other industries", *Montenegrin Journal of Economics,* vol. 14, no. 1, pp. 109-120, 2018.
[http://dx.doi.org/10.14254/1800-5845/2018.14-1.8]

[19] D. Han, C. Zhang, J. Ping, and Z. Yan, "Smart contract architecture for decentralized energy trading and management based on blockchains", *Energy,* vol. 199, p. 117417, 2020.
[http://dx.doi.org/10.1016/j.energy.2020.117417]

[20] S. Wang, L. Ouyang, Y. Yuan, X. Ni, X. Han, and F.Y. Wang, "Blockchain-Enabled Smart Contracts: Architecture, Applications, and Future Trends", *IEEE Trans. Syst. Man Cybern. Syst.,* vol. 49, no. 11, pp. 2266-2277, 2019.
[http://dx.doi.org/10.1109/TSMC.2019.2895123]

[21] B.K. Mohanta, S.S. Panda, and D. Jena, "An Overview of Smart Contract and Use Cases in Blockchain Technology", *in 2018 9th International Conference on Computing, Communication and Networking Technologies, (ICCCNT),* Bengaluru, India, 2018, pp. 1-4.
[http://dx.doi.org/10.1109/ICCCNT.2018.8494045]

[22] D. Khan, L.T. Jung, and M.A. Hashmani, "Systematic literature review of challenges in blockchain scalability", *Appl. Sci.,* vol. 11, no. 20, p. 9372, 2021.
[http://dx.doi.org/10.3390/app11209372]

[23] D. Meva, "Issues and Challenges with Blockchain A Survey", *Int. J. Comput. Sci. Eng.,* vol. 6, no. 12, pp. 488-491, 2018.
[http://dx.doi.org/10.26438/ijcse/v6i12.488491]

[24] S. Jani, and T. Shah, "Applications of Blockchain Technology in Banking & Finance", Technical Report, Faculty of Management Studies, Parul University, Vadodara, India, 2018.

CHAPTER 5

Blockchain in Agricultural Information Systems and Networks: Foundation and Future Potentialities - A Scientific Review

P. K. Paul[1,*], **M. Kayyali**[2], **Nilanjan Das**[3] and **Ritam Chatterjee**[1]

[1] *Department of Computer & Information Science, Raiganj University, Raiganj, India*

[2] *Department of Quality Assurance and Accreditation Directorate, Al Maaref University of Applied Sciences, Sarmada, Syria*

[3] *Siliguri Institute of Technology, Siliguri, India*

Abstract: Smart Agriculture, also known as Digital Agriculture, has emerged as an essential paradigm in today's agricultural landscape. The rapid development of this field is fueled by the growth and application of Agricultural Informatics, which significantly enhances various agricultural practices. These practices span from crop and seed cultivation to plant and vegetable farming, livestock management, and post-harvest activities.

Advanced Agricultural Information Systems (AIsS) deploy effective methodologies and cutting-edge technologies to optimize cultivation processes, aiming to improve productivity and efficiency. These Agroinformatics technologies are specifically designed to support more commercially intensive agricultural operations and streamline the management of large-scale systems. Agro Information Systems incorporate diverse components of Information Technology (IT), such as databases, networks, web technologies, software solutions, and multimedia systems, all of which contribute to a more connected and data-driven agricultural environment.

With the rapid evolution of IT, new technologies such as cloud computing, data analytics, big data, the Internet of Things (IoT), and Blockchain are becoming increasingly vital in modern agriculture. Among these, Blockchain technology is revolutionizing agriculture by enabling faster, more secure, and highly efficient systems for agricultural development. Blockchain applications in agriculture ensure transparency, traceability, and security in various processes, from farm-to-fork supply chains to smart contract-based transactions.

In this context, the integration of Blockchain and Machine Learning (ML) technologies plays a pivotal role in shaping Agriculture 4.0. By combining Blockchain's secure and decentralized nature with ML's predictive analytics and data-driven decision-making

---

* **Corresponding author P. K. Paul:** Department of Computer & Information Science, Raiganj University, Raiganj, India; E-mail: pkpaul.infotech@gmail.com

Keshav Kaushik, Rewa Sharma & Ayodeji Olalekan Salau (Eds.)
All rights reserved-© 2026 Bentham Science Publishers

capabilities, these technologies offer unprecedented opportunities for improving farming practices. This paper explores the current applications of Blockchain and Machine Learning in agriculture, focusing on their potential and prospects in transforming the industry. Furthermore, it delves into how blockchain and Machine learning-based agrosystems can foster sustainable agricultural practices, supporting the future of farming by enhancing productivity, reducing waste, and promoting environmental stewardship.

Keywords: Agro ICT, Agriculture 4.0, Agro informatics, Digital agriculture, ML, Machine learning applications, Sustainable development.

INTRODUCTION

Agricultural development through the use of technology and appropriate techniques is crucial for the advancement of the sector. The application of Information and Communication Technology (ICT) and Information Technology (IT) has given rise to fields like Agricultural Information Technology (AIT), Agricultural Information Systems (AIS), and Agricultural Information Sciences (AISc), among others. Blockchain technology plays a significant role in the realm of computing and information technology, offering a wide range of potential applications for the future.

Blockchain functions as both a technology and a system within Information Technology, designed to maintain encrypted records of data. It is also used in the creation and management of distributed databases, which are critical for facilitating data transactions and various types of contracts. As a distributed database, Blockchain aims to maintain accurate and independent records, often referred to as digital ledgers. These systems are decentralized, ensuring accessibility across multiple platforms. In addition, Blockchain serves as a platform for digital monetary services, facilitating transactions involving digital currencies, such as Bitcoin. Both tangible and intangible assets can be recorded within a specific network or blockchain framework [2, 3, 27].

Blockchain has emerged as a highly sought-after tool for improving financial management. An effective Blockchain system relies on various processes that ensure efficient business transaction management. The rapid expansion of Blockchain applications across diverse industries has led to its recognition as a formal academic discipline, with many universities around the world offering courses related to it.

Since Blockchain enables the effective management of financial transactions without the need to share personal data with third parties, it adheres to strong encryption standards, reducing the risk of data breaches. Despite ongoing concerns about large-scale data breaches and cyber-attacks, Blockchain's fraud-resistant features have revolutionized business practices, making them more secure and transparent. In comparison to traditional business processes, Blockchain offers greater efficiency and effectiveness, making it applicable across various sectors.

Machine learning algorithms, which are widely used across different industries, can also play a crucial role in enhancing agricultural productivity. When integrated with Blockchain technology, machine learning contributes to the development of smart agriculture, improving agricultural informatics practices. As a result, agro-ICT systems that focus on quality, quantity, and productivity are increasingly being adopted in both developed and developing countries. The combined power of Blockchain and machine learning can also be applied in underdeveloped regions to significantly boost agro-product production [6, 7, 10].

WORK OBJECTIVE AND AIM

This work, *'Blockchain in Agricultural Information Systems and Networks: Foundation and Future Potentialities - A Scientific Review,'* is a scientific review with the following objectives:

- To provide updates about the fundamentals of Agricultural Information Systems (AIS), including its features and related subjects.
- To gather information about allied technologies of agricultural information systems, especially their enhancement using Blockchain Technologies.
- To examine the basic features, foundation, and general applications of blockchain and machine learning technologies.
- To explore the fundamental and emerging applications of agricultural information systems using blockchain.
- To understand the fundamental concept of Agriculture 4.0, its features, and possible impact in the context of machine learning-supported blockchain technologies.
- To identify the latest issues and challenges in agricultural robots, emphasizing agro informatics development.

METHODS

The work titled *"Blockchain in Agricultural Information Systems and Networks: Foundation and Future Potentialities - A Scientific Review"* is a scientific review focusing on the role of Blockchain in agricultural information systems, particularly in the context of agricultural robots. This review involves the study of existing literature, including journals, academic papers, communications, and reference books. Additionally, various Blockchain-based companies that offer services in the agricultural sector have been analyzed by reviewing information from their official websites, government agencies, and ongoing projects to explore the potential applications and opportunities of Blockchain in agriculture.

In the literature review, the roles of Blockchain, Artificial Intelligence (AI), and Machine Learning (ML) are also examined. All gathered information has been critically analyzed and systematically presented in this work as scientific documentation, organized into different sections for clarity and coherence.

Related Existing Works

The present work reviews various existing sources and presents them scientifically based on the theme of the study.

1. **Alobid M., Abujudeh S., and Szűcs I. (2022) [1]** This study explores the transformative potential of Blockchain technology in the agricultural sector. Known for its application in secure and transparent financial transactions, Blockchain is proposed as a game-changer for agriculture. The authors investigate how Blockchain's unique features can address challenges in agriculture, enhancing efficiency, security, and sustainability. The study focuses on improving traceability and transparency within the agricultural supply chain, offering an immutable record of transactions that ensure a reliable and clear trace from the origin of products to consumers. This is crucial for maintaining food safety and quality standards. The study also discusses how Blockchain can optimize agricultural supply networks by reducing dependency on middlemen, thereby cutting costs and enhancing operational efficiency. Moreover, Blockchain facilitates better connectivity between producers and consumers, contributing to a fairer and more environmentally sustainable economy.
2. **Dal Mas F., Massaro M., Ndou V., and Raguseo E. (2023) [12]** This paper presents a comprehensive literature review on the adoption of Blockchain in the agri-food sector, with a particular emphasis on sustainability. The authors aim to bridge the gap between academic research and practical business applications by reviewing the current state and future possibilities of Blockchain in the agri-food industry. They discuss the pressing issues facing the sector, including inefficiencies in the supply chain, food fraud, and the need for greater transparency and traceability. The paper reviews numerous academic studies on Blockchain's potential to improve supply chain transparency, and food safety, reduce waste, and promote equitable market access. It also examines case studies and pilot projects, providing insights into

the benefits and limitations of Blockchain in real-world applications. Additionally, the paper investigates how businesses in the agri-food sector are adopting Blockchain, the motivations behind these initiatives, the types of Blockchain systems being developed, and the challenges to widespread adoption.

3. **Kassanuk T., and Phasinam K. (2022) [24]** This paper outlines a conceptual Blockchain-based framework designed to enhance safety and security in agriculture. Despite its brief nature, the article presents an in-depth analysis of how Blockchain can be integrated into agriculture to create a "smart" system that addresses critical safety and security issues. The authors emphasize the importance of safety in agriculture, not only to protect consumer health but also to sustain the economic viability of the industry. The paper explores various threats to safety, such as contamination, disease, fraud, and inefficiencies, and proposes Blockchain as a solution. The proposed smart agriculture framework uses Blockchain's tamper-proof and transparent nature to automate operations and enforce contracts through smart contracts. The authors discuss how data such as cultivation, harvesting, processing, and distribution can be recorded on Blockchain to improve traceability and accountability throughout the supply chain.

4. **LB K. (2022) [30]** This study provides a detailed review of how Blockchain is being applied within the agricultural sector. The article outlines the fundamental qualities of Blockchain, such as decentralization, immutability, and transparency, and discusses how these features can address issues like inefficiencies in the supply chain, food fraud, and the lack of transparency between farmers and buyers. The author examines current applications of Blockchain in agriculture, including case studies from around the world that demonstrate how Blockchain is used to improve traceability, accountability, fairer payment methods, and sustainable farming practices. The paper categorizes applications based on areas like supply chain management, data management, financial transactions, and compliance with quality and safety regulations. It also discusses the future of Blockchain in agriculture, acknowledging both its potential benefits and the challenges that need to be addressed.

5. **Pakseresht A., Yavari A., Kaliji S. A., and Hakelius K. (2023) [42]** This article examines the synergy between Blockchain technology and the concept of a circular economy in the agri-food sector. The authors explore how these two revolutionary concepts can contribute to enhanced sustainability and efficiency in food production and distribution. They define the circular economy as an approach that minimizes waste and maximizes resource use, contrasting it with the traditional "take, make, dispose" model. Blockchain's features of transparency, security, and immutability are discussed as key tools

for supporting circular economy practices in the agri-food sector. The paper explores how Blockchain can improve supply chain transparency, promote information sharing among stakeholders, and offer a verifiable record of product origins, processing, and distribution. The authors provide recommendations for overcoming barriers to implementing these concepts, offering guidance to policymakers, industry professionals, and researchers.

6. **Patel H., and Shrimali (2023) [43]** In this study, the authors introduce "AgriOnBlock," a proposed system aimed at improving data collection security and efficiency in agriculture using Blockchain technology. The paper highlights the importance of accurate and timely data in agriculture, such as information on soil conditions, weather patterns, crop health, and market pricing, all of which are crucial for informed decision-making. However, challenges related to data integrity, security, and sharing are also noted. "AgriOnBlock" is presented as a solution to these challenges, providing a decentralized platform for securely collecting, storing, and exchanging agricultural data. The paper discusses the system's design, the Blockchain protocol used, and how it integrates with other technologies such as IoT devices and data analytics tools to enhance data management in agriculture.

BASICS OF BLOCKCHAIN AND ML: THE STORY BEHIND BLOCKCHAIN IN THE AGRO FIELD

Blockchain is no longer just a tool of IT; it is now considered a transformative technology—functioning not only as a database but also as a digital financial record management system that offers enhanced digital trust. David Chaum first coined and proposed the concept of 'Blockchain' in 1982. Later, in 1992, Stuart Haber and W. Scott Stornetta expanded upon these concepts [4, 5, 33]. However, the implementation of the ledger-based Blockchain network became crucial with the introduction of Satoshi Nakamoto's Bitcoin digital currency. Blockchain technology cannot be owned, and its various phases are illustrated in Fig. (**1**) [50].

Technologies in Supply Chain Management and Agriculture

Various technologies are employed to manage the supply chain associated with agricultural production. Machine learning algorithms are particularly useful in analyzing consumer requirements and predicting market demand. From seeding to production, harvesting to procurement, and from farmers to consumers, the agricultural supply chain is complex and difficult to maintain. Additionally, reducing transportation costs and time is essential for delivering products to customers efficiently. Proper storage mechanisms are also necessary to maintain the nutritional value of food and keep it fresh.

Blockchain Technology in Agriculture

Blockchain is a system, tool, and technology supported by protocols that enable the development of cryptocurrencies, underpinned by cryptography. Blockchain transactions are immutable and distributed across multiple locations on a computer network, with the strategies used extending beyond cryptocurrencies [34, 47].

Some of the significant Development in respect of Blockchain Technology	
Year	**Development Phase**
1991	For the first time the cryptographically secure chain of Blocks is described by Stuart Haber and W Scott Stornetta
1998	'Bit gold', a decentralized digital currency mechanism designed by Computer Scientist Nick Szabo
2000	Theory of cryptography secured chains and the idea of potential implementation has been published by Stefan Konst
2008	White Paper Model for Blockchain Technology has been published by pseudonymous Satoshi Nakamoto
2009	First Blockchain as the public leader for transactions made using Bitcoin has been implemented by Nakamoto
2014	Blockchain 2.0 is invented and citing applications beyond currency. Blockchain technology has been separated from currency and its potential for other financial inter-organizational transactions has been explored.
2015	Ethereum Frontier network launched. One of the biggest decentralized applications of Blockchain technology that could be deployed in a live network.
2019	Walmart launched a supply chain system that is based on the Hyperledger platform
2022	Eco-friendly Blockchain networks emerged and Blockchain applications increased among companies

Fig. (1). A few development phases of Blockchain from concept to Blockchain Technology.

There are several types of Blockchains, the main ones being public, private, and hybrid Blockchains. Public Blockchains, which run on decentralized computer networks, are accessible to those interested in a transaction. Users validate transactions and receive rewards. Public Blockchain operates on two models:

1. Proof-of-Work

2. Proof-of-Stake [50].

Examples of public Blockchain include Bitcoin and Ethereum (ETH). Blockchain features include sophisticated security, openness, anonymity, transparency, and advanced distributed systems.

Private Blockchains are restricted and not open to the public. They operate on a permission-based model, where a system administrator plays a vital role. These Blockchains offer full privacy, high efficiency, faster transaction speeds, and better scalability [28, 29, 48].

Hybrid Blockchains combine elements of both public and private Blockchains. They offer better control and integrate both centralized and decentralized features. Although they are not entirely open, they offer features like integrity, security, and transparency, with customizable records and confidentiality within private networks.

Machine Learning in Agriculture

Machine learning (ML) algorithms are capable of learning and improving independently, without the need for external programming. These algorithms improve based on current outputs and historical data. Machine learning is a form of statistical data analysis [5, 8], used for data classification, analytics, pattern recognition, decision-making, predictive modeling, and more.

ML processes large datasets, classifying them and identifying patterns. The system draws conclusions by analyzing the data and learning from it. As a result, ML helps in decision-making and predicting the best possible solutions. Based on the results, the algorithm updates itself, enhancing the predictive capabilities.

Agriculture as a Career and the Role of Technology

Agriculture, one of the oldest professions, continues to be a significant industry that provides both direct and indirect job opportunities. It plays an essential role in pre- and post-agricultural activities, supported by advanced computing practices [8, 9, 26]. In recent years, core and emerging technologies, particularly in AI and machine learning, have been applied to agriculture. However, there are still challenges in achieving effective and sustainable agricultural practices.

AGRO INFORMATICS AND AGRICULTURE 4.0 FOR SOPHISTICATED AGRO DEVELOPMENT

Agricultural Informatics, as a field or sub-field, emerged rapidly and is closely associated with other subjects, helping in the proper development of agricultural systems. As far as increased productivity is concerned, Agricultural Informatics plays a leading role. It is an interdisciplinary area, combining agricultural sciences and information sciences. Agro Informatics helps build advanced agriculture, digital agriculture, and more, using proper tools, techniques, and the latest core and sub-technologies of Information Technology, such as databases, networks, web systems, and multimedia [11, 14, 16]. The latest technologies, such as cloud computing, big data, usability engineering, and Blockchain, contribute to proper agricultural documentation and advanced agro development.

Since agriculture is crucial for any country, it plays a significant role in the country's growth. Agriculture is essential to meet the basic needs of the population. Agricultural 4.0 is the fourth generation of agricultural evolution and refers to a technology-based smart agriculture system [5, 13, 15]. Various basic and emerging technologies are used in Agriculture 4.0. With the incorporation of these technologies, traditional farming has become smart farming. This shift is incredibly useful for farmers to produce crops using various agricultural technologies. By using different kinds of sensors, farmers can easily predict the moisture content in the soil and the different kinds of nutrients present.

With the help of technology, farmers receive predicted weather reports and plans for farming. With accurate weather forecasts, farmers can take appropriate measures and select the best crops according to weather conditions. Agriculture 4.0 is not just about using heavy machinery like tractors, harvesters, and crushers in farming. It is data-driven farming. Various data are generated and received from agricultural field sensors, processed, and used to take appropriate action. Basic technologies like Information Technology (IT) and ICT help in data procurement and establishing network connectivity among all nodes. Emerging technologies like cloud computing, Big Data Analytics, IoT, and Blockchain are also supporting Agriculture 4.0. Artificial Intelligence, machine learning, and data mining are used to analyze real-time data collected by sensors and make informed decisions. These technologies help instruct actuators to perform accordingly [19, 32, 51].

Agriculture 4.0 is a sustainable farming technology. Sensors like temperature, humidity, and soil condition work continuously and send data for further processing. By controlling various parameters, it is easy for the farmer to maintain the proper requirements for crops. These sensors control water consumption, making it easier for farmers to maintain optimal water requirements for crops. It has been observed that crops are damaged due to excessive water supply. By properly controlling the water supply, it is possible to maintain proper soil moisture and keep crops healthy.

Farmers also use excessive fertilizers to increase production. However, unnecessary fertilizer use has been found to affect crop growth and waste money [20, 21, 49]. Sensors also analyze soil nutrients and inform the farmer to use the correct amount of fertilizer, which is beneficial for both the environment and sustainable development.

Agriculture 4.0 is also responsible for genome analysis of crops. Modern technologies aid in gene analysis. Through proper analysis and smart breeding, new seed variants can be produced to increase crop production. Farmers can also continuously monitor the health of crops. IoT devices play a crucial role in the continuous monitoring of crops. IoT technologies are also helpful for indoor farming methods such as greenhouse farming, vertical farming, precision farming, hydroponics, aquaponics, and more [22, 23, 46]. Sensors detect data such as temperature, soil condition, water level, humidity, and light intensity.

IT and ICT technologies handle the transfer of this data. Big Data Analytics, data mining, artificial intelligence, and machine learning help analyze the data collected by sensors and IoT devices, forming the necessary actions accordingly. Network technologies, web technologies, database technologies, and software technologies all contribute to Agriculture 4.0. Additionally, Geographic Positioning System (GPS), Geographic Information Systems (GIS), and satellites play vital roles in Agriculture 4.0. Agricultural robots, autonomous tractors, and drones are modern technological tools used in Agriculture 4.0.

The integration of mobile technologies makes the operation of the entire system easier. The system can be controlled and monitored through mobile phones and personal computers. Agriculture 4.0 provides a complete framework for crop management systems [17, 25, 44].

It consists of a farm management system, grain elevator management system, livestock management, greenhouse monitoring system, autonomous vehicles, and machinery management system, weather management system, agricultural robotics operation system, and so on. Fig. (**2**) shows ML, blockchain, and other technologies used in the promotion of Agriculture 4.0.

There are different farm management software (FMS) that have used various types of machine learning algorithms to manage agriculture. Different types of FMS help farmers with better decision-making, soil management, irrigation management, pest control, and selecting crops based on weather conditions. By providing proper management solutions for agriculture, machine learning algorithms are helping to maintain sustainable development. They strive to maintain the balance of production and suggest the best crops for the farmer and society to maintain food balance. They encourage organic farming and aim to maintain the quality of food. Additionally, they are concerned with food safety.

FUNDAMENTALS AND EMERGING BLOCKCHAIN APPLICATIONS IN THE AGRICULTURAL SECTOR

Blockchain as a system, tool, and technology is emerging and applicable in various areas such as financial services, healthcare and the medical sector, government and administration, travel systems, and retail management [31, 35]. Blockchain Technology is generally required in a variety of mentioned areas but not limited to:

- For security as well as proper sharing of medical data.
- For proper NFT marketplaces.
- In tracking proper music royalties.
- In cross-border payments.
- For sophisticated and real-time IoT management.
- In the enhancement of personal identity security.
- Regarding the anti-money laundering tracking system.
- In proper and efficient emerging supply chain and logistics monitoring.
- Effective logistics and allied monitoring.
- In proper and advanced voting mechanism development.
- For advanced and digital advertising.
- For the development of original content.
- For the exchange of cryptocurrency.
- For the processing of real estate, *etc* [27, 50].

Fig. (2). ML, blockchain, and other technologies in the promotion of agriculture 4.0.

Blockchain, though has ample opportunities, has certain *challenges in the development as well as implementation phases*. As far as awareness is concerned, limited understanding of Blockchain is one of the major challenges for its applications in the financial services sector. As far as legacy infrastructure is concerned proper technical understanding of the field is also needed of the hour [36, 37]. Further here cultural shift from traditional to scientific transition is treated as a major shift regarding the whole process. The regulation of the Blockchain is important including the concern of data privacy. In addition to these, security-related concerns are also considered valuable in major roadblocks. It is a fact that internationally many countries are not yet ready to enact Blockchain Technology in all respects, however, this is the need of the hour.

The agriculture sector is currently experiencing a substantial transition due to the introduction of advanced technologies in recent times. Out of all these options, Blockchain emerges as a groundbreaking power, with the potential to tackle enduring obstacles and unleash novel efficiencies. Diverse possibilities of Blockchain concerning agriculture and allied fields are included in this section encompassing several aspects such as enhancing transparency in supply chains and empowering farmers financially. By further exploring this advanced technology, we intend to analyze how Blockchain has the potential to not only transform the sector but also provide practical solutions that could fundamentally alter the entire food ecosystem. The agriculture sector, typically perceived as conservative and hesitant to adopt new practices, is on the verge of a technological revolution in which Blockchain technology emerges as a prominent participant. This technology, renowned for its durability and clarity, has unparalleled possibilities to address problems such as food deception, inefficiencies in the supply chain, and limited financial accessibility [38, 39, 41]. As we examine the capabilities of Blockchain, we also contemplate its consequences for individuals and organizations involved in many sectors - ranging from small-scale farmers in isolated regions to large multinational agriculture corporations. This introduction establishes the foundation for a thorough examination of how Blockchain technology could serve as the cornerstone in constructing a more effective, open, and environmentally-friendly agricultural future.

Blockchain Technologies in Agro and Food Sectors

The agricultural and food industries are progressively adopting blockchain technology to address intricate problems and enhance operational effectiveness. Blockchain, a decentralized digital ledger system, has various benefits that can dramatically enhance the transparency, safety, and sustainability of food and agricultural supply chains. This section goes into the various advantages of adopting blockchain technology in diverse areas.

Among the important advantages of blockchain in agriculture and the food business is the ability to track the flow of items from farm to table in real time [4]. Each transaction or movement of products is recorded as a block of data that is linked to the preceding and following blocks, forming an immutable and visible chain. This capability is vital in detecting the cause of concerns such as contamination, hence enabling quicker reactions and decreasing the scope of product recalls. Consumers increasingly want transparency regarding the origin and processing of their food, and blockchain technology can provide this information with remarkable precision and reliability [54]. Blockchain's capacity to enable real-time tracking and unchangeable records dramatically enhances food safety. By having complete information about the origin, handling, and the route of food goods, companies can promptly isolate and treat potential sources of contamination [40, 52, 53]. This capability not only protects consumers but also boosts the reputation of firms that can guarantee the safety and quality of their products. In the event of a food safety concern, blockchain can immediately identify and trace back the affected product to its source, considerably decreasing the danger to public health and the related economic damages.

The agricultural and food industries regularly suffer from fraud and counterfeiting, which can range from mislabeling the origin of items to diluting high-value goods with cheaper replacements. Blockchain's transparent and tamper-proof technique guarantees that every participant in the supply chain can independently confirm the validity and authenticity of their products. This form of verification is particularly crucial for protecting the integrity of organic and fairly traded labels, which often demand a premium price in the market.

Blockchain can dramatically simplify supply chain operations by automating transactions and providing a more efficient flow of commodities. Smart contracts, which are self-executing contracts with terms explicitly put into code, can automatically trigger actions such as payments and shipments once certain conditions are met [54 - 56]. This automation lowers the need for intermediaries, consequently saving costs and reducing the time products spend in transit. The increased efficiency not only benefits businesses by enhancing their bottom line but also contributes to a more sustainable operation by decreasing waste and energy usage.

Blockchain technology can benefit small-scale farmers by giving them access to new markets and financial services [4]. By providing a clear record of their products and processes, farmers can show their adherence to quality and sustainability requirements, thereby entering markets that need such verification. Moreover, blockchain-based financial services can give farmers a more secure and efficient means of receiving payment, which is typically a significant difficulty in rural and underbanked areas.

The incorporation of blockchain technology in the food and agricultural sectors promises to bring about changes in the way we grow, sell, and consume food. By enhancing accountability, safety, and effectiveness, blockchain stands to deliver huge benefits to all stakeholders involved. As technology advances and more actors in the business use it, we could anticipate a more transparent, safe, and effective food industry to emerge [11, 57, 58].

Blockchain with Machine Learning Technologies in Improving Supply Chain Management in Agriculture

The agricultural supply chain is a complex network involving various stakeholders, including farmers, suppliers, processors, merchants, and consumers. Traditional supply chain systems often suffer from inefficiencies, lack of transparency, and susceptibility to fraud. Blockchain technology, with its decentralized and immutable ledger, offers a transformative solution to these issues—providing a more transparent, efficient, and secure agricultural supply chain [31].

Traceability is crucial in the agricultural supply chain to ensure food safety, quality, and compliance with regulations. Blockchain enables an immutable record of the entire journey of agricultural goods from farm to fork. Each transaction or exchange is recorded as a block, forming a chain that documents every stage of the product's movement. This traceability is essential for swiftly identifying and responding to issues such as contamination or disease outbreaks, significantly reducing risks to consumers and the economic impact on stakeholders.

Fraudulent practices, such as mislabeling and adulteration, are serious concerns in the agricultural supply chain [56]. Blockchain's transparent and secure system helps combat these by providing a reliable record of a product's origin, handling, and quality. Consumers and stakeholders can verify the authenticity of goods, ensuring that they receive what is advertised—be it organic produce, fair-trade coffee, or single-origin spices.

Blockchain also enables the use of smart contracts—self-executing agreements that activate once predefined conditions are met. In agriculture, smart contracts can streamline processes such as payments, certifications, and quality checks. For example, a smart contract might automatically release payment to a farmer once a shipment is confirmed at its destination. This speeds up transactions, reduces reliance on intermediaries, and minimizes costs and potential fraud.

Smallholder farmers often struggle to secure financing due to a lack of verified data about their operations. Blockchain can provide a transparent and trustworthy record of a farmer's production history, product quality, and transaction history [33, 59, 60]. This information helps financial institutions more accurately assess credit risk, thereby increasing access to loans and other financial services, and supporting the growth of small-scale agriculture [2].

Despite its potential, the implementation of blockchain in agriculture faces challenges. These include the need for adequate technical infrastructure, digital literacy among stakeholders, and standardization of data formats. Additional concerns include data privacy and the environmental impact of certain blockchain systems. Overcoming these challenges requires collaboration among technology providers, industry participants, and policymakers to create a conducive environment for blockchain adoption.

In summary, blockchain technology has the potential to revolutionize agricultural supply chains by enhancing traceability, reducing fraud, streamlining operations, and expanding financial access. As stakeholders continue to explore and implement this technology, the sector may move toward a more transparent, efficient, and resilient future—supporting global food security and sustainability [14].

Blockchain Applications and Agro Enhancement

Blockchain technology has emerged as a promising solution to various challenges faced by the agricultural sector. Its applications span from improving supply chain transparency and enabling financial transactions to optimize data management [23]. However, like any emerging technology, blockchain presents both benefits and drawbacks that must be carefully evaluated [61, 62]. Below is an overview of its key advantages and limitations in the context of agriculture.

Enhanced Transparency and Traceability

Blockchain creates an immutable and transparent ledger of all transactions, enabling end-to-end traceability from farm to table. This is crucial for validating the authenticity of agricultural products, ensuring food safety, and building consumer trust. Each stage in the supply chain is recorded, allowing stakeholders to trace the origin of products and verify certifications such as "organic" or "fair trade."

Improved Efficiency and Cost Reduction

By automating transactions and reducing the need for intermediaries, blockchain enhances efficiency and lowers operational costs. Smart contracts can execute transactions automatically once conditions are met, reducing the time, labor, and potential errors associated with manual processes.

Increased Security and Fraud Prevention

Blockchain's decentralized and tamper-resistant design enhances data security, making unauthorized manipulation highly unlikely. Altering any recorded data requires consensus from the network, significantly reducing the risk of fraud.

Empowerment of Small-Scale Farmers

Blockchain can empower small-scale farmers by improving their access to markets, ensuring transparent pricing, and enabling faster payments. With verifiable records of farming practices and production quality, smallholders can enter premium markets and receive fair compensation [50, 63].

Blockchain holds vast potential to enhance the agricultural sector by increasing transparency, efficiency, and trust across supply chains. However, addressing implementation challenges such as infrastructure, privacy, and data standardization is crucial. By carefully weighing the pros and cons and pursuing strategic solutions, stakeholders can maximize the benefits of blockchain for a more sustainable and inclusive agricultural future [31, 64].

Machine Learning Applications in the Agricultural Sector

The main objective of utilizing machine learning algorithms in agriculture is to increase crop production. Machine learning algorithms are used to monitor the overall health of plants. They are analyzed to detect different types of plant diseases. They also recommend the proper amount of nutritional requirements and water for the plants. Machine learning algorithms analyze historical data on weather, soil conditions, and geographical data to predict optimal crop production. This helps farmers reduce the uncertainty of production. Accurately predicting rainfall is crucial for farming, as crop production largely depends on weather conditions. By forecasting weather in advance, farmers can make informed decisions about which crops to plant, ensuring they choose the most suitable ones to maximize productivity. This proactive approach helps optimize resources, improve yields, and reduce the risks associated with unpredictable weather.

The use of emerging technologies, in conjunction with machine learning, will help increase crop production. Cloud computing, big data analytics, and the Internet of

Things (IoT) will play a crucial role in maximizing productivity when integrated with machine learning. Different sensors will help collect real-time data that are essential for obtaining accurate information. The sensors will provide actual data on soil composition and moisture content. Machine learning algorithms can then suggest the appropriate amount of fertilizer needed to increase production. They can also predict the probability of floods and warn about the rate of soil erosion. Machine learning algorithms are responsible for the overall monitoring of soil conditions.

Pests are another threat to plants. The attack of different types of pests harms the plants and decreases production. Image processing, combined with machine learning, analyzes the leaves and stems of plants to continuously monitor pest attacks. The efficient machine learning algorithm also suggests the proper pesticide name and the correct dosage to apply to the plant. It has been observed that some pests attack during particular seasons and weather conditions. Machine learning algorithms can also alert farmers about pest invasions.

Weeds are another threat to plants. The unwanted growth of weeds obstructs plant growth and consumes the nutrition required for healthy plant development. Machine learning algorithms can efficiently detect and distinguish between plants and weeds. The algorithm also suggests the proper herbicide and weed-renewal techniques.

Irrigation management is another important aspect of agricultural production. It is necessary to supply the correct amount of water for crop growth. For example, during the rainy season, there is a reduced need for external water supply through irrigation, while in summer or winter, more water is required. Machine learning analyzes weather and soil conditions to predict the water requirements of crops. Based on an actual analysis of the data, the automatic irrigation system adjusts and supplies water as needed. Machine learning algorithms can calculate the water requirement for crops and instruct the automatic irrigation system to deliver the precise amount of water. Machine learning algorithms are helping to install smart irrigation systems to improve agricultural productivity.

To increase productivity, it is necessary to use different types of devices and equipment in farming. Machine learning algorithms have the potential to control and operate various types of farming equipment. It can be used in robots, automatic tractors, harvesters, agricultural drones, and more. Different types of automatic devices can also be employed in agricultural production, such as automatic plant seeding, automatic harvesting, and automatic fertilizer and pesticide spraying. Drones can also be used to spray different types of liquids for various purposes on crops.

ISSUES, CHALLENGES, AND PROBABLE SOLUTIONS IN AGRO MANAGEMENT USING BLOCKCHAIN SYSTEMS AND MACHINE LEARNING

Various basic technologies and emerging technologies have been used in Agriculture 4.0. Blockchain technology is one of the emerging technologies that are used in Agriculture 4.0. Implementing Blockchain technology in agro management has faced many issues and challenges. Technological feasibility is one of the big challenges for Blockchain technology. It is a tough task to build a fully functional Blockchain mechanism for the Agriculture 4.0 system. To build a secure system, technological constraint is a big challenge. Agriculture 4.0 is a large system So, implementing Blockchain technology in the whole system makes the system very complex. As the system grows, the complexity increases exponentially. It is tough to manage a huge amount of data. It is also a tough task for the resource person to understand the complexity of the system. After implementing Blockchain technology, the system becomes less scalable. It is difficult to migrate the whole system from the existing one to the new system [5, 65]. It is a tough task to maintain the compatibility of the new system with the previous system. It is tough to maintain the bridge between the third generation of agriculture and the fourth generation of agriculture. It is also a challenging task to maintain Blockchain interoperability. As the whole system is completely network-dependent, any problems in the network affect the whole system.

It is also challenging for the Blockchain mechanism to create a new ecosystem with a fully functional Agriculture 4.0. The main challenge the Blockchain mechanism faces is that it lacks adaptability to current systems. It is very tough to get the proper workforce. The lack of skill and technical knowledge of the human resource is also a big challenge. Developing proper skills among the resource persons is one of the basic criteria of the Blockchain system. It is very tough to train the farmers to adopt the new system. The farmers are very familiar with the traditional farming mechanism. Providing the proper training to the farmers is also a very challenging task in Agriculture 4.0. The trust issue is another challenging task for Agriculture 4.0. There is a lack of trust between the user and the service provider. Since the system is fully controlled by the automation system, it is very challenging to control the automated system. Agriculture 4.0 is a collection of different systems like the farm management system, grain elevator management system, livestock management, greenhouse monitoring system, autonomous vehicles and machinery management system, weather management system, agricultural robotics operation system, and many more. It is very tough to make the collaboration between different systems. The Blockchain mechanism of one system may create difficulty in interacting with the Blockchain mechanism of another system [6, 66]. Maintaining the logical complexity of the different systems may create a big issue in implementing the Blockchain mechanism in Agriculture 4.0.

Blockchain technology is a new technology. Implementing Blockchain technology in Agriculture 4.0 is associated with financial challenges. Implementing Blockchain technology requires a huge financial investment. To build the system, it needs proper planning and designing issues. It is also tough to design the whole system to maintain the existing farming technology. As Agriculture 4.0 is a collection of different systems, it is very challenging to invest in different technologies and different systems. As Blockchain technology is mainly used for securing the system, it is necessary to invest in Blockchain technology. Providing proper training to the farmer also needs financial involvement. As farming areas are spread worldwide, the number of users providing the service is huge. A huge financial investment is required to maintain a large system, train a large number of people, and access various locations spread across the globe.

Another challenge of Agriculture 4.0 is the lack of standardization. There is no standardized guideline for the creator. Different institutions maintain different approaches to implementing Blockchain technologies in their systems. There is no fixed policy for the companies. There is no policy framework by the government regarding Blockchain technology. There is very little regulation for the creators of the system. There are very few legal guidelines for the system. The lack of proper guidelines makes the system very unsafe. There is also a chance of misuse of the technology. Poor governance and lack of standardization are big challenges to implementing the Blockchain mechanism in Agriculture 4.0.

High Implementation Costs: Setting up a Blockchain system might be expensive, requiring major investment in technology and infrastructure, which may be beyond the means of small-scale farmers and small companies. The fee includes not just the technology but also training for users and continuous maintenance.

Complexity and Technical Challenges: Blockchain technology is sophisticated and may be difficult for all stakeholders to understand and embrace, especially in places with poor digital literacy. The success of Blockchain depends on the engagement of all actors in the supply chain, which might be tough to achieve.

Scalability Issues: Blockchain platforms may have scalability challenges, struggling to process a high number of transactions swiftly and efficiently. As the agricultural supply chain contains several stakeholders and innumerable transactions, the chosen Blockchain system must be able to grow properly.

Regulatory and Legal Uncertainties: The regulatory environment for Blockchain is still growing, and there may be legal difficulties around the usage of Blockchain for specific applications in agriculture. Stakeholders may be hesitant to adopt Blockchain due to worries about compliance with current and future rules.

Various processes need to be adopted to overcome the problems and challenges of Blockchain technology and to find possible solutions in agricultural management using Blockchain systems. It is necessary to divide the whole system into smaller portions and to implement the Blockchain technologies within these portions. After the fully functional smaller portion, it needs to be integrated to create a larger portion. With the integration of a smaller portion, it can create a fully functional system. By dividing the system into smaller partitions, it can make the system more scalable and robust. It increases the interoperability of the system. It reduces the complexity of the system and helps in easy understanding of the system. The resource person will easily understand the whole system and be able to detect any anomaly present in any portion of the system. Dividing the system into smaller partitions gives easy maintenance of the system. By following proper planning and designing, it is possible to reengineer the whole system to adopt the fourth generation of agriculture [10, 65].

To overcome the financial challenges, it is necessary to collect funding from different sources. Another solution to financial problems is to invest partially in the system instead of investing as a whole. It is also possible to raise funding from different institutions. To resolve the trust issue, it is necessary to choose the vendor properly. It is a big challenge to train a large number of people. To provide training to a large number of people, it is necessary to integrate the online-based education system and digital education for training purposes. Dividing the population into smaller groups and arranging various types of workshops is also important. Providing farmers with online-based customized cultivation plans and farming education can help. To reduce the gap between existing systems and Agriculture 4.0, it is necessary to build a user-friendly automation system.

The government also needs to frame a proper policy for the use of different kinds of emerging technologies. It is necessary to frame a proper policy and regulations for the utilization of Blockchain technologies. It is necessary to adopt different kinds of strategies to overcome the various issues and challenges in agro management using the Blockchain system. Fig. (**3**) shows different issues and challenges of the Blockchain system.

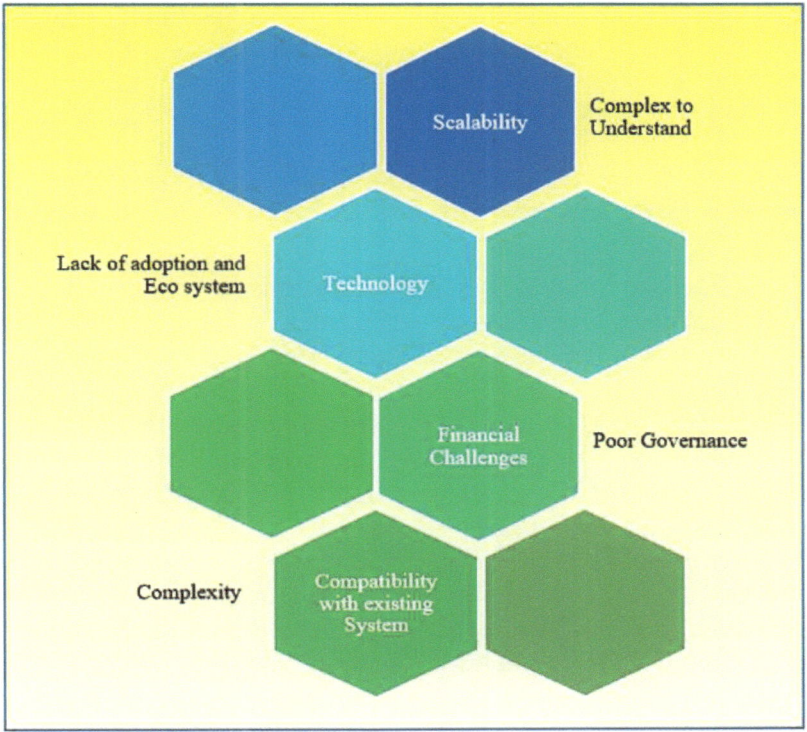

Fig. (3). Major issues and challenges of the Blockchain system.

Blockchain, supported by various sub-technologies of IT, helps advance and modernize agro-systems, ultimately dedicated to reaching efficient agricultural systems with proper agricultural monitoring required in agro-based product management. The expansion of agro-systems is positively enhanced with Blockchain for the development of commercial agriculture as well. As far as the cleaning and purity of the agro-system are concerned, Blockchain is useful and also indirectly helps in managing pesticides, fertilizers, *etc*. Speedy agricultural systems can be achieved with Blockchain applications along with the support of other allied technologies such as IoT, cloud and fog computing, Big Data, and HCI. These lead to proper Agricultural Informatics practices and the advancement of digital agricultural systems, which can ultimately contribute to quality production and simultaneously improve pre- and post-production agricultural systems. Soil, crop, weather management, and monitoring systems enhance quality production for effective quantity enhancement of agro-products, leading to the betterment of different products, crops, and plants through automated agro-harvesting, agro-medication, and agro-based treatment. In terms of developing livestock management, Blockchain and allied technologies also help in creating proper and advanced supply chain management systems, modern agro-marketing, and better agro-business development, among others.

Core Challenges of ML in Agriculture

Implementing machine learning algorithms in agriculture is a very difficult and challenging task. Some of the challenges are as follows:

- It is very difficult to predict weather conditions accurately. The weather is uncertain and does not follow any specific rules or patterns, especially during a particular monsoon. Therefore, predicting floods or droughts is extremely difficult.
- It is difficult to obtain accurate data regarding soil, pest patterns, weather conditions, and so on. This results in a trust issue concerning the quality of the data. Different types of data can be collected in real time, but the data are heterogeneous, and various types of noise may be present. Extracting the actual data from the collected dataset is challenging.
- The agricultural system is highly complex. Decoding this system and designing it based on a localized and personalized approach is very challenging.
- Infrastructure is another challenge to implementing machine learning in agriculture. The lack of devices and equipment such as robots, automatic tractors, drones, *etc.*, hinders progress.
- The lack of a communication system and a strong network also creates a significant problem in collecting real-time data.
- The lack of training and expertise is another constraint in implementing machine learning in agriculture. Farmers are still not familiar with digital systems, and training a large number of farmers to incorporate smart agricultural production is very tough.
- Integrating modern farming techniques with existing farming techniques is a major challenge.
- The initial setup cost of technology-based, automatic smart agriculture systems is very high, which discourages farmers from installing the complete system for agricultural production.
- There are no standardization protocols or policies for data security and privacy in the digitized system. The incorporation of machine learning algorithms in agriculture creates concerns regarding data security. There are trust issues with the machine learning algorithms used to design predictive models.

Future Potentials of Blockchain & Machine Learning-Supported Agricultural Systems

The future of agriculture holds significant promise with the integration of Blockchain and Machine Learning (ML) algorithms. These technologies are poised to revolutionize agricultural systems by enhancing automation, efficiency, and sustainability. Below are some potential advancements:

Full Automation in Agricultural Production: Blockchain and ML algorithms will enable fully automated agricultural processes, including seeding, harvesting, pest control, irrigation management, soil condition monitoring, and fertilizer requirements, reducing human intervention and optimizing production.

Personalized Farming Solutions: Given the varying soil conditions and weather patterns in different regions, these technologies will provide tailored solutions to farmers. By analyzing local conditions, Blockchain and ML will offer customized recommendations to maximize crop yield and productivity.

Self-Sufficient Decision-Making Systems: Blockchain and ML can create autonomous systems that minimize human involvement, allowing machines to analyze data and make informed decisions based on real-time inputs. This will ensure efficient use of resources, such as water, fertilizers, and pesticides.

Climate Data Analysis for Optimal Crop Growth: By analyzing climate data, Blockchain and ML algorithms can predict the ideal conditions for growing specific crops, helping farmers make informed decisions about planting and harvesting, improving crop yield, and reducing waste.

Support for Diverse Farming Techniques: These technologies will encourage various farming models such as organic farming, greenhouse farming, vertical farming, and aquaponics. By providing data-driven insights, Blockchain and ML will support sustainable and efficient agricultural practices suited to different environments.

Sustainable Agriculture Management: Blockchain and ML algorithms will play a crucial role in managing the entire agricultural value chain—from production to procurement to supply chain optimization—ensuring long-term sustainability by reducing waste, improving traceability, and enhancing resource management.

Advanced Agricultural Analytics: Modern techniques like genome analytics and breeding control will be used to suggest optimal strategies for cross-breeding, pest control, disease resistance, and climate-specific farming. This will enhance plant health and increase agricultural productivity.

Global Food Safety: Blockchain and ML will enhance global food safety by ensuring transparent tracking and traceability of food products throughout the supply chain, guaranteeing quality control and preventing food fraud.

Encouraging Collaborative Farming: These technologies will facilitate networking and communication among farmers across different geographical locations, promoting collaborative farming. This could lead to shared resources, data, and strategies for improved crop yields and reduced risks.

CONCLUDING REMARKS

The integration of Blockchain technology with Machine Learning (ML)-based algorithms has the potential to transform the agricultural sector, ushering in a new era of transparency, efficiency, and sustainability. From farm to table, these technologies offer solutions to long-standing challenges, empowering stakeholders across the agricultural value chain. Beyond operational improvements, Blockchain and ML could foster a more equitable agricultural system, ensuring fair compensation for farmers and promoting global food security.

As we look to the future, the possibilities offered by these combined technologies are vast. Blockchain and ML can serve as catalysts for socio-economic change, boosting food production, environmental sustainability, and economic equity worldwide. However, widespread adoption will require overcoming several challenges, including technical, regulatory, and educational hurdles.

The successful integration of Blockchain and ML in agriculture demands collaboration among policymakers, technologists, and farmers. A collective effort is required to establish frameworks that ensure these technologies are accessible, scalable, and beneficial for all sectors of the agricultural ecosystem. Although the journey toward full-scale adoption is complex, the potential benefits make it a challenge worth pursuing.

Blockchain and ML technologies are not only valuable for improving agricultural processes in developed countries but also for driving innovation and efficiency in the developing world. By enabling smart agro-systems, these technologies can contribute to the growth of sustainable agriculture, helping to address challenges like climate change, pest infestations, and disease management. This will lead to enhanced agro-nutritional systems and better business development opportunities in the agriculture sector.

With the increasing involvement of multinational corporations, private organizations, government agencies, and institutions in the agricultural digital revolution, the next step is to establish proper regulatory policies and frameworks. These will ensure that Blockchain and ML technologies are utilized effectively in creating intelligent, sustainable, and inclusive agricultural systems worldwide.

REFERENCES

[1] A.A. Barakabitze, K.G. Fue, and C.A. Sanga, "The use of participatory approaches in developing ICT-based systems for disseminating agricultural knowledge and information for farmers in developing countries: The case of Tanzania", *Electron. J. Inf. Syst. Dev. Ctries.*, vol. 78, no. 1, pp. 1-23, 2017. [http://dx.doi.org/10.1002/j.1681-4835.2017.tb00576.x]

[2] A. A. Mukherjee, R. K. Singh, R. Mishra, and S. Bag, "Application of blockchain technology for sustainability development in agricultural supply chain: Justification framework", *Oper. Manag. Res.*, vol. 15, pp. 46–61, 2022.

[3] D. Xie, L. Chen, L. Liu, L. Chen, and H. Wang, "Actuators and sensors for application in agricultural robots: A review," *Machines*, vol. 10, no. 10, pp. 913, 2022.

[4] S. Awan, S. Ahmed, F. Ullah, A. Nawaz, A. Khan, M. I. Uddin, A. Alharbi, W. Alosaimi, and H. Alyami. "IoT with blockchain: A futuristic approach in agriculture and food supply chain," *Wireless Communications and Mobile Computing*, vol. 2021, pp. 1–14, June 2021. [http://dx.doi.org/10.1155/2021/5580179]

[5] K. S. Kumar, S. Balakrishnan, and J. Janet, "A cloud-based prototype for the monitoring and predicting of data in precision agriculture based on internet of everything," *Journal of Ambient Intelligence and Humanized Computing*, vol. 12, no. 9, pp. 8719–8730, 2021.

[6] A. D. Nugroho, "Agricultural market information in developing countries: A literature review," *Agric. Econ. – Czech*, vol. 67, no. 11, pp. 468–477, 2021.

[7] A. Pakseresht, A. Yavari, S.A. Kaliji, and K. Hakelius, "The intersection of blockchain technology and circular economy in the agri-food sector", *Sustainable Production and Consumption*, vol. 35, pp. 260-274, 2023. [http://dx.doi.org/10.1016/j.spc.2022.11.002]

[8] J. Nurgazina, U. Pakdeetrakulwong, T. Moser, and G. Reiner, "Distributed ledger technology applications in food supply chains: A review of challenges and future research directions," *Sustainability*, vol. 13, no. 8, p. 4206, 2021.

[9] M. A. Dayıoğlu and U. Turker, "Digital transformation for sustainable future-agriculture 4.0: A review," *Journal of Agricultural Sciences*, vol. 27, no. 4, pp. 373–399, 2021.

[10] H. F. Atli, "Digital marketing in the agricultural sector and digital transformation in agricultural marketing," in *Proc. 8th Int. Tokyo Conf. Innovative Studies of Contemporary Sciences*, pp. 415–424, 2024.

[11] Z. M. Hurst and S. Spiegal, "Design thinking for responsible agriculture 4.0 innovations in rangelands," *Rangelands*, vol. 45, no. 4, pp. 68–78, 2023.

[12] K. K. S. Liyakat, "Model for agricultural information system to improve crop yield using IoT," *Journal of Open Source Development*, vol. 9, no. 2, pp. 16–24, 2022.

[13] T. Duckett, S. Pearson, S. Blackmore, B. Grieve, W. H. Chen, G. Cielniak, et al., "Agricultural robotics: The future of robotic agriculture," *arXiv preprint arXiv:1806.06762*, 2018.

[14] M. Fiore and M. Mongiello, "Blockchain technology to support agri-food supply chains: A comprehensive review," *IEEE Access*, vol. 11, pp. 75311–75324, 2023.

[15] F. da Silveira, F.H. Lermen, and F.G. Amaral, "An overview of agriculture 4.0 development: Systematic review of descriptions, technologies, barriers, advantages, and disadvantages", *Comput. Electron. Agric.*, vol. 189, 2021.106405 [http://dx.doi.org/10.1016/j.compag.2021.106405]

[16] F. Dal Mas, M. Massaro, V. Ndou, and E. Raguseo, "Blockchain technologies for sustainability in the agrifood sector: A literature review of academic research and business perspectives", *Technol. Forecast. Soc. Change.* vol. 187, p. 122155, 2023.
[http://dx.doi.org/10.1016/j.techfore.2022.122155]

[17] F. A. Kitole, E. Mkuna, and J. K. Sesabo, "Digitalization and agricultural transformation in developing countries: Empirical evidence from Tanzania agriculture sector," *Smart Agricultural Technology*, vol. 7, p. 100379, 2024.

[18] K. Hushvakhtzoda, "Management accounting in the agricultural enterprise information system," in *E3S Web of Conferences*, vol. 390, p. 03022, 2023.

[19] D. P. Sakas, N. T. Giannakopoulos, A. G. Panagiotou, N. Kanellos, and C. Christopoulos, "Search engine results optimization for supply chain SMEs through digital content management and fuzzy cognitive models," *Journal of Computational and Cognitive Engineering*, vol. 4, no. 2, pp. 161–172, 2025.

[20] R. R. Naikwade, B. K. Patle, V. S. Joshi, N. D. Pagar, and S. B. Hirwe, "Agriculture 5.0: Future of smart farming," in *Proc. Nat. Conf. Innovative Global Technology Trends in Art, Design, Technology, Management, Vedic Science, Education and Architecture, Film & Media*, MITADT School of Engineering, Pune, India, 2021, pp. 1-6.

[21] M. Rafi, A. I. Abueid, M. Umar, and A. B. Miled, "Big data based smart sensing for precision agriculture using artificial intelligence," *Utilitas Mathematica*, vol. 121, pp. 174–188, 2024.

[22] H. Patel, and B. Shrimali, "AgriOnBlock: Secured data harvesting for agriculture sector using blockchain technology", *ICT Express,* vol. 9, no. 2, pp. 150-159, 2023.
[http://dx.doi.org/10.1016/j.icte.2021.07.003]

[23] A. A. Mukherjee, R. K. Singh, R. Mishra, and S. Bag, "Application of blockchain technology for sustainability development in agricultural supply chain: Justification framework," *Operations Management Research*, vol. 15, no. 1, pp. 46–61, 2022.

[24] V. D. Gowda, M. S. Prabhu, M. Ramesha, J. M. Kudari, and A. Samal, "Smart agriculture and smart farming using IoT technology," in *J. Phys.: Conf. Ser.*, vol. 2089, no. 1, p. 012038, Nov. 2021.

[25] M. Javaid, A. Haleem, R.P. Singh, and R. Suman, "Enhancing smart farming through the applications of Agriculture 4.0 technologies", *International Journal of Intelligent Networks*, vol. 3, pp. 150-164, 2022.
[http://dx.doi.org/10.1016/j.ijin.2022.09.004]

[26] B. Demirtaş and A. İldeş, "Evaluation of the effects of agricultural information sources in the extension of producers," *Economics and Administrative Sciences Modern Analysis and Researches*, vol. 119, 2023.

[27] K. Kaushik, S. Dahiya, and R. Sharma, "Role of Blockchain Technology in Digital Forensics", In: *In Handbook of Research on Digital Forensics and Investigation.*, K. Kaushik, S. Dahiya, R. Sharma, Eds., Taylor & Francis, 2022, pp. 267-285.

[28] "Survey on the Applications of Blockchain in Agriculture", *Agriculture,* vol. 12, no. 9, p. 1333, 2022.
[http://dx.doi.org/10.3390/agriculture12091333]

[29] K. Kaushik, "Demystifying Blockchain in 5G and Beyond Technologies", *Journal of Mobile Multimedia*, vol. 18, no. 05, pp. 1379-1398, 2022.
[http://dx.doi.org/10.13052/jmm1550-4646.18513]

[30] K. Kaushik, and S. Dahiya, "Scope and Challenges of Blockchain Technology", In: *Recent Innovations in Computing.*, P.K. Singh, Y. Singh, M.H. Kolekar, A.K. Kar, P.J.S. Gonçalves, Eds., vol. Vol. 832. Springer: Singapore, 2022, pp. 361-370.
[http://dx.doi.org/10.1007/978-981-16-8248-3_38]

[31] M. A. Dayıoğlu and U. Turker, "Digital transformation for sustainable future-agriculture 4.0: A

review," *Journal of Agricultural Sciences*, vol. 27, no. 4, pp. 373–399, 2021.

[32] M. Alobid, S. Abujudeh, and I. Szűcs, "The role of blockchain in revolutionizing the agricultural sector", *Sustainability,* vol. 14, no. 7, p. 4313, 2022.
[http://dx.doi.org/10.3390/su14074313]

[33] G. Kootstra, X. Wang, P. M. Blok, J. Hemming, and E. Van Henten, "Selective harvesting robotics: Current research, trends, and future directions," *Current Robotics Reports*, vol. 2, no. 1, pp. 95–104, 2021.

[34] C. Niyonzima, "The role of robotics in agriculture: Enhancing productivity and sustainability," *Research Output Journal of Biological and Applied Science*, vol. 3, no. 2, pp. 28–31, 2024.

[35] K. Phasinam, T. Kassanuk, P. P. Shinde, C. M. Thakar, D. K. Sharma, M. K. Mohiddin, and A. W. Rahmani, "Application of IoT and cloud computing in automation of agriculture irrigation," *Journal of Food Quality*, vol. 2022, no. 7, pp. 1-8, 2022.

[36] S. I. Moazzam, U. S. Khan, W. S. Qureshi, M. I. Tiwana, N. Rashid, W. S. Alasmary, J. Iqbal, and A. Hamza. "A patch-image based classification approach for detection of weeds in sugar beet crop," *IEEE Access*, vol. 9, pp. 1–14, 2021.

[37] S. P. Tiwari, "Information and communication technology initiatives for knowledge sharing in agriculture," *arXiv preprint arXiv:2202.08649,* 2022.

[38] J. D. Borrero and J. Mariscal, "A case study of a digital data platform for the agricultural sector: A valuable decision support system for small farmers," *Agriculture*, vol. 12, no. 6, p. 767, 2022.

[39] L. F. Oliveira, A. P. Moreira, and M. F. Silva, "Advances in agriculture robotics: A state-of-the-art review and challenges ahead," *Robotics*, vol. 10, no. 2, p. 52, 2021.

[40] P. K. Paul and S. K. Jena, "Economical, financial and allied concerns in healthy agricultural information systems practice: The context of developing countries," *Economic Affairs*, vol. 68, no. 04, pp. 2161-2170, December 2023.

[41] P. K. Paul, R. R. Sinha, P. S. Aithal, R. Saavedra, B. Aremu, and S. Mewada, "Cloud computing vis-à-vis agricultural development towards digital and smarter agricultural informatics practice," *Asian Journal of Engineering and Applied Technology*, vol. 9, no. 1, pp. 18–24, 2020.

[42] P. K. Paul, A. Bandyopadhyay, M. Hoque, and S. K. Jena, "Agricultural information networks and systems: Necessity, components—A scientific review," *Int. j. appl. sci. eng,* vol. 12, no. 1, pp. 17–27, 2024.

[43] P. K. Paul, "Data analytics vis-à-vis agricultural development: International scenario and Indian potentialities—A techno and managerial context," in *Demystifying Big Data Analytics for Industries and Smart Societies,*, K. Kaushik, M. Dahiya, and A. D. Dwivedi, Eds., Chapman and Hall/CRC, 2023, pp. 193–209.

[44] P. K. Paul, "Usability engineering and HCI for promoting root-level social computation and informatics practice: A possible academic move in the Indian perspective," *International Journal of Asian Business and Information Management (IJABIM)*, vol. 12, no. 2, pp. 96–109, 2021.

[45] P.K. Paul, "Emerging Blockchain Technology vis-à-vis Limitations and Issues: Emphasizing the Indian Context", In: *In Advancements in Quantum Blockchain With Real-Time Applications*. IGI Global, 2022, pp. 56-79.
[http://dx.doi.org/10.4018/978-1-6684-5072-7.ch003]

[46] P. K. Paul, P. S. Aithal, and R. M. Saavedra, "Blockchain in educational development: Potentialities and issues-towards sophisticated digital education systems", *Int. J. Appl. Sci. Eng.*. vol. 11, no. 2, pp. 75–86, 2022.
[http://dx.doi.org/10.30954/2322-0465.3.2022.1]

[47] S. Sindhu and D. Sindhu, "Information dissemination using computer and communication technologies for improving agriculture productivity," *Development*, vol. 6, no. 6, 2017.

[48] A. Narendra Babu, M. C. Blossom, A. Praneetha, P. Shirisha, P. M. Kishore, F. M. Mounika, et al., "Internet of Things (IoT) based pesticide spraying robot—A revolution in smart farming," *Indian Journal of Science and Technology*, vol. 16, no. 22, pp. 1676–1681, 2023.

[49] D. Badar and B. ul Islam, "Design and fabrication of the automatic multipurpose agriculture robot (AMAR)," *Computer and Decision Making: An International Journal*, vol. 1, pp. 340–356, 2024.

[50] P. Indira, I. S. Arafat, R. Karthikeyan, S. Selvarajan, and P. K. Balachandran, "Fabrication and investigation of agricultural monitoring system with IoT and AI," *SN Applied Sciences*, vol. 5, no. 12, p. 322, 2023.

[51] S. Awan, S. Ahmed, F. Ullah, A. Nawaz, A. Khan, M.I. Uddin, A. Alharbi, W. Alosaimi, and H. Alyami, "IoT with blockchain: A futuristic approach in agriculture and food supply chain", *Wirel. Commun. Mob. Comput.*, vol. 2021, no. 1, 2021.5580179 [http://dx.doi.org/10.1155/2021/5580179]

[52] Y. Shen, "Construction of a wireless sensing network system for leisure agriculture for cloud-based agricultural Internet of Things," *Journal of Sensors*, vol. 2021, Art. no. 3021771, 2021.

[53] M. Vahdanjoo, R. Gislum, and C. A. G. Sørensen, "Operational, economic, and environmental assessment of an agricultural robot in seeding and weeding operations," *AgriEngineering*, vol. 5, no. 1, pp. 299–324, 2023.

[54] A. B. Santoso, S. S. Girsang, B. Raharjo, A. B. Pustika, Y. Hutapea, M. Kobarsih, A. Suprihatin, E. D. Manurung, D. R. Siagian, S. Hanapi, T. Purba, D. Parhusip, S. W. Budiarti, Y. P. Wanita, R. U. Hatmi, M. A. Girsang, L. Haloho, Waluyo, Suparwoto, Yustisia, and Sudarmaji. "Assessing the challenges and opportunities of agricultural information systems to enhance farmers' capacity and target rice production in Indonesia," *Sustainability*, vol. 15, no. 2, p. 1114, 2023.

[55] S.O. Araújo, R.S. Peres, J. Barata, F. Lidon, and J.C. Ramalho, "Characterising the agriculture 4.0 landscape-emerging trends, challenges and opportunities", *Agronomy*, vol. 11, no. 4, p. 667, 2021. [http://dx.doi.org/10.3390/agronomy11040667]

[56] Y. Zheng, Y. Xu, and Z. Qiu, "Blockchain traceability adoption in agricultural supply chain coordination: An evolutionary game analysis," *Agriculture*, vol. 13, no. 1, p. 184, 2023.

[57] S. Vashisht, S. Gaba, S. Dahiya, and K. Kaushik, "Security and Privacy Issues in IoT Systems Using Blockchain", In: *Security and Privacy in Internet of Things (IoT): Challenges and Solutions.*, R. Hussain, A. Kumar, V. Bhatia, Eds., CRC Press: Boca Raton, FL, 2022, pp. 155-178. [http://dx.doi.org/10.1201/9781003193425-8]

[58] K. Kaushik, S. Tayal, S. Dahiya, and A.O. Salau, "Sustainable and advanced applications of blockchain in smart computational technologies", In: *Chapman and Hall/CRC*, 2022. [http://dx.doi.org/10.1201/9781003193425]

[59] A. Botta, P. Cavallone, L. Baglieri, G. Colucci, L. Tagliavini, and G. Quaglia, "A review of robots, perception, and tasks in precision agriculture," *Applied Mechanics*, vol. 3, no. 3, pp. 830–854, 2022.

[60] R. P. dos Santos, N. Fachada, M. Beko, and V. R. Leithardt, "A rapid review on the use of free and open source technologies and software applied to precision agriculture practices," *Journal of Sensor and Actuator Networks*, vol. 12, no. 2, p. 28, 2023.

[61] N. Mahalingam and P. Sharma, "An intelligent blockchain technology for securing an IoT-based agriculture monitoring system," *Multimedia Tools and Applications*, vol. 83, no. 4, pp. 10297–10320, 2024.

[62] O. Mapiye, G. Makombe, A. Molotsi, K. Dzama, and C. Mapiye, "Information and communication technologies (ICTs): The potential for enhancing the dissemination of agricultural information and services to smallholder farmers in sub-Saharan Africa," *Information Development*, vol. 39, no. 3, pp. 638–658, 2023.

[63] D. Patel, M. Gandhi, H. Shankaranarayanan, and A. D. Darji, "Design of an autonomous agriculture

robot for real-time weed detection using CNN," in *Advances in VLSI and Embedded Systems: Select Proceedings of AVES 2021*, Singapore: Springer Nature Singapore, pp. 141–161, 2022.

[64] Y. Liu, X. Ma, L. Shu, G.P. Hancke, and A.M. Abu-Mahfouz, "From Industry 4.0 to Agriculture 4.0: Current status, enabling technologies, and research challenges", *IEEE Trans. Industr. Inform.*, vol. 17, no. 6, pp. 4322-4334, 2021.
[http://dx.doi.org/10.1109/TII.2020.3003910]

[65] W. Byamukama, P. M. Businge, and R. Kalibwani. "Mobile Telephony as an ICT Tool for Agricultural Information Dissemination in Developing Countries: A Review", *East African Journal of Agriculture and Biotechnology (EAJAB),*, vol. 6, no. 1, pp. 35-43, Feb. 2023.

[66] E. M. Pechlivani, G. Gkogkos, N. Giakoumoglou, I. Hadjigeorgiou, and D. Tzovaras, "Towards sustainable farming: A robust decision support system's architecture for Agriculture 4.0," In: *Proc. Int. Conf. Digital Signal Processing (DSP),* Rhodes Island, Greece, June 2023, pp. 1–5.

CHAPTER 6

Deep Learning-based Intrusion Detection System for IoT-based Blockchain System

J. Jayaganesh[1,*], **Sreenivas Mekala**[2], **M. Kalyan Chakravarthi**[3], **R. Sundarrajan**[4], **Belsam Jeba Ananth M.**[5], **Mohit Tiwari**[6] and **Manika Manwal**[7]

[1] *Department of Computer Science, Government Arts and Science College Perumbakkam, Chennai, India*

[2] *Department of Information Technology, Sreenidhi Institute of Science & Technology, Hyderabad, India*

[3] *School of Electronic Engineering, Vellore Institute of Technology, Andhra Pradesh, Amaravathi, India*

[4] *Department of Information Techology, Kalasalingam Academy of Research and Education (Deemed to be University), Virudhunagar, India*

[5] *Department of Mechatronics Engineering, SRM Institute of Science and Technology, Kattankulathur, India*

[6] *Department of Computer Science and Engineering, Bharati Vidyapeeth's College of Engineering, Delhi, India*

[7] *Department of Computer Science and Engineering, Graphic Era Hill University, Dehradun, India*

Abstract: Security and privacy concerns, which are made worse by the growing number of Internet-connected devices, are the primary obstacles to the Internet of Things (IoT) widespread implementation. Everyone is now very concerned about Internet of Things security, including businesses, governments, and consumers. Even though no system can ever be completely protected from attacks, effective system defense depends on real-time threat detection. There is a dearth of studies on intrusion detection systems that work well in IoT-based blockchain systems. In this study, we present a novel approach to intrusion detection in the Internet of Things-based blockchain systems by employing the DL (Deep Learning) subfield of machine learning to identify security abnormalities. This detection platform provides security as a service and allows interoperability with numerous network communication protocols utilized by the Internet of Things. We go into great details about the suggested system's architecture and intrusion detection method. Real network traces are evaluated along with simulated data to illustrate the scalability of the proposed intrusion detection system to prove its viability. Our results confirm that the proposed intrusion detection system can correctly detect real intrusions.

---

* **Corresponding author J. Jayaganesh:** Department of Computer Science, Government Arts and Science College Perumbakkam, Chennai, India; E-mail: everjays@gmail.com

Keshav Kaushik, Rewa Sharma & Ayodeji Olalekan Salau (Eds.)
All rights reserved-© 2026 Bentham Science Publishers

Keywords: Smart contracts, Blockchain, Deep learning, IoT, Intrusion detection.

INTRODUCTION

A network of common physical things that can be linked to the Internet and utilized to transmit data and combine it with other network resources is known as the Internet of Things, or IoT [1]. These items are either sensors or networked digital gadgets that can exchange data *via* the World Wide Web after being collected. New applications and services are produced as a result of these interactions among people, processes, sensors, and connectivity. In the Internet of Things, these electronic gadgets or sensors are called "things." IoT networks are essentially formed by connecting IoT devices that are within a user's range, usually within ten meters. These networks feature an unstable topology that is subject to alter over time [2]. IoT technology is being utilized more and more in a variety of fields, including business-augmented services, health care, national security, and, on a smaller scale, smart home environments. IoT networks are getting more and more popular, which makes them more vulnerable to security breaches. Attacks on cyberspace are turning into one of the biggest risks to IoT security [3]. Blockchain technology is driven mostly by the need for decentralization. Blockchain's open and accessible record ensures that a single node breakdown has no impact on the entire network. Blockchain transformed the transactional networking structure from a constellation to a point-to-point (P2P) design. This changed architecture enables 2 entities to connect openly through the use of encrypted and safety depending on coding and algorithmic safety. Therefore, it is crucial to secure IoT-based blockchain systems and build intrusion-resistant IoT networks to protect sensitive data.

Research Objective

The objectives of this research are as follows:

- To have a thorough understanding of IoT and its constituent parts.
- To research anomaly detection approaches and construct an intrusion detection model for Internet of Things networks based on deep learning.
- To assess the model and offer suggestions for improving its development.

Scope and Limitations of Study

To facilitate safe data transfer among Internet of Things devices that are located close to one another, this study aims to develop an intelligent, portable intrusion detection system. The goal of this system is to examine textual or numerical real-world data that is contained in network packets. At present, this technology is not designed to handle encrypted or raw/unformatted data. Moreover, this intrusion detection system can only identify anomalies at the transport layer. As such, it will be difficult to find more sophisticated or physical attacks that could use this method to alter or tamper with the hardware of Internet of Things devices. Despite being designed to be portable, the recommended intrusion detection system is meant to be a logical control that is, software rather than a physical control for Internet of Things networks.

LITERATURE REVIEW

Internet of Things Definition

All current gadgets that can generate data and send it *via* the Internet are collectively referred to as the IoT. According to a recent study, the total number of internet-connected devices is predicted to surpass 6.4 billion by 2016 and reach 20.8 billion by 2020 [4]. The iPhone, iPad, iWatch, Smart TVs, and many other gadgets are on this list.

IoT Security Issues and Existing Intrusion Detection Methods

The characteristics of hacker groups involved in cybercrime are covered by some researchers [5]. They define cybercrime, discuss its potential, meaning, and the theoretical and practical difficulties in dealing with these cyber offenders, and come to the conclusion that state actors' cybercrime and protest-oriented cybercrime are more structured and specialized than regular forms of protest. They contend that although cybercriminals operate in loose networks, even in cases where their attacks span national borders, they are still physically close to one another. Research efforts are focused on mitigating security risks associated with IoT network protocols, such as the Constrained Application Protocol (CoAP) [6], which holds great potential for the ambitious vision of a Smart City Environment. They recommend a modular rule-based intrusion detection framework, but their results highlight the advantages of a hybrid approach that blends anomaly- and rule-based intrusion detection. Furthermore, the IDS system they had in place was limited to mitigating routing assaults. Using behavioral modeling, Arrington *et al.* suggest identifying anomalies connected to non-playing characters (NPCs), or people acting out various roles within or around a smart home, as a means of detecting intrusions in smart homes [7]. The proposed work claims to create cost-effective, easily verifiable autonomous monitoring for intrusion detection, but it does not specify which hardware implementation or IA was utilized.

IoT Security Vulnerabilities

This section lists the many attacks that can be launched against Internet of Things networks and discusses the general danger landscape for these networks. We examine several potential network-based assaults that might be launched towards a network that is linked to smart homes. In a smart home scenario, a malicious network trace can be used to reveal or delete data, alter or interfere with the behavior of IoT devices, or even physically injure end users [8 - 10]. IoT networks are quite vulnerable to several types of attacks. Researchers have recently managed to trigger an autopilot automobile collision [11], which might be deadly in the event of an actual attack. We list comparable IoT-specific attacks that we have studied in this section.

Attack by Remote Control

Attackers utilize denial-of-service, man-in-the-middle, and botnet techniques to target distant, and linked IoT devices. After successfully intercepting the genuine communication, the attacker can control the remote device's actions.

Bricking Attack

Bricking attacks target Internet of Things (IoT) communication protocols with ease. A payload, typically a worm, is primarily responsible for spreading the assault. It is sent from a remote device that is connected to the victim's network. By simply moving from one device to its nearby ones, the worm multiplies by taking advantage of their physical closeness.

Weaponization of Devices

Smart hub microphones, TV cameras, and baby monitors are just a few examples of Internet of Things gadgets that can see and record their hosts. An attacker using a device weaponization attack must be able to take control of these gadgets to monitor their victim.

Attack using Wormhole Tunnel

A wormhole tunnel attack uses two attacker nodes connected by a virtual private connection to target Internet of Things networks. When the victim node in this attack receives a network packet, it first sends it *via* the wormhole so that it can be replayed later. The RPL network then begins to generate non-optimized routes as a result.

Enhanced Rank Attack on RPL

RPL is a low-powered, lossy IPv6 routing mechanism. Every device in the RPL network has a rank value given to it. An indirect assault on IoT networks called an RPL rank attack seeks to create enormous path loops by increasing the rank value, which leads to network-wide inconsistencies.

Attacks Using Sinkholes

A rogue node must advertise fictitious routing information to draw a sizable amount of network traffic. It must then drop the packets to negatively impact network performance as a whole.

Attack by Ballot Stuffing

In this attack, a hostile node could degrade a well-behaved node's confidence with destructive recommendations. Its chances of getting chosen for the service will thus be reduced [12].

Attacks using Opportunistic Services

Self-interest drives the self-promoting or opportunistic service attack; a malicious node may start by offering excellent service to establish a solid reputation among peer nodes [13]. Consequently, it may result in biased, subpar service and harm the overall quality of service (QoS) of the network.

Attacks that Distribute Denial of Service

Tiny IoT networks, like smart homes, are readily disruptible in terms of services and minimum service level operation by a relatively tiny cluster of external devices. A smart home IoT network's quality of service can be severely reduced by flooding it with a lot of network packets, each of which has a big payload.

Botnet Participation

IoT devices that run unsafe exploitable code, are often provided with malicious defaults, and permit unauthorized access to management systems are all reasons why botnet masters find them appealing.

Ransomware

Ransomware, sometimes known as "jack-ware," is specifically designed by attackers to target connected devices. Jack-ware is a tactic used by attackers to threaten to take down vital services or do damage to the Internet of Things devices until the victim pays up.

METHODOLOGY

Network Architecture

Sensor outputs, triggers, status messages, and other information are exchanged between IoT (smart things) devices *via* communication [14]. Blockchain can increase the safety of gadgets by decentralizing the storage and transmission of communication notifications, which are instructions that govern system-wide activity. Blockchain also contributes to the development of confidence among many stakeholders by utilizing an agreed-upon smart contract to manage system functioning and agent conduct. Brokers enable the network to adapt downward and up, making it better suited to dealing with various IoT context architectures and communication standards.

Fig. (1) depicts the architecture for the proposed IDS in an IoT network where the edge router acts as the IoT hub. Every Internet of Things device linked to the network is under the supervision of the IoT coordinator, which is also referred to as an IoT hub. To get to their destination, all connections from IoT devices pass through the IoT hub. 40 kbps is sufficient for the majority of home automation devices because it can handle the demands of low-powered control systems [15].

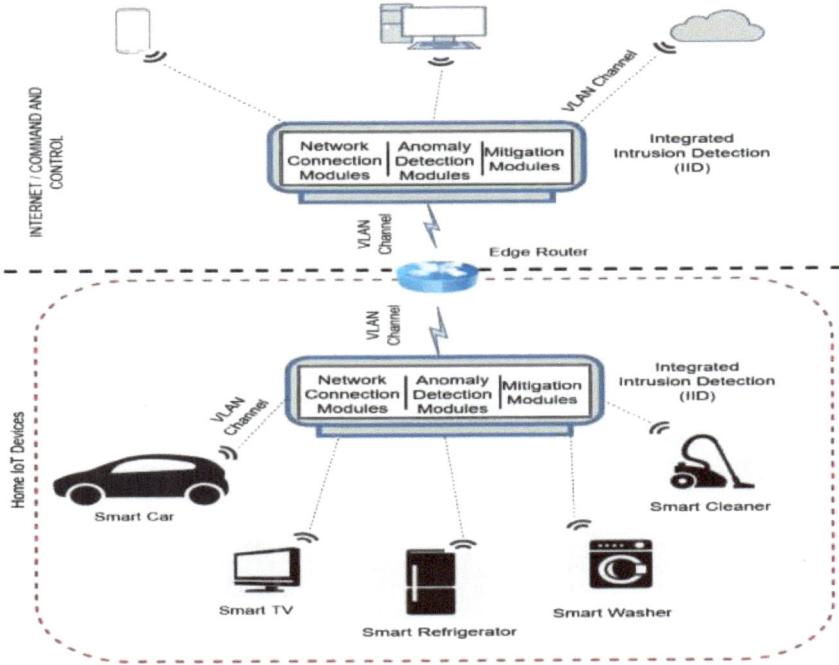

Fig. (1). Network topology overview.

Architecture of the System

Our suggested intrusion detection system for IoT networks aims to stop assaults by offering on-demand security services. The ability to recognize its surroundings, the capacity to listen incessantly to wireless communication traffic in its immediate environment, and the early identification of intrusions are the main duties of the suggested intrusion detection system.

The network connection phase, anomaly detection phase, and mitigation phase are the three primary stages of the suggested IDS, as shown in Fig. (**2**). The recommended intrusion detection system searches for and deploys the appropriate network adapter during the Network Connection stage, allowing network translation and the interpretation of intercepted network packets from its surroundings. Utilizing a feed-forward deep learning algorithm, the recommended intrusion detection system searches for anomalies in the network traffic inside the IoT network during the anomaly detection phase. As a result, it follows a predefined process in the Mitigation Phase to address any intrusions that may be discovered.

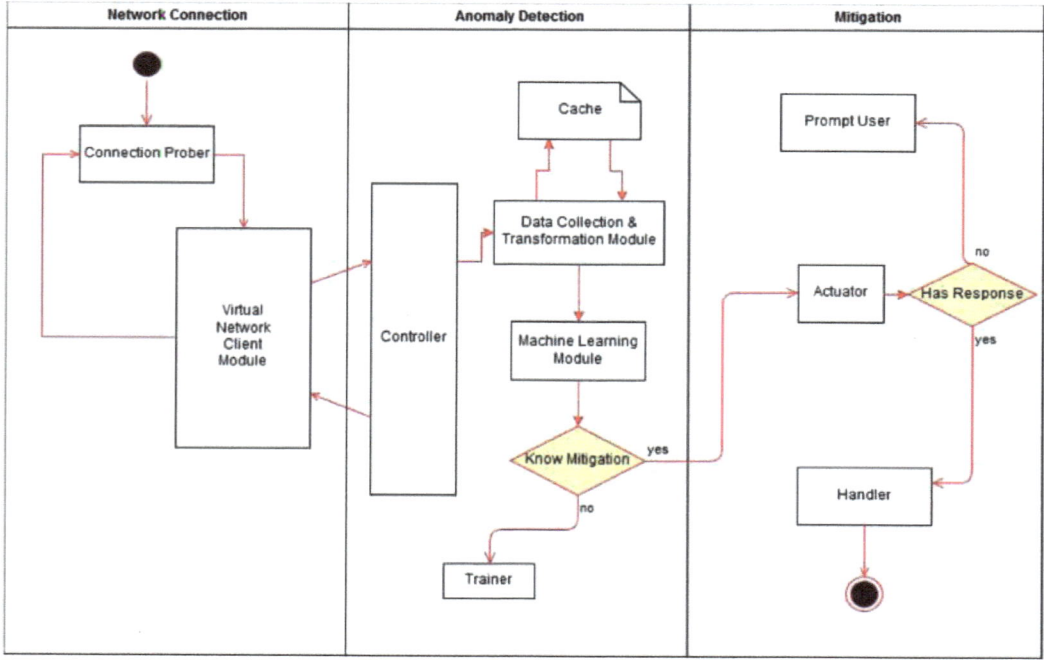

Fig. (2). Overview of IDS architecture.

Phase of Network Connection

A variety of network communication protocols can be used by the many devices that make up the Internet of Things networks to facilitate communication. To monitor the Internet of Things network, the proposed intrusion detection system makes use of Virtual Network Connections (VNCs) during the Network Connection phase. Different network translation adapters can be used with any virtual network connection. VNC can listen to many wireless communication streams at once by using multiple translation adapters concurrently. Just three IoT communication protocols are supported by the prototype created for this research: 6LoWPAN, ZigBee, and Bluetooth as proof-of-concept. Table 1 contains a collection of these protocols' technical requirements.

Table 1. Targeted IoT protocol specifications.

Protocol	Frequency	Range	Data rates
6LoWPAN	900 MHz	30 m	100 Kbps
ZigBee	2.4 GHz	10-100m	250Mbps
Bluetooth	2.4.GHz	50 -150m	1 Mbps

Identification of Anomalies

Perceptual learning is the machine learning technique used in the suggested intrusion detection system for anomaly identification. The Data Collection and Transformation module offers the machine learning module with the primary features (header tags) obtained from the network packets for binary classification after accepting the network traffic from the Virtual Network Client module. The following section covers the implementation of the Data Collection and Transformation module and the Machine Learning-based Anomaly Detection module, as shown in Fig. (2).

Phase of Mitigation

When an intrusion is discovered, the mitigation phase is in charge of initiating a mitigation response or a preventive activity. The Actuator and Handler modules are the two modules used by the proposed intrusion detection system to facilitate the mitigation reaction if an intrusion is discovered. The primary objective of this study is to create an intrusion detection system, not to provide a mitigation technique. The Machine-Learning module has detected an intrusion; it is the Actuator module's responsibility to identify the intrusion and start a mitigation process to address it. As a result, the recommended intrusion detection system employs a basic incident response approach. Instead of responding on its own, the actuator uses the signatures of the found malicious network trace to instruct the Handler module on the proper course of action. However, the Handler module's only duty is to carry out the appropriate subroutine in response to the Actuator module's mitigation response.

Deep Learning-based Detection

Network traffic provides the characteristics that the proposed intrusion detection system uses. The computational power-to-performance ratio and computing capability of lightweight, resource-constrained portable Internet of Things devices were taken into consideration when choosing these features. Conversely, the properties of the network packet come directly from the bit stream of IoT network traffic, which is the representation of the IPv6 protocol's header. The IPv6 protocol's header length is constant; hence feature extraction is carried out as a procedure with a fixed time complexity. It is implied by the feature extraction process from the bit stream that decoding is not required.

Anomaly Detection based on Deep Learning

We create a feed-forward Deep Belief Network (DBN) with a Deep Neural Network (DNN) as the perceptual learning model. A model with n number of neural nodes in each layer connected by undirected links is called a deep belief network. To put it simply, a DNN is an Artificial Neural Network that builds itself forward by adding new data to a Deep Belief Network. While there are other methods to create a DNN, one benefit of starting with a DBN model is that unsupervised learning algorithms can be used to train the DBN layers. This allows for the creation of DNN from a pre-trained model quickly compared to supervised learning through unsupervised learning. In this study, we created a five-layer deep learning model, as shown in Fig. (3), containing one input layer, three hidden perceptual layers, and one binary classifier layer as an output layer.

As shown in Fig. (4), we build a DNN model using the pre-trained layers of the DBN model. Fig. (4) illustrates how unsupervised training yields the weights for each hidden layer in this DBN model, denoted by w_i. As a result, just the first set of weights is assigned using the learning parameters from this unsupervised training. After evolution is completed successfully, the DBN becomes a feed-forward Artificial Neural Network (ANN), which is another name for a Deep Neural Network. At the top layer of this DBN model, label information (a) for each network transaction and a binary classification layer are integrated to build a unique deep learning model.

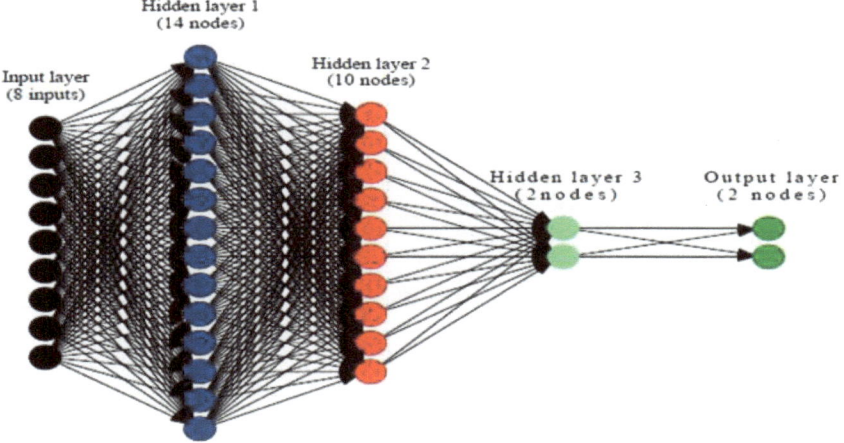

Fig. (3). For the suggested intrusion detection system, a deep learning model.

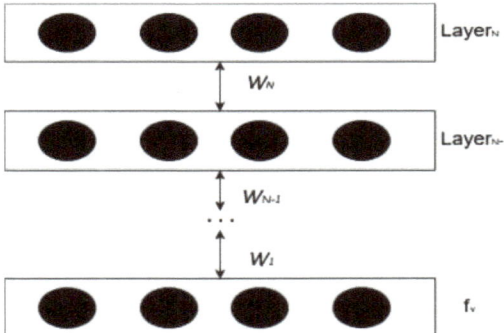

Fig. (4). Structure of DBN.

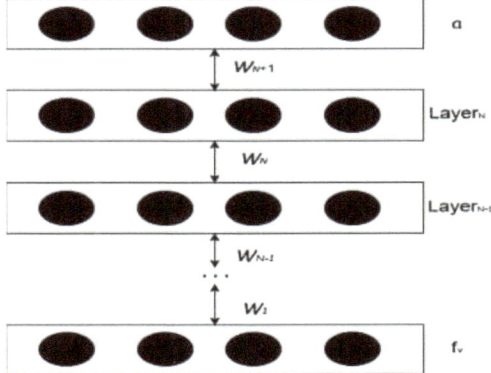

Fig. (5). Structure of DNN.

Fig. (**5**) illustrates how the DBN is enhanced to become a Deep Neural Network by adding label and binary classification layer information. Now, the label data is used to train this DNN model using a bottom-up supervised learning methodology. During the supervised learning phase, each node in a DNN layer is assigned a weight parameter. This parameter can be altered by using the gradient descent methodology. The main function of the recommended DNN model, a binary cross entropy loss function, seeks to lower the total cost of the system, as shown in Algorithm 1.

Algorithm 1: Deep learning-based intrusion detection model.

```
Require: N - List of all header tags from all packets in network interface queue.
 1: function PREDICT(Cache)        /*where cachePipe - is the pipe established with
    cache*/
 2:     matrix ← Cache        /*translate packets to matrices*/
 3:     Extract features from matrix
 4:     Define dataset_train & dataset_test
 5:     Initialize Sequential deep-learning model
 6:     if initialized then
 7:         Compile binary-crossentropy classifier
 8:         m ← Sequential deep-learning model
 9:     end if
10:     Training: m ← dataset_train
11:     if Training is complete then
12:         Prediction: m ← dataset_test
13:         if Predictions are correct then
14:             Re-Train the model
15:         else
16:             Invoke Mitigation Phase
17:         end if
18:     end if
19:     Store: classificationStore ← Predictions    /*store the classifier model*/
20: end function
```

For training and evaluating the predictions, the deep neural network model is retrofitted. This classifier is kept by the machine learning module in the classification store, a secondary storage unit. To build the suggested intrusion detection system, we separated the dataset into subsets for training and testing. As instructed, we compare the training dataset with the testing dataset to test the proposed intrusion detection system. If the predictions made during testing do not match the results from the testing dataset, the system merges the training and testing datasets and retrains itself *via* cross-validation.

RESULTS

This section of the study describes the results of testing the proposed intrusion detection system on Cooja Simulations for the blackhole, wormhole, distributed denial of service, sinkhole assaults, and opportunistic

The five metrics—recall, precision, F1 score, and training time—that the recommended intrusion detection system must meet throughout 150 separate runs are graphically displayed in this section. A training cycle and a testing cycle make up each run.

Blackhole Attack

The accuracy and recall of the suggested IDS are assessed in Figs. (**6** and **7**) using various studies for the detection of blackhole attacks. A suggested intrusion detection system continuously demonstrates a precision of 0.9, while other intrusion detection systems give an average precision of 0.7. However, our IDS's recall is on par with previous efforts. As seen in Fig. (**8**), the suggested IDS regularly outperforms previous efforts in terms of F1 score.

Opportunistic Service Attack

As Figs. (**9** and **10**) show, the precision for opportunistic service attacks normalizes to 0.9 from the beginning, yet it is significantly higher than the precision shown by other IDSs. However, compared to previous intrusion detection systems, the suggested IDS has a significantly higher recall rate of 0.95. The suggested IDS and existing IDSs have a comparable F1 score (Fig. **11**) because of comparable precision.

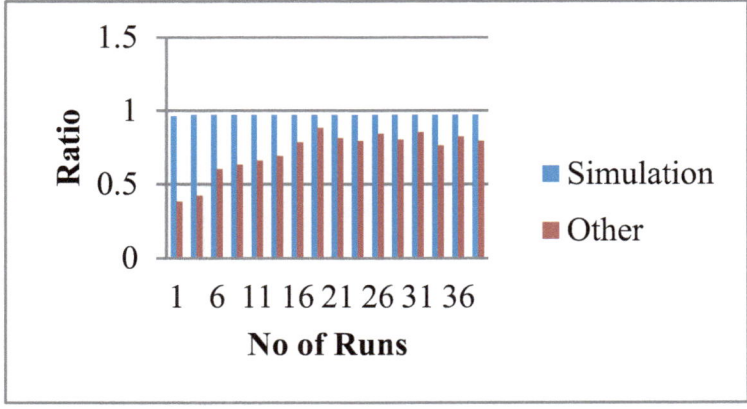

Fig. (6). Blackhole attack precision.

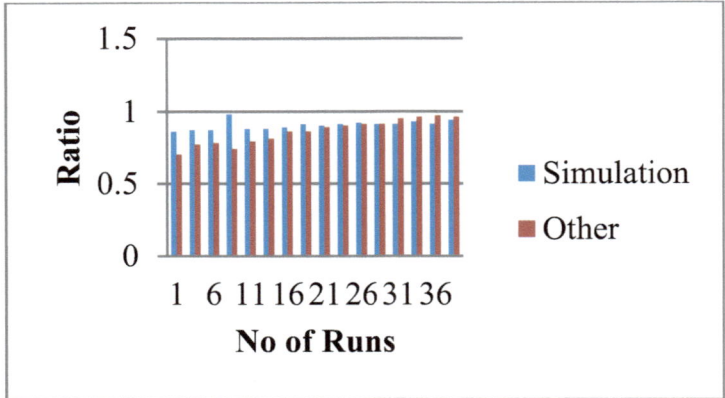

Fig. (7). Blackhole attack recall.

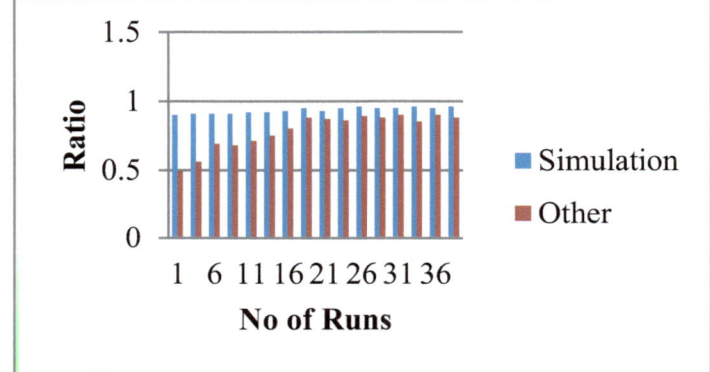

Fig. (8). Blackhole attack F1 score.

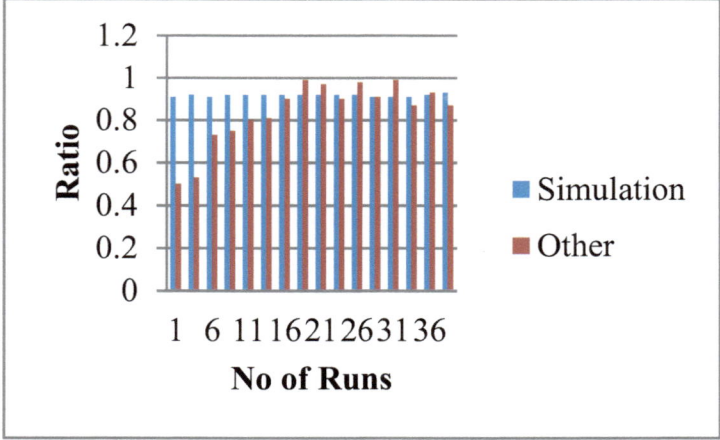

Fig. (9). Opportunistic attack precision.

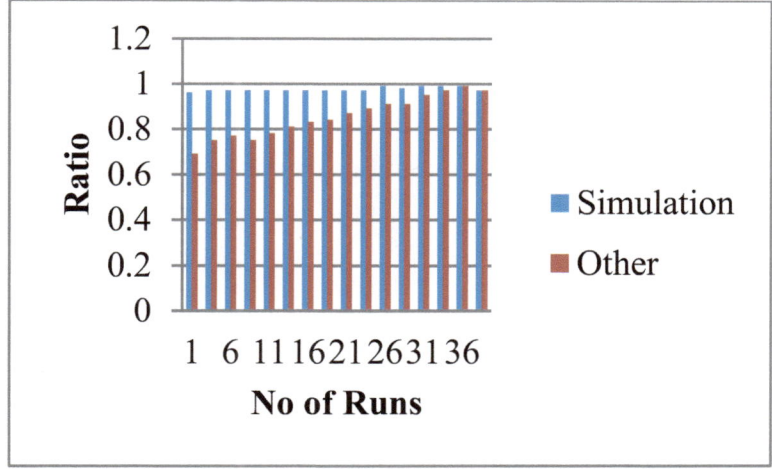

Fig. (10). Opportunistic attack recall.

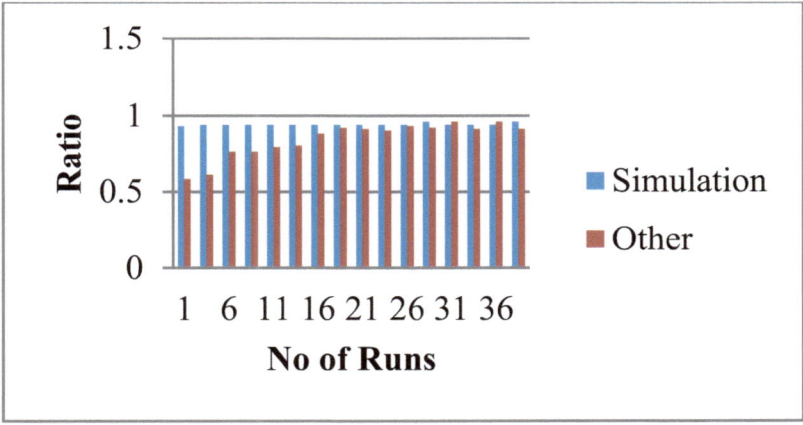

Fig. (11). Opportunistic attack F1 score.

DDoS Attack

The suggested IDS considerably outperformed other IDSs, which only displayed 0.8 precision and 0.9 recalls, as seen in Figs. (**12** and **13**). Its precision (0.9) and recall (0.93) rates were also significantly higher. Every intrusion detection method outperforms DDoS attacks (Fig. **14**). However, the suggested IDS and other IDSs have F1 scores that fall between 0.8 and 0.9. We put the recommended intrusion detection system through wormhole and sinkhole assaults in a test bed constructed with real IoT sensors.

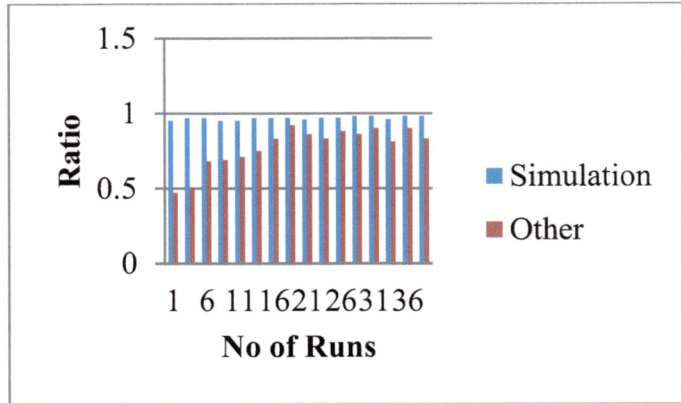

Fig. (12). DDoS attack precision.

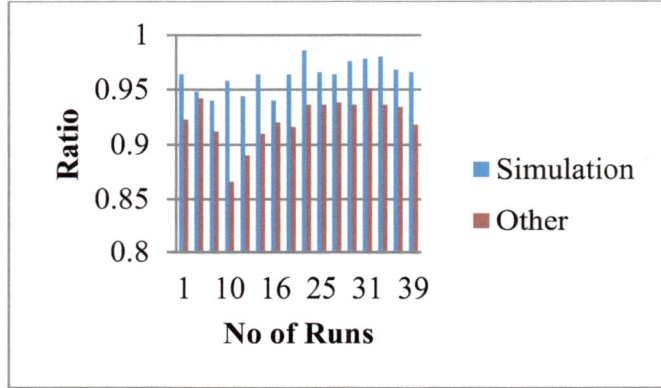

Fig. (13). DDoS attack recall.

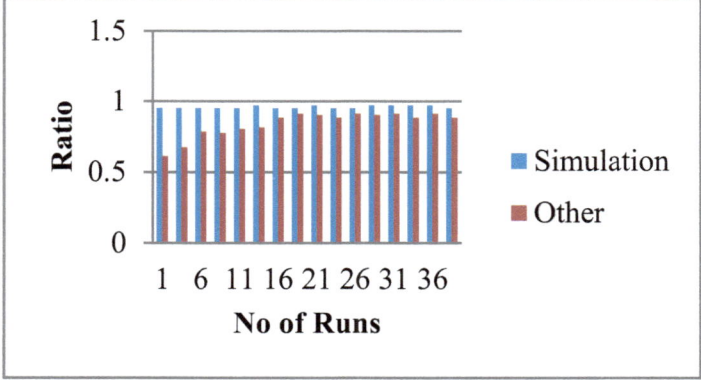

Fig. (14). DDoS F1 score.

Sinkhole Attack

Fig. (**15**) illustrates how the suggested IDS's precision for sinkhole attacks normalizes to 0.95 in the IoT sensor test bed and simulation test bed. However, recall for the IoT sensor test bed decreased significantly, as seen in Fig. (**16**), going from 0.96 to 0.9. The lossy wireless transmission medium in the test bed for IoT sensors is the cause of this reduction. In both test beds, the F1 score (Fig. **17**) was similar despite the decline in the recall rate.

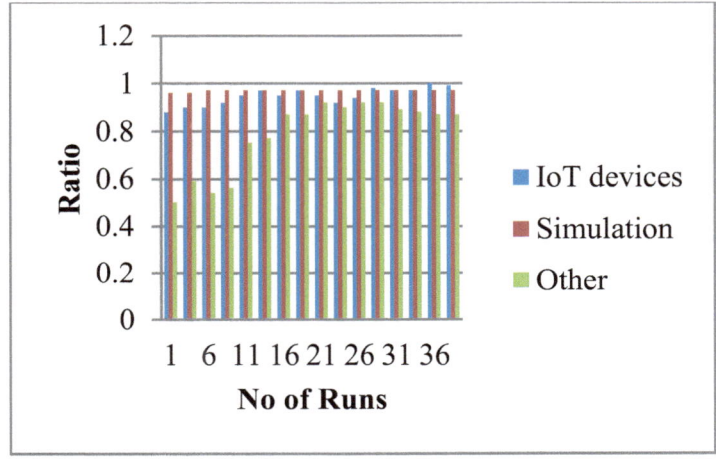

Fig. (15). Sinkhole attack precision.

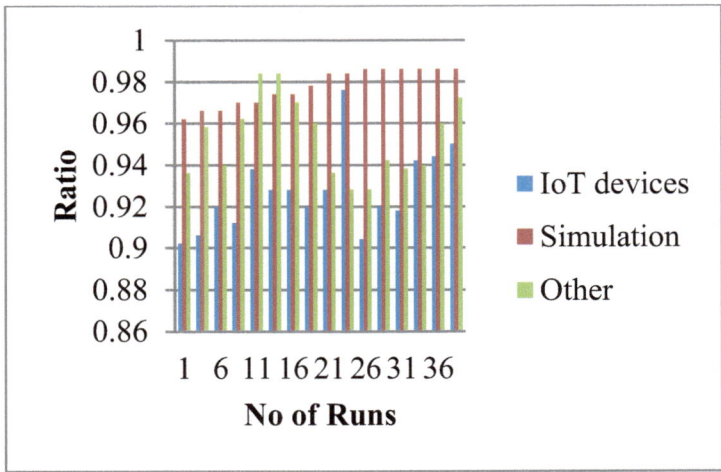

Fig. (16). Sinkhole attack recall.

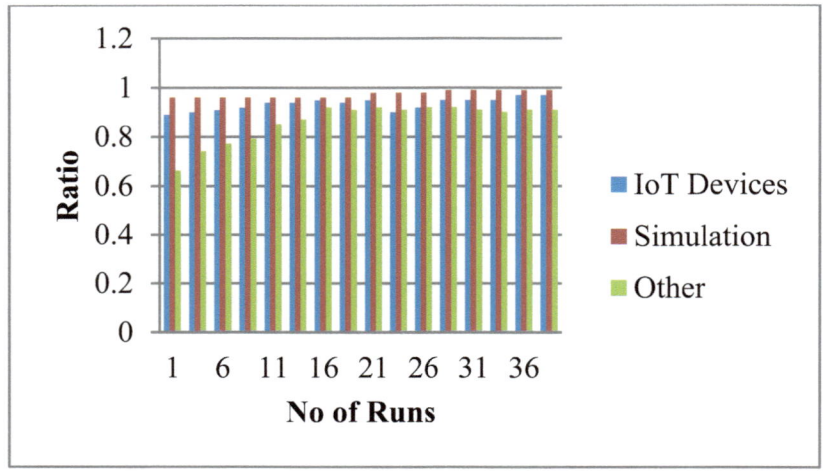

Fig. (17). Sinkhole attack F1 score.

Wormhole Attack

The precision, recall, and F1 score values for our IDS and other works normalize to an average rate of 0.9, as shown in Figs. (**18, 5, 19** and **20**).

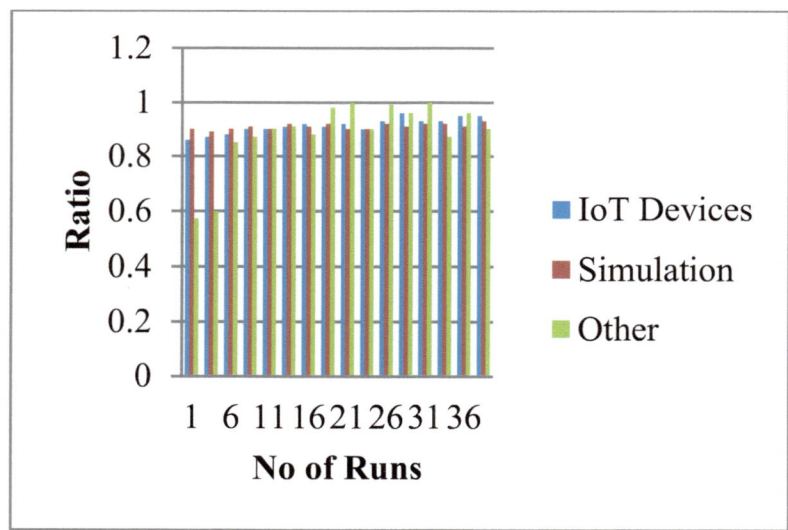

Fig. (18). Wormhole attack precision.

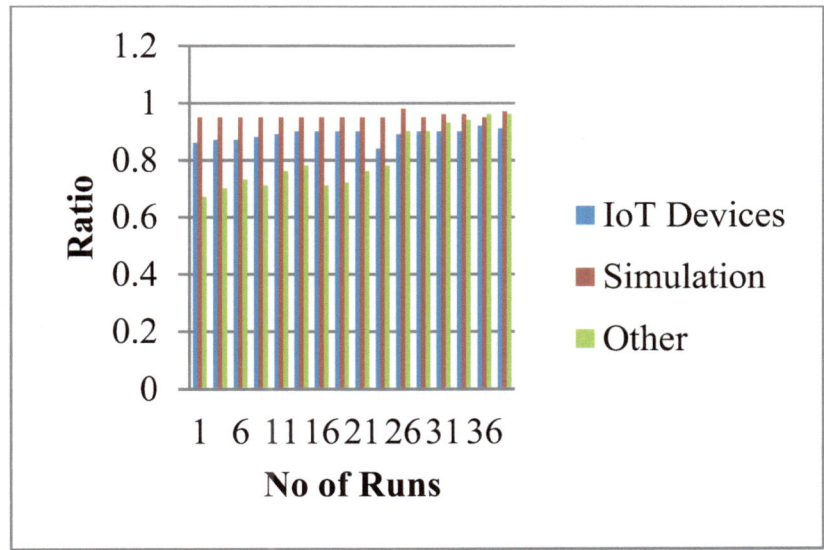

Fig. (19). Wormhole attack recall.

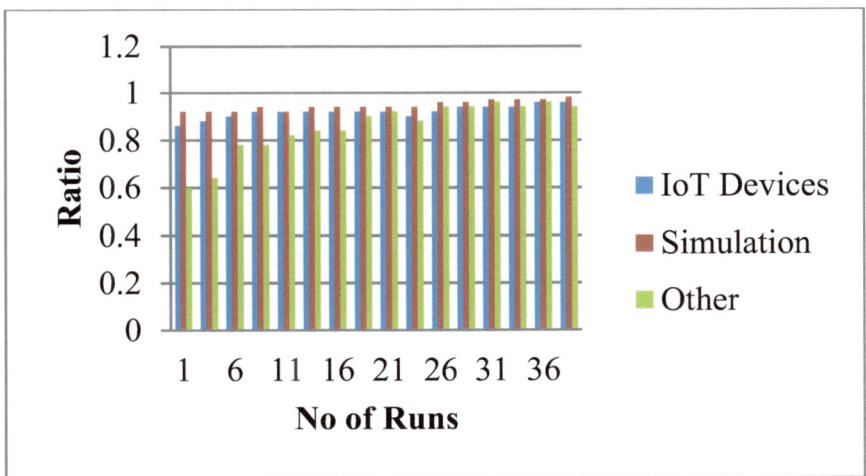

Fig. (20). Wormhole attack F1 score.

The training time for the IID is unchanged because it was trained once before these tests, which is an essential point to notice. The suggested intrusion detection system performs similarly in real-world network configurations as it does in simulated network traffic. To compare our intrusion detection systems with those in the literature, we also build a variety of them using rules-based, Inverse Weight Clustering, and signature-based methodologies. We put them to the test in a simulated network environment, looking for the five threats listed above.

DISCUSSION

Analysis

The proposed intrusion detection system, which leverages deep learning for anomaly detection in IoT networks, was assessed using the labeled testing dataset. The six values that make up each record in the testing dataset are transmission mode, duration, source and destination IP address transmission rates, reception rates, data-value information, and binary label information. Together, these records make up 33.333% of the input dataset. The length, data-value information, source-IP, and destination-IP readings were obtained using the IoT sensors of the Cooja simulator; the transmission rate, reception rate, transmission-to-reception ratio, and transmission mode values were determined using additional simulation components.

Whether a network transaction is malicious or benign is indicated by the binary label information. Three hundred and six hundred labeled training datasets, or 66.668% of the input dataset, were used to train the Deep Neural Network. After that, it was tested using the testing dataset, but the binary label information specifying the binary classification to which each record in the testing dataset corresponded was not given to it. Stated differently, the testing dataset without binary labels was used to train the Deep Neural Network. The testing dataset had 39687 unlabeled records; therefore, 39687 predictions in the form of "0" or "1" are produced by the deep-learning model.

Following that, each record's original labels from the testing dataset were compared with the test results, and the findings indicate:

- 9837 projected invasions turned out to be anomalies in all. As a result, the intrusion detection system's true positive (TP) value is:

$$TP = 9837$$

- There were 476 expected invasions out of which the actual number was regular traffic. As a result, the intrusion detection system's true positive (FP) value is:

$$FP = 476$$

- 226 projected normal charts turned out to be anomalies in all. As a result, the intrusion detection system's true positives (FN) value is:

$$FN = 226$$

The following actual values are required to compute the performance measures of the suggested model, such as the F1 score, sensitivity, and precision:

Considering that Dt is the testing dataset's entire number of entries,

$$D_t = 19845$$

There are 9495 genuine normality values in the testing dataset. If the testing dataset's actual number of normality is represented by Dnormal, then.

$$D_{normal} = 9495$$

The testing dataset has 10350 abnormalities in total. Using the testing dataset as an example, let $D_{anomaly}$ denote the real number of anomalies.

$$D_{anomaly} = 10350$$

The suggested intrusion detection system's sensitivity, or recall, for identifying anomalies is 0.950434.

$$\frac{TP}{D_{anomoly}} = \frac{9837}{10350} = .950434$$

The suggested intrusion detection system's accuracy in sounding an alarm when abnormalities are discovered is 0.953844.

$$\frac{TP}{FP + TP} = \frac{9837}{9837 + 476} = .953844$$

The suggested intrusion detection system has an F1 score of 0.952195.

$$\frac{2 * (precision * recall)}{(precision + recall)} = \frac{1.8131315}{1.904278} = 0.9521359$$

The accuracy and false positive rate of anomaly detection are typically used to assess them. However, additional performance criteria including precision, F1 score, and sensitivity are also important. On the other hand, the suggested intrusion detection system based on deep learning has demonstrated 95.38% accuracy in correctly labeling the aberrant network traffic in an Internet of Things network. The high accuracy percentage suggests that anomaly-based intrusion detection using deep learning can yield very accurate results. Moreover, it has been demonstrated that employing deep neural networks for classification yields higher accuracy than utilizing clustering algorithms.

The suggested intrusion detection system has an overall accuracy of 95.38%, which is higher than that of previous work. The results indicate that the number of classifiers has no bearing on the IoT environment because binary classifiers appear to be sufficient for achieving detection accuracy. Furthermore, the suggested intrusion detection system outperforms conventional intrusion detection systems in terms of performance.

CONCLUSION

The suggested intrusion detection system skillfully makes use of a deep learning algorithm in conjunction with network virtualization to effectively adjust to the needs of Internet of Things networks. Various network adapters are utilized to intercept network traffic and convert communication protocols into a comprehensible format. Preprocessing is done on this data to extract various network traffic aspects. Throughout the testing and deployment stage, these attributes are put into a lightweight deep neural network, which trains itself to create a binary classifier that can distinguish between malicious and benign network traffic. An average detection rate accuracy of 85% was obtained after 150 runs of evaluating the suggested IDS against five different attack types: wormhole, distributed denial of service, blackhole, opportunistic service, and sinkhole. Up to the first thirty runs, the detection rate increases steadily; after that, the accuracy normalizes at 95%. This suggests that within the first thirty runs, the suggested intrusion detection system was fully trained. Before it was fully trained, the proposed intrusion detection system was seen to have an average false-positive rate of 4%.

This pattern demonstrates that the suggested intrusion detection system may secure Internet of Things networks effectively and dependably while using a minimal amount of computing and power resources. We can infer, based on test findings from an actual sensor-based Internet of Things network that deploying the suggested intrusion detection system in an IoT network to differentiate between authentic attacks and those that appear to be legitimate is both feasible and practicable.

REFERENCES

[1] A. Paul, and R. Jeyaraj, "Internet of Things: A primer", *Hum. Behav. Emerg. Technol.*, vol. 1, no. 1, pp. 37-47, 2019.
[http://dx.doi.org/10.1002/hbe2.133]

[2]   A. Shahraki, A. Taherkordi, O. Haugen, and F. Eliassen, "A survey and future directions on clustering: From WSNs to IoT and modern networking paradigms", *IEEE Trans. Netw. Serv. Manag.*, vol. 18, no. 2, pp. 2242-2274, 2021.
[http://dx.doi.org/10.1109/TNSM.2020.3035315]

[3]   I. Butun, P. Österberg, and H. Song, "Security of the Internet of Things: Vulnerabilities, attacks, and countermeasures", *IEEE Commun. Surv. Tutor.*, vol. 22, no. 1, pp. 616-644, 2020.
[http://dx.doi.org/10.1109/COMST.2019.2953364]

[4]   N. Herencsar, "Ubiquitous Connectivity of Consumer IoT Devices", *IEEE Consum. Electron. Mag.*, vol. 11, no. 4, pp. 9-10, 2022.
[http://dx.doi.org/10.1109/MCE.2022.3177030]

[5]   R. McCusker, "Transnational organized cyber crime: distinguishing threat from reality", In: *Transnational Financial Crime.* Routledge, 2017, pp. 415-432.
[http://dx.doi.org/10.4324/9781315084572-23]

[6]   K.P. Naik, and U.R. Joshi, "Performance analysis of constrained application protocol using Cooja simulator in Contiki OS", in *Proc. 2017 Int. Conf. Intelligent Computing, Instrumentation and Control Technologies (ICICICT),* Kannur, India, 2017, pp. 547–550.
[http://dx.doi.org/10.1109/ICICICT1.2017.8342622]

[7]   B. Arrington, L. Barnett, R. Rufus, and A. Esterline, "Behavioral modeling intrusion detection system (BMIDS) using Internet of things (IoT) behavior-based anomaly detection via immunity-inspired algorithms", In: *Proc. 2016 25th Int. Conf. Computer Communication and Networks (ICCCN),* Waikoloa, HI, USA, Aug. 2016, pp. 1–6.

[8]   K. Gupta, and S. Shukla, "Internet of Things: Security challenges for next generation networks", *2016 International Conference on Innovation and Challenges in Cyber Security (ICICCS-INBUSH),* Greater Noida, India, 2016, pp. 315-318.
[http://dx.doi.org/10.1109/ICICCS.2016.7542301]

[9]   T. Xu, J.B. Wendt, and M. Potkonjak, "Security of IoT systems: Design challenges and opportunities", *2014 IEEE/ACM International Conference on Computer-Aided Design (ICCAD),* San Jose, CA, USA, 2014, pp. 417-423.
[http://dx.doi.org/10.1109/ICCAD.2014.7001385]

[10] M. Azrour, J. Mabrouki, A. Guezzaz, and A. Kanwal, "Internet of Things security: challenges and key issues", *Secur. Commun. Netw.*, vol. 2021, pp. 1-11, 2021.
[http://dx.doi.org/10.1155/2021/5533843]

[11] O. Solon, "A team of hackers takes remote control of a Tesla Model S from 12 miles away", *The Guardian,* p. 20, 2016.

[12] A. Mayzaud, R. Badonnel, and I. Chrisment, "A Taxonomy of Attacks in RPL-based Internet of Things", *Int. J. Netw. Secur.*, vol. 18, no. 3, pp. 459-473, 2016.

[13] A.O. Bang, U.P. Rao, P. Kaliyar, and M. Conti, "Assessment of routing attacks and mitigation techniques with RPL control messages: A survey", *ACM Comput. Surv.*, vol. 55, no. 2, pp. 1-36, 2023.
[http://dx.doi.org/10.1145/3494524]

[14] M. Khan, B.N. Silva, and K. Han, "Internet of things based energy-aware smart home control system", *IEEE Access,* vol. 4, pp. 7556-7566, 2016.
[http://dx.doi.org/10.1109/ACCESS.2016.2621752]

[15] W.A. Jabbar, M.H. Alsibai, N.S.S. Amran, and S.K. Mahayadin, "Design and implementation of IoT-based automation system for smart home", In: *Proc. 2018 Int. Symp. Networks, Computers and Communications (ISNCC),* Rome, Italy, 2018, pp. 1–6.
[http://dx.doi.org/10.1109/ISNCC.2018.8531006]

CHAPTER 7

E-analysis and Notarization of Social Media based on Blockchain Technology

K. Santhanalakshmi[1,*], **G. Madhumita**[2], **Martin Selvakumar Mohanan**[3], **Sathish Kumar R.**[4], **Belsam Jeba Ananth M.**[5], **Subhrajit Chanda**[6] and **Gunjan Chhabra**[7]

[1] *Faculty of Management, SRM Institute of Science and Technology, Kattankulathur, India*

[2] *Department of Management Studies, Vels Institute of Science Technology and Advanced Studies (VISTAS) Chennai, India*

[3] *Department of Organization & Human Resource Management, Great Lakes Institute of Management, Chennai, India*

[4] *Department of Artificial Intelligence and Machine Learning, Faculty of Engineering and Technology, Jain University (Deemed-to-be-University), Bengaluru, India*

[5] *Department of Mechatronics Engineering, SRM Institute of Science and Technology, Kattankulathur, India*

[6] *Jindal Global Law School, OP Jindal Global University, Sonipat, India*

[7] *Department of Computer Science and Engineering, Graphic Era Hill University, Dehradun, India*

Abstract: Social media has completely changed how people communicate on a worldwide scale by offering a robust platform for idea sharing, contract negotiations, and the submission of fresh business concepts. However, a number of problems, such as inaccurate information, inadequate content screening, copyright infringement, hacking, identity theft, and fake news, limit the use of social media. This paper presents a proof-of-credibility (PoC) and notarization service-based blockchain strategy for identifying fake news and preventing its spread through social media. Social media platforms are using machine learning methods as part of their marketing strategies. On social media, however, deliberately created screenshots and bogus news are constantly created and shared. Blockchain technology is a good platform for notarizing online activity because it can store data in a safe, unchangeable manner. The Proof-of-Concept methodology was tested on two datasets of notable tweets gathered from various news sources on Twitter. We propose a framework for the authenticated archiving of social media content using blockchain technology. A text message scenario is given as a proof-of-concept based on the suggested strategy, and the results demonstrate how well the suggested approach works in identifying rumors and halting their spread.

---

[*] **Corresponding author K. Santhanalakshmi:** Faculty of Management, SRM Institute of Science and Technology, Kattankulathur, India; E-mail: santhank@srmist.edu.in

Keshav Kaushik, Rewa Sharma & Ayodeji Olalekan Salau (Eds.)
All rights reserved-© 2026 Bentham Science Publishers

Keywords: Blockchain, E-analysis, Fake news, Machine learning, Notarization, PoC, Social media.

INTRODUCTION

Social media refers to internet sites that let users create social networks or engage with others who have similar interests, pastimes, life experiences, or connections [1]. It is now very difficult to share essential materials on social media sites like Facebook, Twitter, and Instagram if you do not first evaluate its credibility. The spread of incorrect information and fake news on social media platforms poses a severe threat to academics and Social Network Service Providers (SNPs) [2]. Furthermore, because people are more prone to disseminate fake information across their social networks farther, faster, and deeper than real information, on social media, this false information spreads like wildfire [3]. Furthermore, it is challenging to prosecute criminals due to the absence of credible digital evidence.

This study provides a revolutionary technique to notarize social media content using blockchain technology, together with Proof of Credibility (PoC) that can detect false information spread throughout social networks and validate shared information [4].

Businesses use machine learning findings to better understand customer perspectives and to enhance their marketing tactics. Machine learning instruments can help electronic advertisers more effectively indicate and understand data, which is an advantage. By maintaining apprised of consumer tastes and providing the required information, one may forecast the actions of online customers. The generation and dissemination of information could be altered by developing blockchain-based solutions [5]. When creating a trusted social system, blockchain technology can offer transactions that are transparent, verifiable, trustworthy, immutable, and dependable [6].

A blockchain is an ever-expanding collection of blocks that include transaction data, a timestamp, and a cryptographic hash of the previous block [7]. Data integrity is immediately guaranteed by blockchain technology once transaction data is recorded there. Blockchain is the perfect platform for notarization services because of this feature. Ensuring that input data are not changed before being incorporated into a block is an important but difficult issue. Then, if you want to notarize user-provided content that is unchangeable, an official social media service provider can be of great assistance. Specifically, official service providers can submit a document or photo with a digital signature in response to requests from users on social media accounts. The document's validity can be confirmed through the use of a public key infrastructure (PKI) protocol.

Any document that lacks an authentic signature from the official service provider shall be regarded as fraudulent according to the PKI standard. Furthermore, it is anticipated that the malevolent actions of spreading false information would significantly reduce because any attempt at shifting public opinion using fake news will be permanently stored in the blockchain.

We look into the idea of applying blockchain theory to the creation of a unique Proof of Credibility (PoC) protocol that may be used to identify false information spread *via* social networks and validate shared information. 1003 notable tweets pertaining to the famous hashtag #ISIS and 802 remarkable tweets pertaining to the well-known hashtag #Halamadrid, collected from multiple news outlets on Twitter, are used to evaluate the proposed technique. The results demonstrated that a standard blockchain consensus could be established to verify the accuracy of information and stop misinformation from spreading on social media. Proof of Concept (PoC) will be the first blockchain solution to address the issue of false information and fake news on social media.

Objective of Study

- To look into the potential of applying blockchain theory to the creation of a revolutionary Proof of Credibility (PoC) protocol that can be used to identify false information on social media networks and validate material that has been posted.
- To examine how social media posts can be notarized using blockchain technology.
- To get over the primary problems with censorship, fake news, and privacy on social media.

LITERATURE REVIEW

Notarization

Notarization usually involves a variety of procedures to assure the parties to a transaction (such as business formation, patent applications, and intellectual estate protection) that the documents certifying the transaction are legitimate [8]. Every one of those processes involves a number of parties, from the party seeking notarization to the central authority, which essentially verifies the accuracy and validity of the required documents and the signatures placed on them. To put it simply, by monitoring the procedure, the central organization assures the legitimacy of the transaction.

Let us examine the situation from the standpoints of the IT administrator, the notary public, and the person who granted the power of attorney. Thanks to

Arredondo's [9] study from these three different angles, we have a basic understanding of a few of the necessary conditions to set up a blockchain-based notarization service. It becomes clear that one of the most important things to consider is the date of data registration on the blockchain, as already mentioned by Maesa and Mori [10]. There may even be a few-hour lag between when the blockchain data registration request is made and when it is completed, depending on the level of congestion on the blockchain network. Furthermore, it becomes necessary to store the supplied papers in a repository in some manner so that they may be accessed in the event that their validity needs to be confirmed [11].

There are currently a number of decentralized and centralized blockchain-based notarization programs available on the market. We determined the attributes and capabilities that notarization software ought to have in order to compare them. These are the notarization apps:

- Blockchains supported
- Hash custody
- Free space size
- Centralized or decentralized archive server type
- Customized notarized file template
- File custody
- Multiple digital signatures
- File sharing
- Large-scale file upload
- P2P file custody
- Notarization Report (PDF)

History of Blockchain

Distributed, always-available, immutable, irreversible, and duplicate-able public data storage is what a blockchain is. Without the assistance of a third party, it enables trustless individuals to agree on an immutable and auditable piece of data [12]. Put differently, blockchain technology enables the creation of an append-only secure database that depends on a distributed, decentralized agreement mechanism to determine what newly added data is valid. Different blockchain versions differ in terms of who can join the network and how data is stored there.

When everyone can read a blockchain and utilize it to conduct transactions, as well as when everyone can take part in reaching a consensus, the blockchain is said to be public [13]. Consequently, there is not a centralized register or a trustworthy third party.

On the other hand, if a small and predetermined number of participants can only reach a consensus, the blockchain is referred to as private (or semi-private). Organizations grant write access and read permissions can be restricted or made public. Consensus processes for private blockchains are typically simple and straightforward.

Transactions or data are often stored on the blockchain. This guarantees that the chain will behave in an ACID (Atomicity, Consistency, Isolation, and Durability) manner [14]. As a result of the blockchain's logic, many users must maintain duplicates of everything. Even if data is lost or corrupted in one node, it is simple for it to synchronize with additional nodes in the network. As a result, it might offer durability.

Attack using False Data

The technology of Blockchain is generally thought to be a useful tool for maintaining the integrity of transaction data. Diverse sectors are starting to make an effort to capitalize on this feature. Notary services are one of the blockchain's most promising application areas [15]. Provable digital proof can be obtained with a blockchain-based notary service since the notarized content's integrity is verified cryptographically.

Despite the blockchain's suitability for notary services, a significant security flaw exists. That's an example of a fabricating data attack: adding fake data to a blockchain in order to trick other people, like in Fig. (**1**). When it comes to cryptocurrencies, the blockchain can be used for all transaction verification. About the notarization service, it is not the case, nevertheless. Before being notarized, the contents must be verified; however, the blockchain network's nodes lack the necessary data to verify the input data's accuracy. It indicates that the legitimacy of an input document cannot be determined by the blockchain system alone.

However, several services were introduced without taking into account the negative consequences of the attack that falsified data [16]. Put another way, it is possible to notarize fake data using the present blockchain notary services. Even if they only check to see if a document was saved by a particular user at a particular time, notary services nevertheless assert that their service may replace the current notary system. Such notary services are difficult to trust unless they offer an open verification process. Building a system that is resistant to the fabricating data attack is therefore essential.

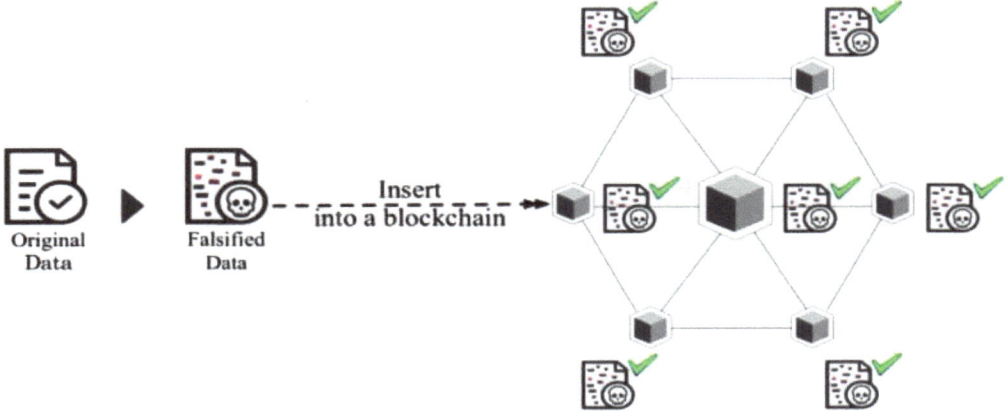

Fig. (1). An example of an assault using falsified data. Nodes in a blockchain network are unable to determine whether incoming data is legitimate.

Social Media Security based on Blockchain

Identifying rumors automatically and preventing their spread are extremely difficult tasks for trustworthy social network designers. Several tactics have been developed to counteract misleading material on social media sites [17, 18]. The advantages of machine learning-based methods are being used in recent studies to identify false information [19, 20]. Sentiment analysis combined with IP network analysis has been used in several methods to discover social network rumors [21]. Additionally, a few studies attempted to use Natural Language Processing techniques to overcome this issue [22]. These studies, however, are very limited in what they can detect and yield imprecise results when it comes to fake news.

LinkedIn uses algorithms to predict which people would be the best candidates for a given position. Employing machine learning methods, it finds potential who are searching for novel possibilities or who are more inclined to respond. With the latest update to its assistance, Twitter now lets users create thumbnails from full images employing machine learning or crop images employing facial recognition. As a result, on rare occasions, it could commit numerous False Positive and False Negative mistakes. Blockchain technology can therefore be used to redevelop social network systems for P2P communication, giving users back control over their shared posts. The following are the main benefits of using blockchain-based methods to identify false information:

- Improved security and privacy.
- Architecture of decentralized social networks.
- User control through content distribution.

- Automatic online verification of shared data.
- Provides strong authentication and guarantees privacy.

METHODOLOGY

Notarization Approach

In this part, an inventive technique for preventing a data fabrication attack on a blockchain-based notarization service is provided. The idea is that, instead of users, a social media service provider creates a digital signature and a snapshot of a document that needs to be certified. This technique can prevent users from attempting to fake a snapshot because they do not have the service provider's private key. The system effectively inhibits forgery by users, service providers, and unauthorized parties since the processes for creating and inserting digital evidence are run independently of each other. Subsequently, the PKI protocol can be followed to quickly verify the evidence. The process's sequence diagram is shown in Fig. (**2**). People may quickly weed out material that is not verified or has an incorrect digital signature using this method. The system is therefore able to thwart the attack of fabricating data.

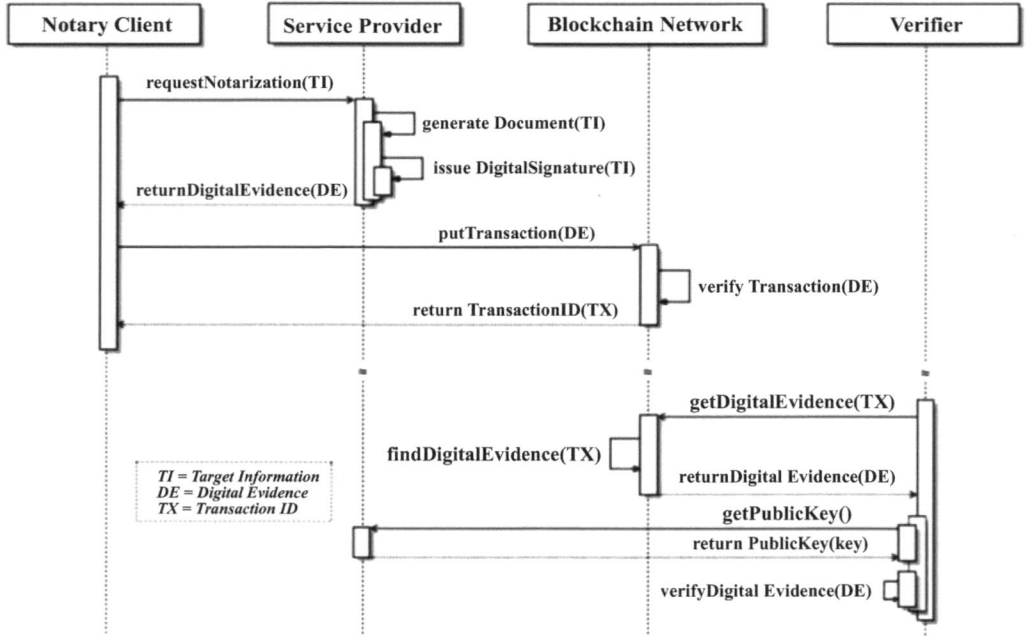

Fig. (2). An illustration of the suggested method's flow.

Approach for Proof of Credibility (POC)

In this study, we present Proof of Credibility referred to as PoC, a novel Blockchain method for identifying and blocking bogus news on social networks. Peer-to-peer computing PoC is the idea of re-engineering social networks as decentralized systems in which peers represent users. A distributed ledger is an unchangeable, cryptographically secured log of rumors that are contributed to by each peer. A fresh quantity of rumors that have been detected is indicated by each block in the blockchain, which makes up the framework of the distributed ledger. For instance, if the blockchain algorithm finds ten rumors, a new block is added to the chain. The PoC chain code, which is utilized with all peers on the social network platform, is used to create the recognition feature. They can run POC chain code through a blockchain browser. Fig. (**4**) outlines the protocol's design paradigm, whereas, Fig. (**3**) depicts the blockchain-based social network system.

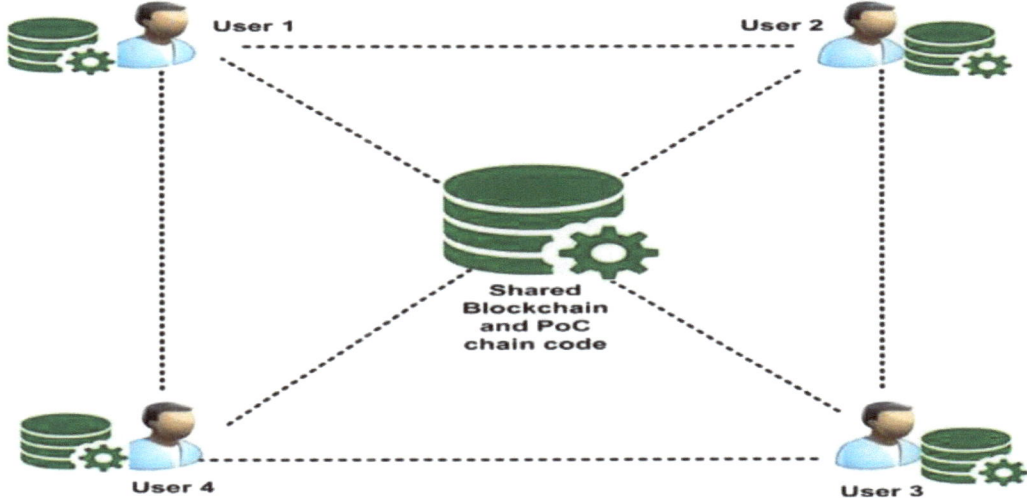

Fig. (3). A diagram illustrating the Blockchain-based Social Network System.

PoC is founded on the idea of evaluating the information source's dependability. We may find noteworthy content from an online newspaper, magazine, TV news channel, radio station, wire service, or user-generated blog. The Best Match method (BM25F) measure serves as the foundation for PoC functionality [23]. It can be applied to assess the reliability of newsworthy internet sources [24].

Two dependent elements can be used to calculate the trustworthiness of a source. The first factor, which determines the believability weight (W) value for information sources, is related to Equation (**1**).

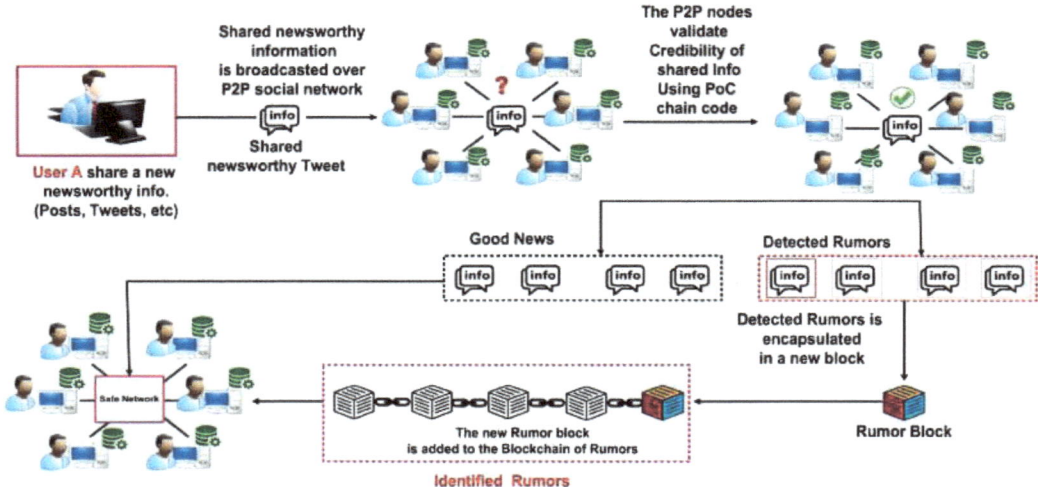

Fig. (4). Model of proof of creditability.

$$W(S_i) = \frac{Occuree \times Boost}{[(1-b)+b \times \frac{\#post}{\#Followers}]} \quad (1)$$

Where "occuree" is the total amount of tweets and shared posts about the source within a specific trending subject at a specific time t. As seen in Table **1**, the use of Boost, sometimes referred to as the boost factor, depends on the kind of information source. The boost figures come from News Trust, a review platform that evaluates news reports based on journalistic merit rather than mere readership.

Table 1. Boost the values of the most popular newsworthy information sources.

Source of News	Values of Boost
Magazines	3.69
Blogs	3.57
Newspaper	3.30
Radio	3.61
Online sites	3.70
TV news channels	3.55

The PoC-chain code can be developed similarly to Algorithm 1 in order to implement the detection methodology and assess the reliability of the information.

```
Algorithm 1: PoC Detection Methodology

1: Input: Time $T = \{t_1, t_2, t_3, \ldots t_n\}$
2: Input: News $= \{N_1, N_2, N_3 \ldots N_p\}$
3: Output: Blockchain of Rumors $BR = \{B_1, B_2, B_3, \ldots B_n\}$
4: Procedure Rumors Detection
5: While ( is share news() )
6: for each $N \in News$ in $t_i$ Do
7: if ($N_i$. url IsTrue ()) Then
8: Source_News $\leftarrow N_i$
9: else
10: Blog_News $\leftarrow N_i$
11: End if
12: End for
13: for each $N_i \in Source\_News$
14: $Score(N_i) = SC (N_i. source)$
15: $Cred_{Threshold\ 1} = \sum_{i=1}^{i=n1} \frac{score(N_i)}{n1}$
16: if $(Score(N_i) < Cred_{Threshold})$
13: $B_j \leftarrow N_i$
14: else
15: Good info $\leftarrow$ Ignore $(N_i)$
16: End if
17: End for each
18: for each $N_i; \in Blog\_News$
19: $Score(N_i) = \frac{\#Reshare}{\#Followers} \times 100$
20: $Cred_{Threshold\ 1} = \sum_{i=1}^{i=n2} \frac{score(N_i)}{n2}$
21: if $(Score(N_i) < Cred_{Threshold})$
22: $B_j \leftarrow N_i$  // Add $N_j$, to the Block $B_j$
23: else
24: Good Info $\leftarrow$ Ignore $(N_i)$
25: return $B_j$
26: $BR \leftarrow B_j$,  // Add $B_j$, to the blockchain
27: Open (New Block $B_{j+1}$)
28: End While
29: End Procedure
```

RESULTS

Proof-of-concept

This section describes a smartphone instant messaging app that was created with the recommended methods as a proof-of-concept. Blockchain network (BN), Service provider (SP), and Notary client (NC) are the three key companies. Fig. (**5**) shows the system's overall workflow.

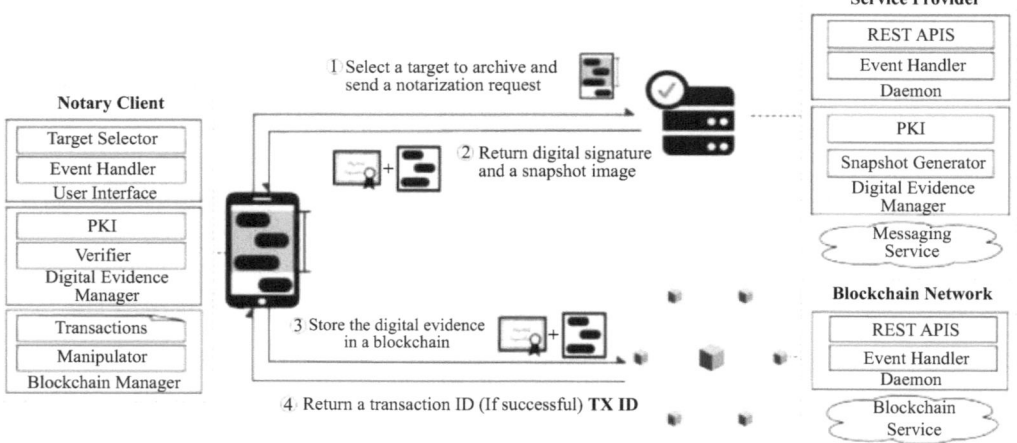

Fig. (5). Entire blockchain-based notarization service procedure..

Users can ask SP, a messaging service provider, to notarize content, such as conversation histories on their platforms. Users can designate particular content (such as a variety of conversation histories) to be preserved, and SP captures a digital proof of that content—that is, the digital signature and snapshot and emails it to the users. The digital signature is signed using the SP's private key. Because of this, a cryptographic module can verify the truths, which are corroborated by the veracity of the information and the presence of events on the social media picture.

A client application called NC serves as a bridge between BN and SP. NC offers a user interface (UI) for notarizing occurrences on social media networks. NC notifies SP of a target event and user details in a notarization request. NC initiates a transaction to upload the digital evidence to BN after receiving a photo and digital signature from SP. A user can retrieve a snapshot and confirm the list of valid transactions that are displayed by NC and saved in BN.

An all-purpose blockchain system called BN is used to record notary transactions. By using a distributed consensus process, nodes are able to securely validate transactions and add them to new blocks. Nodes cannot use data that is accessible in the actual world for transaction validation, as was covered in Section 2. Consequently, transaction validation is the procedure of determining if a digital piece of evidence has been authenticated by an authorized organization. When a new block containing numerous verified transactions is appended to the end of the old chain, the altered blockchain is synced across all nodes.

PoC Results

Two datasets gathered from Twitter have been used in a simulation experiment to examine the viability and efficacy of the suggested PoC technique. The two datasets are characterized as two popular subjects (#Halamadrid and #ISIS) that have a number of noteworthy tweets shared by various news outlets. A software application has been developed to gather tweets related to each trending subject over four-time intervals: the Twitter R library utility [25]. Table 2 provides a summary of the two dataset's general descriptions.

Table 2. Description of two datasets: #Halamadrid and #ISIS.

	#ISIS					#Halamadrid				
Source	Tweets	t1	t2	t3	t4	Tweets	t1	t2	t3	t4
Magazines	145	45	33	37	30	152	46	27	36	43
Blogs	115	24	22	38	31	103	29	21	25	28
Newspaper	277	65	72	58	82	179	38	45	56	40
Radio	95	24	15	21	35	97	28	32	16	21
Online sites	110	21	34	29	26	93	15	25	18	35
TV news channels	128	35	28	42	23	104	24	21	42	17
Wire service	105	25	37	25	18	46	13	14	9	10
Total	975	239	241	250	245	774	193	185	202	194

Based on the simulation findings applied to the two datasets, the PoC algorithm was capable of identifying bogus news as follows: Table 3 displays the number of tweets for each block: 201 in block 1, 266 in block 2, 204 in block 3, and 205 in block 4.

Table 3. The quantity of false information found in the #Halamadrid and # ISIS datasets over a four-time period.

Sources	t1		t2		t3		t4	
	ISIS	Halamadrid	ISIS	Halamadrid	ISIS	Halamadrid	ISIS	Halamadrid
Magazines	19	10	22	16	18	28	12	11
Blogs	5	11	24	16	13	18	10	20
Newspaper	40	15	43	22	21	13	33	16
Radio	7	8	10	16	14	9	15	17
Online sites	14	11	23	12	6	8	16	9
TV news channels	23	8	19	3	9	16	14	2

(Table 3) cont.....

Sources	t1		t2		t3		t4	
	ISIS	Halamadrid	ISIS	Halamadrid	ISIS	Halamadrid	ISIS	Halamadrid
Wire service	11	19	24	16	13	18	10	20
Total	B1=201		B2=266		B3=204		B4=205	

The overall amount of false news for each of the seven categories of information sources is also shown in Fig. (6).

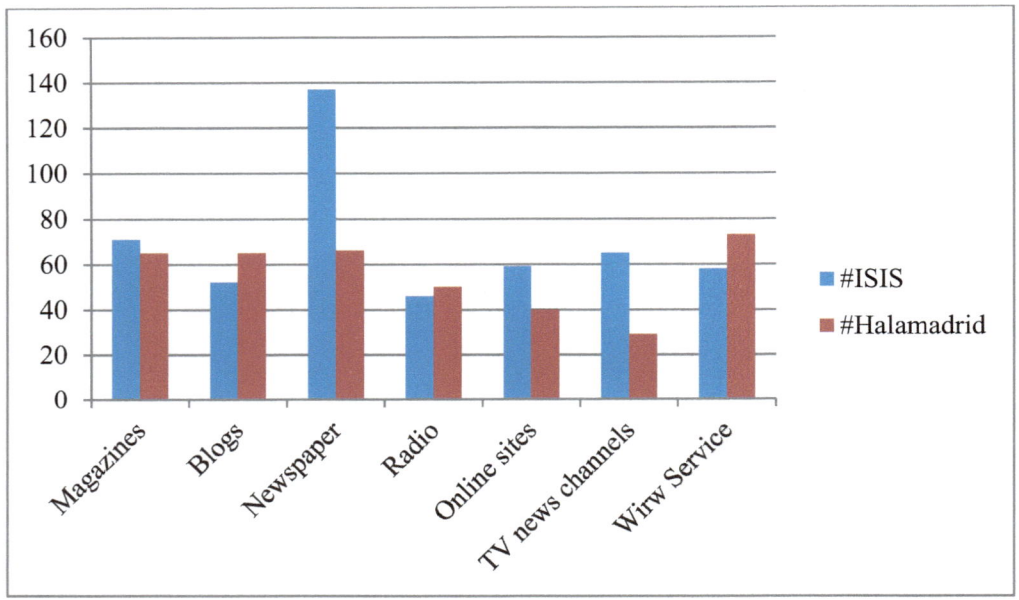

Fig. (6). The total amount of false information for the seven information type sources in the two examined datasets following the formation of four blockchain blocks.

The results suggest that online newspapers are the most popular source of fake news in the #ISIS dataset, whereas wire services are the top popular source in the #Halamadrid dataset. The percentages of bogus news found in the two datasets under examination are shown in the pi plot in Fig. (7).

The set of detected fake news (876 tweets) and good news (873 tweets) is outsourced to the Xpertin platform for verification of the acquired results. It employs a group of top social media service specialists. Only 790 tweets total or 90% of detected fake news are real, according to Xpertin's verification results and feedback, whereas 85% of detected good news is real or, in other words, only 691 tweets total are good news. This indicates, based on Xpertin's comments, that 86 tweets were identified as fraudulent and 59 as legitimate *via* the PoC technique. In light of the True Negative as TN, True Positive as TP, False Negative as FN, and False Positive as FP, the following formulas can be used to compute precision, recall, and accuracy: 2, 3, 4. Fig. (**8**) shows the accuracy, precision, and recall of the PoC technique.

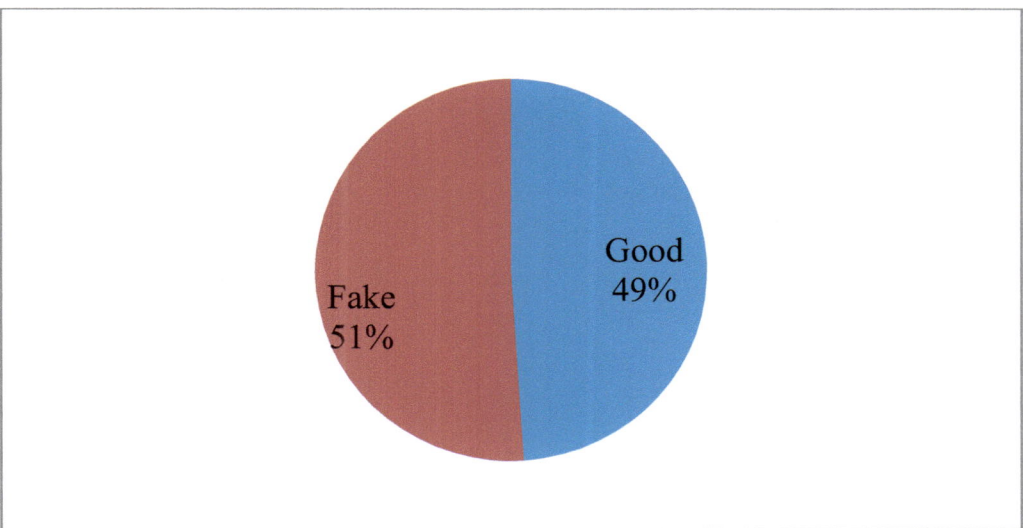

Fig. (7). The two data sets' total percentages of found fake news.

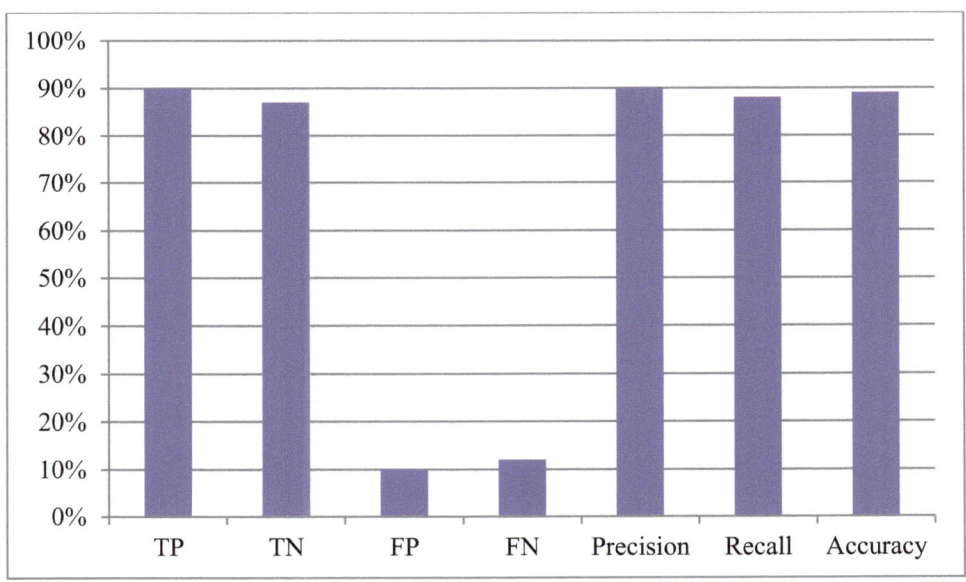

Fig. (8). Results for TN, TP, FN, FP, recall, precision and accuracy.

$$Precision = \frac{TP}{TP + FP} \tag{2}$$

where the number of tweets that are False Positives is equal to the number of tweets that are True Positives.

$$Recall = \frac{TP}{TP + FN} \tag{3}$$

Here, the quantity of False Negative tweets (FN) is equal to the quantity of True Positive tweets (TP).

$$Accuracy = \frac{TP + TN}{P + N} \tag{4}$$

Such that N = (TN + FP) and P = (FN + TP), TN is the True Negative tweet.

Furthermore, the PoC mechanism's Fall-Out, Specificity, Negative Predictive Value (NPV), and False Discovery Rate (FDR) are evaluated with the aid of formulae 5, 6, 7, and 8, and the results are displayed in Fig. (9).

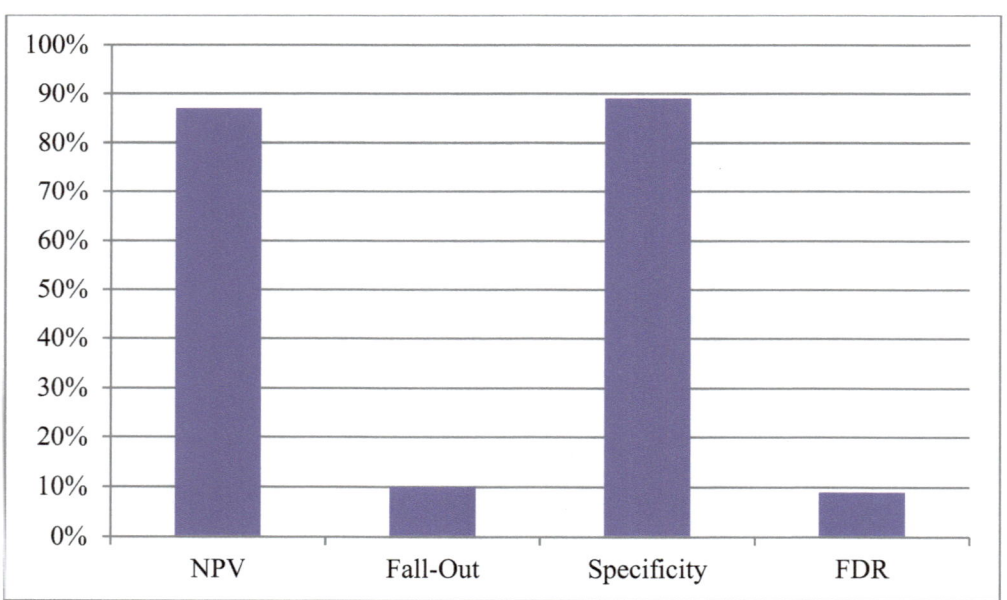

Fig. (9). Results for fall-out, NPV, FDR, and specificity.

$$NPV = \frac{TN}{TN + FN} \quad (5)$$

$$Fall - Out = \frac{FP}{FP + TN} \quad (6)$$

$$Specificity = \frac{TN}{TN + FP} \quad (7)$$

$$FDR = \frac{FP}{FP + TP} \quad (8)$$

Other research has underlined the need to apply blockchain technology to identify and stop misleading material in social networks, but it has not offered a fresh or practical blockchain solution to address this issue [26, 27]. This research was constrained to discussing the problem's state of the art alone, failing to provide a revolutionary blockchain-based algorithm that could identify false information in social media. Presenting Proof of Credibility (PoC), the first blockchain consensus, was the aim of this study in order to detect and suppress rumors and deception on social media. The study's most intriguing conclusion is that, despite the fact that the suggested blockchain algorithm is only a preliminary one, it can still need additional features and metrics in the future to detect false news with a satisfactory accuracy rate of 89%. Other noteworthy findings are the poor scores of Fall-Out and FDR (9% and 10%, respectively) in identifying rumors and fake news. Finding that 52% of all tweets in the two studied datasets are categorized as fake news is a little startling. This unexpected result implies that, in order to accurately assess the credibility of newsworthy content handled online, greater attention should be paid to other aspects (such as news coherence and consistency, as well as public acceptability and commons) [27]. Nonetheless, these results validate and promote the use of blockchain algorithms to regulate and govern the spread of information within social networks. There are no similar components that we may look into because this finding has never been released before and all prior research has handled the issue as a theoretical investigation and a review of the literature [29, 30]. But in order to distinguish false information in social networks, this work presents the first working blockchain algorithm that can be compared to other blockchain-based algorithms that may be created in the future. The outcomes should be regarded with caution since the suggested approach is only simulated on a limited collection of important tweets obtained from two well-known Twitter subjects. For more reliable analysis and assessment, the suggested method should be improved and tested on benchmarks and standardized datasets. It should also be tested over longer timeframes to examine the spread of rumors on the blockchain in more tracing. Even yet, this preliminary research indicates that the first blockchain-based algorithm should be used to manage and control the spread of information in social networks in order to identify false information and fake news [31]. Two other critical aspects should be the focus of future research: expanding the information credibility metrics in the suggested technique and modeling its effectiveness in benchmark and standardized datasets.

CONCLUSION

This study looked at the use of a unique blockchain-based algorithm for identifying and preventing disinformation and fake news on social media. Additionally, a blockchain application for social media platform content notarization was presented. Proof of Credibility (PoC), a novel blockchain consensus for spotting false information on social media platforms, was presented in the study. It also introduced a new kind of attack on a blockchain called a fabricating data attack and suggested a countermeasure for it.

Letting legitimate service providers deliver authentic data signed with their private key is the essential concept. It is difficult for people to escape accountability for the material they post under this system. People will soon be able to avoid posting false stuff on social media thanks to this. Future studies should tackle the scalability problem and the need for a reputation system to lessen reliance on an official service provider.

The study's simulation of the suggested algorithm on two popular Twitter topics produced positive initial findings. Based on the results of the experiment, PoC is able to identify fake news with an accuracy of roughly 89%, and fall-out and false discovery rate of roughly 10% and 9%, respectively. These findings imply the potential for more blockchain algorithms to be suggested and analyzed in order to manage and control the diffusion of online information across social networks. The concept of using blockchain technology to identify false news was just anecdotal prior to this investigation. The lack of a benchmark and standardized datasets to more accurately investigate PoC efficiency was a limitation of this work. However, this study offers insightful information about using Blockchain technology and creating new consensuses to better manage and regulate the spread of rumors on social media. Further investigation utilizing controlled trials and benchmark datasets is required to enhance PoC performance and effectiveness in identifying fake news and rumors in the upcoming studies.

REFERENCES

[1] Y. Amichai-Hamburger, and T. Hayat, "Social networking", *The international encyclopedia of media effects*. P. Rössler, Ed., Wiley-Blackwell, 2017.

[2] S. Vosoughi, D. Roy, and S. Aral, "The spread of true and false news online", *Science,* vol. 359, no. 6380, pp. 1146-1151, 2018.

[3]   G. Pennycook, Z. Epstein, M. Mosleh, A.A. Arechar, D. Eckles, and D.G. Rand, "Shifting attention to accuracy can reduce misinformation online", *Nature,* vol. 592, no. 7855, pp. 590-595, 2021.
[http://dx.doi.org/10.1038/s41586-021-03344-2] [PMID: 33731933]

[4]   J. Paschen, "Investigating the emotional appeal of fake news using artificial intelligence and human contributions", *J. Prod. Brand Manage.,* vol. 29, no. 2, pp. 223-233, 2020.

[6]   W.J. Tee, and R.K. Murugesan, "Trust network, blockchain and evolution in social media to build trust and prevent fake news", *2018 Fourth International Conference on Advances in Computing, Communication & Automation (ICACCA)* Subang Jaya, Malaysia, 2018, pp. 1-6.
[http://dx.doi.org/10.1109/ICACCAF.2018.8776822]

[7]   Y. Chen, Q. Li, and H. Wang, "Towards trusted social networks with blockchain technology", *arXiv preprint,* arXiv:1801.02796, 2018

[8]   A. Narayanan, J. Bonneau, E. Felten, A. Miller, and S. Goldfeder, "Bitcoin and cryptocurrency technologies", *CursoElaborado Pela,* vol. 1, no. 1, pp. 1-308, 2021.

[9]   T. Palmisano, V.N. Convertini, L. Sarcinella, L. Gabriele, and M. Bonifazi, "Notarization and anti-plagiarism: a new blockchain approach", *Appl. Sci.,* vol. 12, no. 1, p. 243, 2021.
[http://dx.doi.org/10.3390/app12010243]

[10]   A. Arredondo, *Blockchain and certificate authority cryptography for an asynchronous on-line public notary system,* M.S. thesis, Dept. of Electrical and Computer Engineering, Univ. of Texas at Austin, Austin, TX, USA, 2017.

[11]   D. Di Francesco Maesa, and P. Mori, "Blockchain 3.0 applications survey", *J. Parallel Distrib. Comput.,* vol. 138, pp. 99-114, 2020.
[http://dx.doi.org/10.1016/j.jpdc.2019.12.019]

[12]   G. Karame, and S. Capkun, "Blockchain security and privacy", *IEEE Secur. Priv.,* vol. 16, no. 4, pp. 11-12, 2018.
[http://dx.doi.org/10.1109/MSP.2018.3111241]

[13]   N. Alexopoulos, J. Daubert, M. Mühlhäuser, and S.M. Habib, Beyond the hype: On using blockchains in trust management for authentication, *In Proc. 2017 IEEE Trustcom/BigDataSE/ICESS,* Sydney, NSW, Australia, Aug. 2017, pp. 546–553.

[14]   B. Cao, Y. Li, L. Zhang, L. Zhang, S. Mumtaz, Z. Zhou, and M. Peng, "When Internet of Things meets blockchain: Challenges in distributed consensus", *IEEE Netw.,* vol. 33, no. 6, pp. 133-139, 2019.
[http://dx.doi.org/10.1109/MNET.2019.1900002]

[15]   G. Wang, Q. Wang, and S. Chen, "Exploring blockchains interoperability: A systematic survey", *ACM Comput. Surv.,* vol. 55, no. 13s, pp. 1-38, 2023.
[http://dx.doi.org/10.1145/3582882]

[16]   T.K.L. Moraes, *Originalmy: Decentralising notary and authenticity services with blockchain-based technology,* Mestrado Profissional em Gestão para Competitividade - Tecnologia da Informação, Fundação Getulio Vargas, Escola de Administração de Empresas de São Paulo, São Paulo, Brazil, July 2019.

[17]   G. Song, S. Kim, H. Hwang, and K. Lee, "Blockchain-based notarization for social media", In: *Proc. 2019 IEEE Int. Conf. Consumer Electronics (ICCE),*. Las Vegas, NV, USA, Jan. 2019, pp. 1–2.

[18]   M. A. Hisseine, D. Chen, and X. Yang, "The application of blockchain in social media: A systematic literature review," *Applied Sciences*, vol. 12, no. 13, 2022.

[19]   E. Mustafaraj, and P.T. Metaxas, "The fake news spreading plague: was it preventable?", In: *Proc. 2017 ACM Web Science Conf. (WebSci '17),* Troy, NY, USA, June 2017, pp. 235–239.
[http://dx.doi.org/10.1145/3091478.3091523]

[20]   S. Singhania, N. Fernandez, and S. Rao, "3HAN: A deep neural network for fake news detection," in *Neural Information Processing: 24th Int. Conf., ICONIP 2017,* Guangzhou, China, Nov. 14-18, 2017,

Proc., vol. 10635, Part II, pp. 572-581, Springer International Publishing.

[21] H. Ahmed, I. Traore, and S. Saad, Detection of online fake news using n-gram analysis and machine learning techniques. In *Intelligent, Secure, and Dependable Systems in Distributed and Cloud Environments: First Int. Conf., ISDDC 2017, Vancouver, BC, Canada, Oct. 26–28, 2017,.* Proc., vol. 10618, pp. 127–138, Springer International Publishing.

[22] H. Rashkin, E. Choi, J.Y. Jang, S. Volkova, and Y. Choi, "Truth of varying shades: Analyzing language in fake news and political fact-checking", *in Proc. 2017 Conf. Empirical Methods in Natural Language Processing (EMNLP),* Copenhagen, Denmark,. 2017, pp. 2931–2937.
[http://dx.doi.org/10.18653/v1/D17-1317]

[23] R. Oshikawa, J. Qian, and W.Y. Wang, "A survey on natural language processing for fake news detection", *arXiv preprint arXiv:1811.00770, 2018.,* .

[24] M. Alrubaian, M. Al-Qurishi, M.M. Hassan, and A. Alamri, "A credibility analysis system for assessing information on twitter", *IEEE Trans. Depend. Secure Comput.,* vol. 15, no. 4, pp. 661-674, 2016.

[25] A. Rahiman, and S.A. Sattar, A Comparative Analysis on Rumor Microblogs Detection from Social Network Sites. In *Advances in Computational Intelligence and Informatics,* Proc. ICACII 2019, vol. 119, pp. 389–396, Springer Singapore, 2020.

[26] M. Torky, E. Nabil, and W. Said, "Proof of credibility: A blockchain approach for detecting and blocking fake news in social networks", *Int. J. Adv. Comput. Sci. Appl.,* vol. 10, no. 12, 2019.
[http://dx.doi.org/10.14569/IJACSA.2019.0101243]

[27] S. Paul, J.I. Joy, S. Sarker, S. Ahmed, and A.K. Das, "Fake news detection in social media using blockchain", *In 2019 7th international conference on smart computing & communications (ICSCC), ,* 2019 Sarawak, Malaysia, 2019, pp. 1-5.
[http://dx.doi.org/10.1109/ICSCC.2019.8843597]

[28] A. Campan, A. Cuzzocrea, and T.M. Truta, "Fighting fake news spread in online social networks: Actual trends and future research directions", *2017 IEEE International Conference on Big Data (Big Data),* 2017 Boston, MA, USA, 2017, pp. 4453-4457.
[http://dx.doi.org/10.1109/BigData.2017.8258484]

[29] A. Zareie, and R. Sakellariou, "Minimizing the spread of misinformation in online social networks: A survey", *J. Netw. Comput. Appl.,* vol. 186, p. 103094, 2021.
[http://dx.doi.org/10.1016/j.jnca.2021.103094]

[30] R. Kumar and R. Sharma, "Managing trust in IoT using permissioned blockchain," in *Internet of Things and Cyber Physical Systems,* 1st ed., CRC Press, 2022, pp. 23–40.

[31] S. Huckle, and M. White, "Fake news: A technological approach to proving the origins of content, using blockchains", *Big Data,* vol. 5, no. 4, pp. 356-371, 2017.
[http://dx.doi.org/10.1089/big.2017.0071] [PMID: 29235919]

CHAPTER 8

Development of Smart City using Blockchain and Artificial Intelligence

Chetan Shelke[1,*], Preeti Gupta[2], Binod Kumar[3], Abhijeet Kaiwade[4], Belsam Jeba Ananth M.[5], Sumeet Gupta[6] and Satvik Vats[7]

[1] *Alliance College of Engineering and Design, Alliance University, Bangalore, India*

[2] *Department of Computer Science and Engineering, Jain University (Deemed-to-be-University), Bangalore, India*

[3] *Department of Computer Applications, JSPM's Rajarshi Shahu College of Engineering, Pune, India*

[4] *Institute of Management and Research., Abhinav Education Society's Institute of Management and Research, Pune, India*

[5] *Department of Mechatronics Engineering, SRM Institute of Science and Technology, Kattankulathur, India*

[6] *Global Economics and Finance Cluster, School of Business, University of Petroleum and Energy Studies, Dehradun, India*

[7] *Department of Computer Science and Engineering, Graphic Era Hill University, Dehradun, India*

Abstract: The rapid uptake of blockchain and artificial intelligence (AI) technologies like machine learning (ML) in particular has brought about a paradigm change that is elevating the digital ecosystem for smart cities. The development of new technology can be used to create intelligent societies within smart cities in this era of rapid digital communication. Uses of blockchain technology and ML technologies are proliferating, guaranteeing solutions for issues in a multitude of sectors, such as financial services, cryptocurrency, threat intelligence, social and public services, and the Internet of Things. These "smart cities" are constructed using various technologies, including artificial intelligence and blockchain. As a result, the way these technologies are applied in smart cities both present and future will alter not only the character of governance and human interaction but also the way business is done. The research suggests doing an experimental study to find out how blockchain technology and artificial intelligence are affecting the creation of smart cities. It tries to set the scene for queries like how traditional business models are getting ready for this disruption, what obstacles they might encounter, and what effects both technologies might have on the organization's growth. Blockchain technology and artificial intelligence have a lot

---

[*] **Corresponding author Chetan Shelke:** Alliance College of Engineering and Design, Alliance University, Bangalore, India; E-mail: binod.istar.1970@gmail.com

Keshav Kaushik, Rewa Sharma & Ayodeji Olalekan Salau (Eds.)
All rights reserved-© 2026 Bentham Science Publishers

of potential to help create smart cities. The results of the research will provide corporations with the rationale to start concentrating on these technologies and putting early adoption strategies into place, which will eventually cause them to change their smart city business models advance.

Keywords: Artificial intelligence, Blockchain, Development, Electronic commerce, Smart city.

INTRODUCTION

Smart cities are high-tech urban areas with intelligent subsystems linking individuals and institutions. These cities have the capacity to provide quick access to high-quality public services, hence improving the quality of life for all stakeholders, by using big data collections. Information and communication technology foster economic progress. In addition to enhancing city administration, they may have had the greatest impact on promoting social interaction and the sharing concept [1].

By 2030, 66% of people on Earth will reside in big cities, according to UN estimates [2]. This means that in order to maintain social sustainability, we must address a number of challenges. Additionally, this type of city structure presents social and environmental challenges. Municipalities are using up about half of the world's resources. It creates problems when distributing these resources using current technology in a uniform manner [3]. Thus, ICT (information and communication technology) might be very important to the idea of smart cities.

As the world grows more interconnected, the fourth industrial revolution—fueled by inventions like the internet is speeding up. In order to perform transactions securely and quickly, new sectors are emerging as a result, such as smart cities, which combine internet connectivity, blockchain technology, and online payment [4]. Moreover, Schwab and Davis [5] assert that data is the driving force behind the fourth industrial revolution. As a result, data-intensive methods like cloud computing, artificial intelligence, machine learning (ML), and the Internet of Things (IoT) will become more valuable and widely used. The purpose of this research is to demonstrate how blockchain technology and artificial intelligence can be used to further the development of smart cities (Fig. **1**).

Pervasive sensors are transforming urban transportation, improving security, and making it easier to collect enormous amounts of data that artificial intelligence (AI) computers can analyze. They enable the city to monitor and react to resident mobility, as well as to communicate with its own infrastructure. The conditions of the city can therefore be optimized. ML is built to gather, analyze, and interpret data accurately and efficiently while requiring no human intervention. ML is still a away from becoming self-sufficient, but it may learn and develop by collecting and evaluating new data that must be supplied and stored correctly. Because of its distributed registry architecture, which allows data to be stored concurrently on all network nodes, blockchain technology is advantageous in this respect. Complete decentralization of data is made possible by this, improving the efficiency and "democratic" nature of data access.

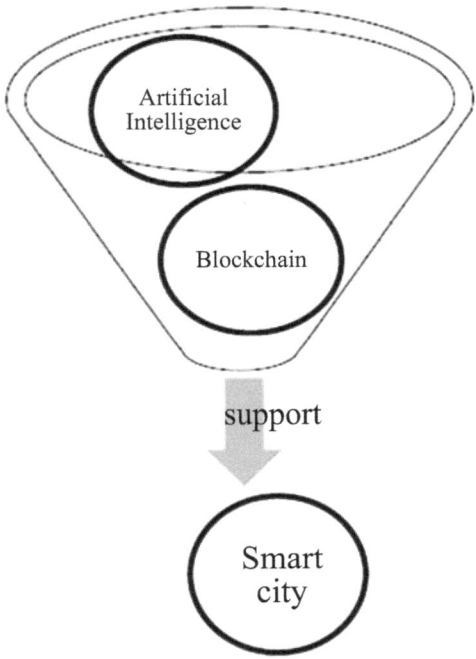

Fig. (1). AI and blockchain as elements supporting the creation of smart cities.

However, since these smart cities are constructed on consolidated facilities, attacks that take benefit of a single point of failure can target them. For instance, even though it might not be as convenient, a bank has the authority to charge astronomically high fees for each transaction. In addition, the bank may not always be online or might have a breach, providing dishonest attackers with access to customer data, as the recent Capital One data leak demonstrates [6]. Moreover, the increased demand for personal data, such as credit card numbers, passport details, and medical histories, on the dark web exposes citizens of smart cities to needless risk [7].

Blockchain technology was inspired by Satoshi Nakamoto's Bitcoin paper, and it is necessary to solve these and other problems that smart cities have [8]. Blockchains can perform peer-to-peer atomic transactions that eliminate middlemen and their costs, and they are safe, decentralized, and resilient to failure (Byzantine fault tolerance) [9]. When smart cities combine the decentralized nature of blockchain technology with the adaptability of AI; they have the potential to grow while enhancing their shortcomings. Nevertheless, using blockchain-based technologies in smart cities has drawbacks. Decentralized networks, such as blockchains, function autonomously from governing bodies and their regulatory departments. As a result, certain countries have banned blockchain technology altogether, particularly Bitcoin, and consider other decentralized apps (DApp) to be harmful [10]. Thus, this article offers a summary and explanation of blockchain and AI methods in connection to the building of smart cities.

Study Objective

- To look into how AI (artificial intelligence) and Blockchain technologies are being used to develop smart cities.
- Should look into how the existing business models are getting ready for change.
- To explore the challenges faced for the development of Business.
- To demonstrate how blockchain technology and artificial intelligence fit into the development of smart cities.

LITERATURE REVIEW

A Sneak Peek at the Two Business Plans

The application of two business models AI and Blockchain as well as their interactions with the e-commerce models utilized in smart cities are examined in this research. Furthermore, although blockchain and AI can be used alone, their combination produces a product that is more potent than the sum of its parts. This section lists successful instances and describes the current business strategy based on blockchain and AI.

AI Business Model

The systematic approach of incorporating sensors into an already-existing system and extracting data from it is known as artificial intelligence or AI. Three out of every four AI firms fail, despite the fact that the market was expected to be worth $11 trillion in 2015 [11]. Nevertheless, AI appliances are widely used in households and cities, ranging from TVs to refrigerators to smart alarm clocks [12]. The high failure rate is due to the fact that the majority of individuals and businesses utilizing AI in their operations have access to data but do not understand how to use it as a source of revenue or a competitive advantage. Like how information is the cash of the fourth modern unrest, it is the premise of man-made consciousness and related enterprises [5]. The many business models that are based on AI and ML are presented in the paragraphs that follow.

Due to the high risk, high cost, and widespread impact of accidents on the social, political, environmental, and economic dimensions of commercial operation, aircraft, oil mining, and other industries are tightly controlled. Establishing compliance requirements and scheduling routine human inspections of the machinery and plants were the conventional approaches to guaranteeing safety [13]. However, companies use ML to guarantee compliance by affixing sensors where real-time plant monitoring is possible. Consequently, businesses may take a proactive approach to safety without having to pay extra. In the aircraft industry, this is standard procedure. Jet engines are fitted with sensors that provide real-time tracking, alerting, and effective evaluation of supplier engine health data [14].

Preventative maintenance is the second business model that uses AI. Low-cost AI systems may be utilized to keep an eye on facilities and operating systems and notify users when problems occur from unfavorable operating conditions [15]. As an alternative, plants or equipment might be planned for routine maintenance schedules that include shut-down times. Notwithstanding, by executing deterrent upkeep methodology, particularly in hardware and plants whose activity and support are confounded, the monetary effects of these blackouts can be kept away from [16]. With AI-empowered sensors in the breeze turbine edges, General Electric has successfully utilized precaution upkeep to change the pitch point in light of neighborhood wind current and plan free time for turbine support when there is no wind.

Not to mention, the field of remote diagnostics has made extensive use of AI sensors and systems, particularly in the medical and agricultural sectors. For instance, greenhouse managers employ AI sensors to remotely monitor and regulate ideal plant growth environments, including CO_2, temperature, light, and humidity [17]. Artificial intelligence (AI) systems are being used in the medical field for fitness tracking, therapy (like insulin pumps), and patient state monitoring (using wearable technology) [18].

The benefit of the membership model is steady revenue as compared to selling the product in a single exchange and charging customers for subsequent overhauls. This model is comparable to the Software as a Service (SaaS) cloud design and strategy [19]. As an alternative, an AI developer and manufacturer may decide to market the intended result rather than their product. This based-on-results business strategy focuses on meeting the needs of the client rather than creating a product that a customer may determine suits their needs. As opposed to just providing motors as per the particulars determined by the airplane developer or administrator, Rolls-Royce is one illustration of an organization that offers help that incorporates nonstop motor well-being and execution observing for each motor it sells and keeps up with in activity [20].

The underlying concept of these artificial intelligence business models is that consumers and companies build, and produce while employing these AI platforms (hardware and software) based on their knowledge. In actuality, though, there are now a variety of business models that focus on offering technical expertise in order to construct the products that end users use as the foundation for their businesses [21]. For instance, a developer and supplier of AI devices may offer subscription leasing for their goods particularly software that operates on specialized cloud servers as well as round-the-clock customer assistance.

Blockchain Business Model

The potential for excessive connectivity in smart cities is one of its drawbacks, which might change their usefulness from advantageous to annoying. Consider the internet as an example, where targeted advertising has become so popular that businesses are now creating user profiles and selling the information to other businesses. Furthermore, user and browser fingerprinting has progressed to the point that it is now stepping into murky ethical waters [22]. A man-in-the-middle attack or other similar attacks could expose business secrets, private information, or other sensitive data collected by a variety of AI devices and sensor networks. Furthermore, as demonstrated by the acts of the Chinese government and the mobile phone corporation Huawei, faith in the devices themselves is not even assured [23]. Fig. (**2**) shows the critical Blockchain business model design.

Thus, the consolidation of AI and blockchain would fuel smart city areas' inadequacies. Notwithstanding, what exactly is blockchain? A blockchain is a dispersed record with sections that are time-stepped and cryptographically endorsed to guarantee their permanence [24]. In addition to being decentralized and exhibiting Byzantine fault tolerance, a business model based on blockchain technology would be peer-to-peer transacted in a network where the business model enforces trust [25].

Thus, the cornerstones of every blockchain-based business model are decentralization, permanence, and transparency [26]. There are three primary techniques in which these plans of action utilize the blockchain foundation. In order to ensure that the information is meticulously crafted, they first save all of their data on the blockchain [27]. Additionally, they improve the usability and usefulness of current foundations, like supply chains, by influencing the straightforwardness portion of blockchains [28]. Finally, the more sophisticated business model puts its AI frameworks on top of blockchains to create a decentralized AI framework [29]. The various business models that have been established around or inspired by blockchains are explained in the paragraphs that follow.

Fig. (2). A business model based on blockchain.

On the other hand, the utilization and transfer of tokens with intrinsic value within the blockchain is the core of a vital token business model. Token economics, another name for this business model, functions similarly to traditional banks, with the exception that it is decentralized and that no single entity, like the government, controls the creation, use, or destruction of tokens [30]. Furthermore, the value of the tokens comes from the users' perception of them rather than, say, their backing in gold reserves. Because of this, utility token business models only turn a profit when the value of each token rises.

On the other hand, a corporation that uses a more modern blockchain business model termed securities is selling tokens known as securities, which are expected to appreciate in value as more people buy them. Put otherwise, holding a blockchain security token is equivalent to having legitimate ownership of an asset [31]. Therefore, the purpose of the blockchain is to authenticate the token owners and control the production and usage of security tokens. Verified owners are also permitted to utilize their tokens as collateral in addition to trading them under this business model. As a result, the securities business model offers a means of redefining ownership as we know it and distributing money across many parties without devaluing the token [32].

The most straightforward strategy for a non-specialized company to coordinate blockchain innovation into their current framework and strategy is through the Blockchain as a Service business model. This is on the grounds that the environment makes it feasible for organizations to make, test, and execute their items while abstracting endlessly low-level infrastructural components [33]. The Ethereum Blockchain as a Service, which was developed and managed by a joint venture between Microsoft and ConsenSys, is one example.

The Business Models' Effect

By 2020, it is predicted that AI will have grown to over 20 billion devices, with 4.5 billion of those devices coming from Europe [34]. In addition, it is estimated that more than 65% of the total populace will live in cities by 2040. Thus, the developing smart city communities will depend on streetlamp-fueled neighborhoods notwithstanding customary remote organizations for availability. These organizations can shape a wide area network (WAN) or lattice organization. Besides, on the grounds that the quantity of associated artificial intelligence gadgets in smart city communities is developing dramatically, there is a higher risk of undesirable admittance to private and delicate information continued wide area network. In this way, blockchain innovation should be utilized to safeguard these discussions as well as keep up with classification and validity. Thus, the implications for how blockchain technology and artificial intelligence could impact the development of smart cities will be discussed next.

All developers and some end users are aware of the issue of AI security. This is due to examples showing how readily an AI device's security can be exploited, particularly with regard to the data it collects and transfers. These systems encrypt data using conventional cryptographic techniques, which involve exchanging private keys and sending cipher text-based data *via* a network.

However, considering the worldwide cost of cybercrime, the potential damage to smart cities would be exponential and might even cause a metropolis to collapse [35]. This implies that, in the case of an AI network based on blockchain technology, an attacker must compromise the security of the entire network, or at least 52% of it, rather than just one or two devices, requiring a different form of security architecture. Because controlling a blockchain network comes with a high cost, hostile attackers find it extremely difficult to accomplish so. Therefore, developers and users can be protected from most risks by employing blockchain technology to safeguard AI networks, with the exception of those persons or institutions that are ready to pay a charge [36].

Additionally, e-commerce is another aspect of smart cities that will be touched by blockchain and AI. The smart cities of the future, built on top of these two technologies, will improve the local services and goods that are offered to people in close proximity to their homes or places of employment. The desire to promote local distinctiveness will inspire locals to use blockchain technology and artificial intelligence to develop goods and services, therefore displacing national and excessively commercial brands with locally owned businesses that cater to the needs of the community. However, for this to be successful, there needs to be compatibility and interoperability across the various AI platforms and blockchain applications [37].

Despite their flaws, blockchain and artificial intelligence will form the foundation of smart cities in the present and the future. This is due to the two platforms' seamless integration, great adaptability, and simplicity of usage. The way these two technologies alter public transportation is one such effect they will have in smart cities. A great many city occupants and laborers have been utilizing public transportation all the more oftentimes during the beyond 20 years to get from point A to point B, for example, from home to work [38]. Given the rising pattern of environmental mindfulness and the drive to restrict future contamination by bringing down discharges from copying petroleum derivatives, it is guessed that the number would increment. For example, the Maltese government has employed the confidential firm Omnitude to utilize blockchain innovation to create and give answers for the issues influencing the country's public transportation framework [39]. It is anticipated that this system will serve as a payment hub for various public transportation systems, enhancing operational and sector transparency.

Additionally, e-commerce is another aspect of smart cities that will be touched by blockchain and AI. The smart cities of the future, built on top of these two technologies, will improve the local services and goods that are offered to people in close proximity to their homes or places of employment. Promoting local uniqueness will encourage residents to employ blockchain technology and artificial intelligence (AI) to create products and services, which will cause nationally recognized and overly commercial brands to lose market share to locally held companies that serve the needs of the community. However, for this to be successful there needs to be compatibility and interoperability across the various AI platforms and blockchain applications [40].

An Overview of Smart Cities and Emerging Markets

With the introduction and widespread adoption of electrical and electronic home and communication technologies, such as computers, modems, cable TV, and the initial version of the contemporary internet powered by the World Wide Web (and

HTTP), the 1990s brought in an era of unprecedented advancement [41]. New markets like social networking, online shopping, e-commerce, and advertising have all grown as a result of this trend. Businesses can now make over 61% of their revenue from online activities such as adverts, thanks to technology [42, 43]. E-commerce sales, for example, increased dramatically from $6 billion to over $25 trillion in 2014 and beyond. Consequently, there is currently room for growth and development in smart cities. All that is required to get things going are the business models that accompany the underlying technologies.

METHODOLOGY

The following part outlines the research approach and techniques used to ascertain the effects of blockchain and artificial intelligence on the creation of smart cities. This implies the application of both qualitative and quantitative research techniques. The quantitative analysis of the studies will provide more information, particularly regarding the participants' subjective and objective perspectives on the topic, in addition to shedding light on the statistical features of the research.

Qualitative Methodology

The qualitative strategy will collect and analyze secondary data about model companies in order to address the research topic. Businesses that employ blockchain and AI models will make up the study's population. Most of the businesses that will be included in the study's sample are situated in emerging markets and smart cities across the globe. To avoid sampling and information bias in the findings of the research, a random sample technique will be employed. A study of earlier research on the topic and related studies would be one of the many outplays that the sampling approach would take into account.

The limitation of the qualitative approach is the ever-evolving nature of technologies. Therefore, the results may not accurately reflect the situation in the industry as it stands right now. As a result, secondary data is either infrequently ignored when new models replace older ones or are not updated frequently enough. Emerging markets and smart cities are two instances of how bankers and consumers heavily rely on technology (blockchain, artificial intelligence, or a combination of both). The two models offer ways to make transactions more flexible and transparent while also cutting down on transaction times. When adopting such business models, charts and other graphical representations will be used to help explain the principles and determine how they affect e-commerce.

The Quantitative Method

In addition, a quantitative strategy will be used in the study to solve the research topic. The method will be helpful in gathering data regarding the viewpoints of professionals in the field regarding the numerous advancements and dynamics of blockchain technology and artificial intelligence.

Population Target

Academics and industry experts, including firm managers and blockchain and AI pioneers, university professors, and pioneers in the field, will be the focus of this study. The participants will come from a variety of industries and businesses. As a result, 65 volunteers will be enrolled in the study to provide the necessary data. Although 65 is not enough to bolster the validity of the research's conclusions, it is appropriate for a pilot study on a fact-finding expedition.

Research Instrumentation

To obtain quantitative data for the study, interviews will be conducted. There will be both closed- and open-ended questions during the interviews. The statistical information gathered from the closed-ended questions will allow the researcher to gauge public opinion and the acceptance of various perspectives on the topic. Conversely, the open-ended questions will facilitate the collection of in-depth information on the topics by allowing participants to explain their answers.

Analyzing Data

Excel software will be used to analyze the gathered data and record it in tables. The researcher will create charts and graphical representations of the study's results using the Excel application.

Ethical Consideration

This research project will comply with the standard ethical guidelines governing research endeavors. These involve getting the sampled and accepted study participants' informed consent before the research begins and honoring their choice to withdraw for any reason. Second, the interview subjects were given the go-ahead to use their free will and supply the required data after being made aware of the research's goals. In light of this, no subject was forced to participate in the research. Lastly, the participants were granted secrecy and anonymity because their personal information, including names, was never recorded during the study's use of alphanumeric codes.

RESULTS

This section will discuss the research findings following data analysis. The following is a list of the several topics (aspects) from the qualitative and quantitative research designs that will be looked at.

Blockchain and AI's Contributions to Business Development

The ratings for how diverse people would employ blockchain and AI together, as well as what they liked and believed might be improved about both technologies' integration as they are utilized in creating smart cities, are given in Table **1** and Fig. (**3**).

Table 1. Impacts on the emerging market and smart city.

Infrastructure and transaction	Rating
Faster transaction	5
Loan processing and access	3
Process and transaction transparency	4
Inventory monitoring and management	3
Prevention of wastage and fraud	5
Development of online infrastructure	3

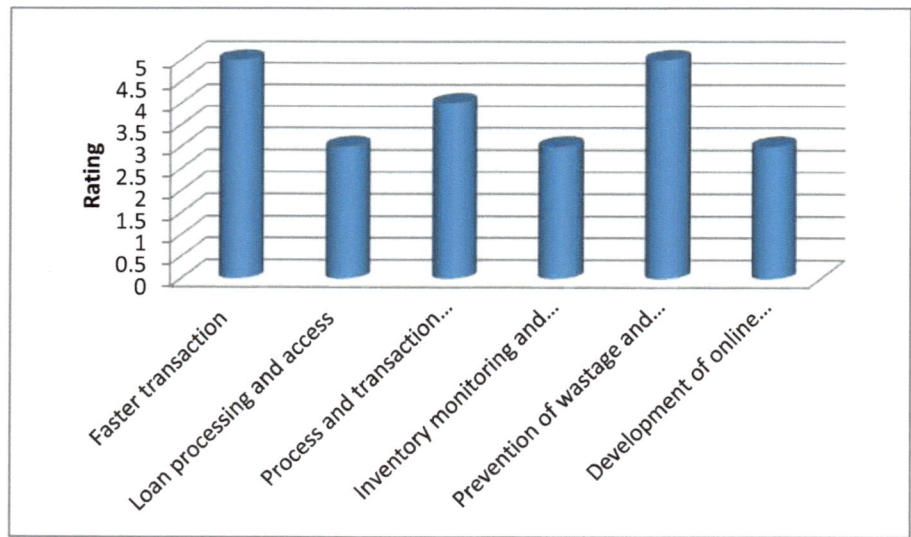

Fig. (3). The significance of business models in developing economies and smart city.

These include five-star ratings for openness throughout the entire infrastructure and transactions that are speedier and more scalable. Conversely, radio frequency identification is used by blockchain and artificial intelligence technology to verify product quality, specifications, and individual needs. Customers who have a preference for frozen dairy goods or cold red meats, for example, might use these models to signal their preferences when placing purchases. When used with blockchain, AI facilitates ongoing product evaluation.

In addition, the end-to-end link between sellers and buyers helps in the real-time rectification of inaccurate product specifications through the implementation of blockchain platforms and artificial intelligence (AI). As a result, buyers are guaranteed high-quality products. In addition, they provide me with regular information on service enhancements and modifications to the websites or gadgets so that we may stay current with market trends. Again, in the event that deliverables are specifically collected, employment in the courier and warehousing services may be created in the context of reducing middlemen.

These are only a few of the numerous ways that blockchain technology and artificial intelligence are affecting the growth of smart cities, and the information gathered for this study will support these assertions. Figs. (**4** and **5**) in this context provide an overview of the domains that blockchain and AI are affecting and how their applications are anticipated to interact with smart city communities.

Fig. (4). The impact of AI analysis on business and commerce.

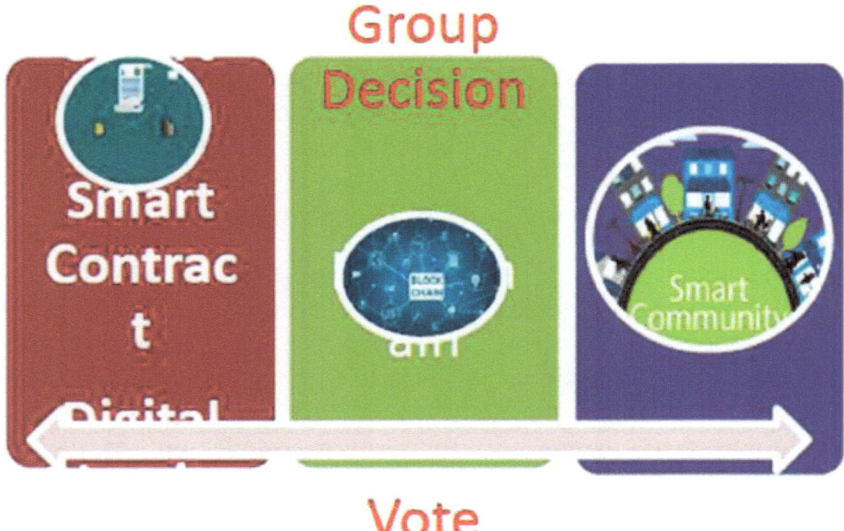

Fig. (5). Application of blockchain in emerging markets.

However, there are worries that this kind of study design is not sound and could lead to confirmation bias. However, the study's investigators took this into account and took steps to prevent it from happening by applying statistical techniques, such as formulating a null hypothesis that will either be supported or refuted based on the information gathered.

Modern Businesses' Readiness to Adopt Blockchain and AI Technologies

Participants will be asked during the interview if their companies can use blockchain and artificial intelligence. They will also be questioned about whether they have the resources needed to be profitable in addition to being competitive in developing smart cities. This will make it easier to comprehend concerns about how well-suited the current company models are to change and adapt to the times. Of the 65 respondents, 27 stated that their businesses were prepared to pursue the shift in its entirety. However, 38 of the respondents said that their businesses' structural and human resource reforms are necessary for them to fully accept the new changes.

Obstacles in the Adoption of Blockchain and AI Technology

The participants will also be asked to list the difficulties that their businesses have faced, or anticipate facing, as AI and blockchain technology advance. This will make it easier to identify the people and mentalities needed for the changeover and day-to-day operations of the blockchain-integrated AI business models. The study also looks for these problems since there is business potential for present and future entrepreneurs to take advantage of them. These are added together and shown as follows in Fig. (**6**).

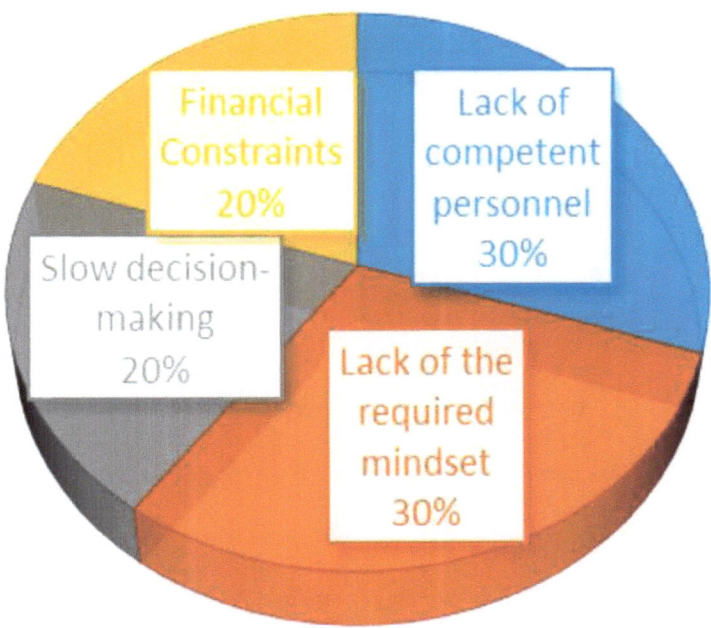

Fig. (6). Challenges Blockchain and AI Face.

Contributions, both Theoretical and Practical

The results of this research will be crucial in providing details on the advantages of blockchain and artificial intelligence for enterprises. As a result, this study provides a justification for businesses to use the technology. Additionally, the study highlights the difficulties that businesses have while implementing the technology, laying the groundwork for future research on how to remove these obstacles in order to promote corporate growth.

CONCLUSION

The global shift from rural to urban areas indicates that smart cities are the next stage of growth. Blockchain and AI promise to bring forth previously unheard-of advancements in every sphere of human society. Furthermore, due to their complementary nature, blockchain and AI ought to be able to tackle the majority of problems that arise in businesses, especially when introducing new and untested business models. This article proposed research to ascertain how blockchain and artificial intelligence technology can affect smart city development. When the study is finished, it will shed light on a number of topics, including the contributions made by these two technologies and the difficulties that people and companies may have while changing their business strategies. Subsequent research endeavors will build upon this paper by broadening its scope and utilizing larger sample sizes. Despite these drawbacks, time and budgetary restrictions played a significant role in deciding the study's sample size.

REFERENCES

[1] A. Visvizi, and M.D. Lytras, "Rescaling and refocusing smart cities research: from mega cities to smart villages", *Journal of Science and Technology Policy Management,* vol. 9, no. 2, pp. 134-145, 2018.
[http://dx.doi.org/10.1108/JSTPM-02-2018-0020]

[2] S.E. Bibri, and J. Krogstie, "Smart sustainable cities of the future: An extensive interdisciplinary literature review", *Sustain Cities Soc.,* vol. 31, pp. 183-212, 2017.
[http://dx.doi.org/10.1016/j.scs.2017.02.016]

[3] X. Li, P. Jiang, T. Chen, X. Luo, and Q. Wen, "A survey on the security of blockchain systems", *Future Gener. Comput. Syst.,* vol. 107, pp. 841-853, 2020.
[http://dx.doi.org/10.1016/j.future.2017.08.020]

[4] S. Perätalo, and P. Ahokangas, "Toward smart city business models", *Journal of Business Models,* vol. 6, no. 2, pp. 65-70, 2018.

[5] K. Schwab, and N. Davis, *Shaping the future of the fourth industrial revolution.* New York, NY, USA: Currency, 2018..

[6] J. Lu, "Assessing the cost, legal fallout of Capital One data breach", *Law360 Expert Analysis.,* 2019.

[7] B. Luthi, "Here's what your data sells for on the dark web," *Experian Blog,* 2025.

[8] N. Stifter, A. Judmayer, P. Schindler, A. Zamyatin, and E. Weippl, "Agreement with satoshi–on the formalization of nakamoto consensus", *Cryptology ePrint Archive.,* 2018.

[9] O. Sohaib, H. Lu, and W. Hussain, "Internet of Things (IoT) in E-commerce: For people with disabilities", *In: Proc. 2017 12th IEEE Conf. Industrial Electronics and Applications (ICIEA),* Siem Reap, Cambodia, June 2017, pp. 419–423.

[10] B. Kewell, and P.M. Ward, "Blockchain futures: With or without Bitcoin?," *J. Strateg. Change,* vol. 26, no. 5, pp. 471–480, Sept. 2017.
[http://dx.doi.org/10.1002/jsc.2149]

[11] J. Bughin, E. Hazan, S. Ramaswamy, M. Chui, T. Allas, P. Dahlström, N. Henke, and M. Trench, "Artificial intelligence: The next digital frontier?," McKinsey Global Institute, Discussion Paper, 2017.

[12] M. M. Kaya, Y. Taşkıran, A. Kanoğlu, A. Demirtaş, E. Zor, İ. Burçak, M. C. Nacak, and F. T. Akgül, "Designing a smart home management system with artificial intelligence & machine learning," *Mach. Learn.,* 2021.

[13] C. Coglianese, and J. Nash, "Compliance management systems: Do they make a difference?", *The Cambridge Handbook of Compliance,* D. D. Sokol and B. van Rooij, Eds., Cambridge University Press, pp. 20–35, 2021.

[14] A.F. El-Sayed, *Aircraft propulsion and gas turbine engines..* 2nd ed., Boca Raton, FL, USA: CRC Press, 2017.

[15] A. Chaudhuri, "Predictive maintenance for industrial iot of vehicle fleets using hierarchical modified

fuzzy support vector machine", *arXiv preprint, arXiv:1806.09612, 2018.*.

[16] A. Massaro, S. Selicato, and A. Galiano, "Predictive maintenance of bus fleet by intelligent smart electronic board implementing artificial intelligence", *IoT,* vol. 1, no. 2, pp. 180-197, 2020.
[http://dx.doi.org/10.3390/iot1020012]

[17] C. Maraveas, "Incorporating artificial intelligence technology in smart greenhouses: Current State of the Art", *Appl. Sci.,* vol. 13, no. 1, p. 14, 2022.
[http://dx.doi.org/10.3390/app13010014]

[18] D. Nahavandi, R. Alizadehsani, A. Khosravi, and U.R. Acharya, "Application of artificial intelligence in wearable devices: Opportunities and challenges", *Comput. Methods Programs Biomed.,* vol. 213, p. 106541, 2022.
[http://dx.doi.org/10.1016/j.cmpb.2021.106541] [PMID: 34837860]

[19] T. Tzuo, and G. Weisert, *Subscribed: Why the subscription model will be your company's future-and what to do about it,* . New York, NY, USA: Penguin, 2018.

[20] R. Royce, *The jet engine.*. 5th ed., Chichester, UK: John Wiley & Sons, 2015.

[21] W. Reim, J. Åström, and O. Eriksson, "Implementation of artificial intelligence (AI): a roadmap for business model innovation", *AI,* vol. 1, no. 2, pp. 180-191, 2020.
[http://dx.doi.org/10.3390/ai1020011]

[22] A. Lerner, A.K. Simpson, T. Kohno, and F. Roesner, "Internet jones and the raiders of the lost trackers: An archaeological study of web tracking from 1996 to 2016", *in Proc. 25th USENIX Security Symposium (USENIX Security 16),* , 2016 Austin, TX, USA, Aug. 2016, pp. 1–16.

[23] M. Kwan, "Can Huawei sue the US government for defamation?", *IALS Student Law Review.* vol. 7, no. 1, pp. 53–62, 2020.

[24] D. Puthal, N. Malik, S.P. Mohanty, E. Kougianos, and C. Yang, "The blockchain as a decentralized security framework [future directions]", *IEEE Consum. Electron. Mag.,* vol. 7, no. 2, pp. 18-21, 2018.
[http://dx.doi.org/10.1109/MCE.2017.2776459]

[25] F. Hawlitschek, B. Notheisen, and T. Teubner, "The limits of trust-free systems: A literature review on blockchain technology and trust in the sharing economy", *Electron. Commerce Res. Appl.,* vol. 29, pp. 50-63, 2018.
[http://dx.doi.org/10.1016/j.elerap.2018.03.005]

[26] W. Nowiński, and M. Kozma, "How can blockchain technology disrupt the existing business models?", *Entrep. Bus. Econ. Rev.,* vol. 5, no. 3, pp. 173-188, 2017.
[http://dx.doi.org/10.15678/EBER.2017.050309]

[27] J. Hwang, M. Choi, T. Lee, S. Jeon, S. Kim, S. Park, and S. Park, "Energy prosumer business model using blockchain system to ensure transparency and safety", *Energy Procedia,* vol. 141, pp. 194-198, 2017.
[http://dx.doi.org/10.1016/j.egypro.2017.11.037]

[28] N. Emmadi, and H. Narumanchi, "Reinforcing immutability of permissioned blockchains with keyless signatures' infrastructure", *in Proc. 18th Int. Conf. Distributed Computing and Networking (ICDCN '17),* , 2017 Hyderabad, India, 2017, pp. 1–6.
[http://dx.doi.org/10.1145/3007748.3018280]

[29] K. Salah, M.H.U. Rehman, N. Nizamuddin, and A. Al-Fuqaha, "Blockchain for AI: Review and open research challenges", *IEEE Access,* vol. 7, pp. 10127-10149, 2019.
[http://dx.doi.org/10.1109/ACCESS.2018.2890507]

[30] P. Tasca, "Token-based business models", *Disrupting finance: FinTech and strategy in the 21st century,* pp. 135-148, 2019.

[31] D. Tapscott, and A. Tapscott, *Blockchain revolution: how the technology behind bitcoin is changing money, business, and the world.*. New York, NY, USA: Penguin, 2016.

[32]   Y. Chen, "Blockchain tokens and the potential democratization of entrepreneurship and innovation", *Bus. Horiz.,* vol. 61, no. 4, pp. 567-575, 2018.
[http://dx.doi.org/10.1016/j.bushor.2018.03.006]

[33]   J. Singh, and J.D. Michels, "Blockchain as a service (BaaS): Providers and trust", *2018 IEEE European Symposium on Security and Privacy Workshops (EuroS&PW),* , 2018 London, UK, 2018, pp. 67-74.
[http://dx.doi.org/10.1109/EuroSPW.2018.00015]

[34]   M. Sallaba, D. Siegel, and S. Becker, IoT powered by Blockchain: How Blockchains facilitate the application of digital twins in AI, Deloitte, Point of View Report, 2018.

[35]   J. Singh, M. Sajid, S. K. Gupta, and R. A. Haidri, "Artificial intelligence and blockchain technologies for smart city", *Intelligent Green Technologies for Sustainable Smart Cities,* pp. 317-330, 2022.

[36]   M.S. Ali, K. Dolui, and F. Antonelli, "IoT data privacy *via* blockchains and IPFS," in *Proc. 7th Int. Conf. Internet of Things (IoT '17),* Linz, Austria, 2017, pp. 1-7.
[http://dx.doi.org/10.1145/3131542.3131563]

[37]   S. Singh, P.K. Sharma, B. Yoon, M. Shojafar, G.H. Cho, and I.H. Ra, "Convergence of blockchain and artificial intelligence in IoT network for the sustainable smart city", *Sustain Cities Soc.,* vol. 63, p. 102364, 2020.
[http://dx.doi.org/10.1016/j.scs.2020.102364]

[38]   I. Eyal, A. E. Gencer, E. G. Sirer, and R. Van Renesse, "Bitcoin-NG: A scalable blockchain protocol," in *Proc. 13th USENIX Symp. Networked Systems Design and Implementation (NSDI 16),* Santa Clara, CA, USA, Mar. 2016, pp. 45–59.

[39]   A. Kumar, S. Sharma, and R. Singh, "Blockchain-based model for secure and trusted IoT system," in *Proc. Int. Conf. Adv. Comput. Commun. Technol. (ICACCTech),* 2023, pp. 743–748.

[40]   S. Kauf, "Artificial intelligence and blockchain for smart city", *Organizacja i Zarządzanie: Kwartalnik Naukowy,* vol. 3, no. 55, pp. 49–62, 2021.

[41]   J. Ruan, and Y. Shi, "Monitoring and assessing fruit freshness in IOT-based e-commerce delivery using scenario analysis and interval number approaches", *Inf. Sci.,* vol. 373, pp. 557-570, 2016.
[http://dx.doi.org/10.1016/j.ins.2016.07.014]

[42]   S.Q. Liu, and A.S. Mattila, "Airbnb: Online targeted advertising, sense of power, and consumer decisions", *Int. J. Hospit. Manag.,* vol. 60, pp. 33-41, 2017.
[http://dx.doi.org/10.1016/j.ijhm.2016.09.012]

[43]   B. Aslam, and H. Karjaluoto, "Digital advertising around paid spaces, E-advertising industry's revenue engine: A review and research agenda", *Telemat. Inform.,* vol. 34, no. 8, pp. 1650-1662, 2017.
[http://dx.doi.org/10.1016/j.tele.2017.07.011]

CHAPTER 9

Blockchain, Big Data, and Deep Learning-based Fraud Detection System for Credit Card Fraud

Nur Mohammad Ali Chisty[1,*], **Shweta Gakhreja**[2], **Yogita Satish Garwal**[2], **Belsam Jeba Ananth M.**[3], **Tripti Tiwari**[4], **Dharamvir**[5] and **Kamreed Udham Singh**[6]

[1] *Cyber Crime Wing, Anti-Terrorism Unit, Bangladesh Police, Dhaka, Bangladesh*

[2] *Manipal University Jaipur, Jaipur, India*

[3] *Department of Mechatronics Engineering, SRM Institute of Science and Technology, Kattankulathur, India*

[4] *Department of Management Studies, Bharati Vidyapeeth (Deemed to be University) Institute of Management and Research, Delhi, India*

[5] *Department of Computer Application, The Oxford College of Engineering, Bengaluru, India*

[6] *School of Computing, Graphic Era Hill University, Dehradun, India*

Abstract: Companies in the financial industry are among those who are implementing their operations online as a result of the internet's rapid growth in usage. Because of the enormous economic damages that arise from financial fraud, it is becoming an important concern as financial frauds are becoming more common and sophisticated globally. An economic fraud detection system (FDS) must be able to identify risks such as unusual assaults and unauthorized entry. The last few decades have seen a widespread application of data mining and machine learning (ML) methods to address this problem. These techniques still require improvement, though, to handle big data quickly and recognize unidentified trends in attacks. The importance of data safety and evaluation systems for big data has changed recently due to the enormous volume of data and its continuous growth. Big data is defined as information that is difficult to handle, store, and evaluate using standard software tools and databases. Big databases exhibit considerable quantity, speed, and diversity, necessitating the development of novel methods for handling them. Thus, employing blockchain and a deep learning-based (DL) approach for FDS is suggested in this work for credit card frauds. The objective of this framework is to improve the accuracy of identification in the context of big data in a private-permissioned blockchain network, while also improving the existing detection methods. A present DL algorithm called the Auto-encoder algorithm

---

[*] **Corresponding author Nur Mohammad Ali Chisty:** Cyber Crime Wing, Anti-Terrorism Unit, Bangladesh Police, Dhaka, Bangladesh; E-mail: nmachisty@gmail.com

Keshav Kaushik, Rewa Sharma & Ayodeji Olalekan Salau (Eds.)
All rights reserved-© 2026 Bentham Science Publishers

and a few other ML algorithms are contrasted with the outcomes of the suggested framework's evaluation using a real database of credit card frauds. According to the study findings, the LSTM performed flawlessly, achieving 99.9% accuracy in roughly a minute.

Keywords: Big data, Blockchain, Credit card frauds, Deep learning, Fraud detection system.

INTRODUCTION

The variety of bank operations using credit cards has increased dramatically in the past few decades, as has the incidence of fraud and card burglary. According to the 2018 Organization for Financial Analysts Settlements Fraud Poll [1,] there has been a rise in transactions scams. As per the research, a record-breaking seventy-eight percent of every company experienced fraudulent payments last year, totaling seven hundred treasury and finance experts. Finance organizations have dropped billions of dollars because of credit card fraud since the emergence of electronic payments [2]. As a result of this problem, financial companies and banks encounter the difficulty of developing efficient and assertive fraud detection systems (FDS).

Illegal economic operations are highly complex and difficult to detect. With the advancement of contemporary innovations, especially inside the economic industry, fraud is on the rise. There are many kinds of fraud in finance structures, including internet banking deception, credit card deception, fake loans, documentation deception, Phishing, fraud, and fake logins, among many others. Fraud charges cost economic institutions millions of dollars each year, negatively impacting the institution's economic position and client trust [3].

Worldwide economic organizations and corporations are suffering huge damages as a result of several economic frauds. Daily, there are reports of credit card information being hacked. An illegal activity employing debit and credit card information without the consent of the true client is ringing a warning for financial institutions, clients, and authorities all over the globe [4].

Monetary fraud has become an enormous issue. Unapproved access and unique assaults are detected by employing an approach to identify banking fraud. Banking organizations should regularly improve their processes to identify fraud. In recent years, machine learning (ML) and data mining techniques have become widely utilized to address this issue [5]. Nowadays, ML is frequently employed in financial services and industries for a variety of uses, including portfolio administration, dealings, risk evaluation, avoidance, and fraud detection. In the financial sector, for instance, ML is employed to create Chatbots, which are artificial intelligence programs that communicate with clients and react to their inquiries [6]. Decision Dealing Support Devices, also known as Computational Dealing, are employed in dealing with making highly rapid choices. Furthermore, among the main applications of ML in the financial services sector is fraud detection. Identifying illicit behavior became less difficult with the assistance of ML methods. Built on the transaction history, ML demonstrated novel approaches for analyzing client behavior and determining whether or not there is fraud [7].

Nevertheless, these methods must be enhanced in the areas of computing expenses, memory expenses, and handling big data, which is becoming an aspect of modern economic deals. Economic fraud detection is a difficult issue because of 4 essential causes: (1) fraudulent conduct is continually transforming, (2) there is no process for monitoring data on a fraudulent deal, (3) present identification methods (such as ML methods) have specific constraints, and (4) economic fraud databases are extremely biased, making it difficult to train methods [8]. Previous research has explored the potential of blockchain-based technologies and smart contracts in cooperative and distributed DL. Maintaining confidentiality is crucial for a secure collaborative environment. The objective of this study is to suggest a FDS centered on a deep learning (DL) method. This system is designed to detect skeptical financial transactions and notify suitable officials so that suitable measures can be taken. As an outcome, the suggested approach could be a helpful instrument for the banking industry in reducing possible losses.

LITERATURE REVIEW

DL is outlined in a study[9] as an excellent option for dealing with scams in banking transactions by causing the most effective utilization of financial institutions' big data. DL is a catch-all term for ML that employs an advanced multiple-layer artificial neural network (ANN). It is a physiologically encouraged system of human cells made up of multifaceted hidden layers of nonlinear computational units, with every neuron capable of sending data to another neuron within the hidden layers [10]. The research conducted by some authors [11] presents a blockchain-based progressive outlier clustering method that is both mathematically efficient and successful in terms of functionality. Blockchain innovation is being employed to improve system safety, while DL methods are employed for prediction purposes.

They constructed an approach for detecting fraudulent use of credit cards depending on data gathered from purchases made with credit cards. The findings demonstrated the significance of categorizing characteristics such as kinds of goods, purchases kinds, and places, among others, in detecting the fraudulent use of credit cards. The application of a Logistic Regression (LR) method for identifying fraud, on the other hand, is not an effective strategy since it can just anticipate a categorized result. Furthermore, this method is renowned for being susceptible to over-fitting [12].

METHODOLOGY

The phases of the suggested economic FDS are outlined in this part. The system is separated into three phases: the pre-applying phase, the implementing phase, and the post-applying phase. The phases are depicted in Fig. (**1**) and are covered in greater depth in the ensuing subdivisions.

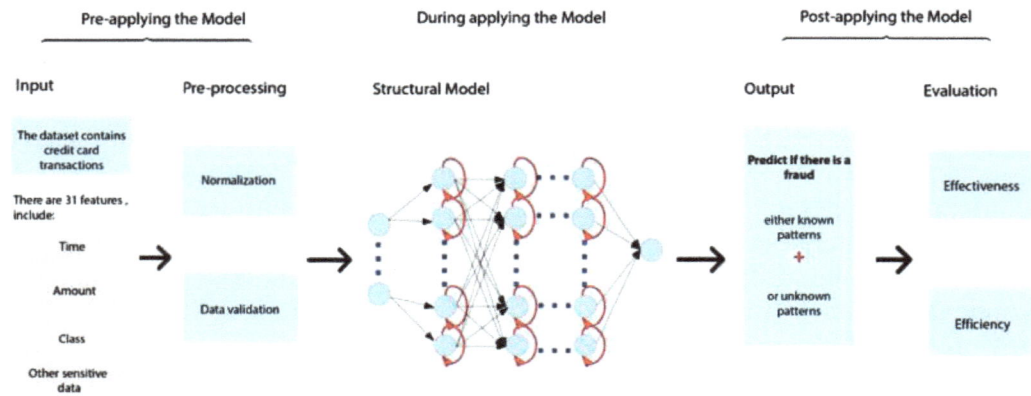

Fig. (1). The suggested framework.

Pre-applying Phase

This phase is divided into smaller phases, the first of which is the data sub-phase, which includes preparing the database instances for the system's training and testing. The database includes credit card operations that occurred within two days; out of 284,807 actions, there are 492 frauds. This leads to a significant imbalance in the database, which explains 0.17 percent of every activity in the favorable class (fraudulent conduct). In addition, there are thirty-one characteristics in this collection, including sensitive characteristics like class, quantity, and duration. Several investigators have employed it as a standard database. Three steps must be taken before the framework is implemented in the collection: verification of data, normalization, and division.

a. The verification of data

This phase is used to verify the accuracy of the data in the database, such as period data that are negative, empty figures, or negative.

b. Normalization

The framework adjusts the factors to lie in a spectrum of -1 to 1 to produce a reliable outcome. This phase is required to convert the database's numerical column data to a prevalent size without destroying any data or distorting the spectrum of figures. Eq. (**1**) is used in the process of normalization.

$$x(i) = \frac{x(i) - \bar{x}}{s(x)} \qquad (1)$$

c. Database Sample Divide

To obtain an accurate performance evaluation, the data instances must be split into testing and training groups. Thirty percent of the database was set aside to be tested and seventy percent was designated for training in the suggested system.

Implementing Phase

This phase involves two subdivisions that employ the suggested long short-term memory (LSTM), which is the core of the suggested DL system. The LSTM framework is created and its variables are established during the subdivisions.

An expansion of recurrent neural networks (RNNs), which are DLNNs with recollection, is the LSTM method, which is the basis for the DL economic FDS suggested in this article. Because of its prior understanding of the relationship between predicted outcomes and archival input information, it is particularly suitable for detection. The LSTM layout facilitates learning *via* extended reliance on a series of predicted problems. It can retain an extended memory and is helpful for longer-term trends. Additionally, it has the standard conduct that stores data for an extended amount of time. As per the researchers, this makes it an ideal instrument for operations involving forecasting and detection. The pre-applying system phase's collected information is introduced into the implementing paradigm phase, where it is analyzed by the tiers containing LSTM cells. In Fig. (**2**), the LSTM cell's framework is displayed.

The memory structures, or cells, that make up the LSTM network's architecture are depicted in Fig. (**2**) as having multiple phases and gates. The cell phase is the primary channel of data movement. It permits the data to proceed in an unchanged manner. The forget gate (ft) controls what data should be eliminated or retained. Both the present input (Xt) and the statistics from the previous hidden state (ht1) are processed through the sigmoid operation. The figures between 0 and 1 are found by the sigmoid operation (r); measurements closer to 0 indicate to forget, and measurements closer to 1 indicate to retain. Additionally, the cell's condition vector Ct1 charges the components that will be forgotten. Calculating the forget gate is explained by Eq. (2):

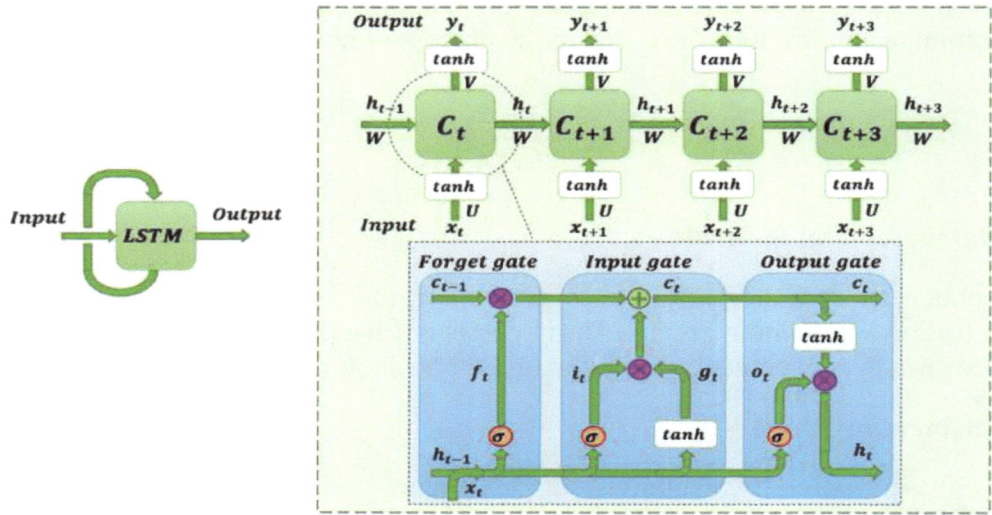

Fig. (2). LSTM cell framework.

Below time step t, the overall calculation process is as follows:

a. Forget gate calculation: Entries xt and ht-1 are passed *via* the source gate to compute the forget gate ft. The result is a value (0 aproxiamtes 1), which is then transmitted to the cell state data Ct-1 to determine if the previous cell state Ct-1 is preserved.

$$f_t = \sigma(W_f x_t + U_f h_{t-1} + b_f) \qquad (2)$$

b. Source Gate: Change the source details i_t and the applicant cell condition (Equation 3-4) $\bar{C}_t$.

$$\bar{C}_t = tanh(W_c x_t + U_c h_{t-1} + b_c) \qquad (3)$$

$$i_t = \sigma(W_i x_t + U_i h_{t-1} + b_i) \qquad (4)$$

c. Upgrade cell condition: The cell condition of t time stage C_t is upgraded based on the upgraded applicant cell condition $\overline{C_t}$ as well as the cell condition of t the prior period stage C_{t-1} (Equation **5**).

$$C_t = f_t \times C_{t-1} + i_t \times \overline{C_t} \tag{5}$$

d. Outcome gate: Use result cell state and result entry OT to obtain result data Ct (Equations **6-7**).

$$o_t = \sigma(W_o x_o + U_o h_{o-1} + b_o) \tag{6}$$

$$h_t = o_t \times \tanh C_t \tag{7}$$

The process of activation is expressed as: (Equations 8-9)

$$\sigma(x) = \frac{1}{1 + e^{-x}} \tag{8}$$

$$\tanh(x) = \frac{e^x - e^{-x}}{e^x + e^{-x}} \tag{9}$$

LSTM Variables and Performance Measurements

To enhance the outcomes, the framework utilizes several variables known as hyperparameters. Four variables are employed, as listed in Table **1**, to assess the effectiveness of the suggested system: optimizer, batch count, periods, and matrix. Table **2** displays a selection of the many optimization techniques that have the potential to distinguish between distinct designs.

The Post-applying Phase

The outcome is obtained and then evaluated in two parts in this phase. It will determine whether or not there is fraud by displaying the database's results. Next, an analysis and evaluation of the acquired data will be conducted. The system's variables are adjusted, and it is evaluated on varying numbers of tiers and repetitions as part of the assessment procedure. Determining which adaptable variables offer the greatest implementation duration and prediction accuracy is the aim. Additionally, determine how many layers and repetitions will yield the most beneficial outcomes by testing these values.

Table 1. LSTM variables and performance measurements.

Variables	Definition
Batch count	Relates to how many data windows we pass around at once.
Optimizing technologies	Variables that operate to improve the performance. There are several varieties, including Adam and RMSprop.
Epochs	It describes the quantity of forward and backpropagation repetitions that the system must perform.
Measure	Assess performance using metrics such as accuracy, and so on.

Table 2. Optimizing technologies of the LSTM framework.

Optimizing technologies	Definitions
Adagrad	An optimizing method depending on gradients is called Adaptive Gradient (Adagrad). Adagrad adjusts variables by the adaptable learning pace. It makes more modest changes. Because of this feature, it is helpful in situations involving limited information.
Adam	Adaptable moment estimation (ADAM) is a technique used in DL ANN methods that flexibly modifies the learning speed calculation for each variable. The initial and subsequent moments of the gradient are used to accomplish this aim. Further, ADAM is helpful for issues involving a lot of statistics.
RMSprop	Geoff Hinton suggested Root Mean Squared Propagation (RMSprop). It is a private descent-based optimization method intended for ANN. A well-liked option for an adaptable learning pace method is RMSprop.

Database of Credit Card Fraud Detection

Numerical columns referred to as characteristics are present in the database utilized for this research, as explained in Part "Pre-applying the system. "These characteristics include various types of data, such as:

1. "Time" is defined as the interval of seconds between two credit card operations.
2. The term "Amount" describes how the transaction's amounts are structured.
3. Certain delicate characteristics in "V1 to V28".
4. The term "class" describes the forged operation; a column value of ¼1 indicates fraud, while a column value of ¼0 indicates there was no scam.

Research Setup

To provide strong proof that the LSTM framework helps identify abnormalities in the finance sector, the system construction is carried out in this part. The various tasks, including pre-processing and choosing a model, are programmed using operations from the Python Sklearn library. The LSTM framework is implemented with the aid of the Keraslibrary. The objective is to quantify the economic detection fraud's accuracy, loss rates, and duration of operation. Furthermore, it demonstrates that the LSTM framework is capable of identifying both recognized and unidentified trends in fraud.

The evaluation and performance measures, together with techniques for contrasting the recommended system performance, are covered in this subpart. Understanding the interpretations of different evaluation criteria and the data they seek to convey is important for comparing since the underlying processes of these metrics may differ. These metrics include, among others, accuracy, loss rate, and implementation duration. This set of measurements is reliant on a "confusion matrices."

The uses of credit card fraud detection determine the relative significance of these four parts. Accuracy is described as a ratio of precise forecasts and total estimates (Equation **9**).

$$Accuracy = \frac{TN + TP}{TN + FN + FP + TP} \quad (10)$$

The loss rate is an operation that evaluates the distinction between the true result and anticipated results during training to accelerate the procedure of learning. Additionally, the loss rate is employed to minimize mistakes and assess system performance. Equation (**9**) may be used to determine the loss rate. Where Y stands for predicted results and YPred for true results (Equation **11**).

$$Loss = Y - \log Y_{prd} + (1 - Y) - \log(1 - Y_{prd}) \quad (11)$$

The amount of duration the system spends completing the operation is known as the implementation duration. The purpose of computing the implementation duration is to ascertain how long the system needs to identify frauds and to ensure that the system accomplishes its objective effectively. The calculation of implementation duration is explained in Equation (**10**).

$$Duration = Duration_{end} - Duration_{start} \quad (12)$$

RESULTS

This part examines the outcomes of using the suggested framework. Additionally, an examination of the published findings is also done.

Research Outcomes

The system's initial results showed that it could achieve 99.9 percent accuracy and a 0.46 percent rate of loss in 307 seconds. As indicated in Table **3** and Fig. (**3**), this study employed the Adagrad optimizing algorithm, a hundred repetitions, and three layers for encoding and decoding.

Table 3. Initial study outcomes.

Optimization algorithm	No. of tiers	No. of repetition	Training Accuracy (%)	Verification Accuracy (%)	Loss (%)	Duration (s)
Adagrad	3	100	99.9	99.93	0.46	307

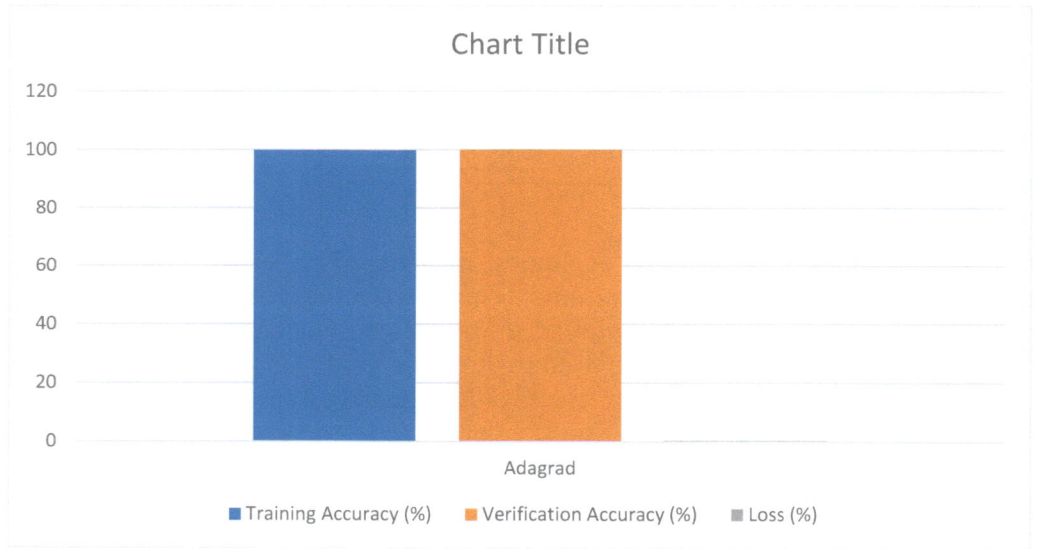

Fig. (3). Initial study outcomes.

The optimization algorithm Adam was additionally examined on multiple tiers and a varied number of repetitions because, as demonstrated by the results in Table **4** (Fig. **4**), it produced excellent outcomes. As Table **5** and Fig. (**5**) show, there has been no discernible improvement in accuracy with increasing the number of layers. The outcomes indicate that the number of repetitions has also not altered significantly; ten repetitions yielded 99.9 percent accuracy and 0.31 percent loss rate, while 100 repetitions produced 99.9 percent accuracy and 0.21 percent loss rate. Additionally, 99.9 percent accuracy and 0.18 percent loss rate were attained after 200 repetitions as indicated in Table **6** and Fig. (**6**).

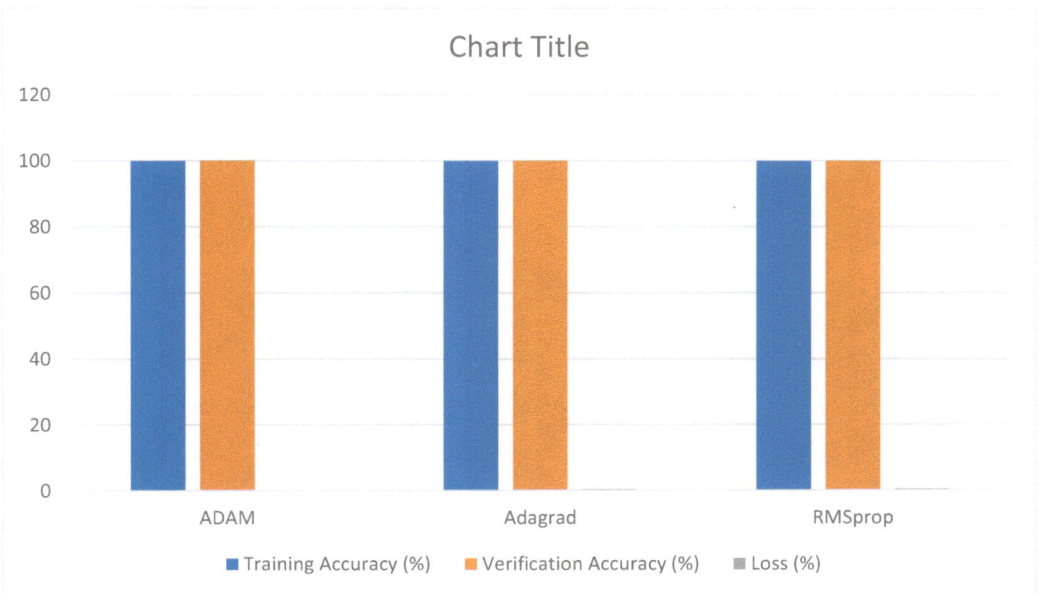

Fig. (4). Study outcomes with various optimization algorithms.

Table 4. Study outcomes with various optimization algorithms.

Optimization algorithm	No. of tiers	No. of reptation	Training Accuracy (%)	Verification Accuracy (%)	Loss (%)	Duration (s)
ADAM	3	100	99.96	99.96	0.21	405
Adagrad	3	100	99.9	99.93	0.46	307
RMSprop	3	100	99.94	99.94	0.35	385

Table 5. Adam optimization algorithm output with varying layer counts.

No. of Layers	No. of Reptation	Training Accuracy (%)	Verification Accuracy (%)	Loss (%)	Duration (s)
2	100	99.9	99.9	0.22	400
3	100	99.9	99.9	0.21	405
5	100	99.9	99.9	0.22	468

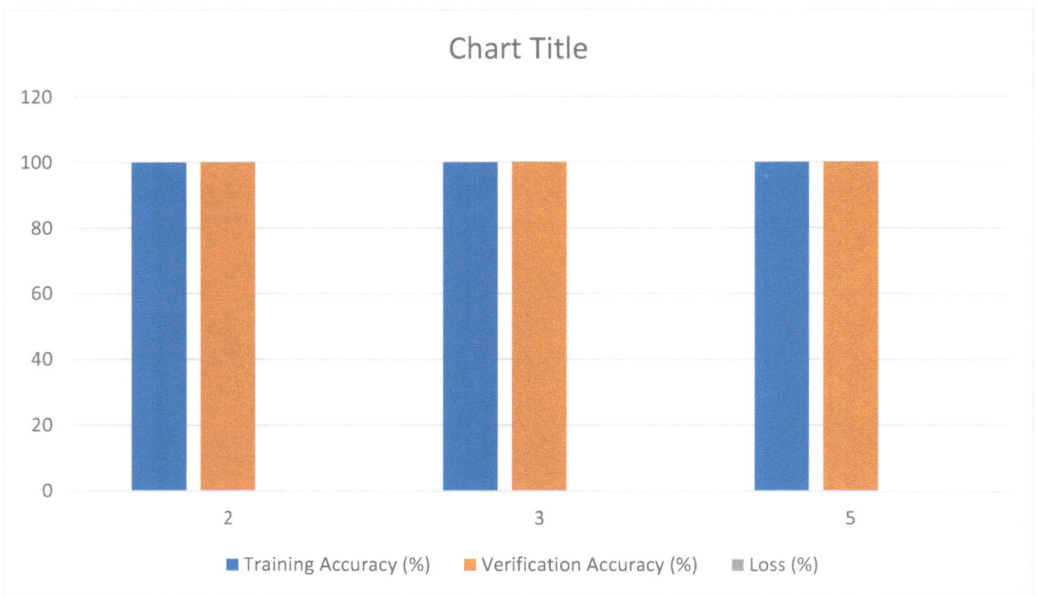

Fig. (5). Adam optimization algorithm output with varying layer counts.

Table 6. Adam optimization algorithm output with varying repitition counts.

No. of Layers	No. of Reptation	Training Accuracy (%)	Verification Accuracy (%)	Loss (%)	Duration (s)
3	10	99.95	99.95	0.31	45
3	100	99.96	99.96	0.21	405
3	200	99.9	99.96	0.18	868

Result Assessment

Depending on the use of LSTM cells, the system detects economic fraud rapidly and effectively. Many optimization algorithms can be utilized in this system; nevertheless, choosing the best optimization algorithm outcomes is an important boost in outcomes. The number of tiers and repetitions failed to create any significant distinction in the study. Furthermore, the outcomes show that the number of repetitions and the number of tiers affect the duration. The outcomes demonstrated a significant relationship between accuracy and the number of repetitions. Furthermore, the number of repetitions has a negative association with loss rates. As demonstrated in Fig. (**7**), there is a negative association between accuracy and loss rates; as accuracy rises, loss rates decline.

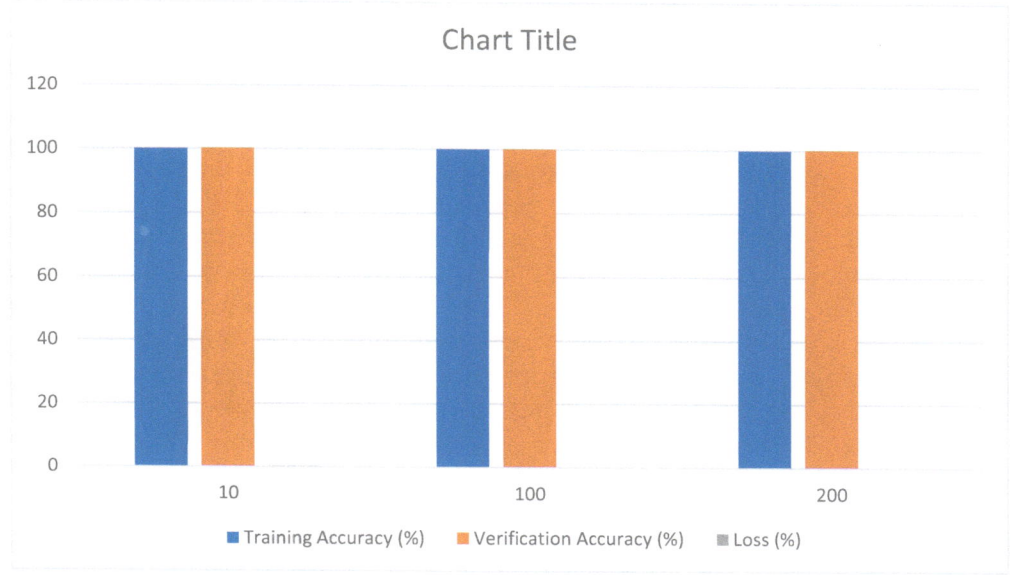

Fig. (6). Adam optimization algorithm output with varying reptation counts.

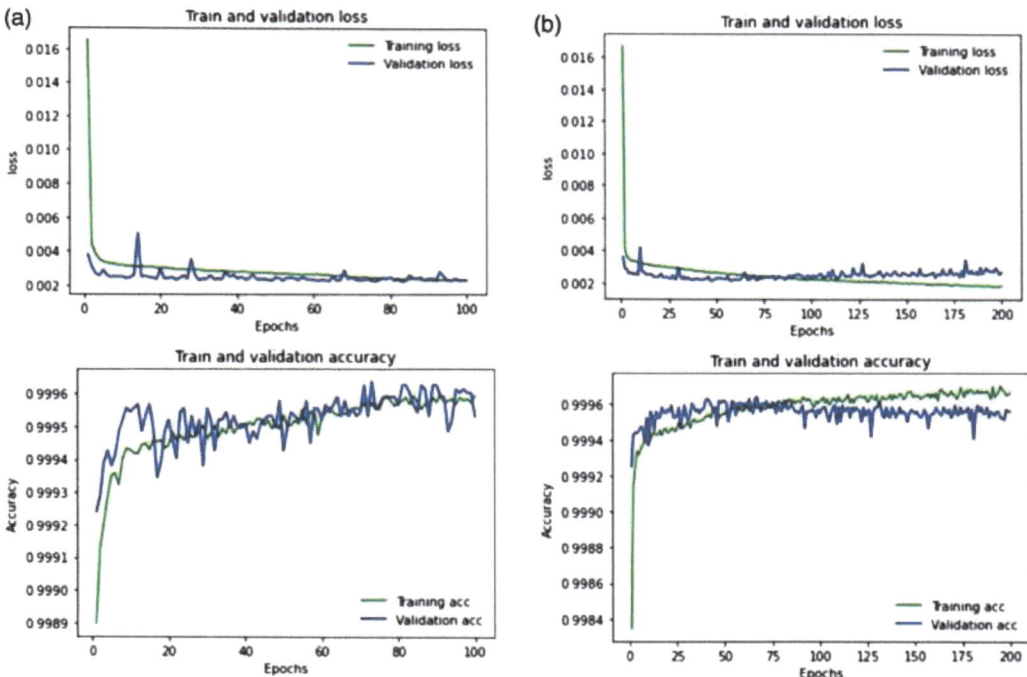

Fig. (7). The outcomes **(a)** displayed the loss and accuracy after 100 repetitions and the outcomes **(b)** displayed the loss and accuracy after 200 repetitions.

Comparison with Other DL Algorithms

The suggested framework is contrasted with the Autoencoder system to demonstrate its efficacy. Studies demonstrate that the Adam optimization algorithm outperforms other optimization techniques in terms of accuracy and pace; thus, the Adam optimization algorithm with three levels and 100 repetitions is used in this comparison. According to the outcomes in Tables **7** and **8**, the LSTM approach surpassed the Auto-encoder system. In 405 seconds, the LSTM model achieved 99.9 percent accuracy and a 0.21 percent loss rate. In comparison, the Autoencoder system achieved 70.27% accuracy and a loss rate of 96.08% in 318 seconds. The outcome demonstrated that the LSTM framework may be trained even from complicated information trends. Furthermore, the LSTM framework can cope with large amounts of data more effectively.

Table 7. Comparing with auto-encoder.

System	Optimization algorithm	No. of tiers	No. of reptation	Training Accuracy (%)	Verification Accuracy (%)	Loss (%)	Duration (s)
Auto-encoder	Adam	3	100	70	69	69	318
LSTM	Adam	3	100	99	99	0.21	405

Table 8. Comparing the outcomes with ML Algorithms.

System	Duration (s)	Accuracy (%)	Disadvantages
LR	10	99.88	• LR can only produce a category-based result. • Its susceptibility to excessive fitting.
SVM	435	99.87	• SVM is not suitable for big and complicated datasets. • SVM needed data with annotations for training, making it ineffective for detecting novel trends in fraud. • The outcomes of SVM are not transparent.
RF	200	99.9	• RF can produce good outcomes with a small number of statistics. • RF rapidly approaches a stage where it can no longer improve accuracy. • It is necessary to train the data to anticipate the outcomes.

Comparing with Current ML-based Methods

The LSTM-oriented economic FDS has been contrasted to current ML-based algorithms such as Random Forest (RF), Logistic Regression (LR), and Support Vector Machine (SVM). These methods for ML were utilized with identical data collection, and the outcomes are displayed in Table **8** and Fig. (**9**). RF achieved the same accuracy as LSTM after ten times of modification. However, RF needed a longer duration to execute and extensive data training for predicting the outcome. As a result, detecting novel trends in fraud was ineffective. SVM, on the other hand, achieved 99.8 percent accuracy in 435 seconds. SVM produced lesser outcomes in terms of pace and accuracy. As a result, it is unsuitable for large amounts of complicated statistics. LR additionally accomplished 99.8 percent accuracy in 10 seconds. Although LR got shorter to complete, it produced a smaller accuracy than LSTM. As per (Fig. **8**), LR is entitled to a categorical result. Even though certain methods of ML have produced excellent outcomes, they are not capable of anticipating novel trends or coping with big data since they might get to an extent where they cannot improve accuracy. DL-based techniques, on the other hand, are capable of learning *via* complicated information trends and dynamically adjusting to novel trends in fraud. Table **8** and Fig. (**9**) detail the disadvantages of every ML method in the setting of the economic fraud identification issue.

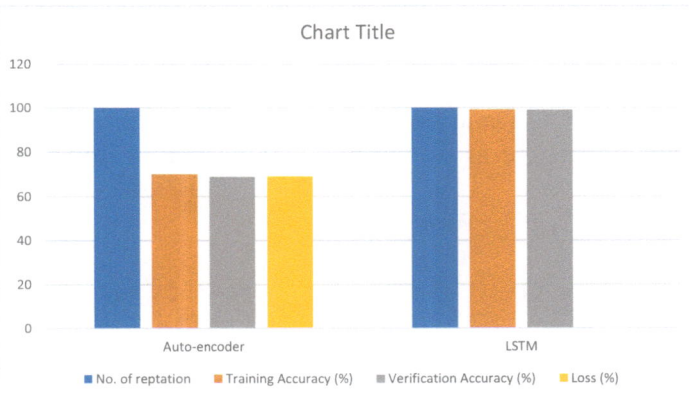

Fig. (8). Comparing with auto-encoder outcomes.

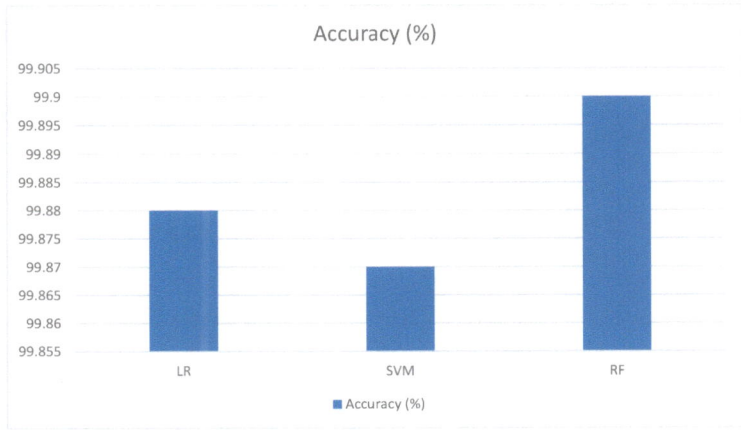

Fig. (9). Comparing the outcomes with ML Algorithms.

CONCLUSION

The issue of economic fraud has broad ramifications for key players and the financial industry. In the past decade, the problem has gotten worse due to a greater dependence on growing technologies. The importance of safeguarding data and analytics platforms for big data has changed recently due to the emergence of enormous quantities of data and its continuous growth. In the era of big data, conventional methods are no longer successful. Consequently, employing actual credit card fraud statistics, the study created a framework for economic FDS depending on the LSTM method. The purpose of this framework was to improve the accuracy of identification in the context of big data while also improving the existing identification methods. It used DL methods to swiftly and accurately detect trends, thereby addressing the issue of detecting complex and unidentified trends in fraud. Additionally, the suggested framework depending on the LSTM algorithm was used to tackle the issue of the ineffectiveness of the current methods. Lastly, a contrast of the LSTM approach with Auto-encoder and other ML methods currently in use demonstrated that it may function flawlessly when handling identifying fraud issues. In the years to come, an algorithm could be created to carry out several functions, such as determining the precise place and timing of a fraud.

REFERENCES

[1] J. Yomas, and C. Kiran, "Critical analysis of the evolution in the e-payment system, security risk, threats, and vulnerability", *Communications on Applied Electronics,* vol. 7, no. 23, pp. 21-29, 2018.
[http://dx.doi.org/10.5120/cae2018652800]

[2] A.M. Fayyomi, D. Eleyan, and A. Eleyan, "A Survey Paper On Credit Card Fraud Detection Techniques", *International Journal of Scientific & Technology Research,* vol. 10, no. 09, 2021.

[3] R. Kumar and R. Sharma, "Leveraging blockchain for ensuring trust in IoT: A survey," *J. King Saud Univ. – Comput. Inf. Sci.,* vol. 34, no. 10, pp. 8599–8622, 2022.

[4] Y. Jain, N. Tiwari, S. Dubey, and S. Jain, "A comparative analysis of various credit card fraud detection techniques", *International Journal of Recent Technology and Engineering,* vol. 7, no. 5, pp. 402-407, 2019.

[5] V. Patil, and U.K. Lilhore, "A survey on different data mining & and machine learning methods for credit card fraud detection. International Journal of Scientific Research in Computer Science", *Engineering and Information Technology,* vol. 3, no. 5, pp. 320-325, 2018.

[6] S.V. Suryanarayana, G.N. Balaji, and G.V. Rao, "Machine learning approaches for credit card fraud detection", *Int. J. Eng. Technol,* vol. 7, no. 2, pp. 917-920, 2018.
[http://dx.doi.org/10.14419/ijet.v7i2.9356]

[7] H. Naik, and P. Kanikar, "Credit card fraud detection based on machine learning algorithms", *Int. J. Comput. Appl.,* vol. 182, no. 44, pp. 8-12, 2019.
[http://dx.doi.org/10.5120/ijca2019918521]

[8] A. Singh, R.K. Ranjan, and A. Tiwari, "Credit card fraud detection under extreme imbalanced data: a comparative study of data-level algorithms", *J. Exp. Theor. Artif. Intell.,* vol. 34, no. 4, pp. 571-598, 2022.
[http://dx.doi.org/10.1080/0952813X.2021.1907795]

[9] A. Kaul, M. Chahabra, P. Sachdeva, R. Jain, and P. Nagrath, "Credit Card Fraud Detection Using Different ML and DL Techniques", *In: Proc. of the International Conference on Innovative Computing & Communication (ICICC),* 2021

[10] F.K. Alarfaj, I. Malik, H.U. Khan, N. Almusallam, M. Ramzan, and M. Ahmed, "Credit card fraud detection using state-of-the-art machine learning and deep learning algorithms", *IEEE Access,* vol. 10, pp. 39700-39715, 2022.
[http://dx.doi.org/10.1109/ACCESS.2022.3166891]

[11] C. Yang, "Incremental outlier feature clustering algorithm in blockchain networks based on big data analysis", *IETE J. Res.,* vol. 69, no. 11, pp. 1-9, Apr. 2022.

[12] F. Itoo, Meenakshi, and S. Singh, "Comparison and analysis of logistic regression, Naïve Bayes and KNN machine learning algorithms for credit card fraud detection", *International Journal of Information Technology,* vol. 13, no. 4, pp. 1503-1511, 2021.
[http://dx.doi.org/10.1007/s41870-020-00430-y]

CHAPTER 10

IoT-driven Blockchain System for Prediction of Heart Disease Using Smart Healthcare Monitoring Deep Learning Model

Mrunal K. Pathak[1,*], Shaik Balkhis Banu[2], Anupama Chadha[3], Gaurav Kumar[4], Shashi Kant Mishra[5], Tarun Jaiswal[6] and Vikrant Sharma[7]

[1] *Department of Information Technology, AISSMS Institute of Information Technology, Savitribai Phule Pune University, Pune, India*

[2] *Department of Physiotherapy, Fatima College of Health Sciences, Al Ain, UAE*

[3] *Department of Computer Applications, Manav Rachna International Institute of Research and Studies, Faridabad, India*

[4] *School of Computer Application, Lovely Professional University, Phagwara, Punjab, India*

[5] *Guru Nanak Institute of Technology, Hyderabad, India*

[6] *National Institute of Technology, Raipur, India*

[7] *Department of Computer Science and Engineering, Graphic Era Hill University; Adjunct Professor, Graphic Era Deemed to be University, Dehradun, India*

Abstract: The Internet of Things (IoT) is utilized to enhance conventional healthcare organizations in a variety of ways, such as monitoring patient habits. Sensor data from the IoTs is critical for medical facilities. Due to confidentiality and safety concerns, data should be safeguarded from unwanted alterations. On the contrary, Blockchain innovation offers a variety of ways to protect data from alterations. Deep learning (DL), as a subsection of machine learning (ML), has the revolutionary possibility to reliably analyze enormous amounts of data at very fast rates, provide insightful conclusions, and effectively resolve complex problems. Preventive treatment and prompt intervention for individuals at risk depend heavily on rapid and precise disease prediction. The capacity to handle consecutive time-series data with recurrent neural network variations of DL depends on developing prediction systems with improved accuracy, which is crucial given the increased usage of electronic clinical documents. Prediction analysis is used for the electronic clinical data kept in the cloud regarding patient records by the proposed framework, which acquires data from IoT gadgets. With an accuracy of 98.8 percent, specificity of 98.8 percent, precision of 98.9 percent, and F-value of 98.8 percent, the bidirectional long short-term memory-based intelligence medical network for monitoring and precisely predicting heart disease threat outperforms the current Intelligent cardiovascular illnesses prediction structures.

---

* **Corresponding author Mrunal K. Pathak:** Department of Information Technology, AISSMS Institute of Information Technology, Savitribai Phule Pune University, Pune, India;
E-mail: mrunal.pathak@aissmsioit.org

Keshav Kaushik, Rewa Sharma & Ayodeji Olalekan Salau (Eds.)
All rights reserved-© 2026 Bentham Science Publishers

Keywords: Blockchain, Deep learning, Internet of things, Heart disease, Prediction.

INTRODUCTION

The advancement of science and technology has coincided with the emergence of humankind. Innovations in the fields of medical services, agriculture, transport, and logistics, among others, have been made possible by the progress made in information and communication technology (ICT). The IoT Internet of Things is a significant factor behind the technological growth of ICT and is guiding future industries toward automated and decentralized intelligence [1]. The Internet of Things is constantly changing, influencing every aspect of our lives and acting like a living thing. The IoT links individuals, information, things/objects, and processes—from robots in industries to domestic gadgets. In the meantime, cloud computation offers flexible service-on-demand with nearly limitless processing and storage capacity. Parts of cloud computing and the IoTs support one another even if they have evolved independently and uniquely [2]. The two innovations eventually developed together in the last few years, and the resultant convergence was dubbed the Cloud-IoT model [3, 4]. This presented enormous opportunities for launching brand-new, cutting-edge services .

Since information technology uses started to distantly gather, route, and manage the condition of patients, wellness-based uses were driving advances in science and technology. As a result, IoT is driving and revolutionizing current advancements in healthcare by using wearable technology and sensor systems to collect patient physiological information [5]. The Cloud-IoT leverages the vast capacity of the Cloud to store and handle massive amounts of patient medical files, comprising sensing statistics from healthcare IoT for investigation in the medical industry.

Analytics follows the methodical, statistical, and qualitative examination of medical data for effective decision-making, while prediction analyses come from enhanced statistics aiming to evoke the prediction of prospective incidents utilizing accessible statistics [6]. Among other critical responsibilities in healthcare, statistics is used for medical decision assistance, prediction risk evaluation, and distant health monitoring. A large portion of healthcare involves risk prediction and reduction using historical and present patient statistics. The combination of humongous datasets from different resources encompassing electronic clinical data (ECD), healthcare imaging, testing outcomes, and administration data warranting rapid judgments is effectively handled by medical statistics [7]. Clinicians frequently have to make highly unpredictable decisions, but because of advancements in prediction analysis, such decisions will be better enlightened than ever. With the use of these state-of-the-art prediction analysis techniques, one may prevent hospital readmissions, minimize overhead costs, avoid complications, enhance long-term disease care, and detect problems early on. Microservices have prompted a shift from centralized to decentralized frameworks among developers and scholars. The benefits of blockchain innovation are discussed, as well as its possible uses in healthcare institutions.

Healthcare prediction analysis uses a range of methods, from sophisticated machine learning (ML) and artificial intelligence (AI) methods to traditional linear frameworks [8]. A branch of machine learning called deep learning (DL) is strong and dependable enough to manage and acquire knowledge from massive amounts of complicated medical data autonomously. It also provides useful knowledge and solutions to challenging situations. Its use in a broad range of healthcare settings has outperformed the outcomes of conventional systems. In particular, the recurrent neural network (RNN) [9] has gained popularity in the investigation of temporal occurrences and time-sequential activities and is capable of handling the ongoing connections of input statistics. The current period is driven by Industry 4.0, which involves implementing high-touch technologies and developing blockchains for real-time utilization of patient clinical data employing deep learning (DL).

Hence this aims to investigate the heart disease prediction rate using the DL algorithm. In this study, a fuzzy information system (FIS) is used for initial classification activity. Bidirectional long short-term memory (Bi-LSTM) is precisely employed to predict the risk of heart disease.

LITERATURE REVIEW

Incorporating blockchain and cloud technology creates a multitier structure for incorporating IoT into healthcare systems. Various techniques have been proposed recently for the prediction of heart disease. An accuracy of 85.4 percent is shown by deploying multiple ensemble classifiers to improve the accuracy of cardiovascular disease risk prediction [10]. A study proposed a fog strategy for handling healthcare data that combines blockchain and the cloud [11]. The primary purpose of the approach is to offer patients the ability to manage their personal information. Fog nodes are deliberately located near detectors to create a distributed blockchain with an authorization tier for data access by users. This article presents an instance analysis that evaluates the efficacy, openness, and availability of the proposed design in several settings, such as resident medical services.

A hybrid ML algorithm that predicts heart disease [12] by fusing methods from random forest (RF) and linear method (LM) has an 88.7 percent performance accuracy.

A neuro-fuzzy healthcare decision support platform combined with a coronary artery disease prediction system is provided. The accuracy, specificity, sensitivity, and precision of this framework, which consists of an artificial neural network (ANN) and an adaptable neuro-FIS, are 94.15%, 91.44%, 95.5%, and 92.6%, accordingly [13]. An automated cardiac disease prediction system utilizing cluster-based Bi-LSTM is suggested. This model has 94.78% accuracy when evaluated on the UCI database [14].

A novel IoT architecture utilizing deep convolutional neural networks (DCNN) is proposed. This structure is coupled with a smart sensor that monitors a patient's blood pressure (BP) and electrocardiogram (ECG). With 98.2 percent accuracy, this method outperforms both current DL neural networks (NN) and logistic regression (LR) [15].

METHODOLOGY

IoT serves as the vital collection element for countless real-time services that encourage communication between objects and people. The broad set of statistics generated by IoT gadgets is a serious obstacle to the medical framework's ability to interpret, store, and handle data.

Fig. (1) illustrates the several components that comprise the suggested smart medical platform for cardiovascular disease risk prediction. These parts comprise the data collection level, data pre-processing, and the condition prediction tier.

Data Collection Layer

There are 2 main resources of data that are gathered by the proposed medical network. Patients' everyday health monitoring provides physiological statistics, which include BP, heart rate, blood glucose/sugar threshold, cholesterol threshold, breathing rate, blood oxygen, action, electroencephalogram (EEG), ECG, and electromyogram (EMG). These statistics are transmitted *via* Bluetooth/Zigbee to connected distant portal gadgets, after which they are transmitted to a cloud data center for pre-processing and disease prediction. The individual's health record, such as a record of tobacco use and diabetes, observation records, and thorough medical (laboratory) records are all included in the ECD, which is another source of statistics. The ECD is kept in a cloud record and provides useful data on disease prediction.

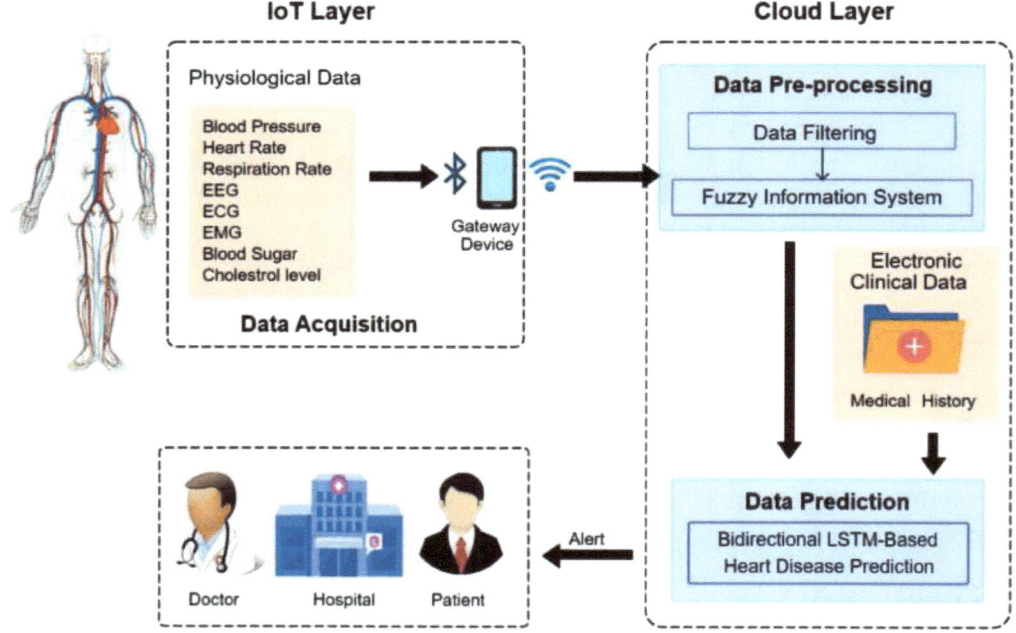

Fig. (1). Framework of cardiovascular disease risk prediction.

In this study, the Cleveland and Hungarian databases from the UCI ML repository are taken into consideration to identify the presence of cardiac illness from heart patient statistics. The suggested approach was applied to a collection of 14 characteristics related to hearts.

Data Preprocessing Layer

Since real-world statistics are often inconsistent, sparse, and noisy, pre-processing datasets have become essential before deploying ML algorithms. Proper treatment of missing data, feature selection, and normalization are necessary for effective cardiovascular disease prediction from a cardiovascular disease database. Signal anomalies, like noise and missing scores, can affect statistics obtained from wearable sensing devices. This can lead to inaccurate results or, in the instance of cardiovascular disease prediction, chaotic outcomes. To remove noise, inconsistencies, and duplicate entries from the data this chapter applies a widely recognized method called Kalman filtering. It just needs a small amount of processing power because of its straightforward structure. This unsupervised filtering technique is specialized to manage large real-time sensing device statistics and furnish results nearer to that of the actual readings from the sensing devices without distortion. Furthermore, this chapter employs two additional unsupervised filters during the data filtering phase: replacing missing values and eliminating worthless data. Substantial characteristics are eliminated by the first filter with an additional ninety percent of maximal variation. The subsequent filter fills in any data lacking from the organized database with the mean and median of the current dataset.

FIS

The word "fuzzy" describes something ambiguous or inexplicit, and the necessity of modeling ambiguous real-world occurrences served as the inspiration for the fuzzy network. A fuzzifier, an inference motor, a knowledge foundation, and a defuzzifier are the 4 parts that make up the typical fuzzy network. Fuzzy collections and language values may be used as data to a normal fuzzy structure, along with numerical data. Fuzzification is the procedure by which a crisp input gets assigned the appropriate fuzzy group by the fuzzifier. A collection of fuzzy conditioned constraints in the knowledge foundation serves as indicators of professional expertise, and the inference system uses them to connect the values of the input parameters to the language values of the output factor using an appropriate approximation reasoning technique. The knowledge foundation, which is comprised of a dataset and a rule base, applies domain expertise. Language management criteria are stored in the database, and domain professional information is stored in the rule base. If numerical data output is required, defuzzification adds crisp statistics to the generated fuzzy collection in addition to language values. A FIS is utilized to categorize the dangers of cardiovascular disease depending on individual wellness statistics.

The BP, ECG, and maximal heart rate data are generated, passed into the member operation, and fuzzified into fuzzy collections employing a fuzzy value spectrum. The operation of FIS for predicting the danger of cardiovascular disease is shown in Fig. (2).

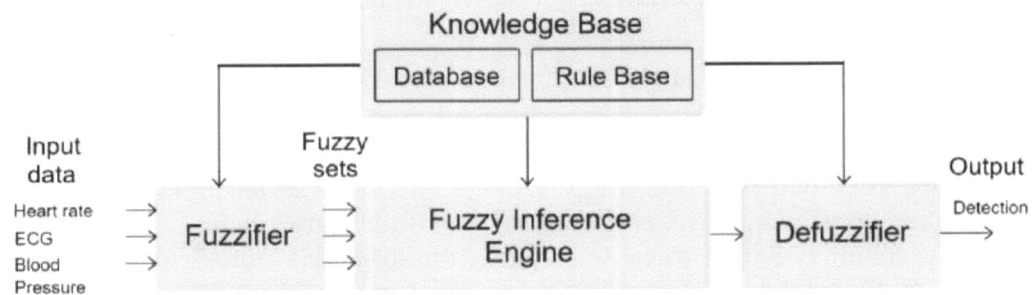

Fig. (2). Risk prediction of cardiovascular disease using FIS.

The resulting fuzzy collections are fed into the FIS so that it can categorize patients according to their medical records. The language parameters and the fuzzy collection of the FIS that corresponds to them are shown in Table **1**. The BP variable's member functionality and range are displayed in Table **2**.

Table 1. FIS-fuzzy collection and language factor.

Language Variable	Fuzzy Collection
BP	High, Normal, Low risks
Maximal heart rate	High, Normal, Low risks
ECG	High, Normal, Low risks

Table 2. BP-Member operation and range.

Member Operation	Range
High	90/130 and above
Normal	40/90–70/100
Low	70/110–80/120]

Using an appropriate approximation reasoning technique provided as fuzzy conditional constraints in the knowledge foundation, the value of the input parameter is translated into the language values of the output parameter. Together with matching member functions, the outcomes are categorized in the rule base according to these fuzzy rules. Patients who pose significant hazards are notified, and the cloud is used for storing and analyzing the individual's overall risk position in the future.

Prediction Data Layer

Sequence prediction issues have been around for a while and are frequently considered to be among the hardest to solve in the data science industry.

RNN

In recent times, DL methods have been widely used and studied to extract data from various forms of data. NNs are capable of learning patterns and uncovering previously unknown patterns. Many DL systems, like as the DNN, CNN, and RNN, take into account various characteristics of the source data. CNN and DNN generally function badly when managing time-oriented statistics in the feed. Textual, audio, and video areas involving consecutive input are dominated by RNNs. A cyclical connection, which permits the improvement of the current status depending on supply and previous conditions, is a common component of

RNN layouts. The recurrent or hidden layers of the RNNs are made up of recurrent cells. The input that is currently being received includes comments links and past moods that affect the moods of the recurrent cells. Different RNNs can be created by arranging recurrent tiers in different ways. Therefore, the recurrent unit and network architecture set RNNs apart. RNN performance is determined by different cells and the links inside them.

These networks have demonstrated extraordinary efficacy in certain scenarios. Examples of these systems are complete RNNs and selected RNNs, which are composed of standard recurrent modules (sigma and Tanh cells). Unfortunately, long-term connections are difficult for RNNs with normal recurrent cells to manage since it can be difficult to find the linking data when there is a significant lag in the relevant input data.

LSTM

In actuality, the LSTM NN is an RNN that has been uniquely improved by RNN. It appears that the basic RNN has a self-linked hidden layer that is not available in conventional NNs. RNN is suitable for time-series data analysis because it may improve the hidden layer state at the current period with the hidden layer state at the past era. However, due to the "neglecting" of basic time-series features, RNN gets harder to learn as time series length rises, and the gradient either vanishes or rises. By contrast, LSTM addresses the problem of RNN, which is often used to address the problem of long-term dependency but is unable to fully exploit sequential facts. Using three inputs (forget, input result), LSTM adds a memory cell state to the hidden layer neural endpoint to store historical information and regulates the improvement and disregarding of sequential data. Fig. (3) depicts the LSTM NN architecture.

Below time step t, the overall calculation process is as follows:

a. Forget gate calculation: Entries xt and ht-1 are passed *via* the source gate to compute the forget gate ft. The result is a value (0 approximates 1), which is then transmitted to the cell state data Ct-1 to determine if the previous cell state Ct-1 is preserved.

$$f_t = \sigma(W_f x_t + U_f h_{t-1} + b_f) \quad (1)$$

b. Source Gate: Change the source details i_t and the applicant cell condition $\bar{C}_t$.

$$\bar{C}_t = tanh(W_c x_t + U_c h_{t-1} + b_c) \quad (2)$$

$$i_t = \sigma(W_i x_t + U_i h_{t-1} + b_i) \tag{3}$$

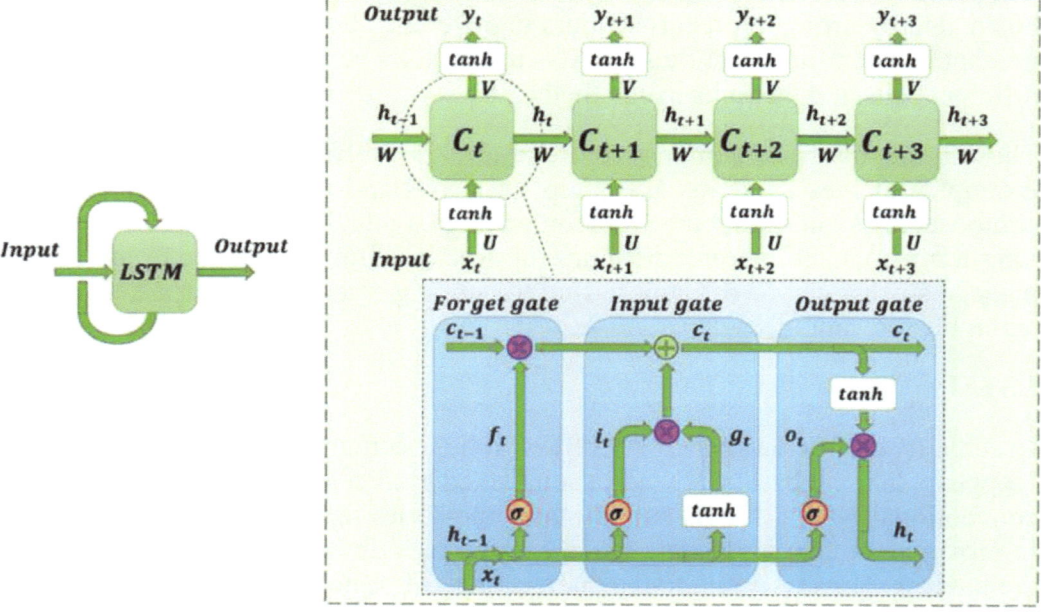

Fig. (3). The structure of LSTM NN.

c. Upgrade cell condition: The cell condition of t time stage C_t is upgraded based on the upgraded applicant cell condition $\bar{C}_t$ as well as the cell condition of t the prior period stage C_{t-1}.

$$C_t = f_t \times C_{t-1} + i_t \times \bar{C}_t \tag{4}$$

d. Outcome gate: Use result cell state and result entry OT to obtain result data Ct.

$$o_t = \sigma(W_o x_o + U_o h_{o-1} + b_o) \tag{5}$$

$$h_t = o_t \times \tanh C_t \tag{6}$$

The process of activation is expressed as:

$$\sigma(x) = \frac{1}{1 + e^{-x}} \tag{7}$$

$$\tanh(x) = \frac{e^x - e^{-x}}{e^x + e^{-x}} \tag{8}$$

Research Setup

Through the use of DL systems, including the suggested framework and the FIS coupled with the LSTM (FLSTM) framework, this study attempted to assess sequence prediction systems on the cardiovascular disease database. Using data from the University of California, Irvine (UCI) web machine learning and data mining archive, the framework makes use of the Cleveland and Hungarian cardiovascular disease databases. The fourteen characteristics are included in 303 and 294 files, accordingly, from the original databases on cardiovascular disease from Hungary and Cleveland. The sturdiness of the suggested DL framework was tested by increasing these instances to 100,000 data employing the database-generating instrument Mockaroo. One hundred thousand records are used to determine the system, with seventy percent going toward training activities and thirty percent toward testing activities. The suggested NN framework consists of four levels, the dense layer having 7 components, and two hidden layers. With a randomized mass initialization ranging from 0.1 to 0.2, the dropout amount is eighteen percent and the number of units is autonomously chosen depending on accuracy requirements. There is a 0.16 learning speed and a 0.96 decay speed. The batch dimension is 128 and the number of epochs is configured to be configurable. The momentum significance is 0.82. Cloud servers receive the IoT statistics collected *via* wireless body sensing networks (WBSNs) and use them for pre-processing and categorization operations. The study was run using the TensorFlow ML pack with Apache Spark and Cassandra for servers and storing architecture on the i2k2 Cloud system.

Performance Assessment

This part explores the implementation of the suggested system and outlines the results. Three different systems were used for evaluating the data that were left over after the preliminary pre-processing chores of data cleansing and data filtration. One of the algorithms used was the general LSTM for predicting illnesses. The subsequent system, known as FLSTM, blends the FIS and LSTM. Individuals' initial cardiovascular disease risk category is classified using the FIS, but predictions are made using the LSTM framework. The third approach, known as FBiLSTM in the research suggested, blends the FIS and Bi-LSTM for the prediction of cardiovascular disease. The performance measures of accuracy, precision, specificity, and functional measurement of the individual's risk for cardiovascular disease condition are used to evaluate each of these designs.

The evaluation and performance measures, together with techniques for contrasting the recommended system performance, are covered in this subpart. Understanding the interpretations of different evaluation criteria and the data they seek to convey is important for comparing since the underlying processes of these metrics may differ. These metrics include, among others, macro- and micro-averages, F-value, recall, accuracy, and precision. This set of measurements is reliant on a "confusion matrices."

The uses of cardiovascular risk prediction determine the relative significance of these four parts. Accuracy is described as a ratio of precise forecasts and total estimates (Equation **9**). Equation (**10**) defines specificity as the percentage of correctly expected negatives. The ratio of correctly predicted positives to overall positives is known as accuracy, or positive prediction value (Equation **11-13**).

$$Accuracy = \frac{TN + TP}{TN + FN + FP + TP} \tag{9}$$

$$Specifity = \frac{TN}{TN + FP} \tag{10}$$

$$Precision = \frac{\sum_{l=1}^{L} TP_l}{\sum_{l=1}^{L} FP_l + TP_l} \tag{11}$$

$$Recall = \frac{\sum_{l=1}^{L} TP_l}{\sum_{l=1}^{L} FN_l + TP_l} \tag{12}$$

$$F - value = \frac{\sum_{l=1}^{L} 2TP_l}{\sum_{l=1}^{L} FN_l + FP_l + 2TP_l} \tag{13}$$

RESULTS

Experiments are conducted on the types of generic LSTM, FIS integrated with LSTM (FLSTM), and the suggested framework to assess the suggested platform at different numbers of cases (ten percent to one hundred percent).

The performance of the LSTM, FLSTM, and the proposed framework is demonstrated in Tables 3, 4, and 5 along with the assessment indexes of accuracy, precision, recall, specificity, and F1-score.

Table 3. Performance metrics for precision, and accuracy.

-	-	Accuracy	-	-	Precision	-
Data (%)	Suggested	LSTM	FLSTM	Suggested	LSTM	FLSTM
10	94.8	94	94.5	94.9	94	94.6
20	96	94.3	95.5	96.0	94.3	95.5
30	96.7	94.5	96.2	96.7	94.5	96.2
40	97.2	94.6	96.6	97.2	94.6	96.6
50	97.6	94.7	97.0	97.6	94.7	97
60	97.9	94.8	97.3	97.9	94.8	97.3
70	98.2	94.8	97.5	98.2	94.8	97.5
80	98.4	94.9	97.7	98.4	94.9	97.7
90	98.6	95	97.9	98.7	95	97.9
100	98.8	95	98	98.8	95	98

Table 4. Performance metrics for recall and specificity.

	Recall			Specificity		
Data (%)	Suggested	LSTM	FLSTM	Suggested	LSTM	FLSTM
10	94.9	94	94.5	94.8	94	94.6
20	96	94.3	95.6	96	94.3	95.5
30	96.7	94.5	96.2	96.7	94.5	96.2
40	97.2	94.6	96.6	97.2	94.6	96.6
50	97.6	94.7	97	97.6	94.7	97
60	97.9	94.8	97.3	97.9	94.8	97.3
70	98.2	94.92	97.5	98.2	94.8	97.5
80	98.4	94.91	97.6	98.5	94.9	97.7
90	98.7	95	97.8	98.6	95	97.9
100	98.8	95	98	98.9	95	98

Table 5. Performance metrics for F-value.

Data	-	F1-value	-
-	Suggested	LSTM	FLSTM
10	94.8	94	94.5

(Table 5) cont.....

Data	-	F1-value	-
-	Suggested	LSTM	FLSTM
20	96	94.3	95.5
30	96.7	94.5	96.2
40	97.2	94.6	96.6
50	97.6	94.7	97
60	97.9	94.8	97.3
70	98.2	94.8	97.5
80	98.4	94.9	97.7
90	98.6	95	97.9
100	98.8	95	98

The study of the F1-value, recall, specificity, accuracy, and precision shown by the LSTM, FLSTM, and proposed framework are demonstrated in Figs. (**4 – 8**). Data for the study involving the three systems under consideration are raised from ten percent to one hundred percent.

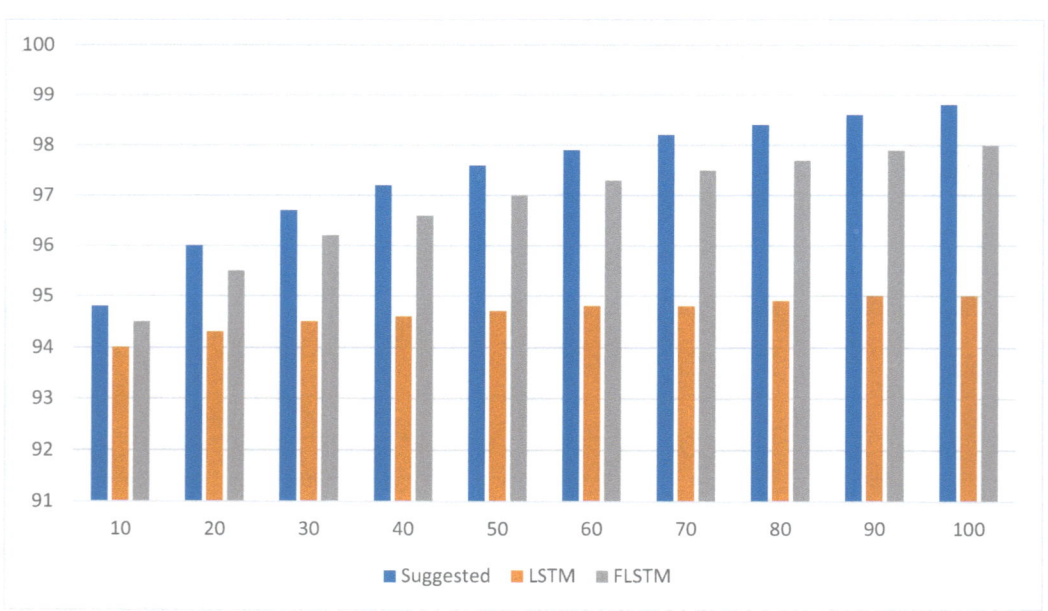

Fig. (4). Outcomes of the accuracy analysis.

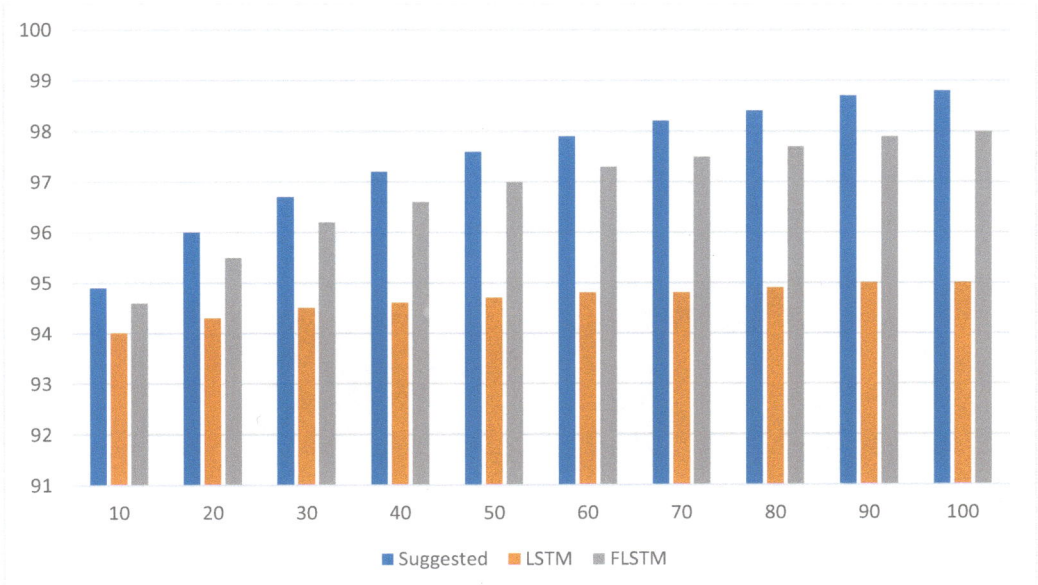

Fig. (5). Outcomes of the precision analysis.

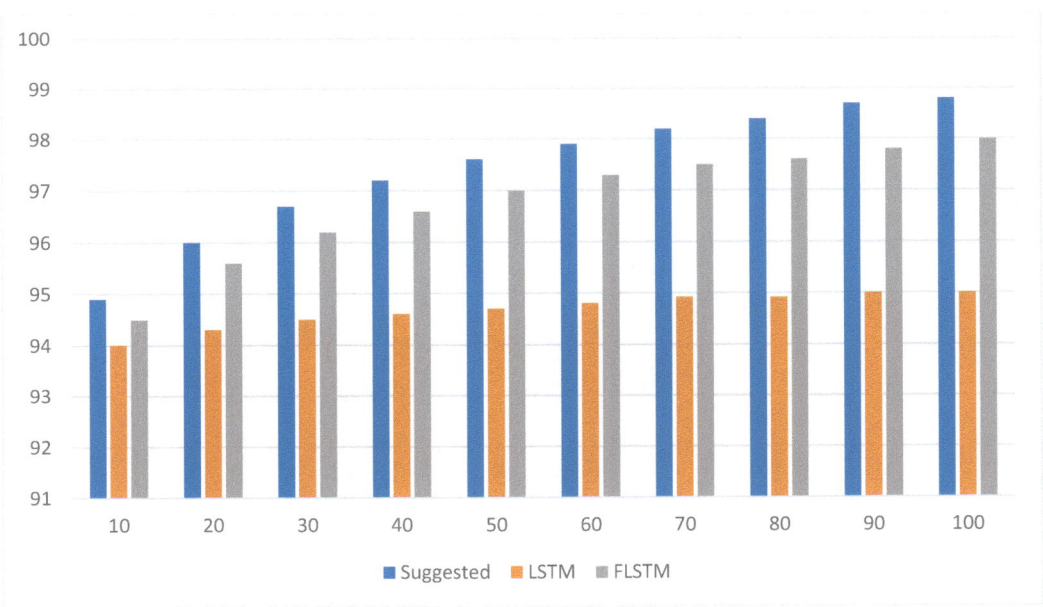

Fig. (6). Outcomes of the recall analysis.

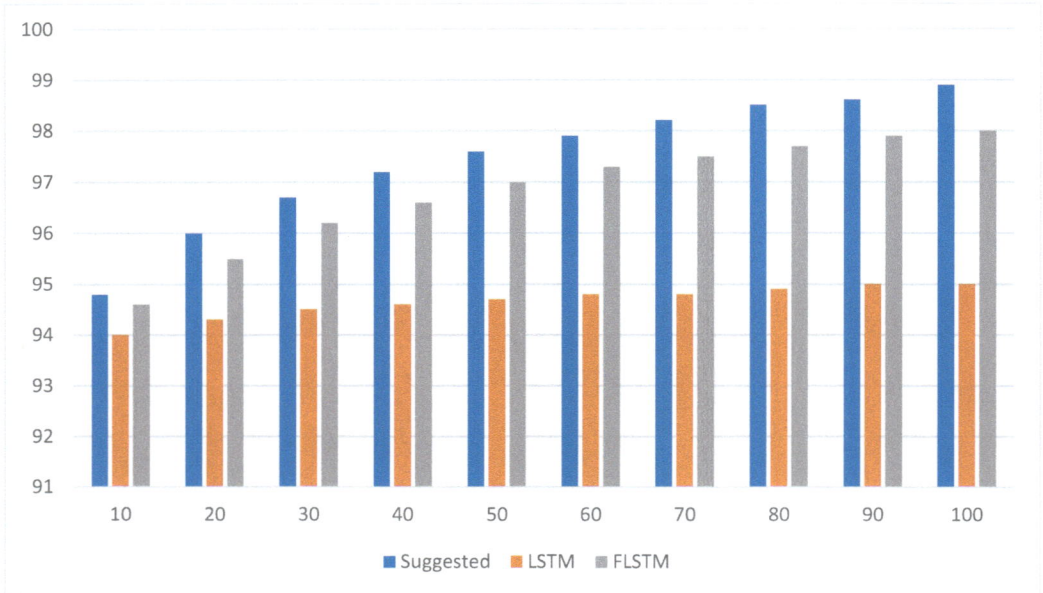

Fig. (7). Outcomes of the specificity analysis.

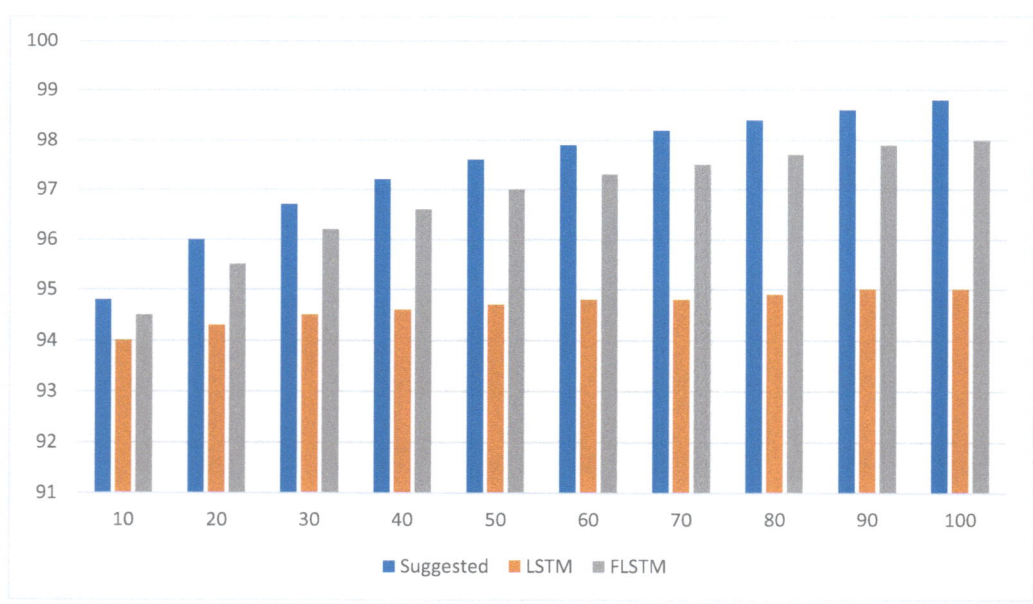

Fig. (8). Outcomes of F1-value.

Analysis of the suggested approach, LSTM, and FLSTM systems' accuracy, precision, specificity, and F1-value reveals that the recommended approach performs better than the other two models.

Table 6 provides an overall functionality comparison of the suggested approach, LSTM, and FLSTM systems.

Table 6. Comparing the suggested system's performance metrics.

Performance Measures (%)	Suggested	LSTM	FLSTM
Accuracy	98.86	95.07	98.04
Recall	98.81	95.06	98.04
Precision	98.9	95.07	98.03
Specificity	98.9	95.07	98.03
F1-value	98.86	95.07	98.03

It is acceptable to conclude that the proposed FIS with the Bi-LSTM structure operates better than the other systems with remarkable results when multiple operational factors are taken into consideration.

When there is a significant gap between the linked input data, RNNs are effective at managing sequential statistics but ineffective at managing long-term dependencies. LSTM was proposed as a solution to conventional RNN problems. LSTM uses a memory cell's hidden unit to store data from the prior input. Data from the past is retained *via* unidirectional LSTM. Bidirectional LSTM, on the other hand, can act on both past and prospective data since it has two separate LSTM hidden layers with similar outputs in different orientations. The UCI cardiovascular disease database, which contains 100,000 records, was used to execute the tests employing generic LSTM systems, an FIS coupled with LSTM, and suggested BiLSTM systems for cardiovascular disease risk prediction. From Fig. (9) FLSTM (FIS plus LSTM) outperforms the 95.0% accuracy of the generic LSTM algorithm with 98.04% accuracy. With 98.8% accuracy, the suggested setup with FIS and bi-LSTM beats the two earlier versions. Comparing the proposed approach to the other two systems, it also performs better in terms of F1-value, precision, recall, and specificity. DNNs are shown to be significantly impacted by the activation method selected, with sigmoid and tanh activation processes being used in the general LSTM system. Swish, Tanh, and Leaky ReLU activation processes are used to model each of the two LSTM cells in the suggested framework; hyperparameter adjustment produced improved outcomes.

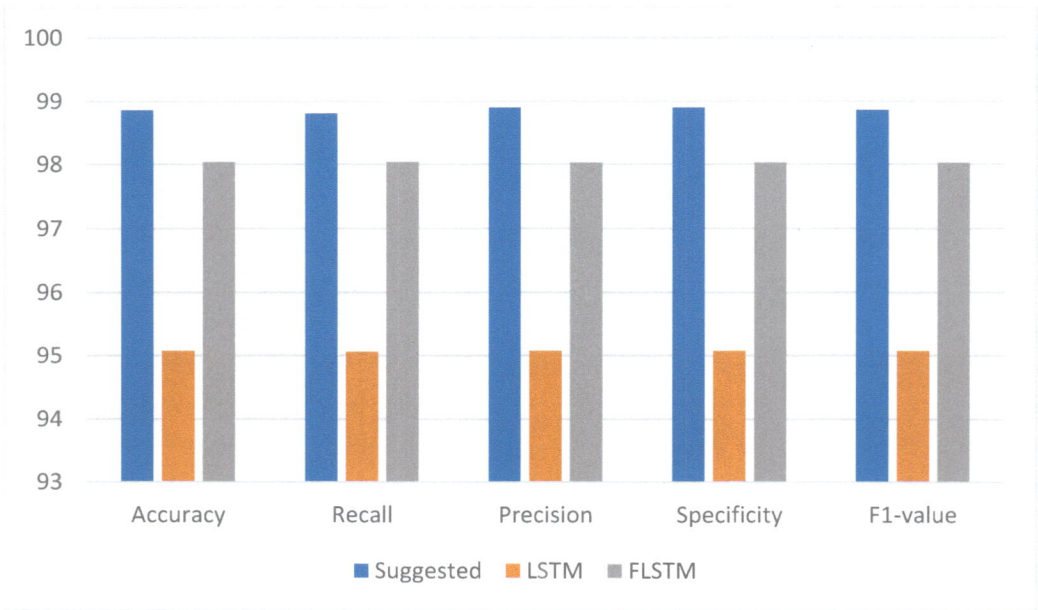

Fig. (9). Performance outcomes of the suggested model.

The prediction accuracy of the suggested research is evaluated using state-of-the-art methods that make use of databases on cardiac disease. Table **7** presents the findings of a comparison investigation that analyzed the accuracy outcomes of the suggested system with the models that are currently in the research, arranged in sequence of accuracy. The comparison of the suggested system's performance outcomes with the current platforms is shown in Fig. (**10**).

Table 7. In-depth contrast with the most recent systems.

Reference Paper	Approach	Accuracy (%)
[16]	Type-2 fuzzy logic	86
[17]	Fuzzy Analytic Hierarchy and ANN	91
[18]	Adaptive neuro-fuzzy	92.3
[19]	Ensemble classifiers	85.4
[20]	Hybrid model of RF and linear approach	88.7
[21]	$\chi 2$ Statistical model and DNN	91.5
[22]	Relief feature selection and DT	92.8
[23]	Adaptive neuro-FIS	94.1
[24]	Sequential forward selection and RF	98

(Table 7) cont.....

Reference Paper	Approach	Accuracy (%)
[25]	Kernel RF	98
[26]	Fuzzy rules and DNN	96.5
[27]	DCNN	98.2
[28]	Ensemble DL method	98.5
[29]	CNN	97
[30]	Linear-SVC and DNN	98.5
[31]	Cluster-based Bi-LSTM	94.7
-	The suggested method	98.8

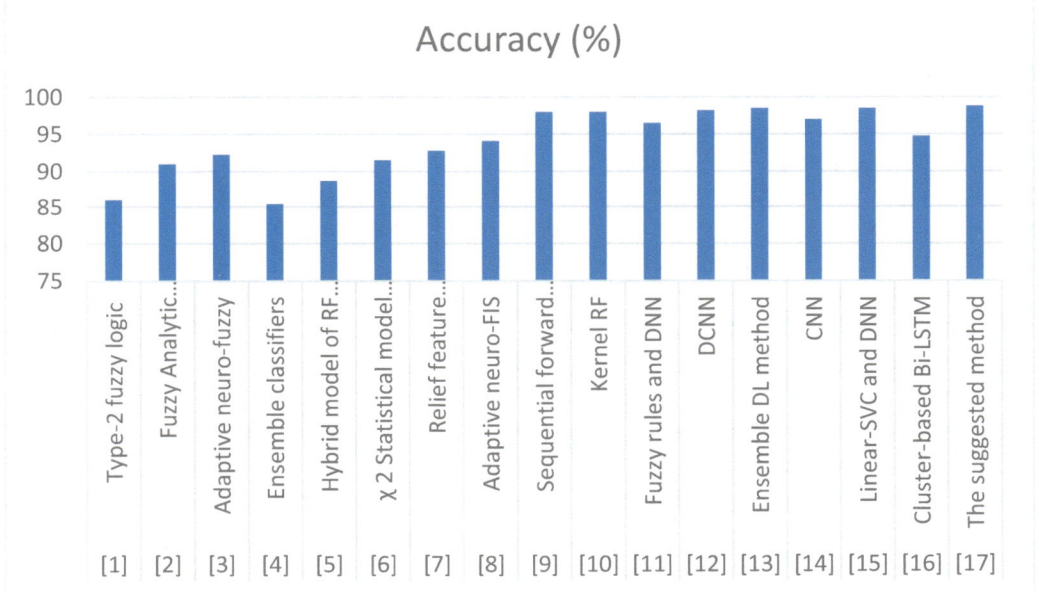

Fig. (10). In-depth contrast with the most recent systems.

The performance of the suggested method outperforms that of the current systems, according to the comparison with relevant state-of-the-art cardiovascular disease prediction methods.

Due to their urgency and context-sensitivity, large-scale IoT-driven activities for real-time intelligent systems in the medical industry require quick analysis. Increased data congestion, high bandwidth usage, and service issues are the results of both the growth in IoT gadget count and the increase in data produced by smart gadget usage. Because of its centralized nature, the cloud computation paradigm is unable to handle the constraints faced by the Cloud-IoT framework, which include lag, connection, and bandwidth utilization. Due to these drawbacks, decentralized edge and fog computation paradigms were made possible, allowing computation and storage to be managed by edge units that are nearer to the data resource. The Cloud is enhanced and extended by these more recent computation innovations, which also make AI operations possible at the edge units. This hierarchy edge-fog-cloud paradigm effectively handles the massive amounts of data collected by IoT gadgets while minimizing lag, which significantly lowers the delay limitations. To manage the rise in IoT data while overcoming the inherent limitations of the cloud, like higher lag and bandwidth consumption, the suggested cloud-based prediction platform can therefore be implemented at the fog/edge tiers in the future.

CONCLUSION

The IoTs have significant uses in a variety of fields, including industrial, healthcare, armed forces, agricultural, and telephony. Technological breakthroughs have facilitated the emergence of several intelligent uses, particularly in the healthcare field. The FIS and the bidirectional LSTM of an RNN are used in this study to develop an IoT-Cloud-based smart medical system for heart disease risk prediction. The estimated system outperforms existing cutting-edge heart disease prediction systems with accuracy, precision, sensitivity, specificity, and F1 values of 98.85%, 98.9%, 98.8%, 98.89%, and 98.85%, respectively. DL algorithms have a great deal of untapped promise in medical study; this is merely one aspect of the field's use of them. The system may be improved to autonomously suggest an individual's nutrition and physical activity based on their medical status and the guidance of a cardiac expert. IoT gadgets are used by the suggested smart heart disease prediction systems to collect data; the cloud is used for other common functions. This research may be expanded in the future to incorporate fog/edge computation, where time-sensitive computational activities might be finished at the fog/edge tiers to get around the Cloud's intrinsic drawbacks, like higher lag and bandwidth usage while managing the rise in IoT data. When fog/edge computation is used, the effectiveness of medical services may be revolutionized with accurate and prompt disease forecasts, combined with quick reactions and flexible decision-making by physicians, which will enhance the total quality of service.

REFERENCES

[1] M. Bhatia, and S.K. Sood, "Game theoretic decision making in IoT-assisted activity monitoring of defence personnel", *Multimedia Tools Appl.,* vol. 76, no. 21, pp. 21911-21935, 2017.
[http://dx.doi.org/10.1007/s11042-017-4611-3]

[2] F. Firouzi, B. Farahani, and A. Marinšek, "The convergence and interplay of edge, fog, and cloud in the AI-driven Internet of Things (IoT)", *Inf. Syst.,* vol. 107, p. 101840, 2022.
[http://dx.doi.org/10.1016/j.is.2021.101840]

[3]   A.A. Nancy, D. Ravindran, P.M.D. Raj Vincent, K. Srinivasan, and D. Gutierrez Reina, *Electronics,* vol. 11, no. 15, p. 2292, 2022. "Iot-cloud-based smart healthcare monitoring system for heart disease prediction *via* deep learning",
[http://dx.doi.org/10.3390/electronics11152292]

[4]   A. Botta, W. de Donato, V. Persico, and A. Pescapé, "Integration of cloud computing and internet of things: a survey", *Future Gener. Comput. Syst.,* vol. 56, pp. 684-700, 2016.
[http://dx.doi.org/10.1016/j.future.2015.09.021]

[5]   G.L. Santos, P. Takako Endo, M.F. Ferreira da Silva Lisboa Tigre, L.G. Ferreira da Silva, D. Sadok, J. Kelner, and T. Lynn, "Analyzing the availability and performance of an e-health system integrated with edge, fog and cloud infrastructures", *Journal of Cloud Computing.* vol. 7, no. 16, pp. 1–15, 2018.
[http://dx.doi.org/10.1186/s13677-018-0118-3]

[6]   S. Suresh, "Big data and predictive analytics: applications in the care of children", *Pediatr. Clin. North Am.,* vol. 63, no. 2, pp. 357-366, 2016.
[http://dx.doi.org/10.1016/j.pcl.2015.12.007] [PMID: 27017041]

[7]   I.P. Sofjan, I. Salik, and P.J. Panzica, "SAP BusinessObjects in Medical Informatics", *Cureus,* vol. 15, no. 6, p. e40208, 2023.
[PMID: 37435258]

[8]   R. Miotto, F. Wang, S. Wang, X. Jiang, and J.T. Dudley, "Deep learning for healthcare: review, opportunities and challenges", *Brief. Bioinform.,* vol. 19, no. 6, pp. 1236-1246, 2018.
[http://dx.doi.org/10.1093/bib/bbx044] [PMID: 28481991]

[9]   S.K. Pandey, and R.R. Janghel, "Recent deep learning techniques, challenges and its applications for medical healthcare system: a review", *Neural Process. Lett.,* vol. 50, no. 2, pp. 1907-1935, 2019.
[http://dx.doi.org/10.1007/s11063-018-09976-2]

[10] A. Muniasamy, S. Tabassam, M.A. Hussain, H. Sultana, V. Muniasamy, and R. Bhatnagar, "Deep learning for predictive analytics in healthcare", *The International Conference on Advanced Machine Learning Technologies and Applications (AMLTA2019), ,* 2020 A. Hassanien, A. Azar, T. Gaber, R. Bhatnagar, and M. F. Tolba, Eds., *Advances in Intelligent Systems and Computing,* vol. 921, Springer, Cham, 2020, pp. 33–42.
[http://dx.doi.org/10.1007/978-3-030-14118-9_4]

[11] A. Latif, A.Z. Arfianto, J.E. Poetro, T.N. Phong, and E.T. Helmy, "Temperature monitoring system for baby incubator based on visual basic", *Journal of Robotics and Control [JRC],,* vol. 2, no. 1, pp. 47-50, 2021.
[http://dx.doi.org/10.18196/jrc.2151]

[12] P. Amin, N.R. Anikireddypally, S. Khurana, S. Vadakkemadathil, and W. Wu, "Personalized health monitoring using predictive analytics", *2019 IEEE Fifth International Conference on Big Data Computing Service and Applications (BigDataService), ,* 2019 Newark, CA, USA, 2019, pp. 271-278.
[http://dx.doi.org/10.1109/BigDataService.2019.00048]

[13] A.G. Alvanou, A. Stylidou, and T.P. Exarchos, "Web-Based Decision Support System for Coronary Heart Disease Diagnosis", *Proc. GeNeDis 2020,* P. Vlamos, Ed., *Advances in Experimental Medicine and Biology,* vol. 1338, Springer, Cham, 2021, pp. 31–38.
[http://dx.doi.org/10.1007/978-3-030-78775-2_5]

[14] R. Kumar and R. Sharma, "AI-driven dynamic trust management and blockchain-based security in industrial IoT," *Computers and Electrical Engineering,* vol. 123, pt. C, 2025.

[15] M. Muzammal, R. Talat, A.H. Sodhro, and S. Pirbhulal, "A multi-sensor data fusion enabled ensemble approach for medical data from body sensor networks", *Inf. Fusion,* vol. 53, pp. 155-164, 2020.
[http://dx.doi.org/10.1016/j.inffus.2019.06.021]

[16] F.D. Fuchs, and P.K. Whelton, "High blood pressure and cardiovascular disease", *Hypertension,* vol. 75, no. 2, pp. 285-292, 2020.

[http://dx.doi.org/10.1161/HYPERTENSIONAHA.119.14240] [PMID: 31865786]

[17] A. Zanchetti, C. Thomopoulos, and G. Parati, "Randomized controlled trials of blood pressure lowering in hypertension: a critical reappraisal", *Circ. Res.,* vol. 116, no. 6, pp. 1058-1073, 2015.
[http://dx.doi.org/10.1161/CIRCRESAHA.116.303641] [PMID: 25767290]

[18] C.B.C. Latha, and S.C. Jeeva, "Improving the accuracy of prediction of heart disease risk based on ensemble classification techniques", *Informatics in Medicine Unlocked,* vol. 16, p. 100203, 2019.
[http://dx.doi.org/10.1016/j.imu.2019.100203]

[19] P. Joseph, D. Leong, M. McKee, S.S. Anand, J.D. Schwalm, K. Teo, A. Mente, and S. Yusuf, "Reducing the global burden of cardiovascular disease, part 1: the epidemiology and risk factors", *Circ. Res.,* vol. 121, no. 6, pp. 677-694, 2017.
[http://dx.doi.org/10.1161/CIRCRESAHA.117.308903] [PMID: 28860318]

[20] P.A. Sapp, T.M. Riley, A.M. Tindall, V.K. Sullivan, E.A. Johnston, K.S. Petersen, and P.M. Kris-Etherton, "Nutrition and Atherosclerotic Cardiovascular Disease", In: *Present Knowledge in Nutrition..* 11th ed., vol. 2: Clinical and Applied Topics in Nutrition, Academic Press, 2020, pp. 393–411.
[http://dx.doi.org/10.1016/B978-0-12-818460-8.00022-8]

[21] M.A. Moreno-Ibarra, Y. Villuendas-Rey, M.D. Lytras, C. Yáñez-Márquez, and J.C. Salgado-Ramírez, "Classification of diseases using machine learning algorithms: A comparative study", *Mathematics,* vol. 9, no. 15, p. 1817, 2021.
[http://dx.doi.org/10.3390/math9151817]

[22] N.C. Long, P. Meesad, and H. Unger, "A highly accurate firefly based algorithm for heart disease prediction", *Expert Syst. Appl.,* vol. 42, no. 21, pp. 8221-8231, 2015.
[http://dx.doi.org/10.1016/j.eswa.2015.06.024]

[23] S. Mohan, C. Thirumalai, and G. Srivastava, "Effective heart disease prediction using hybrid machine learning techniques", *IEEE Access,* vol. 7, pp. 81542-81554, 2019.
[http://dx.doi.org/10.1109/ACCESS.2019.2923707]

[24] H. Ahmed, E.M.G. Younis, A. Hendawi, and A.A. Ali, "Heart disease identification from patients' social posts, machine learning solution on Spark", *Future Gener. Comput. Syst.,* vol. 111, pp. 714-722, 2020.
[http://dx.doi.org/10.1016/j.future.2019.09.056]

[25] A.H.N. Kishore, and V.E. Jayanthi, "Neuro-fuzzy based medical decision support system for coronary artery disease diagnosis and risk level prediction", *J. Comput. Theor. Nanosci.,* vol. 15, no. 3, pp. 1027-1037, 2018.
[http://dx.doi.org/10.1166/jctn.2018.7198]

[26] L. Ali, A. Rahman, A. Khan, M. Zhou, A. Javeed and J. A. Khan, "An automated diagnostic system for heart disease prediction based on χ^2 statistical model and optimally configured deep neural network," in *IEEE Access*, vol. 7, pp. 34938-34945, 2019.
[http://dx.doi.org/10.1109/ACCESS.2019.2904800]

[27] P. Dileep, K.N. Rao, P. Bodapati, S. Gokuruboyina, R. Peddi, A. Grover, and A. Sheetal, "An automatic heart disease prediction using cluster-based bi-directional LSTM (C-BiLSTM) algorithm", *Neural Comput. Appl.,* vol. 35, no. 10, pp. 7253-7266, 2023.
[http://dx.doi.org/10.1007/s00521-022-07064-0]

[28] T. Mazhar, Q. Nasir, I. Haq, M. M. Kamal, I. Ullah, T. Kim, H. G. Mohamed, and N. Alwadai, "A novel expert system for the diagnosis and treatment of heart disease," *Electronics,* vol. 11, no. 23, Art. no. 3989, 2022.

[29] A.K. Paul, P.C. Shill, M.R.I. Rabin, and K. Murase, "Adaptive weighted fuzzy rule-based system for the risk level assessment of heart disease", *Appl. Intell.,* vol. 48, no. 7, pp. 1739-1756, 2018.
[http://dx.doi.org/10.1007/s10489-017-1037-6]

[30] A. Mehmood, M. Iqbal, Z. Mehmood, A. Irtaza, M. Nawaz, T. Nazir, and M. Masood, "Prediction of heart disease using deep convolutional neural networks", *Arab. J. Sci. Eng.*, vol. 46, no. 4, pp. 3409-3422, 2021.
[http://dx.doi.org/10.1007/s13369-020-05105-1]

[31] *Frontiers in Intelligent Computing: Theory and Applications,* S. Satapathy, V. Bhateja, B. Nguyen, N. Nguyen, and D. N. Le, Eds., *Advances in Intelligent Systems and Computing,* vol. 1013, Springer, Singapore, 2020.
[http://dx.doi.org/10.1007/978-981-32-9186-7_21]

CHAPTER 11

Adoption of Machine Learning Techniques in Smart Applications based on Blockchain Technology

K.M. Rashmi[1,*], **Balraj Kumar**[2], **K.T. Thilagham**[3], **Harish Kumar**[4], **S. Aswath**[5], **Mohit Tiwari**[6] and **Rahul Chauhan**[7]

[1] *Department of Electronics and Communication Engineering, Manipal Institute of Technology Bengaluru, Manipal Academy of Higher Education, Manipal, Karnataka, India*

[2] *School of Computer Application, Lovely Professional University, Phagwara, Punjab, India*

[3] *Department of Metallurgical Engineering, Government College of Engineering Salem, Salem, India*

[4] *Department of Computer Science, King Khalid University, Abha, Saudi Arabia*

[5] *Department of Electronics & Communication Engineering, Vel Tech Rangarajan Dr Sagunthala R&D Institute of Science and Technology, Chennai, India*

[6] *Department of Computer Science and Engineering, Bharati Vidyapeeth's College of Engineering, Delhi, India*

[7] *Department of Computer Science, Graphic Era Hill University, Graphic Era Deemed to be University, Dehradun, Uttarakhand-248007, India*

Abstract: The Internet of Things (IoT) has advanced toward smart houses as a result of the widespread detection and supply administration brought about by the advancement of technological advances in the field of sensing devices advancements. Many IoT gadgets in smart houses are represented by gateway links, the safety of which is dependent on the centralized framework. The blockchain structure is thought of as a smart house gateway to handle safety concerns in this system by fending off potential threats and utilizing the machine learning algorithm Deep Reinforcement Learning (DRL). The safety and dependability of the suggested blockchain-oriented smart house strategy were thoroughly assessed in terms of reach, confidentiality, and authenticity. In the data storage and transfer of blocks, blockchain is used to circumvent conventional centralized design. The capacity of networked users to authenticate is caused by the data authenticity within and outside of the smart house. The system that is being exhibited is built on the Ethereum blockchain, and its safety, responsiveness, and accuracy are measured. The results of the study demonstrate that the suggested fix outperforms more current, published works. The most successful parts of the suggested method to enhance structure performance oriented on appropriate values and integrate

---

* **Corresponding author K.M. Rashmi:** Department of Electronics and Communication Engineering, Manipal Institute of Technology Bengaluru, Manipal Academy of Higher Education, Manipal, Karnataka India; E-mail: rashmi.km@manipal.edu

Keshav Kaushik, Rewa Sharma & Ayodeji Olalekan Salau (Eds.)
All rights reserved-© 2026 Bentham Science Publishers

with blockchain in terms of smart house safety oriented on smart gadgets to prevent sharing and confidentiality hackers are found in DRL, a machine learning-based method. This chapter tested the suggested approach using two different kinds of databases and then contrasted it to other state-of-the-art systems. In the subsequent phase, when there are sixteen percent disparities in terms of enhancing the accuracy of smart houses, a DRL with an accuracy of 96.7 percent operates better and produces more powerful results compared to Artificial Neural Networks with an accuracy of 80.05%.

Keywords: Deep reinforcement learning, Blockchain, Machine learning, Smart home, Smart applications.

INTRODUCTION

Over the last few years, data has emerged as a crucial resource of expertise and, *via* smart applications, it has opened up novel avenues for solving issues in real-world industries including finance, bioinformatics, farming, and wireless communications [1, 2]. People can accomplish the intended activity more quickly due to these data-driven applications that integrate relevant information into user expertise [3]. It makes information functional, enhances client communications, personalizes the client's expertise, boosts functional effectiveness, and opens up novel commercial opportunities [4]. A person's life can be made simple by a variety of smart applications, like smart houses, hospitals, cities, *etc*. With the ability to control smart houses and improve human lifestyles, contemporary society is thought to include smart innovations. The gadgets, namely smart devices, can be linked to share data with other gadgets in the house through an Internet of Things (IoT)-based framework [5]. From five hundred million smart house to 700 million gadgets in 2018–2022, the mean annual expansion of smart houses and their technology was over 30 percent [6].

The vast volume of data produced by these apps presents challenges for keeping databases, as well as safety concerns with its communication. A distributed database system called blockchain can be utilized to address these problems [7]. Blockchain, which has a dispersed database system, has been employed to address these problems. It was created in 2008 by Satoshi Nakamoto and comprised a collection of networked devices that work together as a time-stamped, tamper-proof ledger [8]. It is made up of a series of blocks joined by basics in cryptography. The 3 pillars of blockchain are immutability, decentralization, and openness. These three features made it possible for a broad spectrum of uses, such as the presence of electronic currency (currency that doesn't exist physically) and analyses of its appropriateness for smart applications [9]. Even though blockchain guarantees confidentiality and safety, different weaknesses also began surfacing once it was implemented.

Since conventional techniques rely on signatures to identify trends, a strong Intrusion Detection System (IDS) is necessary to address the previously stated problem. However, one of the newer technologies known as machine learning (ML) can be utilized to analyze data traffic and find breach and attack trends [10]. Therefore, creating successful and rapid methods to examine this enormous volume of data is essential for managing blockchain-based smart applications [11]. As a result, ML is widely used in modern society and is used on twelve occasions a day without the user even realizing it. ML allows machines to process information, operate, and research without human oversight [12]. Deep Reinforcement Learning (DRL) is a new technology that may be applied to interruption areas and assault trends in the stream of data assessment [13]. Depending on several uses, like data exchange in the smart house, this paper shows the integration of blockchain and DRL in smart houses.

LITERATURE REVIEW

To safeguard the smart house against threads, a study introduced a blockchain-based safe system that makes use of IoT detection devices [14]. This system's execution demonstrates safe communication amongst the Internet of Things gadgets in a dispersed setting.

The incorporation of blockchain technology and IoT with a smart area concept is presented [15], providing clients with a connection to the electricity grid. The created technology establishes a link between the client and the blockchain within the electricity grid network. The one who accesses the solar panel setup may entertain the system and purchase and trade the power through blockchain.

The application of smart house technologies in household settings is expanding as a result of recent advancements. With the use of gadgets and management systems, it is possible to effortlessly regulate the living space [16].

The smart house connection was introduced [17] using safety flaws. Because of a lack of client data, employing an ISP to manage gadgets and verify certificates is feasible but insufficient for safety.

Blockchain technology and ML were integrated into the smart grid's renewable power supply, as demonstrated in a study [18]. Hyperledger Calliper is the applicable blockchain system, which is chosen depending on speed, delay, and resource utilization. The power crowdsourced structure can benefit from this approach.

METHODOLOGY

Adoption of Blockchain and DRL in Smart House

The blockchain and ML-integrated smart house application is presented in this part. With the advancement of technological advances, the smart house has emerged as a well-known method for securing properties, optimizing the application of IoT gadgets, and resolving the issue of hacker assaults aimed at obtaining user data. This study suggested DRL-integrated blockchain-enabled smart house security during this procedure. DRL is primarily used because it is a learning-based method, which improves smart house performance more than other works now in use. The blockchain-based smart house design with RL is depicted in Fig. (**1**). Data is gathered from various smart gadgets and IoT detectors. The DRL architecture is utilized by the database to eliminate faults like interruption, reiteration, and loss of data value from the blockchain. The associated worries are about data being removed from the DRL architecture. DRL can concentrate on chain sections rather than the method of gathering data. For this purpose, a particular structure for detecting fraud and theft depending on predictions is created.

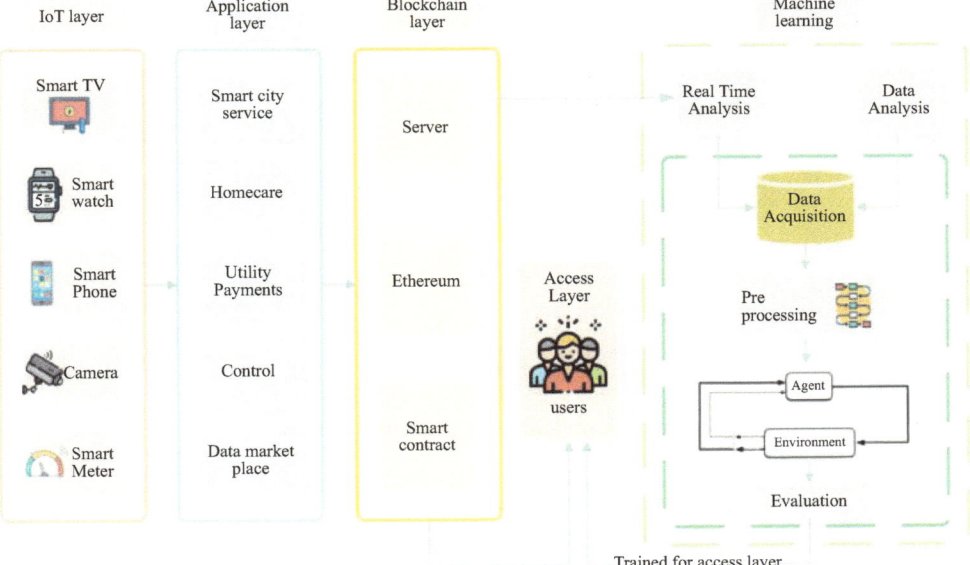

Fig. (1). The blockchain-based smart house design with ML.

DRL

Using ML methods inside the design of a smart house became an everlasting answer for several issues. The most important IoT gadgets for enhancing safety at home are under the management of these methods. The value operation, ecological designs, and approaches are all effectively optimized and expressed in this procedure using the DRL method, which works end-to-end. Employing the initial high-dimensional dataset and the foundation of the management regulations, DRL may construct a framework dependent on pattern extraction. Fig. (**2**) illustrates a decision-control and optimization-based DLR. This method is divided into two primary groups: training and execution. The training portion is a learning-based segment that employs decision-making to optimize the execution of parts to acquire information in an authentic setting. When there is a crisis, the agent adjusts to the changed surroundings by enhancing the collected compensation instead of replacing optimization.

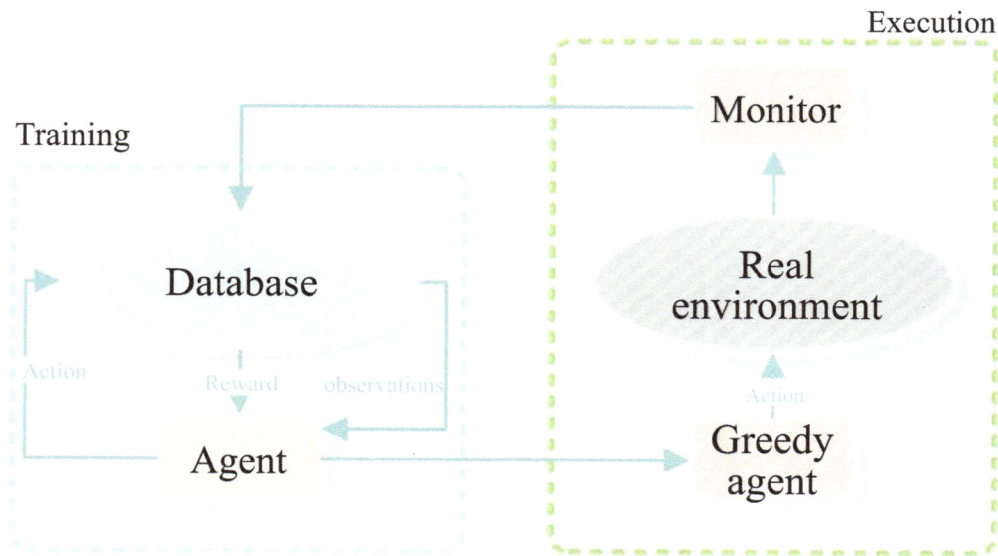

Fig. (2). DRL design in smart house optimization and decision management.

Blockchain-Based Gateway System for Smart Houses

Smart house gateways that use blockchain technology provide decisive data transfer, power, authorization, and gadget trust. A dispersed and centralized system at the blockchain's cloud tier is a smart house. As shown in Fig. (**3**), the proposed blockchain-based smart house is composed of three primary stages: the gadget, the gateway, and the cloud tier. Smart gadgets are gathered in gadget tiers that gather and keep track of data from various IoT gadgets set up in smart houses. Depending on customer requirements, the gateway tier stores data that is produced from the device tier. Every gateway's procedure data and gateway ID are registered in the blockchain by the final layer, known as the cloud layer. Users have shared access to the blocks whenever they require them. The gadgets can gather and store data in blockchain because of the data-gathering procedure. The user can construct blocks, layout, check, and more with this procedure.

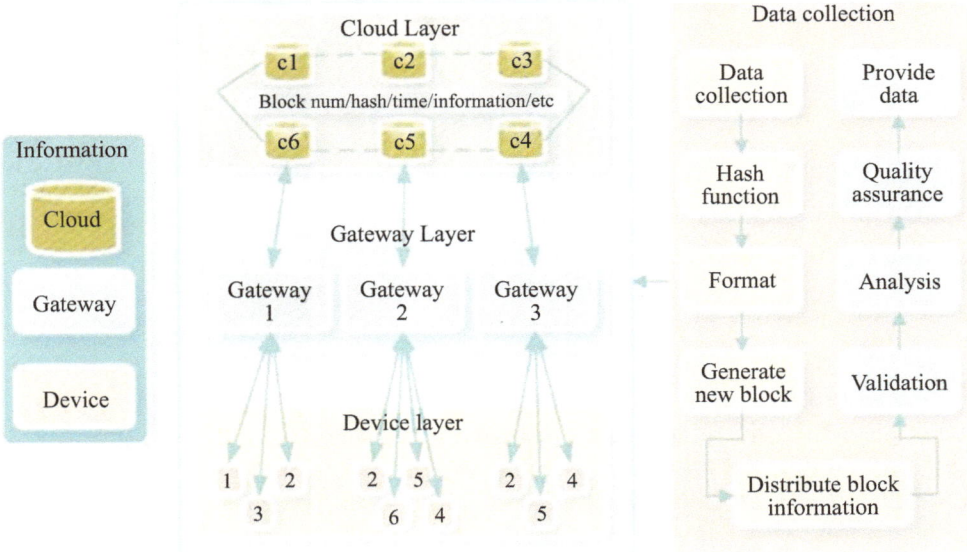

Fig. (3). Smart house gateway design built on a blockchain-enabled cloud infrastructure.

The block architecture in this framework is depicted in Fig. (4). The 5 key parts of the blocks are discussed below:

- **Previous Block Hash:** The blocks constantly save their prior block hash data to maintain the tamper-proof nature of the blockchain system.
- **Timestamp:** The timestamp is included in the block, records as timing data, and saves the metadata to track the beginning and finish duration of any occurrence.
- **Nonce:** The desired number for quantitative assessment used to generate random numbers is called Nonce.
- **FromDeviceID:** Documentation of the future activities of the source gadget.
- **ToDeviceID:** Note the desired gadget transaction location.

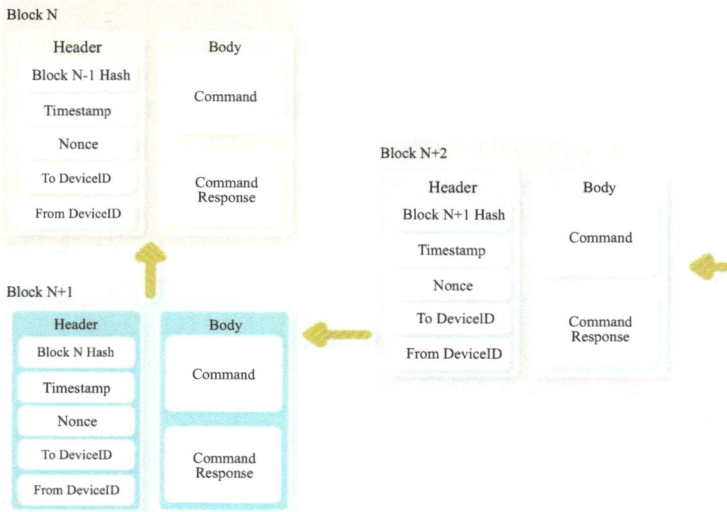

Fig. (4). Blockchain framework.

The steps involved in requesting user permission and validation are shown in Figs. (**5** and **6**). Initially, a smart application must be installed and an individual key must be generated for every account to authorize the user. The next step is to register an individual key using the Rest API. To verify the login, you can log in to the user in the super-node and validate it.

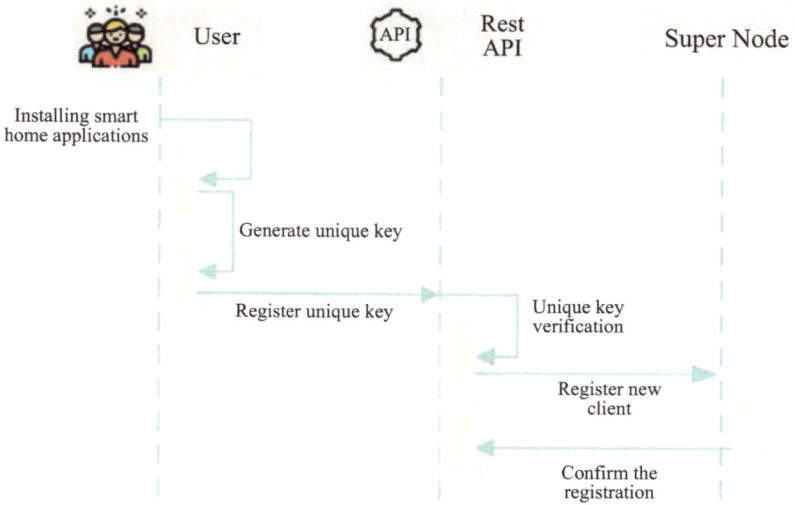

Fig. (5). User authentication procedure.

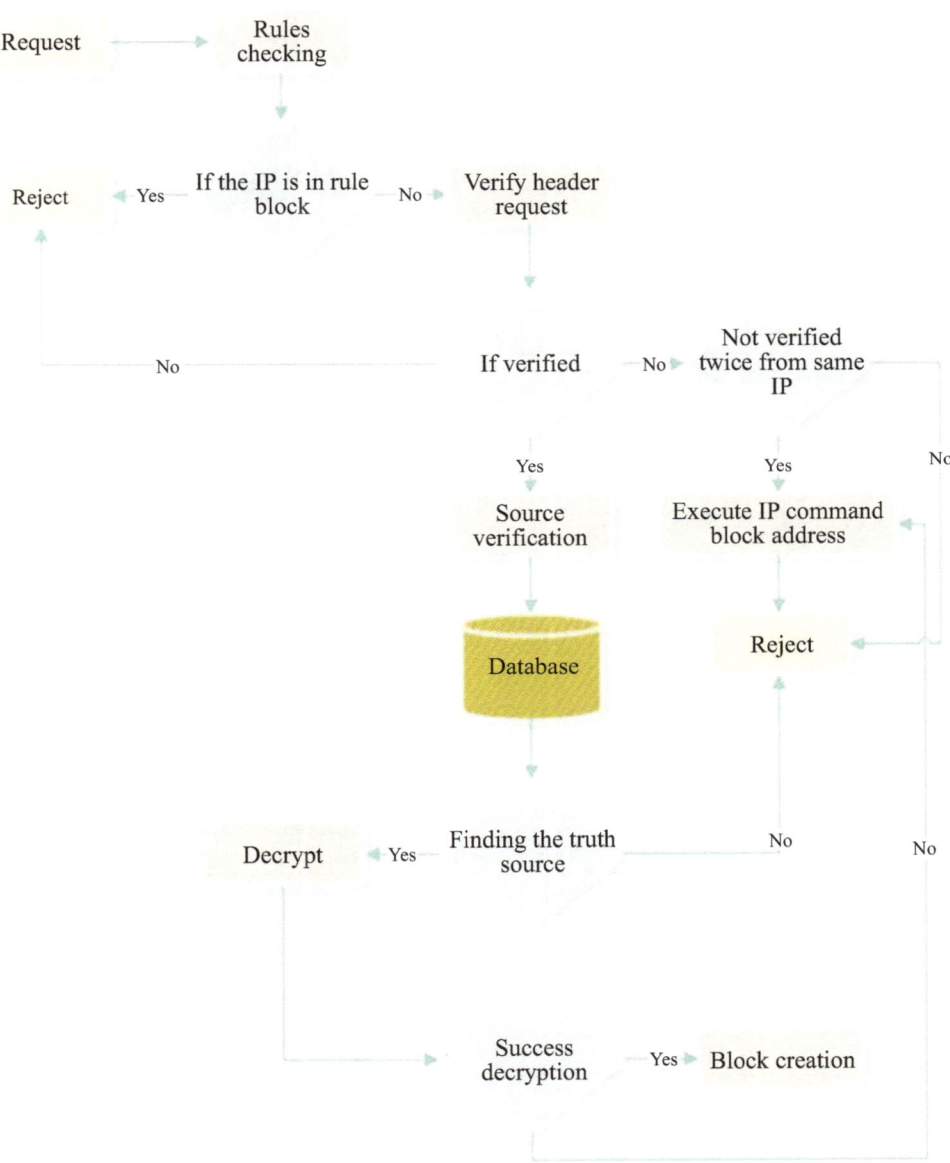

Fig. (6). Validation request procedure.

RESULTS

The research findings and the application of the DRL and blockchain-based smart house design are presented in this part.

Study Setup

The summary of the developed setting is shown in Table **3**. This machine has 32 GB of memory that is in operation. Ethereum is the blockchain architecture that is being shown. DRL is the ML method in use. Table **1** present below shows the research setup.

Table 1. Research setup.

Element	Details
Blockchain design	Ethereum
Memory	32
OS	Ubuntu Linux 18.04.1 LTS
CPU	Intel(R) Core (TM) i7-8700@3.20 GHz
Python	3.6.2
Docker engine	18.06.1-ce version
ML algorithm	DRL
Docker composer	1.13.0 version

Table 2. DRL and blockchain assessment of performance in smart house layout.

S. No.	Duration (s)	
	Training	Validation
1	97.6	94.5
2	4.6	7
3	97.5	92.2
4	97.7	97.3
5	4.5	4.9
6	4.6	9.9
7	98	96.2
8	96.9	94

Table 3. Blockchain-based smart houses with a DRL training collection entry during prediction.

DRL Framework (80 percent Training Statistics)		
N=150.3 (Outcome Y1, Y0)		
Anticipated Outcome (X1, X0)	Assault (Y1)	Regular (Y0)
X0 = 79.4 Regular X1 = 70.8 Assault	2.9 67.3	76.4 3.5
SVM	-	-
X0 = 58.9 Regular X1 = 91.3 Assault	4.7 89.6	54.2 1.7
DT	-	-
X0 = 63.5 Regular X1 = 86.7 Assault	4 84.4	59.5 2.3
ANN	-	-
X0 = 60.7 Regular X1 = 89.5 Assault	3.2 87.5	57.4 2

Data

This structure is used to analyze information that was gathered from smart house IoT sensing devices. The data transition from IoT detection devices to the smart house gateway is demonstrated by this procedure. The provided statistics are entered into the data collection layer of the suggested approach. The information gaps were left out by the particular data cleansing. The blockchain network's gateway data administration is depicted in Fig. (7). The three stages of this procedure are the hashing layer, the pre-processing data layer, and the data collection layer. Moments are spent setting up, obtaining, and preserving data during the data-gathering process. The filtering, standardization, and categorization procedures are included in the data pre-processing. Lastly, the encryption, hashing, and preservation of data are found in the hashing layer. The produced data from the gadget comprises the interaction with the routers at a particular moment. The saved unprocessed information is transmitted to the gate it needs fresh data. Just the data with the gadget ID is stored in the subsequent layer depending on standardization categorization to create ample storage. Ultimately, the created data in the smart house stores vital user data in an encrypted manner requires an authentication code from the user, and is stored in a hash operation.

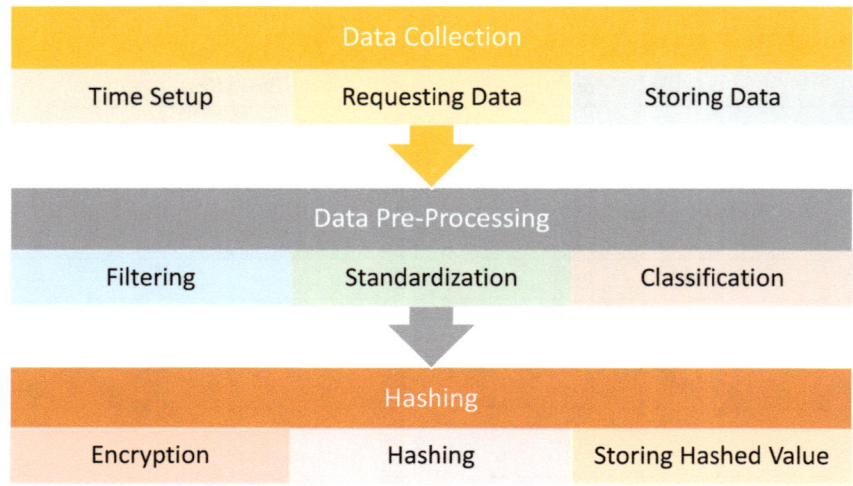

Fig. (7). Data administration of gateway depending on blockchain architecture.

Performance of the Blockchain Architecture in Smart Houses

This part presents the recommended architectural execution to verify the system's performance. The different data points for smart house safety optimization are displayed in Table **2** and Fig. (**8**) for both training and validation purposes. Fig. (**8**) discusses 8 different variables.

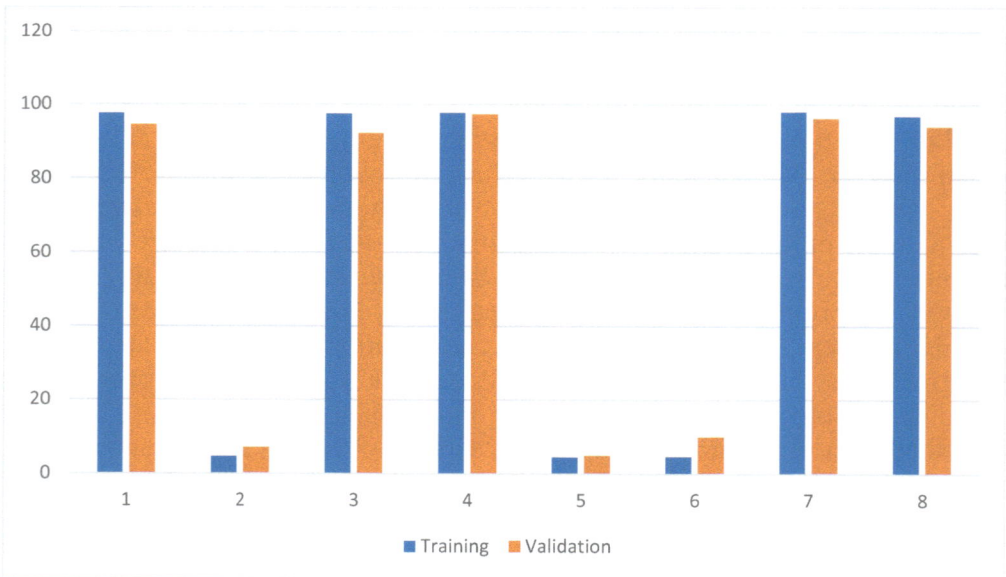

Fig. (8). DRL and blockchain assessment of performance in smart house layout.

Using a DLR prediction collection as a basis, Table 3 displays a blockchain-powered smart house. In the training collection, 150,317 entries overall have been evaluated. Two categories—normal data and assault samples—are used to group such data. 70,852 are the targeted files, while 79,465 are the usual statistics. Furthermore, out of the 67,321 anticipated documents, 3531 are incorrect, and 3531 are illegal.

Performance of DRL in Smart Houses

Depending on Q-learning, the DRL's performance assessment is assessed.

The verification logs for the platform under presentation are displayed in Table 4. 32,955 assault entries and 10,931 regular entries make up the 33,886 verification data overall. In the absence of an apparent assault, 10,348 entries that were witnessed are regarded as regular, and 583 entries as incorrect predictions. In addition, 9,09 entries are unreliable, and 22,046 entries display accurate prediction data.

Table 4. Blockchain-based smart houses with a DRL training collection entry during verification.

DRL Framework (80 percent Training Statistics)		
N=150.3 (Outcome Y1, Y0)		
Anticipated Outcome (X1, X0)	Assault (Y1)	Regular (Y0)
X0 = 10.9 Regular X1 = 22.9 Assault	583 22.04	10.3 909
SVM	-	-
X0 = 8.2 Regular X1 = 25.6 Assault	499 24	7.7 1.6
DT	-	-
X0 = 9.8 Regular X1 = 24 Assault	694 23	9.1 1
ANN	-	-
X0 = 8.7 Regular X1 = 25.1 Assault	799 23.6	7.9 1.5

Fig. (9) illustrates the DRL methods' capabilities based on the operations that were performed. The procedure takes one hour, and the results indicate that the DRL optimization spectrum is large during the hours of two to ten in the early hours and five to nine in the noon.

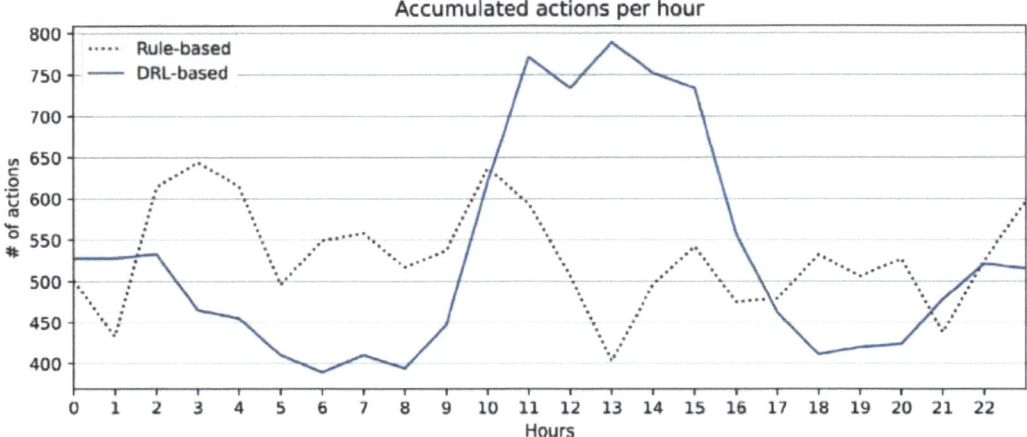

Fig. (9). DRL activity performance in smart house framework.

Table **5** demonstrates the contrary of the performance of the suggested approach with other state-of-the-art. In the given data kind, Artificial Neural Network (ANN) outperforms DRL in the subsequent phase with an accuracy of 80.05. Two different kinds of databases, NSL-KDD and KDD-CUP-99, were processed to create the suggested framework.

Table 5. ML method comparison with DRL.

Method	KDD-CUP-99	NSL-KDD
DRL	97	96.9
SVM	90.8	70.6
ANN	89.4	80
DT	81.1	79

The performance assessment of a smart house depending on several ML methods is shown in Table **6** and Fig. (**10**) as a consequence of anticipated outcomes for false positive, false negative, positive, and negative predicted values.

Table 6. Assessment of performance of prediction compared to suggested methods.

-	Training (%)	Validation (%)
Accuracy	99	95
Rate	5	7
Sensitivity	99.5	98
Specificity	97	96

(Table 6) cont.....

-	Training (%)	Validation (%)
FPV	6	7
FNV	6	8
PPV	97.5	95.5
NPV	95	94

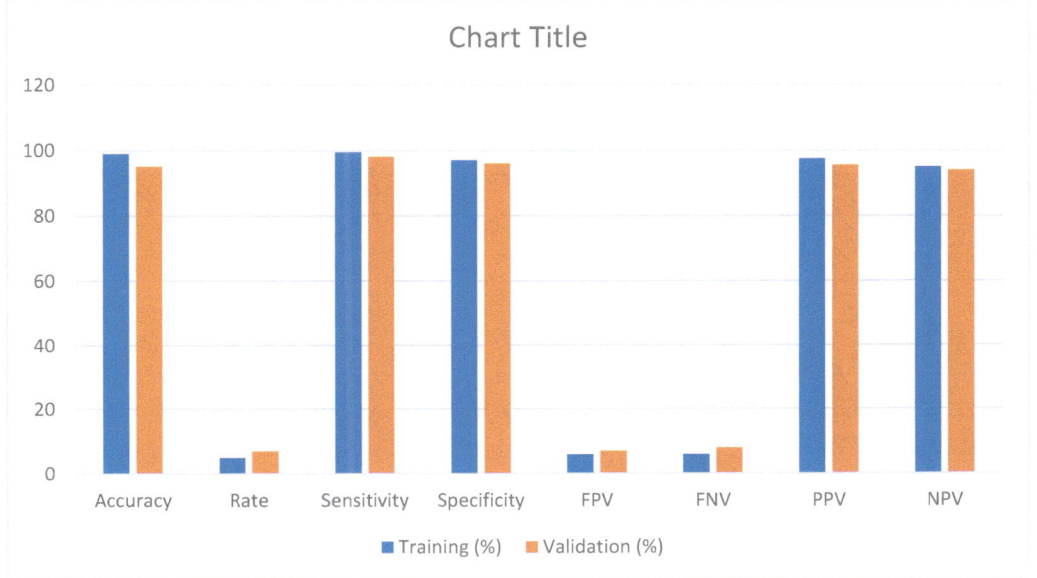

Fig. (10). Assessment of performance of prediction comparing suggested methods.

The reaction duration and precision of entries for safety precautions of data congestion volumes are displayed in Tables **7** and **8**, Figs. (**11** and **12**). Greater safety assessment and quicker reaction are found in the gateway tier. The blockchain-based method that is being offered uses trustworthiness, safety, privacy, and identification for a smart house.

Table 7. Response duration assessment safety in data traffic volume.

Traffic Data Quantity	Response Duration (s)	
-	Suggested Framework	Centralized Framework
0	0	0
2000	5	15
4000	5.1	15.1
6000	7	17

(Table 8) cont.....

Traffic Data Quantity	Response Duration (s)	
-	Suggested Framework	Centralized Framework
8000	7.5	18
10000	8	19
12000	9	20
14000	10	22

Table 8. Assessment accuracy of safety in the volume of data flow.

Traffic Data Quantity	Accuracy	
-	Suggested Framework	Centralized Framework
0	0	0
2000	35	20
4000	61	45
6000	65	50
8000	70	50
10000	71	55
12000	75	60
14000	80	61

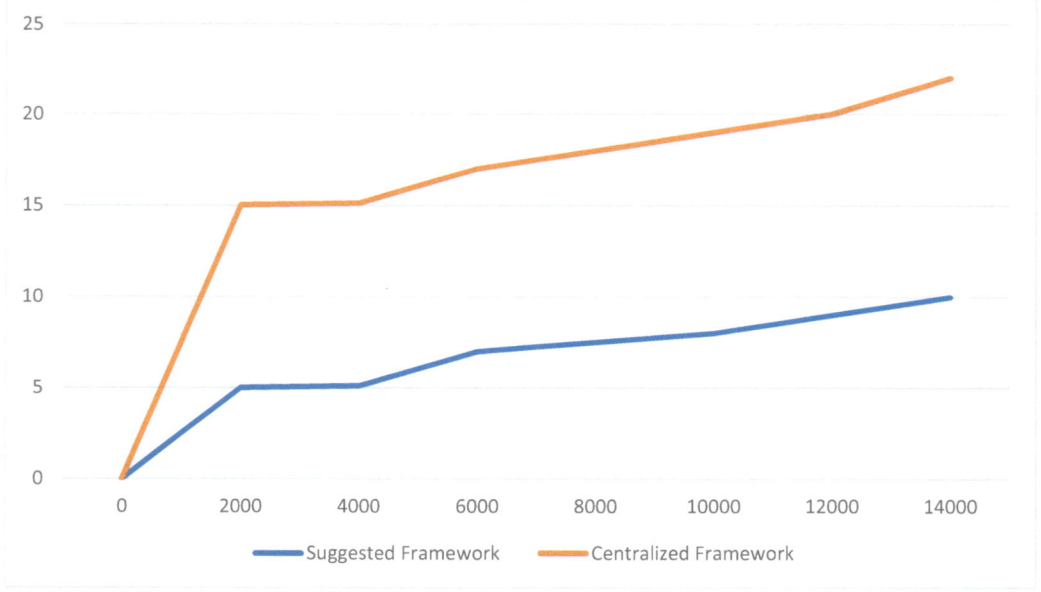

Fig. (11). Response duration assessment safety in data traffic volume.

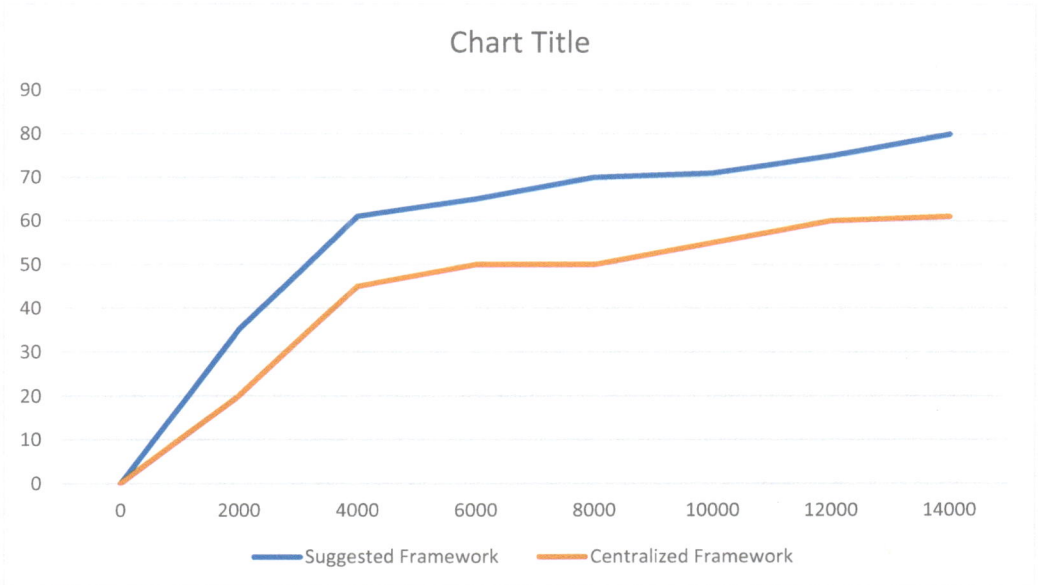

Fig. (12). Assessment accuracy of safety in the volume of data flow.

To verify the suggested layout, this study performed broadcasting and developed a block employing an ESP32 chip. As per the protocol, SN can generate the block and broadcast it for verifying transactions. Mined two blocks are displayed in Fig. **(13)**. The beginning timings of blocks one and two are displayed in the chosen green sections, while the finishing timings of blocks one and two are displayed in the chosen yellow sections. There is a chance that the blocks extracted from duration will be accessible by humans.

In this method, the challenging objective regulates the machine's operating stage to generate novel blocks. In the identical path altering the challenge and mining duration, which are controlled by the program that is compiled in Table **9**, sufficient duration is needed if a novel block is formed within the duration constraint. The challenge and mining duration disparities for block one are displayed in the table. For every block from complexity two, the actual complexity is one and the potential lag duration is 0.22. Fig. **(14)** shows the transactional duration as well as the complexity during the computation period. According to the figure, it requires 60 seconds for a meal at challenging four. The primary goal of evaluating complexity and duration is to display complexity entries expressed in terms of seconds per second.

Table 9. Disparities in block mining complexity and duration.

Complexity	Mining Duration (s)
1	0.5
2	0.2
3	0.3
4	60

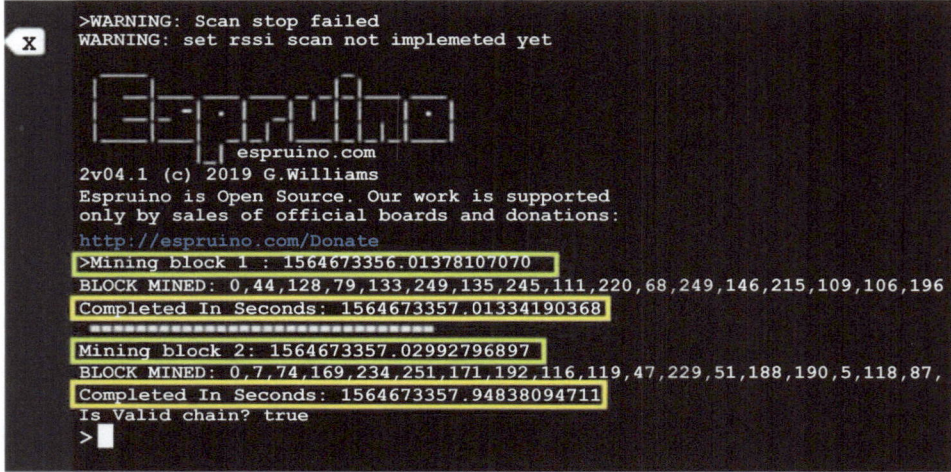

Fig. (13). Outcomes of block mining.

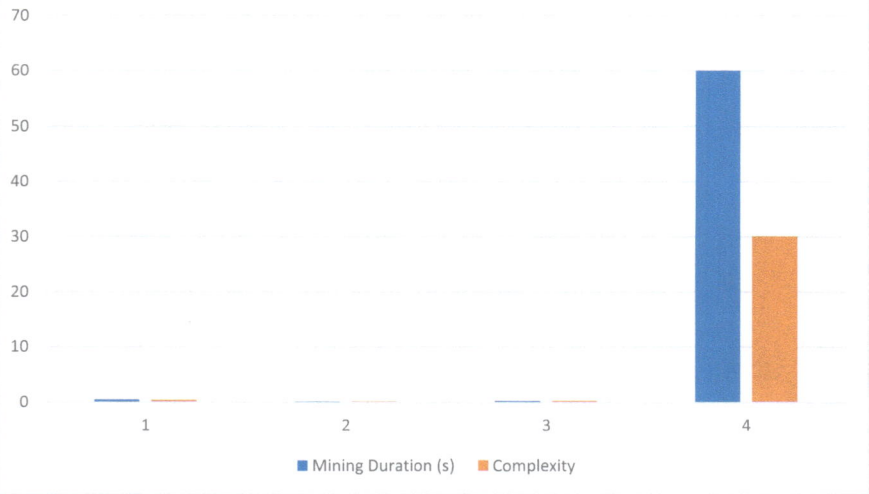

Fig. (14). Complexity level of duration taken for the transaction.

CONCLUSION

Among the most modern innovations in the IoT and sensing architecture is the smart house. The prediction and evaluation of which blockchain and ML have the most opportunity to accomplish this goal are greatly hampered by intervention and the recognition of smart houses. This method makes it difficult to apply the authority and computing limitations associated with the smart house implementation. To reduce the conflicting IoT and centralized gateway issues with authentication, secrecy, and authenticity in smart houses, this chapter has thus introduced DRL incorporation with blockchain. This paper offered a basic concept for a blockchain's safety framework as well as the studies that are currently available for smart house safety. Instead of the user's performance being deleted as a unit in the blockchain architecture, IoT gadgets brought uniqueness to the framework.

REFERENCES

[1] S. Kaneriya, J. Vora, S. Tanwar, and S. Tyagi, "Standardizing the use of duplex channels in 5G-WiFi networking for ambient assisted living", In: *Proc. 2019 IEEE Int. Conf. Commun. Workshops (ICC Workshops)*, Shanghai, China, 2019, pp. 1–6.

[2] S. Tyagi, M.S. Obaidat, S. Tanwar, N. Kumar, and M. Lal, "Sensor cloud-based measurement to a management system for precise irrigation", *In GLOBECOM 2017-2017 IEEE Global Communications Conference* Singapore, 2017, pp. 1-6.
[http://dx.doi.org/10.1109/GLOCOM.2017.8254440]

[3] U. Bodkhe, P. Bhattacharya, S. Tanwar, S. Tyagi, N. Kumar, and M.S. Obaidat, "BloHosT: Blockchain-enabled smart tourism and hospitality management", *In: 2019 International Conference on Computer, information and Telecommunication Systems (CITS)* Beijing, China, 2019, pp. 1-5.
[http://dx.doi.org/10.1109/CITS.2019.8862001]

[4] Y. Ali, S.W. Shah, and W.A. Khan, "Security at the Internet of Things," in *Machine Tools,* 1st ed., CRC Press, 2023, pp. 31–48.

[5] M.R. Alam, M. St-Hilaire, and T. Kunz, "Peer-to-peer energy trading among smart homes", *Appl. Energy,* vol. 238, pp. 1434-1443, 2019.
[http://dx.doi.org/10.1016/j.apenergy.2019.01.091]

[6] M.S. Farooq, S. Khan, A. Rehman, S. Abbas, M.A. Khan, and S.O. Hwang, "Blockchain-based smart home network security empowered with fused machine learning", *Sensors,* vol. 22, no. 12, p. 4522, 2022.
[http://dx.doi.org/10.3390/s22124522] [PMID: 35746303]

[7] A. Kuzmin, and E. Znak, "Blockchain-based structures for a secure and operated network of semi-autonomous unmanned aerial vehicles", *2018 IEEE International Conference on Service Operations and Logistics, and Informatics (SOLI),* , 2018 Singapore, 2018, pp. 32-37.
[http://dx.doi.org/10.1109/SOLI.2018.8476785]

[8] Y. Fu, and J. Zhu, "Trusted data infrastructure for smart cities: a blockchain perspective", *Build. Res. Inform.,* vol. 49, no. 1, pp. 21-37, 2021.
[http://dx.doi.org/10.1080/09613218.2020.1784703]

[9] A. Koulianos, and A. Litke, "Blockchain Technology for Secure Communication and Formation Control in Smart Drone Swarms", *Future Internet,* vol. 15, no. 10, p. 344, 2023.
[http://dx.doi.org/10.3390/fi15100344]

[10] Y. Liu, F.R. Yu, X. Li, H. Ji, and V.C.M. Leung, "Blockchain and machine learning for communications and networking systems", *IEEE Commun. Surv. Tutor.,* vol. 22, no. 2, pp. 1392-1431, 2020.
[http://dx.doi.org/10.1109/COMST.2020.2975911]

[11] N.E. Akrami, M. Hanine, E.S. Flores, D.G. Aray, and I. Ashraf, "Unleashing the potential of blockchain and machine learning: Insights and emerging trends from bibliometric analysis", *IEEE Access,* vol. 11, pp. 78879-78903, 2023.
[http://dx.doi.org/10.1109/ACCESS.2023.3298371]

[12] N. Waheed, X. He, M. Ikram, M. Usman, S.S. Hashmi, and M. Usman, "Security and privacy in IoT using machine learning and blockchain: Threats and countermeasures", *ACM Comput. Surv.,* vol. 53, no. 6, pp. 1-37, 2021.
[http://dx.doi.org/10.1145/3417987]

[13] H. Wang, N. Liu, Y. Zhang, D. Feng, F. Huang, D. Li, and Y. Zhang, "Deep reinforcement learning: a survey", *Frontiers of Information Technology & Electronic Engineering,* vol. 21, no. 12, pp. 1726-1744, 2020.
[http://dx.doi.org/10.1631/FITEE.1900533]

[14] G. Varshney, and H. Gupta, "A security framework for IOT devices against wireless threats", *In: 2017 2nd International Conference on Telecommunication and Networks (TEL-NET)* Noida, India, 2017, pp. 1-6.
[http://dx.doi.org/10.1109/TEL-NET.2017.8343548]

[15] C. Lazaroiu, and M. Roscia, "Smart district through IoT and blockchain", *In: 2017 IEEE 6th International Conference on Renewable Energy Research and Applications (ICRERA)* San Diego, CA, USA, 2017, pp. 454-461.
[http://dx.doi.org/10.1109/ICRERA.2017.8191102]

[16] J. Chandramohan, R. Nagarajan, K. Satheeshkumar, N. Ajithkumar, P.A. Gopinath, and S. Ranjithkumar, "Intelligent smart home automation and security system using Arduino and Wi-fi", *International Journal of Engineering And Computer Science [IJECS],,* vol. 6, no. 3, pp. 20694-20698, 2017.

[17] V. Sivaraman, H.H. Gharakheili, A. Vishwanath, R. Borelli, and O. Mehani, "Network-level security and privacy control for smart-home IoT devices", *In 2015 IEEE 11th International Conference on Wireless and Mobile Computing, networking and Communications (WiMob)* Abu Dhabi, United Arab Emirates, 2015, pp. 163-167.
[http://dx.doi.org/10.1109/WiMOB.2015.7347956]

[18] F. Jamil, N. Iqbal, Imran, S. Ahmad, and D. Kim, "Peer-to-peer energy trading mechanism based on blockchain and machine learning for sustainable electrical power supply in smart grid", *IEEE Access,* vol. 9, pp. 39193-39217, 2021.
[http://dx.doi.org/10.1109/ACCESS.2021.3060457]

SUBJECT INDEX

A

Access Control 29, 62, 70, 71
Actuator 147, 148
Agriculture 4.0 111, 113, 118, 119, 120, 128, 129, 130, 131
Agricultural Informatics 111, 118
Agro-product 131
Agro-systems 131
AgriOnBlock 116
Anti-Money Laundering 40, 52, 92, 121
Anomaly 61, 63, 130, 140, 141, 142, 146, 147, 148, 158, 159
Anonymity 2, 8, 39, 117
Assets 5, 37, 50, 56, 60, 61, 91, 92, 98, 108, 112, 168
   Digital 5, 56, 91, 168
   Tokenization of 50, 60, 61, 92, 98, 108
   Management 37, 60
Auditability 8, 24
Auditing 53, 60, 67, 101, 102

B

Banking 24, 26, 27, 28, 33, 34, 38, 39, 41, 42, 69, 77, 84, 103, 105, 106, 107, 200
   Investment 33
   Mobile 24, 42
   Syndicate 38, 106, 107
Behavioral Analysis 52, 62
Big Data 111, 119, 120, 131, 182, 199, 200, 201, 214, 218
Bi-LSTM 218, 219, 231
Bitcoin 2, 4, 15, 42, 50, 82, 84, 117, 183, 184
Breach 23, 40, 52, 61, 62, 71, 77, 78, 183, 190
   Data 23, 40, 71, 183, 190
   Security 61, 62, 77
Bricking Attack 143
Business Model 184, 185, 186, 187, 188, 189, 190, 192, 195
   Blockchain as a Service 188
   Securities 187
   Token 187
   Utility Token 187
Byzantine Fault Tolerance 59, 184, 186

C

Central Bank Digital Currencies (CBDCs) 37
Clinical Research 17, 18
Cloud Computing 111, 119, 126, 182, 217
Collision Resistance 58
Cost Reduction 73, 77, 126, 141
Counterparty Risk 97
Crowdfunding 40, 97, 98

D

Decentralization 8, 24, 27, 56, 57, 59, 75, 77, 82, 102, 104, 105, 115, 186
   Applications (DApps) 2, 14, 100, 184, 186
   Finance (DeFi) 24, 37, 51, 54, 56, 65, 67, 69, 70, 75, 79, 188
Deep Belief Network (DBN) 148, 150
Deep Neural Network (DNN) 148, 150, 158, 160, 222, 231, 232
Digital 10, 29, 40, 56, 58, 70, 163, 168, 172
   Identity 40, 56, 70
   Signature 10, 29, 58, 163, 168, 172
Drugs 17, 18, 71
Dual Activation Function 231

E

E-commerce 57, 187, 190, 191
EHR (Electronic Health Records) 17
Electronic Clinical Data (ECD) 217, 219
Electronic Payments 200
Elliptic Curve Digital Signature Algorithm (ECDSA) 10
Energy Consumption 40, 89, 103, 104
Ethereum 2, 6, 9, 14, 25, 61, 65, 83, 84, 100, 163, 165, 188, 239, 246

Execution Time 64 Experiment 173, 225, 231, 234, 236

F

Fabricating Data Attack 166, 168, 178
Fake News 162, 163, 164, 171, 174, 175, 177, 178
False Discovery Rate (FDR) 176, 177, 178
Fraud Detection System (FDS) 199, 200, 201, 203, 207, 214
Fraud Prevention 56, 67, 73, 75, 102, 124
Fuzzification 221
Fuzzy Information System (FIS) 218, 221, 222, 225, 231, 234

G

Gas 64, 84, 100
Governance 6, 56, 61, 129, 181
GPS (Geographic Positioning System) 120
H
Hacker 142, 241
Heart Disease 216, 218, 219, 234
Hidden Layers 201, 222, 231, 234
Hybrid Approach 54, 55, 188
Hyperledger Fabric 25, 31

I

Insurance 24, 38, 51, 54, 73, 83, 97, 181
Intellectual Property Rights 71, 72, 91, 164
Intermediaries 42, 53, 56, 69, 75, 76, 77
Interoperability 40, 65, 66, 77, 78
Intrusion Detection System (IDS) 240,
IoT Communication Protocols 143, 147
IPv6 Protocol 148

K

Know Your Customer (KYC) 40, 52, 92, 103, 107
KuCoin Exchange Hack 62

L

Legacy System 23, 104, 122, 128
Logistics 68, 74, 121
Loss Rate 207, 208, 212

M

Malicious Node 144
Man-in-the-middle attack 143, 186
Medical Fraud Detection 17, 18
Merkle Tree Root Hash 9, 10, 90
Mortgage Agreements 97, 98
Multi-signature Wallet 62

N

Negative Predictive Value (NPV) 176, 177
Neuroscience 17, 18
Non-Repudiation 29
Normalization 202, 203, 220
Notarization 162, 163, 164, 165, 166, 168, 172, 178

O

Oracle Security 63
Oracle Price Feeds 62
Outlier Clustering Method 201

P

Parent Block Hash 9, 10
Parity Wallet MultiSig Bug 62
Perceptual Learning 147, 148
Pharmaceuticals 17, 18
Predictive Analytics 51, 52, 62, 111, 185
Private Securities 38
Programmable Financial Logic 76
Pseudonymity 57, 60

Q

Q-learning 249
Quality of Service (QoS) 144
Quantitative Methodology 191

R

Ransomware 144
Rest APIs 172, 244
Ripple 25, 31, 36
RPL Rank Attack 144
RNNs 203, 222, 223, 231, 234
Robots 113, 120, 127, 217

Ronin Network Hack 63
Royalty Agreements 97, 98
RPL 143, 144

S

SHA-256 87
Sinkhole Attacks 144, 151, 155, 156, 160
Solidity 99
Specificity 176, 177, 216, 219, 226, 227, 231, 234
Stock Trading 37, 91, 92
Supply Chain 37, 58, 72, 100, 116, 117, 124, 132
  Management 58, 100, 116, 117, 124, 132
  Finance 37, 72

T

Time-Series Data 216, 223
Tokenization 56, 60, 61, 67, 78, 92, 98, 108
Traditional Finance System 104, 105
Traditional Banking System 106
Transaction Speed 118, 188

U

Unmanned Aerial Vehicles (UAVs) 18
Unspent Transaction Output (UTXO) 8

V

Virtual Environment 50, 53, 54, 64, 65, 66, 74, 75, 79
Virtual Network Connections (VNCs) 147

W

Wallet 12, 62, 70
Wormhole Attack 143, 156, 157, 160